Domesticity and Power in the Earl

In a fascinating and innovative study, Ruby La
women in the Mughal court of the sixteen
Orientalist interpretations of the *haram* that t.
seclusion and sexual exploitation, the author re
men and women negotiated their everyday life
"inner" chambers as well as the "outer" courts. Using Ottoman and Safavid histories
as a counterpoint, she demonstrates the richness, ambiguity, and particularity of the
Mughal *haram*, which was pivotal in the transition to institutionalization and imperial
excellence.

RUBY LAL is Assistant Professor in the Department of Middle Eastern and South
Asian studies at Emory University. Her research focuses on issues of gender relations
in Islamic societies in the pre-colonial world.

Domesticity and Power in the Early Mughal World

RUBY LAL

Emory University

For Ruth —
My lovely friend!
Thank you for your
friendship.
Ruby
London, Aug, 2006

CAMBRIDGE
UNIVERSITY PRESS

CAMBRIDGE UNIVERSITY PRESS
Cambridge, New York, Melbourne, Madrid, Cape Town, Singapore, São Paulo

CAMBRIDGE UNIVERSITY PRESS
The Edinburgh Building, Cambridge CB2 2RU, UK

Published in the United States of America by Cambridge University Press, New York

www.cambridge.org
Information on this title: www.cambridge.org/9780521615348

First published 2005

Printed in the United Kingdom at the University Press, Cambridge

A catalogue record for this book is available from the British Library

ISBN-13 978-0-521-85022-3 hardback
ISBN-10 0-521-85022-3 hardback
ISBN-13 978-0-521-61534-8 paperback
ISBN-10 0-521-61534-8 paperback

To Prabha and Manmohan
and
to Gyan

Contents

Illustrations

Plates

Plans

Acknowledgments

Many different people and institutions have helped in the making of this book. Words cannot convey my gratitude fully, but they are a beginning.

Academic debts: A very special thanks first to Stephen Dale, Afsaneh Najmabadi, Gyan Pandey, Tapan Raychaudhuri, Leslie Peirce, Romila Thapar, and Rita Costa-Gomes for their exacting criticism and unswerving support since the inception of this work. Conversations with colleagues in the US where I converted my D.Phil. thesis into this book have been challenging, critical, and enjoyable. At the Johns Hopkins University, Toby Ditz, Gabrielle Spiegel, Judy Walkowitz, Jane Bennett, and William Connolly read and commented on multiple drafts of this book, or portions of it. Talal Asad, Gyan Prakash, Suzanne Rait, C. M. Naim, Muzaffar Alam, Kathryn Babayan, Veena Das, Naveeda Khan, Caitrin Lynch, and Colin Johnson read my work and moved me to thinking other possibilities in terms of the direction it could take. David Ludden, Barbara and Tom Metcalf, Barbara Ramusack, Nick Dirks, Peter Stearns, Peter Geschiere, Pamela Reynolds, Christine Stansell, Mary Ryan, Tobie-Meyer Fong, William Rowe, David Bell, David Nirenberg, George Fischer, Dina Siddiqi, Ajay Skaria, Sheldon Pollock, Ali Khan, and Hent de Vries were always supportive. I should also mention the unusual kindness and support of Amartya Sen, Homi Bhabha, Colin Lucas, Daniel Weiss, Mubarak Ali, Girish Karnad, Francis Robinson, and Peter Reeves. And, not least, my students at the Johns Hopkins University over the last three years, who have read this book in various versions and made me think through its basics repeatedly by asking the most raw questions.

In England, David Washbrook and Rosalind O'Hanlon provided early conversations and guidance. Homa Bazyar, my Persian tutor, made me hear and "love the sound of the [Persian] language," as she would repeatedly say in our weekly evening lessons. Tapan Raychaudhuri has been a consistent source of ideas, support, and encouragement. The inquiries that have led to this book began when I was a student in Delhi University, where Monica Juneja, Sunil Kumar, Nayanjot Lahiri, Chandrashekhar (for my first lessons in Persian) and Mahesh Rangarajan discussed and encouraged my work. Harbans Mukhia, Saleem Kidwai, Sudhir Chandra, Irfan Habib; Qeyamuddin Ahmad and Imtiaz Ahmad (in Patna); and Gautam Bhadra (in Calcutta) gave much-needed guidance on archives.

I owe thanks to the librarians and staff of the following libraries for their outstanding service: Indian Institute Library, the Oriental Reading Room and the Oriental Institute in Oxford; the British Library, the Victoria and Albert Museum, London; the National Museum, the Indira Gandhi National Center for the Arts, New Delhi; the Khuda Bakhsh Library, Patna; the Walters Art Gallery, Baltimore; the Smithsonian Institute, Washington, D.C.; the Metropolitan Museum of Art, New York; and the Milton-Eisenhower library of the Johns Hopkins University – particularly to Andi Bartelstein and Sue Woodson, who were always ready to chase the most obscure references. For research assistance and technical support, I am thankful to Abigail Baim-Lance, Robert William Kirk, Becky Daniels, Lisa Goldstein, Ann Rose, and Daphne Klautky.

A scholarship from the Inlaks Foundation, London, made possible my research and writing at the University of Oxford between 1996 and 2000. I thank them, as well as the Beit Fund, the Max Mueller Fund, the Radhakrishnan Bequest, the Oxford Centre for Islamic Studies, and not least my exceptionally hospitable college, St. Edmund Hall, for many kinds of support along the way.

I am grateful to Marigold Acland, my marvelous editor at Cambridge University Press for her support and astute suggestions; to Stephen Dale for recommending this book to Cambridge University Press; and to the two anonymous readers for their helpful comments. I am also thankful to Attilio Petruccioli, the British Library, and the Victoria and Albert Museum for giving me permission to reproduce three splendid Fatehpur-Sikri plans and several Mughal miniatures in this book. Parts of chapters 3 and 5 have appeared earlier in a different form. Chapter 3 as "Historicizing the *Harem*: the Challenge of a Princess's Memoir," *Feminist Studies*, 30, 3 (Fall/Winter 2004); and chapter 5 as "The 'Domestic World' of Peripatetic Kings: Babur and Humayun, c. 1494–1556," *Medieval History Journal*, 4, 1 (January–June 2001).

Finally a few personal acknowledgments. Allan Sealy, that master of style, did me the honor of reading the manuscript, combing through it line by line. Sehr Jalal, wonderful practitioner of Modern Mughal miniature art, generously gave me permission to reproduce her "Topkapi Doorway" on the cover. David Page and Ruth Kirk-Wilson have been my family in London and always provided the comfort of "home." Margaret Hardiman generously offered us her splendid cottage in Dorset (where I was meant to write!). I can never forget Lyn and Rod Liddiard's hospitality in Italy; the unbeatable jazz trips with Anish and Susan Mathai in New York; and Mamet-Papet Unterreiner's endless supply of wine in St. Raphael. I cherish greatly my drives and conversations with Mrs. Lillian, my special friendship with Rita Costa-Gomes, as I do Richard Semba's mouth-watering delights, Hashi Di's version of Mughal recipes, and Mrs. Kishore's doses of Shakespeare and *bharva karela*. I recall fondly my drinking sessions with John O'Doherty, Clare Hutton, Grant Lamond, Nilanjan Sarkar, Noelene Reeves, and Jon Wilson.

To my parents, Prabha and Manmohan, who wanted us to be ourselves, and accepted differences with exceptional grace and equanimity, I dedicate this book in admiration. I also dedicate this book to Gyan: thanks for your companionship, criticism, and all that "little" love. I want to acknowledge the unique friendship of my sisters Reena and Gudiya: I wouldn't have written this book without you. Thanks also to Prabhakar, who has celebrated my career and different "ways of being" over the last decade. My nieces, Faani and Aashna, were born during the last four years. They have already had to live with this book, and I hope they will critique and revisit its formulations soon. *Chaiji* is no more, but if she were, she would have been relieved to see "my studies complete." Thanks finally to Sri Kumari Pandey, Asavari, and Nishad for all their affection.

Ruby Lal

Baltimore
September 2004

Note on transliteration and citations

There is no standard system of transliteration from Persian into English. I use the modified version of the *IJMES* (*International Journal of Middle East Studies*) system developed by Layla S. Diba and Maryam Ekhtiar for their edited volume, *Royal Persian Paintings: The Qajar Epoch, 1785–1925* (New York, 1998).

The following page explains the form of transliteration used for different consonants, vowels, and diphthongs. However, I have omitted all diacritical marks. For non-specialists this removes a source of visual distraction and makes the text less cumbersome. The specialist, by contrast, should have no difficulty in recognizing the Persian terms. I have made two exceptions to this rule:

1. I retain the common English form of all well-known names of persons, places, and Persian texts. Thus: *Baburnama* and *Akbarnama*, rather than *Baburname* and *Akbarname*; Agra rather than Agreh; Begum/Beg rather than Bigum/Biyg; and Husain rather than Husiyn.
2. Original spellings have been retained in quotations. As a result, certain names appear with different spellings in my text, on the one hand, and in some quotations, on the other.

The spellings of Turki words have been kept as they appear in the original texts. Dictionaries and other secondary texts used to cross-check the meanings and spellings of these words are listed in the footnotes.

In citations throughout the book, all information included in square brackets is mine.

Consonants, vowels and diphthongs

CONSONANTS

Hamzeh	'	ص	ṣ
ب	b	ض	ż
پ	p	ط	ṭ
ت	t	ظ	ẓ
ث	s	ع	'
ج	j	غ	gh
چ	ch	ف	f
ح	ḥ	ق	q
خ	kh	ک	k
د	d	گ	g
ذ	z	ل	l
ر	r	م	m
ز	z	ن	n
ژ	zh	و	v
س	s	ه	h
ش	sh	ی	y

VOWELS AND DIPHTHONGS

Long		Short		Diphthongs		Other	
ا	ā	ﹷ	a	وُ	aw	(Silent) ه	eh
و	ū	ﹹ	u	ىُ	ay		
ى	ī	ﹻ	i				

Royal Persian Paintings: The Qajar Epoch, 1785–1925, ed. Layla S. Diba with Maryam Ekhtiar (New York, 1998)

CHAPTER 1

Introduction

This book seeks to construct a history of Mughal domestic life in the time of the first three Mughal kings of India, Babur (1487–1530), Humayun (1508–56), and Akbar (1556–1605). It is a study of the "domestic" as a discursive and performed site, which seeks to demonstrate the centrality of this space in the making of the Mughal imperium.

Mughal women and men were partners in the production not only of heirs but also of imperial genealogies and new royal rituals, in the establishment of new traditions, and even the practice of governance. Paradoxically, however, women are depicted as being so invested in the future of the empire – in the form of giving birth to illustrious progeny, and in the maintenance of "established" traditions – that their own present tends to be erased in the very performance of their royalty and womanhood. In a classic replica of patriarchal norms, women's lives are not for living, but for creating other lives, for preserving and nurturing the future of the generations past, and the generations to come.

A history of Mughal domestic life has not so far been written, for reasons that I hope to clarify in the following pages. And yet ironically, while we have no sustained investigation of the details of domestic arrangements and familial affairs, we live with a widely accepted caricature of a mysterious and unchanging *haram*, which is supposed to represent the sum of Mughal private life from the beginning to the end of this remote yet magnificent imperial formation.[1]

Take this statement on the *haram*, as it appears in one of the few academic studies of the subject in English:

The term Mughal Harem conjures up a vision of a sequestered place ensconcing beautiful forms in mysterious magnificence ... the young girls were not exposed to all the celebrations in the *Mahal* [palace] in which sex orgies dominated or the master bargained for beauty and love on occasions like Nauroz and Khushroz ... Naturally, every lady of consequence tried to win the master's undivided love and openly

---

[1] Cf. R. Nath, *Private Life of the Mughals 1526–1803 A.D.* (Jaipur, 1994), a study entirely devoted to the *haram*.

competed to gain ascendancy in the harem. Women's beauty gave them a power as undefined as unique. ... There were other tensions, though not so deep in effect. These may be classed under the generic term jealousy. ... But on this we need not dwell much for the harem was not meant for the old and ailing. It was meant to be a bright place, an abode of the young and beautiful, an arbour of pleasure and retreat for joy.[2]

Extracted from a book published at the end of the 1980s, the above account might be dismissed as the view of a somewhat traditional historian, were its assumptions not so widely and consistently shared.

There is one sentence on the *haram* in the volume on Mughal India, published in the New Cambridge History of India series in 1993: "Ideally, the harem provided a respite, a retreat for the nobleman and his closest male relatives – a retreat of grace, beauty, and order designed to refresh the males of the household."[3] Again, consider R. Nath's description of the *haram* in his *Private Life of the Mughals* (1994). Although Nath comments parenthetically that the "Mughal harem was a very delicate matter and a sweeping generalisation is hardly justified," his book delineates a *haram* that can only be described as fantasaical. "Though Akbar never indulged in excessive sex, he had a taste for young beautiful women whose company he liked. He had in his harem a large number of handsome concubines and slave-girls for his pleasure, besides more than a dozen legally married wives."[4] The emptying of all sense of social life and contradiction continues in his sketching of the "private life" of Jahangir, the fourth Mughal king. This emperor was "a sensuous person and he excessively indulged both in wine and women ..." writes Nath. "By a routine estimate, he had nearly 300 young and beautiful women attached to his bed, an incomprehensible figure in the modern age. This shows his over-indulgence in sex and his excessive engagement in the harem."[5]

A final example, from Ellison Banks Findly's remarks on the Mughal *haram* in her biography of Nur Jahan, Jahangir's wife, should suffice to demonstrate the pervasive hold of this caricatured representation. It is notable that this is one of the first studies that engages critically with Nur Jahan's life and her exercise of power. Nonetheless, Findly continues to work with a simple, stereotypical understanding of the *haram*. "Finding a productive and satisfying place in a society where pleasure (in all its forms) was the main competitive commodity was a substantial task," she writes. The presence of women improved the business: "this process was surely a more vibrant and honest affair given that it took place in the company of women."[6] But "pleasure (in all its forms)" remains the "main competitive commodity."

[2] K. S. Lal, *The Mughal Harem* (Delhi, 1988), pp. 19, 135, 139, 143, and 152.
[3] John F. Richards, *The Mughal Empire* (Cambridge, 1993), p. 62.
[4] Nath, *Private Life*, p. 13.   [5] *Ibid.*, pp. 15, 17.
[6] Ellison Banks Findly, *Nur Jahan: Empress of Mughal India* (New York, 1993), p. 89.

Further, "the enjoyment of palace life was enhanced ... by the frequent use of drugs and alcohol. Intemperance was the Mughal family's main affliction, and despite public abjurations and the clear ban on the use of liquor by Islam, it remained not only a private curse but a public habit."[7] And finally this classic statement, worthy of the most Orientalist of colonial renderings (easily replicated in the case of other imperial *harams* the world over[8]): "Jahangir's harem was, from all accounts, a rowdy and exuberant place to live and Nur Jahan's fulsome charisma played out profitably against its many walls."[9]

In these accounts, a "pleasure principle" constitutes the essence of the *haram*. There is little sense of history in the discussion of the domain of Mughal domestic relations, the establishment and institutionalization of the *haram*, its changing meanings, and contexts.[10] In fact, as the following chapters will show, the *haram* as well-structured physical quarters – and as distinct feminine space demarcated from more clearly marked male domains – came to be institutionalized only during Akbar's reign. In the chronicles of his peripatetic predecessors, we find a wide range of other terms (including the *haram*) that are carefully deployed according to specific narrative contexts. These terms evoke a discriminating sense of near and distant relatives, generations of kinsfolk at work in imperial designs, their association and invocation of a spectacular genealogy, a sense of belongingness to a named bloodline, as well as of interaction and interdependence in noble communities. What is striking in the early chronicles is that there is no fixed realm such as the *haram*; it is under Akbar that the *haram* becomes a predominant symbol of the Mughal domestic world. Despite this history, the Mughal *haram* comes to be denoted in the unchanging form that Lal and others have handed down to us.

The received image of the Mughal *haram* is an apposite entry point for the present study. It leads me straightaway to the two broad propositions that run through this book. First, I am concerned to challenge some of the assumptions that have commonly been made about the existence of separate "public" and "private" domains in the Mughal world. As noted above, our understanding of the latter has been collapsed into the stereotypical image of something called the *haram*. I examine here the complex set of relations in which women of the nobility were involved in their everyday existence, the

---

[7] *Ibid.*, p. 115.
[8] The following two studies provide a good critique of the stereotypical rendering of the *haram*: Leslie P. Peirce, *The Imperial Harem: Women and Sovereignty in the Ottoman Empire* (New York, 1993); Kathryn Babayan, "The 'Aqa'id al-Nisa: A Glimpse at Safavid Women in Local Isfahani Culture," in Gavin R. G. Hambly (ed.), *Women in the Medieval Islamic World: Power, Patronage, and Piety* (New York, 1998), Introduction.
[9] Findly, *Nur Jahan*, p. 126.
[10] Nath, *Private Life*, p. 11, makes the passing comment that the Mughal *haram* was "founded and developed, in the right sense of the term" under Akbar, but there is little detailing of this development, and as the above phrase shows, he works with a persisting sense of the essential *haram* already being given.

public-political affairs that were necessarily conducted in the "inner" quarters as well as in the (outer) courts, and through all this the very different meanings attaching to domestic life. I wish to point to the richness of many of these activities, and to their complex and contradictory character, thus showing that domestic life is not an endless journey between bedroom and kitchen, with the primary function of raising children and caring for husbands.

If domestic life is multifaceted and more contested than the flattened picture of the *haram* suggests, it is also not frozen in time. Domestic life, like political structures, is historically constituted through multifarious struggles and changes. My proposition is that the very coming into being of a more institutionalized and a regulated form of Mughal domestic world was a part of the making of a new Mughal monarchy. This book shows that there were different stages, as well as diverse and complicated procedures, that went into the making of this imperial polity. It was over time that the Mughals became the "Great Mughals" of popular text and memory. It may be noted, for example, that the *Akbarnama* was the first officially commissioned history of the Mughal era; and, again, it was only under Akbar that an elaborate network of statutes arose, regulating everything from the assignment of places to different nobles at the court to the branding of horses. Small indicators of the institutionalization of empire. Thus was the framework of a paramount, majestic polity established. The domestic world and its denizens were not likely to be exempt from this move towards regulation.

The changing political situation and power of a new dynastic regime is indexed in the domestic sphere in several ways: not only in the titles and honors bestowed upon women and other members of the household, but also in the ascription of roles and performance of activities and, indeed, in the living quarters assigned to them. When the term *haram* comes to be applied regularly to the women of the royal household (in Akbar's time), it indicates a changed political and social situation. The term now also comes to describe the residential quarters of the women – a practice that was hardly possible in Babur's peripatetic reign and still not noticeable in Humayun's. It is in Akbar's time that a clearly demarcated, "sacred incarcerated" sphere emerges as the space of the Mughal domestic – although, as already noted, this segregation is anachronistically assumed as the reigning characteristic of the Mughal domestic world for the entire tenure of Mughal rule.

In the following pages, I posit a domain of "domestic life" as a heuristic device. This domain may be thought of as a necessary reproductive, affective unit, dealing with familial relations, reproductive rights and duties, fostering and care, and suffused by a sense of a close intimate circle. This is a realm in which women have a much more obvious presence than in certain other Mughal activities, like military campaigns or the display of power and grandeur in the court. I have marked out this area of domestic life as separate, or separable, from other activities and forms of sociality that Mughal men and women were engaged in. I do this only to allow a long overdue investigation of the formation of subjects and subjectivities, and of the making of new imperial structures, institutions and practices, in an "invisible" space that has so far been treated as always already given.

The burden of my argument in this book, however, is that no such separate domain exists during the time of the early Mughals – at least not until the establishment of Akbar's new imperial order. I have therefore also attempted throughout these pages to adopt a strategy of writing that displaces, or questions, the very notion of a separate domestic sphere, or of distinct public and private domains, even as I use terms like "domestic life," or "familial affairs," or "household matters," to point to the reproductive and affective relationships and activities of the Mughal kings' intimate circle.

It will be clear that terms such as "public–private," "private life," and so on, cannot be applied readily to the lives and experiences of the people under investigation. I have used the term "domestic" throughout these pages because we need a shorthand term in order to initiate a discussion, and because this term comes with less historiographical baggage than that associated with "public and private" or "private life." It may thus allow us to think of a multifaceted and historically changing domain without very clearly marked boundaries. For the domestic life of the early Mughals is perhaps most usefully conceptualized as a realm in which an array of old and new traditions, intricate configurations of critical power structures, and striking convergences between the prescriptive and practice come together to play a central part in the making of Mughal subjects – men and women.

It is in this context that I raise the question of the meaning of public-private distinctions and how to engage effectively with these terms in a pre-modern context. I also ask what it meant to be a mother, a married woman, a wife, a queen, an elder (or a "junior") in early Mughal India. My hypothesis is a simple one: that the meanings of motherhood, wifehood, love, marriage, filial relationships, and sexuality, are not given to us in some fixed, unchanging form. These meanings are historically and culturally constructed – in the light of different experiences, needs, and conditions.

The question of language is important for this exercise. I analyze an extensive Persian vocabulary in the course of building my argument. The changing terminology of the contemporary records projects the extent to which differences in the physical, political, and cultural circumstances of the early Mughals affected the making of domestic relationships. Varied contexts and diverse units of reference were invoked in thinking of kin and intimate relations during the period under study. It is through an appreciation of these that the domestic world itself may be conceptualized.

This book is addressed to three kinds of audience. To begin with, it should be of interest to scholars and students working on the history of Mughal India. At the same time, I hope it will speak to two other, more dispersed, groups of scholars and students, concerned, on the one hand, with the history and diversity of different Islamic societies and polities and, on the other, with questions of gender relations, domestic arrangements, and the organization of "public" and "private" in the pre-modern world. The very diversity of these potential audiences poses something of a challenge, since they work with rather different theoretical lenses. Let me note something of the mode of debate among each of these intellectual groups, showing thereby the possibility of my own engagement and conversation with them.

Towards a social history of the Mughals

Mainstream Mughal historiography continues to this day to be engaged in a fairly conservative manner with the political and economic bases of Mughal power. Issues of social and cultural history, not to mention questions of gender relations, have yet to find a significant place in this writing. In thinking of the reasons for the particular emphases that Mughal history writing has come to acquire, the problem of the inadequacy of source materials is often advanced as being central to the issue. "How will you write a history of the domestic life of the Mughals?" a leading historian of Mughal India asked me when I began this research. "There are no sources for it." This book argues that, in spite of this historiographical ultimatum, a history of domestic life can be written – indeed must be written – for a better understanding of Mughal history as a whole. As I hope to show, the problem is not one regarding sources at all; it is about the politics of history writing. The archive exists for very different kinds of histories, as long as the relevant questions are asked.

Since the 1950s, historians of Mughal India have concentrated heavily on the political-administrative institutions of Mughal rule. Closely allied to these are studies focused on agrarian conditions, economic change, trade relations and the attendant class struggles. There has been considerable writing in the area of what might be called a socioeconomic history, both in the context of agrarian relations and in that of trade and trading networks.[11]

---

[11] Writings on the political-administrative institutions of the Mughals are extensive. Some of the important examples are: M. Athar Ali, *The Mughal Nobility under Aurangzeb* (Bombay, 1966); Satish Chandra, *Parties and Politics at the Mughal Court 1707–1740* (2nd edn, New Delhi, 1972); I. H. Qureshi, *The Administration of the Mughul Empire* (Lohanipur, 1973); John F. Richards, *Mughal Administration in Golconda* (Oxford, 1975); and Muzaffar Alam, *The Crisis of Empire in Mughal North India: Awadh and the Punjab, 1707–48* (Delhi, 1986). For some useful recent bibliographies, see Richards, *Mughal Empire*; Hermann Kulke (ed.), *The State in India 1000–1700* (Delhi, 1997); Muzaffar Alam and Sanjay Subrahmanyam, *The Mughal State, 1526–1750* (2nd edn, Delhi, 2000).
  Among a plethora of writings on economic and social history in the context of agrarian relations, some of the most notable works are: Irfan Habib, *The Agrarian System of Mughal India, 1556–1707* (Bombay, 1963); Michael Pearson, *Merchants and Rulers in Gujarat: The Response to the Portuguese in the 16th Century* (Berkeley, 1976); Ashin Das Gupta, *Indian Merchants and the Decline of Surat: c. 1700–1750* (Wiesbaden, 1979); for a general survey, see Tapan Raychaudhuri and Irfan Habib (eds.), *The Cambridge History of India*, vol. 1: *c. 1200–c. 1750* (Cambridge, 1982).

Apart from the close and detailed investigation of politico-military, administrative, revenue and agrarian matters, the Mughal court has also been studied selectively as a site for factions and party politics. In most of the histories of the Mughal court and "political" institutions, two common features may be discerned. First, the premise for investigation is that these institutions are seats exclusively of high politics. Second, the histories show these institutional sites as fully developed from the moment of their birth, fixed, and uncomplicated in form. All one notices is a change of individuals, factions, and perhaps physical location. Many of these histories begin with Akbar, the third Mughal (whose imperium and power was truly impressive), and a time when the institutions of the grand Mughals were coming to be securely established.[12] Numerous books and articles have been written of the glory of the Mughal empire, presenting it as it appears in the hey-day of Akbar's rule from Fatehpur-Sikri and Agra, with all its regal paraphernalia given from birth: and the picture is projected backwards to cover the time of his two predecessors.

This presentation of a splendid Mughal empire as an unchanging entity for all time hardly speaks to the making of institutions and their changing character. Adjacent to the above genre are other Mughal histories in which scholars have made an effort to study the evolution of political culture built around forms of ritual sovereignty, literary pursuits, art and architectural splendor. A certain attention to ceremonial as it related to the political, and accounts of marriage aimed primarily at political aggrandizement or consolidation, may be located in these writings.[13]

What happens to the history of Mughal social life? In the received literature, this history takes two main forms. The first is a statement that appears under the generic title "social conditions and life of the people" but amounts to no more than a journalistic listing of items of daily use, festivities, and pastimes. These are described in such general, commonsense terms that they give the reader a history that seems to be valid for all times. In compendiums such as the volume on the Mughal Empire, in the Bhartiya Vidya Bhavan Series on the life and culture of Indian people, chapters entitled

---

[12] Alam and Subrahmanyam note that the great bulk of writings in the Mughal state focus on two periods: the reign of Akbar (1556–1605), and that of his great-grandson Aurangzeb (1658–1707). The "pre-Akbar period," the half-century after 1605, as well as the years after 1707, have been neglected in Mughal historiography. Alam and Subrahmanyam, *The Mughal State*, pp. 17–18.

[13] To take a couple of examples: John F. Richards, "The Formulation of Imperial Authority under Akbar and Jahangir," in John F. Richards (ed.), *Kingship and Authority in South Asia* (Madison, 1978); Norman P. Ziegler, "Some Notes on Rajput Loyalties During the Mughal Period," in Richards (ed.), *Kingship and Authority*. In a similar way, discussions of religion are often centered on the development and place of religion in politics, and the various aspects of the religious policy of Mughal kings. Writings in this area are extensive as well. See, for example, S. R. Sharma, *The Religious Policy of the Mughal Emperors* (3rd edn, New York, 1972); S. A. A. Rizvi, *Religious and Intellectual History of the Muslims in Akbar's Reign* (New Delhi, 1975).

"Social Condition" are usually the last ones.[14] The broad entries of the chapter "Social Condition" in this particular book are dress, toilets, diet, ornaments, kitchens and utensils, intoxicants, fairs and festivals, sports, games and pastimes, customs and ceremonies, social etiquette and manners, modes of traveling and conveyance, postal system, position of women, and education.[15] One cannot but be struck by the ahistoricity of a compilation of this kind.[16]

More directly relevant to the subject of the current investigation is a second strand in Mughal social history, which is best described as belonging to the genre of biographies of women worthies. Studies of this kind focus upon the visibility of imperial women and their power. An interesting feature of this writing is that it has come to be seen by male historians as sufficient to its subject (that is women), and there has been little attempt to rethink long-held assumptions about Mughal court and society. This reluctance to think about women's histories as "history" is obviously not restricted to Mughal historiography alone.

Bonnie G. Smith's point about the fate of early practitioners of gender history in the West – that "prestigious professional history based on deep reflection and weighty political topics was for men, while 'amateurish' women pursued a more 'superficial' kind of writing about the past"[17] – applies equally well to the way in which Mughal women's biographical accounts have been received. The most useful of these, aimed at "bringing women to life," were never thought of as serious mainstream histories, nor even as an important part of thinking "Mughal history." In general, such biographies seem to exist in a separate sphere, all of its own. At best they are seen as (mild) "correctives":[18] there were women too, of course – some of them quite talented!

There is greater irony here. While these studies of Mughal women opened up a neglected area of investigation, the women biographers themselves excluded the possibility of querying or even raising new questions about the

---

[14] R. C. Majumdar (ed.), *The Mughul Empire* (Bombay, 1974).   [15] *Ibid.*, ch. XXI.

[16] Within this genre of Mughal social histories, another remaindered category may be noted: "culture," which refers to works of art, architecture and intellectual life. This area has become the domain of specialists, an exclusive preserve of technical "art" history, and its historians. Histories of Mughal art as well as that of architecture are represented as, in the main, the legitimizing indicator of the rule of an emperor and the glory of his rule – to be seen in wondrous art, and splendid buildings designed by his skilled craftsmen. Questioning parts of this legacy, in a recently edited anthology of essays on architectural history of India, Monica Juneja makes some important suggestions regarding the intellectual importance of architectural history for all historians; Monica Juneja (ed.), *Architecture in Medieval India* (Delhi, 2001).

[17] Bonnie G. Smith, *The Gender of History: Men, Women, and Historical Practice* (Cambridge, Mass., 1998), pp. 1, 6. For an extensive discussion of gender-based power struggles in (American) academic settings, see Joan Scott, "The Campaign Against Political Correctness: What's Really at Stake," *Radical History Review*, 54 (1992).

[18] *Ibid.*, p. 2.

accepted boundaries of family and household, public and private spheres, gender relations and political power. In biographies of Mughal women, one finds little to suggest that royal women were a crucial component of the Mughal world – of imperial designs and the making of this monarchy – and therefore that an investigation of their lives and conditions is vital to any understanding of it.

Rekha Misra wrote an early book in this style of making women "visible," with an appropriately indicative title, *Women in Mughal India* (1967).[19] It is a study of aristocratic Mughal women covering the reigns of the grand Mughals, which gives us details of their political activities, commercial engagements, education and artistic talents, construction and supervision of buildings, charities, and organization of marriages. Misra wrote about women mentioned in imperial records and in the narratives of the European travelers. The author presents her study in the form of biographical sketches of the royal women, unsurprisingly ending up replicating the sources.

Twenty-three years later this was still the dominant trend in writings on Mughal women. In 1990, Renuka Nath continued to write in the biographical mode for elite women, merely adding a few more characters to Misra's list. The title of her book, *Notable Mughal and Hindu Women in the 16th and 17th Centuries* (1990) provides a good indication of its contents.[20] In 1993, the same year that Leslie Peirce's extraordinary book on the Ottoman imperial *haram* came out (a book I take up for fuller discussion in the next section), Ellison Banks Findly produced another biography in the same mold as her biographer-predecessors. The subject here is Nur Jahan, the "Empress of Mughal India," as Findly calls her.[21] The historian's chronological summary of the high points of Nur Jahan's life in the prologue to her book is instructive:

After four years of obscurity, the woman who came to be Nur Jahan met Jahangir at a palace bazaar in the spring of 1611 and the two were married a few months later. She was in her midthirties, had already had one child, and was to be Jahangir's last and most influential wife. Almost at once, Nur Jahan and her cohorts took control of the government as Jahangir bowed to the effects of alcohol and opium. She minted coins, traded with foreign merchants, managed promotions and finances at the court, orchestrated new developments in art and religion, and laid out many of the Mughal gardens we now know. Her power over the emperor and in government affairs was almost complete, but came at the cost of internal tensions. Midway through the reign, her stepson Shah Jahan went into open rebellion and her ruling coalition fell apart as the couple increasingly spent their months in Kashmir. By the time Jahangir died in 1627, splintering of the familial center was so substantial that she had no real chance

---

[19] Rekha Misra, *Women in Mughal India 1526–1748 A.D.* (New Delhi, 1967).
[20] Renuka Nath, *Notable Mughal and Hindu Women in the 16th and 17th Centuries A.D.* (New Delhi, 1990).
[21] Findly, *Nur Jahan*.

for power in the next reign. Nur Jahan was exiled to Lahore where she lived in seclusion with her daughter until her death in 1645.[22]

In spite of its brevity, this is a classic representation of Nur Jahan's life, one that may be found (with slight variations) in several other accounts.[23] All of these histories point to the central place that Nur Jahan came to acquire in the *haram* and court of Jahangir after her marriage. Her ascent to this position is portrayed as sudden, uncomplicated and yet almost miraculous – since it fits into no expected pattern. Even at the outset, one can discern Findly's unproblematic detailing of Nur Jahan's power, and ambition, as if all of these existed in a void (or at best, became possible due to her intimate relationship with Jahangir). Although the historian mentions the "many talented [Mughal] women,"[24] we are led to believe that Nur Jahan's power was a bolt from the blue, that there was no forerunner in this kind of practice of authority. Given the numerous examples of traditions of strong and influential royal women in Muslim societies contemporaneous with the Mughals, Findly's historical sketch of this unique empress is not very enlightening.[25]

Aside from the biographical histories of influential royal women, there have also been some studies of "private" life, and the *haram*. I cited extracts from a couple of these at the beginning of this chapter. Mughal private life and the *haram* appear here as nothing but a caricatured arena of fixed behavioral patterns, of unchanging and unmediated sexual and physical pleasure, a peculiarly static "feminine" domain of which a "history" is barely conceivable. The assumption behind these studies, clearly, is that activities and relationships here are fundamentally unchanging and that (almost before we start) we already know all there is to know about this domain. At the least, I hope, my book will dispel this notion by demonstrating that although there is a repetition in the activities and relationships of men and women (here as

---

[22] *Ibid.*, p. 3.
[23] See the following: Vincent A. Smith, *The Oxford History of India: From the Earliest Times to the End of 1911* (Oxford, 1920), pp. 376–377, 383, 385–386, and 394; Misra, *Women in Mughal India*, pp. 33–40; Chandra Pant, *Nur Jahan and Her Family* (Allahabad, 1978); Richards, *Mughal Empire*, pp. 102–103; Wiebke Walther, *Women in Islam* (Princeton, 1992), pp. 126–127.
[24] *Ibid.*, p. 123.
[25] As an aside, one might note that the tradition of powerful, visible women extends further back to the Mongol and Timurid periods. On Mongol women, see Morris Rossabi, "Kublai Khan and the Women in his Family," in W. Bauer (ed.), *Studia Sino-Mongolia* (Wiesbaden, 1979); Mansura Haider, "The Mongol Traditions and Their Survival in Central Asia (XIV–XV Centuries)," *Central Asiatic Journal*, 28, 1–2 (1984); scholarly writings on Timurid women are extensive, see Priscilla P. Soucek, "Timurid Women: A Cultural Perspective," in Hambly (ed.), *Women in the Medieval Islamic World*; Thomas W. Lentz and Glenn D. Lowry, *Timur and the Princely Vision: Persian Art and Culture in the Fifteenth Century* (Los Angeles, 1989), especially pp. 74, 80, 84. On Turkish women in Central Asia from the ninth to the fifteenth centuries, see Isenbike Togan, "Turkic Dynasties: Ninth to Fifteenth Centuries," *Encyclopedia of Women and Islamic Cultures: Methodologies, Paradigms and Sources* (Leiden and Boston, 2003). See also the fantastic account of Ruy Gonzalez de Clavijo about his visit to the court of Timur, *Embassy to Tamerlane: 1403–1406*, trans. Guy Le Strange (London, 1928).

everywhere else), their interaction is not devoid of surprises, but creative and productive, full of interesting twists and turns. "Repetition" often gives rise to "new and distinctive assemblages," new contingencies, new intents, where the repeated action seems to transform itself because "each iteration occurs in an absolutely unique context."[26]

There have of course been significant exceptions to the kind of social history outlined above. Aside from Tapan Raychaudhuri's early and unusual investigation of social life under the reigns of Akbar and Jahangir in Bengal (which was of course not centrally concerned with the life of the Mughal dynasty),[27] a number of recent writings have opened up certain new avenues of investigation in the realm of Mughal social history. Muzaffar Alam's investigation of Persian language inaugurates new possibilities for an understanding of Mughal practices and culture. Alam's article "The Pursuit of Persian: Language in Mughal Politics" focuses upon the centrality that Persian came to acquire in the time of the Mughals, especially the place it acquired as the (declared) official language in the time of Akbar.[28] This choice of Persian, "in consideration of specific Indian conditions," had interesting implications for the making of Mughal political identity, Alam argues in this article.[29] The author especially notes how the "non-sectarian and liberal feature of Persian made it an ideal forum [sic] through which the Mughals could effectively negotiate the diversities of the Indian society."[30]

Again, in a sensitive exploration of Babur's poetry and autobiography, Stephen Dale tells us a great deal about the particular mores and values of the *padshah*'s highly dispersed society.[31] Dale engages closely with the language of Babur's writings, and is able to reconstruct important aspects of the literary culture of the times, and the personality of the *padshah*: what he describes as the *raison d'être* of Babur's life and his "fundamental political assumptions, social values, religious ideals and even artistic standards."[32] Similarly, Monica Juneja's recent commentary on art and architectural history makes a persuasive plea for the intellectual importance of architectural history for all historians, and the incorporation of such hitherto isolated subdisciplines into mainstream debates on social history.[33]

[26] Jane Bennett, *The Enchantment of Modern Life: Attachments, Crossings, and Ethics* (Princeton, 2001), p. 40.

[27] Tapan Raychaudhuri, *Bengal under Akbar and Jahangir: An Introductory Study in Social History* (Delhi, 1969).

[28] Muzaffar Alam, "The Pursuit of Persian: Language in Mughal Politics," *Modern Asian Studies*, 32, 2 (1998), p. 325.

[29] *Ibid.*, p. 348.   [30] *Ibid.*

[31] Stephen F. Dale: "The Poetry and Autobiography of the *Babur-Nama*," *The Journal of Asian Studies*, 55, 3 (August 1996); *idem*, "Steppe Humanism: The Autobiographical Writings of Zahir al-din Muhammad Babur, 1483–1530," *International Journal of Middle East Studies*, 22 (1990); and *The Garden of the Eight Paradises: Babur and the Culture of Empire in Central Asia, Afghanistan and India, 1483–1530* (Leiden and Boston, 2004).

[32] Dale, "Poetry," pp. 1, 39; see also, Dale, *Eight Paradises*, ch. V.

[33] Juneja, *Architecture*, Introduction, p. 2.

More obviously related to familial affairs and domestic conditions of the Mughal royalty are the works of Stephen Blake and Rosalind O'Hanlon. In his study of the Mughal imperial capital, Shahjahanabad, in the years 1639–1739, Stephen Blake makes the argument that the Mughal state was a patrimonial-bureaucratic structure, in which the emperor and his household were of overwhelming importance.[34] The idea of the patrimonial-bureaucratic state is based on Max Weber's prodigious work. According to Blake, a careful reading of the Mughal documents reveals a "remarkable congruence between the state Akbar organized and the patrimonial-bureaucratic empire analysed by Weber."[35] In his reading, the *A'in-i Akbari* depicts the Mughal emperor as a divinely aided patriarch whose household was the central element in government; members of the army were dependent on the emperor, the administration "a loosely structured group of men controlled by the Imperial household," and the emperor's travels were a significant part of administrative activities.[36] Historians John F. Richards, Burton Stein, Noboru Karashima, and G. Berkemer have accepted Blake's formulations, albeit with slight modifications.

The work of these scholars demonstrates that the Mughal monarchy was a personalized one, much dependent on the household, the persona of the emperor, and personal service.[37] Following this line of inquiry, Rosalind O'Hanlon examines Akbar's self-projection as a universal monarch, and the careful construction of imperial masculinity, as a previously neglected part of the strategy of governance under the third Mughal monarch. O'Hanlon draws attention to the essential gender dimension in the investigation of imperial politics and identity. She shows the development of patriarchal power in the sixteenth and seventeenth centuries, calling for a rethinking of both pre-modern as well as modern Indian society and politics.[38]

This welcome attention to the changing images of power, the wilful construction of imperial "charisma" and the related details of spatial arrangements, marital affairs and bodily regulation, still tends to remain emperor-centered. In spite of their proposition that the imperial household was the crucial domain after which images of other realms of the empire were to be built, neither Blake nor O'Hanlon pays much attention to the activities and relationships – or even the identity – of the inhabitants of the household. Thus

---

[34] Stephen P. Blake, *Shahjahanabad: The Sovereign City in Mughal India 1639–1739* (Cambridge, 1993).

[35] Discussed in the Introduction to Kulke (ed.), *State*, p. 38.

[36] Stephen P. Blake, "The Patrimonial-Bureaucratic Empire of the Mughals," in Kulke (ed.), *State*, p. 302.

[37] Richards, "Imperial Authority," and *idem* "Norms of Comportment among Imperial Mughal Officers," in Barbara Daly Metcalf (ed.), *Moral Conduct and Authority: The Place of Adab in South Asian Islam* (Berkeley, 1984).

[38] Rosalind O'Hanlon, "Kingdom, Household and Body: Gender and the Construction of Imperial Service under Akbar," *Indian Economic and Social History Review* (forthcoming). I have used the version of the paper given to me by the author in 1998.

we find little discussion of how the latter adopted and negotiated the prescribed norms and values, and how these were modified in the process of negotiation.

It is almost as if everything is prescribed from an already constituted center. Even the king appears in these accounts as an abstract category, produced in the light of inherited ethical-moral texts. O'Hanlon's concentration on Akbar's construction of a heteronormative masculinity built upon his reading of ethical digests such as the *Akhlaq-i Nasiri* of Nasir al-Din Tusi (1201–74), does not give the reader an elaborate sense of the tension that went into the self-fashioning of this kingly subject. She follows the imperial chronicler Abu-l Fazl in depicting the emperor as the "living embodiment of ... masculine virtues and exemplar for his servants"[39] – wholly in conformity with the prescribed ideal. When the figure of the monarch is represented in this way, it is not surprising that the king's intimate circle, the invisible members of the Mughal domestic world – who struggled to fashion themselves, and surely contributed to the emergence of new attitudes, values, and behavior – form no part of the above investigations. Yet it is all too clear that without such an inquiry, our understanding of the evolving patterns of Mughal domestic life (and Mughal "norms") will remain impoverished.

One final point about the dominant modes of Mughal history writing. Many of these histories are written as if the Mughal world was no more than a preamble to "modern" India. They are conditioned by questions of empire formation in relation to colonial and post-colonial history. Mughal historians have concentrated on grand themes such as the rise and fall of the Mughal state, long-distance trade (the potentialities of capitalist development), the administrative system of the Mughals, and "religious policy" under different rulers (was not Mughal India already secular?). In many of these accounts, Mughal power marks the beginning of the "modern" state, and of a "modern" economy and administration, which the British would inherit and "develop" in various ways.

This book indicates the need for raising different kinds of questions, and attempts to study Mughal history in terms other than those narrowly concerned with the emergence of a bourgeois, secular, democratic, "modern" India. One area in which the emergence of modernity – capitalism, secularism, democracy, and so on – has been relatively slow, and where change has been less readily visible, is that of familial relations, domesticity, and reproductive duties. I take this area as my focus, precisely so that we may open up other questions of social history and insist upon more careful investigation of the different locations and worldviews, struggles and aspirations, that mark not only different periods of history but every individual period of history too. One point to be borne in mind throughout such investigations is that

---

[39] O'Hanlon, "Kingdom, Household and Body," p. 3.

Mughal history cannot be seen as simply the precursor of British rule in India, or as a pale (or less-developed) form of modern institutions and practices.

Through its investigation of the changing character of Mughal domestic life over the sixteenth century, this book attempts to show how Mughal rule itself – its procedures, its prescriptions, and its spirit – evolved over time. Even though the Mughal empire was a "Muslim" empire (in the sense of being a polity with a Muslim ruler at its head), nothing was given, predestined, or inevitable in the character of its political arrangement, its domestic relations, or its religious policy. Like other Muslim empires (and, indeed, like all empires everywhere), this one too established itself according to its particular circumstances, in its particular context.

The question of public–private

This brings me to my other potential audiences, feminist scholars working on Islamic as well as non-Islamic societies who have forcefully criticized conventional histories predicated on a presumed opposition between public and private life.

This book asks questions about the usefulness of the terms "public" and "private" for a study of Mughal society and politics, but *not* in order to suggest that we dispense with these terms altogether. Trying to invent new vocabularies by arguing that these fit local cultures and contingent histories better is, to use Michael Warner's words, a "rather desperate solution."[40] What we need instead is to engage in new ways with vocabularies and debates that have long sought to make sense of diverse and changing conditions.

In order to do this, I want to highlight the argument made by several scholars about the complex and shifting signs of the public and private. What seems to have been picked up from these terms is an "almost instinctual" meaning rooted in common speech.[41] "So although public and private seem so clearly opposed that their violation can produce a sharp feeling of revulsion," Michael Warner argues, "the terms have many different meanings that often go unnoticed." Moreover, these terms are frequently defined against each other, "with normative preference for one term," and that is not always the case.[42] These terms are neither exact parallels, nor polar opposites. Warner sketches a genealogy of how the public and private came to be imagined as binaries, closely aligned in the liberal tradition, reaching back at least to John Locke.[43]

Consider a range of categories that have come to be ineffaceably marked by "definitional binarisms": secrecy/disclosure, knowledge/ignorance, private/public, masculine/feminine, majority/minority, innocence/initiation, natural/artificial, new/old, discipline/terrorism, canonic/noncanonic, domestic/foreign,

---

[40] Michael Warner, *Publics and Counterpublics* (New York, 2002), p. 11.
[41] *Ibid.*, p. 23.   [42] *Ibid.*, pp. 27–28.   [43] *Ibid.*, see ch. 1, "Public and Private."

wholeness/decadence, urbane/provincial, and so on.[44] The problem in using these binaries, as Eve Kosofsky Sedgwick explains in another context, is that the "definitional nodes in the forms of binarisms ... has to do not with a mystical faith in the number two but, rather, with the felt need to schematize in some consistent way the treatment of social vectors so exceedingly various."[45]

Given the host of meanings and forms of public and private, and the modern complex genealogy of these terms, why is it the case that scholars working on pre- and early modern Islamic societies have carried on deploying a sensibility of binaries to the alternate formulations that they are experimenting with? Despite a critique of the public–private, particularly the strict demarcation that came to be associated with these terms, scholars have, it seems unselfconsciously, kept the ethos of the binary that emerged in the liberal tradition. Their new terms are often presented in two, neatly drawn, easily demarcated, and sometimes distinctly opposite, spheres. Is this because we cannot escape the force of modern (bourgeois) language even when we are aware that certain conceptualizations might not be relevant to the historical circumstances we are concerned with? In a sense there is no escaping from such "categories brought into play by modern forces,"[46] but there are ways in which one might engage with and produce interesting convergences with terms such as the public–private.

By emphasizing the problem in employing binarisms, I want to think about the categorization and conceptualization of the pre-modern historical instance of the Mughals. I take the issue of binaries as central to my engagements, not least because it has been at the heart of scholarly concerns in the West since the debate on public–private spheres in women's history took center-stage in the 1970s.[47] Indeed, the binarized character of these terms has been continually tested and broadened. In an anthology entitled *Woman, Culture and Society* (1974),[48] edited by Michelle Rosaldo and Louise Lamphere, an early attempt was made to identify the structural framework necessary to understand the opposition between domestic and public in psychological, cultural, social, and economic aspects of human life. Rayna Reiter took the debate forward by arguing for the socially constructed, fluid, and changeable character of separate public and private domains.[49]

---

[44] Eve Kosofsky Sedgwick, *Epistemology of the Closet* (Berkeley, 1990), p. 11; cf. Warner, *Publics and Counterpublics*, p. 29.

[45] Sedgwick, *Epistemology*, p. 11, n. 19.

[46] Talal Asad, "Conscripts of Western Civilization," in Christine Gailey (ed.), *Dialectical Anthropology: Essays in Honor of Stanley Diamond* (Ithaca, 1992), p. 333.

[47] The issue of rethinking public and private in women's history has been dealt with comprehensively in the following volume: Dorothy O. Helly and Susan M. Reverby (eds.), *Gendered Domains: Rethinking Public and Private in Women's History: Essays from the Seventh Berkshire Conference on the History of Women* (Ithaca, 1992).

[48] Michelle Rosaldo and Louise Lamphere (eds.), *Woman, Culture, and Society* (Stanford, 1974).

[49] Rayna Reiter (ed.), *Toward an Anthropology of Women* (New York, 1975), pp. 12–13. This volume contained the classic essay by Gayle Rubin, "The Traffic in Women: Notes on the 'Political Economy' of Sex."

The question of cultural, historical, and sexual specificity became noticeably pertinent in the debate on the public–private spheres. Rosaldo, along with other scholars, articulated the difficulties and danger of universal categories in the 1980s.[50] The debate among feminist scholars was thus marked by an investigation of the genealogy of particular conceptual categories that we use for understanding different historical moments.[51]

Carole Pateman's *The Sexual Contract* (1998) articulated a major challenge to the received wisdom on the origins of modern political regimes and the relation of public and private domains.[52] Pateman argued that the original social contract was also a sexual one, a story of freedom and of subjection that established patriarchy. Liberal theorists have "naturalised political power in the social or public realm," forgetting, as Pateman put it, politely if ironically, "to discuss domestic life" and how the division of public and private is produced in the first place.[53]

Likewise, the feminist critique of the public–private dichotomy became central to the arguments of socialist feminists who now looked anew at theories explaining class and production from the vantage point of sexuality and patriarchy.[54] Scholars working on non-Western societies had also begun to ask how the model of public and private domains, notions of domesticity and family, and propositions about the making of intimate communities, might appear in the light of historical and cultural specificities, and the extent

---

[50] See Michelle Rosaldo, "The Use and Abuse of Anthropology: Reflections on Feminism and Cross-Cultural Understanding," *Signs*, 5 (Spring 1980), pp. 389–417.

[51] Susan Moller Okin, for instance, examined the treatment of women in the works of four classic political philosophers – Plato, Aristotle, Rousseau, and Mill – to be able to understand how their conceptions of women hinged around the naturalness of family and its separation from the *polis*; Susan Moller Okin, *Women in Western Political Thought* (Princeton, 1979). See also, Jean Bethke Elshtain, *Public Man, Private Woman: Women in Social and Political Thought* (Princeton, 1981).

[52] Carole Pateman, *The Sexual Contract* (Stanford, 1988).

[53] Cited in Helly and Reverby (eds.), *Gendered Domains*, p. 9, as part of a discussion of Pateman's work. In a parallel move, Joan Landes built on the theoretical framework of Jürgen Habermas, exploring the extent to which the bourgeois political life of France rested upon the renaming of public space as male; Joan B. Landes, *Women and the Public Sphere in the Age of the French Revolution* (Ithaca, 1988); for a study of the implications drawing on the opposition between public and private spheres in the context of the Old Regime in France, see Dena Goodman, "Public Sphere and Private Life: Toward a Synthesis of Current Historiographical Approaches to the Old Regime," *History and Theory: Studies in the Philosophy of History*, 31 (1992), p. 15. Of course, Habermas's *The Structural Transformation of the Public Sphere* (Cambridge, Mass., 1989) has been the subject of a much larger debate, including some reductive readings. For a cogent summing of debates on Habermas, see Warner, *Publics and Counterpublics*, pp. 46–56.

[54] Some examples of the earliest works in this direction are: Eli Zaretsky, *Capitalism, the Family, and Personal Life* (New York, 1976); Lise Vogel, *Marxism and the Oppression of Women: Towards a Unitary Theory* (New Brunswick, 1983); and the influential work of Leonore Davidoff and Catherine Hall, *Family Fortunes: Men and Women of the English Middle Class* (London, 1987). For one of the earliest close readings of feminist anthropology and of material bases of structural difference, see also Joan Kelly, "The Social Relation of the Sexes: Methodological Implications of Women's History," *Signs*, 1 (Summer 1976), pp. 809–823.

to which Western paradigms were relevant to the study of non-Western societies.[55]

Cynthia Nelson made an early argument of this kind in relation to pastoral and sedentary societies in the Middle East. She suggested that the "domestic" concerns of women in such societies were nothing if not political, and looked at wide-ranging ethnographic instances to show how women "negotiated their social order." She emphasized women's part in marital alliances, their participation in warfare, in elaborate networks of friendship and gift-exchange, and in the practice of sorcery, to speak of the "influence" of women "without exaggerating" their importance in public life.[56]

Lila Abu-Lughod's 1986 study of Bedouin women's ritual poetry complicated the question of public–private distinctions. By looking at Bedouin women's poetry and codes of behavior, Abu-Lughod showed how these women were not "confined" to a "domestic" sphere; they were dynamic individuals who used highly valuable cultural forms to express their senti-ments, apparently acknowledging an alternative system of beliefs and values, and constituting through these, forms of dissent and subversive discourse.[57]

Investigations of the early modern Islamic courtly world, more directly relevant to the subject of this book, were at the fore in developing this kind of critique. Leslie Peirce's book, *The Imperial Harem: Women and Sovereignty in the Ottoman Empire* (1993), was one of the first to challenge the applicability of the public–private model to the Ottoman setting.[58] This study has made a major contribution to our reevaluation of the Ottoman state, and the sources of its royal women's authority, family politics, and gender relations in the *haram*. I consider Peirce's work extensively for two reasons: one, this was the first work that provided a clear demonstration of the problems that arise in working with a simple public–private model for courtly societies. Second, Peirce's *Imperial Harem* is the only comprehensive history of gender relations at the Ottoman court, and is an excellent sounding-board for my own inquiry.

Peirce asks what the idea of the "private" "might have meant to an Ottoman man or woman."[59] She reflects at one point on the "language that Ottomans themselves used to describe divisions in their society." She reports briefly on the levels of the meanings of a vast terminology that is available to her:

"the *hass* and the *amm*" had both an abstract level of meaning – the private, particular, or singular versus the universal – and a sociopolitical meaning – the elite versus the

---

[55] See the writings of Michel Foucault, Joan Scott, and Gayatri Chakravorty Spivak as path-breaking instances of this new kind of work that challenged the existing modes of analysis.

[56] Cynthia Nelson, "Public and Private Politics: Women in the Middle Eastern World," *American Ethnologist*, 1, 3 (August 1974), pp. 551–552, 553, 555.

[57] Lila Abu-Lughod, *Veiled Sentiments: Honor and Poetry in a Bedouin Society* (Berkeley and Los Angeles, 1986). For a more recent analysis on connections between gender, politics, and the public sphere, see Nilufer Gole, *The Forbidden Modern: Civilization and Veiling* (Ann Arbor, 1996).

[58] Peirce, *Imperial Harem*.   [59] *Ibid.*, p. 7.

common, the ruling class versus the ruled. The word *hass*, however, presumably aroused a more complex range of associations because of its additional meaning of "that which is associated with or belongs to the ruler," that is, anything royal. Many of the institutional manifestations of the royal power were denoted by the word *hass*: for example, the sultan's privy chamber, the *has oda*; privileged attendants of the sultan, male and female, who bore the title *haseki*; and the royal domains, known simply as "hass". . . . More prevalent in the Ottomans' self-description is the dichotomy of inner and outer, the interior and the exterior. Two sets of words, one Turkish and one Persian, were commonly used to describe this division: *ic/iceri* in Turkish and *enderun* in Persian, for the inner or the interior, and correspondingly, *dis/disari* (or *tasra*) and *birun* for the outer or exterior. [60]

While Peirce's move opens up a critique of the anachronistic (and normalizing) use of the public–private dichotomy and attendant notions of family, and private life, her doubts about the public–private dichotomy remain suspended for the rest of her book, and she lapses into binaries of her own. Her assemblage of alternative terms such as the *hass* and the *amm* are dichotomous, as are *ic/iceri*, *dis/disari*, and *enderun/birun*. Peirce's other contention, that "power relationships in Islamic society are represented by spatial division more horizontal than vertical, in contrast to Western metaphors: instead of moving *up*, one moves *in* towards greater authority,"[61] also does not escape the sensibility of binarism: up and down or in and out still remains a binary.

Peirce says at one point that the Ottoman society of the sixteenth and seventeenth centuries "was dichotomized into spheres characterized less by notions of public/commonweal/male and private/domestic/female than by distinctions between the privileged and the common, the sacred and the profane – distinctions that cut across the dichotomy of gender."[62] Recall Sedgwick's warning about the context of the network of normative "definitional binarisms"; Peirce's "privileged and the common, and the sacred and the profane," in fact, can easily be situated along this continuum of neatly distinguishable terms.[63]

---

[60] *Ibid.*, p. 9.   [61] *Ibid.*

[62] The only spatial (and institutional) category that the author stays with is the *haram*. In fact in working extensively with the *haram*, Peirce digs out the many layers of power and authority in the Ottoman context – beyond the seemingly exclusive power of the male sultan, thus bringing out the many dimensions of the *haram* system.

[63] In a separate article on the subjects of the Ottoman Empire, specifically the Anatolian Turkish-speaking peoples, Peirce investigated a variety of words used by them to denote female and male (*liz*, *avret*, and *hatun* for females, and *oglan*, *ergen*, and *er* for males). The most interesting feature of this vocabulary, Peirce illustrated, was the attention given to individual life-stages, and Ottoman society's notions of normative and problematic sexual behavior. Moreover, this vocabulary showed that it was hegemonic neither for males nor for females. Leslie P. Peirce, "Seniority, Sexuality, and Social Order: The Vocabulary of Gender in Early Modern Ottoman Society," in Madeline C. Zilfi (ed.), *Women in the Ottoman Empire: Middle Eastern Women in the Early Modern Era* (Leiden, 1997).

Several other scholars have undertaken parallel investigations of public–private dichotomies in other locales complicating our readings. In an article entitled "Slippers at the Entrance or Behind Closed Doors," Dina Rizk Khoury investigates the use and perception of space by women in eighteenth- and nineteenth-century Mosul, part of Ottoman Iraq at the time.[64] By using court records involving cases of litigation on division of domestic space, she analyzes the meanings of domestic space for women of different social classes. In this regard, Khoury warns us right at the start that although there was no doubt that "urban-based Islamic scholars articulated a discourse on boundaries between men and women, Muslims and non-Muslims," the distinctions between the public and private are "more a product of our century's sensibilities than the realities of the early modern period." She argues elsewhere that the discourse of the urban-based Islamic scholars, until the late nineteenth century, was quite flexible, being shaped by the political and economic conditions of specific societies at specific times.[65]

Khouri observes that

there was a clear distinction in the vernacular of Mosulis between one's domestic space and that of one's neighbor. The multitude of proverbs that stress the importance of getting along with one's neighbor while maintaining one's sense of privacy, points to the constant tension between what takes place behind closed doors and how it is perceived within women's immediate surroundings. ... Scholars have debated the place of the quarter in the urban hierarchy of public and private spaces. Some have posited that while the quarter was public space, it was made private by women's use of it for domestic and familial chores [the author cites Erika Friedl]. Certainly for Mosuli women, the quarter was a familiar but public space in which they participated in public life in a ritualized and negotiated manner [*sic*]. To a large degree, their definition of what was private and public in the quarter depended on whether they wore veils or not.[66]

It is easy to note that a commonsensical ("almost instinctual"[67]) reading of domestic, privacy, and public–private seems to structure Khouri's interpretation of Mosuli texts. The only moment when the author invokes a plurality of meanings of public–private is when she suggests that these were intersecting spaces. This is also the moment when she points to the contingencies that might be at play in the making of spaces, public or private.

---

[64] Dina Rizk Khoury, "Slippers at the Entrance or Behind Closed Doors: Domestic and Public Spaces for Mosuli Women," in Zilfi (ed.), *Women in the Ottoman Empire*, pp. 105–106. This is the only article of Khoury that I discuss here. She raises very similar questions in another article, "Drawing Boundaries and Defining Spaces: Women and Space in Ottoman Iraq," in Amira El Azhary Sonbol (ed.), *Women, the Family, and Divorce Laws in Islamic History* (Syracuse, 1996), pp. 173–187.

[65] Khoury, "Slippers," pp. 106–107. See also Khoury, "Drawing Boundaries and Defining Spaces."

[66] *Ibid.*, pp. 115–116.   [67] Warner, *Publics and Counterpublics*, p. 23.

Special mention may be made here of Kathryn Babayan's investigation of the world of urban women in Isfahan through the *'Aqa'id al-Nisa* (Beliefs of Women), a book of social critiques by females, probably written by a cleric called Aqa Jamal Khwansari during the reign of the Persian king, Shah Sulayman (1666–94).[68] Although Babayan does not directly engage the public–private debate, her article is suggestive in relation to the construction of pre-modern Muslim women's spaces in Iran. She locates the *'Aqa'id al-Nisa* in the time before the accession of Shah Sultan Husain which witnessed "a radical shift in mood" in Isfahan reminiscent of the Islamic Revolution of 1979. In the sixteenth century, Babayan argues, many different cultural traditions and tendencies provided the background for the construction of attitudes concerning gender and gender-differentiated space, and gives an example of a decree from 1694–95 to illustrate the imperial reaction to the "more eclectic and tolerant ... culture of the classical Safavid era."[69] These were the new paradigms and new "locations of authority" that according to the author formulated the roles of women in dynastic politics as members of the royal household.[70]

The "colorful view of the female sex through five Isfahani women"[71] is analyzed in this cosmos. Through the *'Aqa'id al-Nisa*, Babayan engages the reader in the possibilities of negotiation of fluid physical and mental boundaries as the Isfahani women go about their daily activities. She investigates the performance of local rituals and belief systems of the different confessional groups of Isfahan, demonstrating how the Safavid society was geared towards "communal socializing."[72] The author unpacks the dynamics of this Isfahani community as described by Aqa Jamal. Babayan's attempt to conceptualize the notion of intimacy between members of the same sex, both men and women, is particularly notable. She does this by working out the meanings of terms such as "*khwahar khwaneh*," which has come to "imply a lesbian [*tabaq zan*] in modern Persian literary usage,"[73] and argues that in fact "same-sex relationships were not only about sex ... [but also] involved a sharing of things intimate and personal, a fusion of emotions, and antiquated friendships that are rare in the modern world."[74]

These studies help us to ask: once the critique of the public–private dyad has gone so far, what sense does it make to retain the use of this dichotomy – with or without inverted commas? Is it not necessary at this point to consider alternative ways in which to engage with these terms and conceptualize domains of political contest and intimate relations in some other way that

[68] Babayan, "The 'Aqa'id al-Nisa," p. 349. The spelling and English translation of the text *'Aqa'id al-Nisa* are the author's.
[69] *Ibid.*, pp. 358–359.
[70] *Ibid.*, pp. 350–351. Babayan elaborates these ideas in her book, *Mystics, Monarchs, and Messiahs: Cultural Landscapes of Early Modern Iran* (Cambridge, Mass., 2002).
[71] Babayan, "The 'Aqa'id al-Nisa," p. 362.   [72] *Ibid.*, p. 366.
[73] *Ibid.*, p. 370.   [74] *Ibid.*, p. 373.

might bear closer resemblance to the concepts employed by our historical Others? Perhaps I should add that this demand is easier to make than to execute. It requires, to use Sedgwick's words, "a painstaking process of accumulative reading and historical de- and recontextualization."[75] It is to this slow and painstaking process that I hope this book will contribute.

In summary

Like several of my predecessors, I started research on the domestic life of the early Mughals with an attempt to frame the stories from the Mughal texts in the context of the debates around public and private spheres. I tried to examine the extent to which there existed a private domain (family, *haram*), clearly separated from the public (court). In studying the lives of Mughal men and women, it appeared that public–private were originally different parts of the same courtly life, and that the "private" closely intersected with and spilled over into the "public." The private was never completely segregated, or exclusively residential. Many activities took place in this public–private space, a large number of which were of great political significance. In fact, one could argue that there was no distinction between the public and the private – in the sense of the physical separation of the court and the *haram* – in the time of the peripatetic kings Babur and Humayun. The strict demarcation of physical spaces came about only in the reign of Akbar. Alongside, another sense of the "private" emerged: of a royalty "beyond the reach" of, and "mysterious" and inaccessible to, the rest of the population: the majestic emperor, his secluded *haram*, and the aura of his centralized authority.

In the chronicles of the Mughal times, there is a constellation of concepts for "domestic" – giving us a sense of the pre-history of the Mughal *haram* – before the term *haram* came into frequent use in the imperial histories of Akbar. The *ahl va 'ayal*, the *khanivadeh*, or the *kuch va oruk* of Babur's time, and the *ahl-i haram* or the *haraman-i padshah* of Humayun's time (to take but a few examples), evoke flexible structures and the many layers of a peripatetic world. These terms indicate the number and kind of people, the particularity of the inhabited physical spaces, the importance of ancestral connections, the well-entrenched hierarchies in relationships, and emerging patterns of kinship.[76] In this Persian vocabulary, there is a history of the shifting physical-political-cultural circumstances of the nobles, as well as their shifting relationships. None of this vocabulary demarcates a fixed set of relations or bounded spaces which can be reduced to our understanding of the "family" or the "private." These alternative ways of classifying social life project the variable associations that characterize the fluid early Mughal world.

---

[75] Sedgwick, *Epistemology*, p. 12.

[76] There is an extended discussion of these and other cognate terms in chapters 5 and 6. I do not want to provide a quick translation here since any brief translation would be misleading.

Properly understood, this vocabulary cannot be reduced to binaries of any kind.

As I became increasingly aware of the richness and unfamiliarity of this world, I became more hesitant about using the public–private distinction. A binary implies much about ways of thinking and being that are not to be found in the historical conditions that I am concerned with. Moreover, a framework that dichotomizes assemblages that are multiplicitous tends to erode much of the history and individuality of domestic life at the time of the Mughals. My central concern in this book is to excavate a domain, the boundaries of which are very unclear. Part of the purpose of marking out such a domain is to bring to life the denizens of a hitherto invisible Mughal world: the mothers of the royal children, their nurses, and servants, and others who formed part of these (changing) intimate circles.

The place of women in this history is obviously crucial. The activities of women, the very construction of more permanent domestic quarters, the conceptualization of the *haram*, all of these were part of the making of the new regime, and of establishing its power. That the women eventually became *pardeh-giyan* (veiled ones), and were restricted to secluded quarters called the *haram*, does not alter the point that their status and conduct were of critical importance in the establishment of imperial traditions and imperial grandeur, indeed an intrinsic part of the becoming of a (grand) monarchy.

I discuss instances of autonomy and power exercised by Mughal women. It is in this extensive tradition of matriarchal authority that the most conspicuous symbol of influence and supremacy for Mughal historians – Nur Jahan, the so-called Empress of Mughal India – may be appropriately situated. Contrary to what Findly and others would have us believe, Nur Jahan's empress-status is thus far from an originary moment in the complex history of the making of institutions, mores and practices – courtly or domestic.

A crucial question, then, is that of the extent to which Mughal power was concentrated exclusively in the person of the emperor. An investigation of Mughal life immediately shows the many points of initiative and influence that continued to function throughout this period, the tensions that arose, and the contrary claims of different nodes of power that needed to be resolved in the context of new challenges and new crises. What emerges from this is a history of rich and diverse relations, complicated by the workings of different personalities and the limitations of the sources. What emerge also are clear indications of change over time.

The chapters that follow are an attempt to construct an analysis of Mughal domestic life, of Mughal women and men in their personal relations and activities. This history, I should emphasize, is not a comprehensive account with a neat beginning, middle, and an end. The point here is to bring to life moments of another era. Sometimes, in order to do this, one has to bring together historical moments in ways that do not meet the demands of chronological history. For this reason, and to explain the struggle involved in this exercise, chapters 2 and 3 are concerned with the way in which Mughal domestic life has been represented and the manner in which the archive has been constructed and used.

Having laid out the historiographical context of this work in these initial chapters, I then proceed to two sets of two chapters each. One deals with the period of Babur and Humayun, and the other with the time of Akbar. In each set, the first chapter seeks to map the broader political-intellectual configuration of the court society of the time, while the second chapter provides a more detailed account of the domestic arrangements and activities within the domain that might be described as that of a family or intimate circle.

The concluding chapter of the book draws out some of the implications of the findings presented in the earlier chapters, in part by undertaking a comparison of domestic life in the three great sixteenth-century "Muslim" kingdoms – Mughal India, Ottoman Turkey, and Safavid Iran.

CHAPTER 2

A genealogy of the Mughal *haram*

Much of our knowledge of "the *haram*" comes from the detailed and "scandalous" accounts found in the writings of the early European travelers to India. These writings have been read in a particular way to produce "the Oriental *haram*." I argue in this chapter that the knowledge of the *haram* generated from these travel accounts (and through the accounts and representations of other *harams*, most notably that of the Ottomans[1]) came to occupy an entirely different locus, and significance, once colonial power was established and the Orientalist enterprise of "understanding" and representing India had taken off in the nineteenth century.

William Crooke's introduction to Mrs. Meer Hasan Ali's memoir, *Observations on the Mussulmauns of India*,[2] provides a good example of how deeply entrenched colonial views about the civilizations of the East had become by his time. Mrs. Meer Hasan Ali was an Englishwoman who spent twelve years in India, from 1816 to 1828; eleven of those years were spent in the house of her father-in-law at Lucknow.[3] According to Crooke, the author's family name and the date and place of her marriage were unknown. However, she married Meer Hasan Ali, who taught Arabic to British officers in Calcutta. They went to England in May 1810. Hasan Ali had been appointed assistant to an Oriental scholar at the Military College, Adiscombe. He taught at Adiscombe for six years, before returning to India on grounds of ill health. Mr. and Mrs. Meer Hasan Ali sailed together for

---

[1] Cf. Fatima Mernissi's apt observation: "[It is] the Ottoman imperial harem that has fascinated the West almost to the point of obsession. ... Imperial harems, that is, splendid palaces full of luxuriously dressed and lasciviously reclined indolent women, with slaves standing by and eunuchs watching the gates. ... Why have the Ottoman imperial harems had such an impact on Western imagination? One reason could be the Ottomans' spectacular conquest of Constantinople, the Byzantine capital, in 1453, and their subsequent occupation of many European cities, as well as the fact that they were the West's closest and most threatening neighbor." Fatima Mernissi, *Dreams of Tresspass: Tales of a Harem Girlhood* (Reading, Mass., 1994), pp. 33–34, n. 3.

[2] Mrs. Meer Hassan Ali, *Observations on the Mussulmauns of India*, ed. W. Crooke (1917; rpt. Karachi, 1974).

[3] *Ibid.*, Introduction, p. xi.

Calcutta. She went back to England twelve years later, again because of ill health, and never returned.[4]

Crooke's introduction to Mrs. Ali's memoir states that the value of the book lies in its "first-hand [record of the] experiences of an English lady who occupied the exceptional position of membership of a Musalman family." Since she had "free access to the houses of respectable Sayyids," Mrs. Ali was able to gain "ample facilities" for the study of the manners and customs of Muslim families. "Much of her information on Islam was obtained from her husband and his father, both learned, travelled gentlemen, and by them she was treated with a degree of toleration unusual in a Shi'ah household, this sect being rigid and often fanatical followers of Islam," he writes, adding that her picture of life in the women's quarters (*zenana*) "is obviously coloured by her frank admiration for the people amongst whom she lived, who treated her with respect and consideration. It is thus to some extent idyllic."[5]

Crooke compares Mrs. Meer Hasan Ali's memoir with Fanny Parks's "charming" book *The Wanderings of a Pilgrim in Search of the Picturesque* (1850). Fanny Parks benefited from "a literary knowledge of Hindustani," according to Crooke, while Mrs. Meer Hasan Ali "can have been able to speak little more than a broken patois, knew little of grammar, and was probably unable to read or write the Arabic character."[6] He approvingly cites Fanny Parks's judgment on the "reality" of the *zenana*: "a place of intrigue ... those who live within [its] four walls cannot pursue a straight path; ... never was any place so full of intrigue, scandal, and chit-chat as a zenana."[7]

Reproduced here was a particular vision of Eastern reality, which alone was accorded the status of the truth. The only acceptable narratives were those that spoke of a strange, unfathomable society, which had no history. Any other kind of description was idyllic or "coloured by frank admiration" of the Other. In this way, the world of the colonized became fixed, with images of violence, religiosity, indiscipline, divisiveness, laziness, lustfulness, and strangeness – eunuchs and the *haram*. These are the images that many contemporary historians have come to inherit.

Colonial developments

In European travel writings up to the seventeenth century, one rarely encounters general propositions of the inferiority of the East. At some point in the eighteenth and nineteenth centuries, however, a different kind of statement began to emerge, one that was to become a part of the standard British image of India. This new representation rested upon accounts of specific institutions

[4] *Ibid.*, pp. xiii, x–xi.   [5] *Ibid.*, pp. xv–xvi.   [6] *Ibid.*, p. xvi.   [7] *Ibid.*, pp. xvi–xvii.

and practices that were symbolic of the "abject slavery," general "barbarity," and "lamentably debased" condition of the East.[8]

The new discourse was premised upon a hierarchy of civilizations. In the uniformity and repetitiveness of its terms, a far more homogenous and fixed narrative emerged. The *haram* now appeared in a far more tantalizing and debased form. For illustration, let me draw on three well-known nineteenth-century "histories" – James Mill's *The History of British India*, Elliot and Dowson's *History of India as told by its own Historians*, and Stanley Lane-Poole's *Aurangzeb*.

James Mill wrote his *History of British India* (first published in 1818) when two sets of opinions about India were abroad. William Jones and "fellow Sanskritists" were arguing that Hindus had reached "a high degree of civilization."[9] Their work had opened up what Warren Hastings called "a new and most extensive range for the human mind, beyond the present limited and beaten field of its operations."[10] On the other hand, people like Charles Grant and John Shore, representing the evangelical point of view, called for the introduction of Western education and Christianity to change the "hideous state of Indian society."[11]

Mill wrote in line with the latter opinion. He designed a ladder of civilization or scale of civilization "to simplify the legislator's task of prescribing for each society on each particular rung."[12] In a section entitled "Manners" in volume I of his *History*, Mill says, "The lower orders, in other countries, are often lamentably debased; in Hindustan they are degraded below the brutes."[13] On the manners of the Hindus, more specifically:

It is not surprising, that grossness, in ideas and language, respecting the intercourse of the sexes, is a uniform concomitant of the degraded state of the women. ... Inquiry discovers, that grossness in this respect is a regular ingredient in the manners of a rude age; and that society, as it refines, deposits this, among its other impurities.[14]

What is striking in Mill's account is the way in which detailed accounts are now inserted into a structured statement about hierarchy and civilization. The section on "Manners," taken from a chapter in volume II entitled "Mohammedan Civilisation," demonstrates the point yet again:

In truth, the Hindu, like the Eunuch, excels in the qualities of a slave. ... But if less soft, the Mohammedan is more manly, more vigorous. [In both of them however there is] the same insincerity, mendacity, and perfidy; the same indifference to the feelings of others; the same prostitution and venality are conspicuous. ... The Mohammedans are profuse, when possessed of wealth, and devoted to pleasure; the Hindus are almost always penurious and ascetic.[15]

---

[8] James Mill, *The History of British India*, ed. Horace Hayman Wilson, vols. I–II (5th edn, London, 1858), I, pp. 303, 309, 313.
[9] C. H. Philips (ed.), *Historians of India, Pakistan and Ceylon* (London, 1961), p. 220.
[10] *Ibid.*, p. 218.   [11] *Ibid.*   [12] *Ibid.*, p. 220.   [13] Mill, *History*, I, p. 303.
[14] *Ibid.*, I, p. 321.   [15] *Ibid.*, II, pp. 365–366.

The extract is indicative of the terms of a discourse of hierarchy that emerges in Mill's writing. One might refer to this as the "textual strategy" of his *History*. Once the terms for the debasement and barbarity of the East (insincerity, mendacity, perfidy, prostitution and venality, penuriousness and asceticism) are in place, it does not matter any longer whether details of particular institutions or practices are made available. They will all henceforth fit into a discourse about the less than civilized Other.

The sensuality of women, luxury, pleasure, and indolence become ready signifiers of a dehistoricized world. These are a central part of a discourse laden with stereotypes. The nineteenth-century colony is nothing but a collection of the latter. The Mughal *haram*, to the extent that it is detailed in these nineteenth-century colonial histories, becomes a part of a sweeping statement on the inferiority of the East – governed by virtues such as lust, immoderation, and (in the case of the well-to-do) the obscene display of wealth.

Elliot and Dowson's *History of India as told by its own Historians* provides a good example of how colonial structures of knowledge and power conditioned colonial histories. In the collection of records of Indo-Muslim history, Elliot poured scorn on all Muslim chroniclers of India's history:[16]

Indeed, it is almost a misnomer to style them histories. ... They comprise, for the most part nothing but a mere dry narration of events, conducted with reference to chronological sequence, never grouped philosophically. ... [If] "History is Philosophy teaching by examples," then there is no Native Indian Historian ....[17]

In the histories from the "Muslim period," Elliot and Dowson noted, there was little below "the glittering surface, and ... the practical operation of a despotic Government." By turning to the "present Muhammedan kingdoms of India" and "the people subject to their sway," he argued, one could "draw a parallel between ancient and modern times."[18] These are the "parallels" he found: kings "sunk in sloth and debauchery"; officials who were in fact the "chief robbers and usurers"; eunuchs, reveling in the "spoil of plundered provinces"; the "sensuality and drunkenness of the tyrants."[19]

There was little creditable in India according to Elliot and Dowson. No history, no historians. No measure in actions, no method in government. It

---

[16] Philips, *Historians*, p. 226.
[17] H. M. Elliot and John Dowson, *The History of India as told by its own Historians*, vols. I–VIII (1867–77; rpt. New Delhi, 1996), I, Original Preface, pp. xvi–xix. Elphinstone said something along the same lines as Elliot and Dowson in his comment on the sources for a study of Akbar's reign. While recognizing the importance of contemporary court historians, he nonetheless privileged the accounts of the European travelers, which he felt had greater authenticity, effect, richness, and vivacity. He used the accounts of Thomas Roe, William Hawkins, and Purchas's *Pilgrims* extensively in his writing. See Mountstuart Elphinstone, *The History of India* (2nd edn, London, 1843), II, pp. 305–306. Examples of his references to these European writers may be seen on pp. 306–308, and notes.
[18] Elliot and Dowson, *History*, I, p. xx.   [19] *Ibid.*, pp. xx–xxi.

was pleasure and sensuality that governed these animal-like beings. "Should any ambitious functionary entertain the desire of emulating the 'exceedingly magnifical' structures of the Mogul predecessors ... it will check his aspirations to learn, that beyond palaces and porticos, temples, and tombs, there is little worthy of emulation."[20] A period of "medieval darkness" emerges, to quote Partha Chatterjee, the description of which is founded upon "all the prejudices of European Enlightenment about Islam."[21]

In this colonial historiography of civilization and/or its absence, the Mughal *haram* does not need to appear in detail. For example, both James Mill and his successor as an official-historian, Mountstuart Elphinstone, discuss the Mughal *haram* only through minor references to its women. Mughal women are presented as non-entities, existing only for the pleasure of their men, until it comes to an "exception" like Nur Jahan (the "favorite" queen in the European travel accounts of the sixteenth and seventeenth centuries, as we shall see). Nevertheless, even if the *haram* is infrequently discussed, appearing only in sketchy references to particular women, it serves the purpose of adding to the picture of the general degradation of the East. The crucial question here is not one of the amount of space devoted to different kinds of institutions, but of the structuring of even the most scant references to these.

Let me take as a final illustration, a later nineteenth-century history devoted exclusively to the reign of the last of the great Mughals. In this study, Stanley Lane-Poole carries forward the ethos and vocabulary of the earlier texts.[22] In writing about the forefathers of Aurangzeb, Lane-Poole describes Jahangir (based on Thomas Roe) as follows: "He kept his orgies for the evening, and during the day he was sobriety personified."[23] And here is an imaginative summation of Shah Jahan's activities:

His favourite wife [Mumtaz Mahal who now comes into the picture], the lady of the Taj, had died in 1631, in giving birth to their fourteenth child, and her husband had centred his affection upon his eldest daughter, Jahan-Ara, with so much fervour as to cause no little scandal, while he also denied himself none of the more transitory joys of the zenana. He had been a grave stern man in his prime, an energetic soldier, and a prudent counsellor: at the age of sixty-four he was a sensual pleasure-loving pageant of royalty, given over to ease and the delights of the eye. ... The burden of the state interfered with his enjoyment. ... In 1657 he was afflicted with a malady which, in the words of Bernier ... "it were unbecoming to describe." The self-indulgence of the old sensualist had brought its retribution.[24]

Lane-Poole's vocabulary is one that clearly builds upon that of his predecessors, but it appears even more entrenched. Note "the self-indulgence of

[20] *Ibid.*, p. xxiii.
[21] Partha Chatterjee, *The Nation and its Fragments: Colonial and Postcolonial Histories* (Princeton, 1993), p. 102.
[22] Stanley Lane-Poole, *Aurangzib* (Oxford, 1893).   [23] *Ibid.*, p. 12.   [24] *Ibid.*, pp. 16–18.

the old sensualist," the oft-repeated story (in the European travel writings) of Shah Jahan's affection for his eldest daughter, Jahan-Ara, and her "unlimited influence,"[25] the maladies that are unnamable and the inevitable product of such self-indulgent lives.

Another point needs to be noted about these histories. Most of them are written in what may be called a public affairs mode, in which the domain of the family or the place of women figures rarely. Colonial historians did not write extensively about the women of the realm, but simply referred to the barbarism seen in the subordination of women.

Thus a new structure of colonial power produced a new structure of knowledge, both explicitly based on a belief in the hierarchy of civilizations. In the pecking order now drawn up, the British (or the British version of Christian civilization) was at the top. Muslims, Hindus and others ranked far below – with the Muslims sometimes rated better than the Hindus, and the Hindus at times seen as superior to the Muslims. The signs of the inferiority of the latter set were frequently seen in the place assigned to their women. *Parda*, *sati*, child-marriage, and the *haram* became more or less equivalent symbols of that barbaric Other. For a report based on these premises, it would not even be necessary to detail each of these institutions; one barbaric practice could stand in for the others. Of course, it was *not only* the ethos of the detailed observations that were selected by the colonial authors to make their point. Alongside the comprehensive accounts of the European travelers, there were also passing references, one-liners that gained in authority by repetition and these in turn became a part of the accumulating narrative on the knowledge of the East.

Let me turn now to some of the early texts from which these references are traced.

Early impressions

In this section, I look at the very early European writings and demonstrate how these are marked by the absence of a sustained, consistent picture of the *haram*. Fragmentary statements on the *haram* appear in the interstices of a larger discourse on public affairs. As a parallel step, I show that despite the striking variety and inconsistency of the early European travel writings, they contain a tendency to be flippant and profligate – something that could allow them to be woven into the fixed representation of the *haram* that emerged in the nineteenth century.

I include in this section the writings of the Jesuit missionaries who visited Akbar's court in the late sixteenth century, the journals of English diplomats representing James I at the court of Jahangir, and a few commercial and non-commercial accounts. Some of the earliest European sketches on the women

---

[25] *Ibid.*, p. 25.

of the Mughal *haram* (*haraman*) are contained in the letters and journals of the Portuguese missionaries, the Jesuit fathers who went to the Mughal court in the form of three embassies. References to the *haraman* are also found in the accounts of Pietro della Valle, a Roman who arrived in India in February 1623, and in the writings of an Englishman Ralph Fitch (who traveled between 1583 and 1591).[26] Thematically similar to Fitch's writings are the journals of the English representatives at the court of Jahangir, William Hawkins (1606–11) and Sir Thomas Roe (1616–19), which I shall include here. I also refer to the writings of William Finch (1608–11), a merchant who was on the same outward voyage as Hawkins, for some unusual new data that he presents.

To begin with, let us recount briefly how the Jesuits came to the Mughal court. Akbar first met a group of Portuguese in 1573 during the siege of Surat, a town in western India. A year later he received Peter Tavares, a Portuguese commandant at his court, and inquired a great deal about Christianity. At Tavares's recommendation, Akbar sent for Father Gil Eanes Pereira, Vicar General of Bengal, who arrived in Fatehpur Sikri in 1578. Unable to satisfy Akbar's curiosity about Christianity, Pereira put to the emperor the idea of inviting a Jesuit mission to the court.[27] A group of three Jesuit missionaries arrived in February 1580. This mission headed by Rudolf Aquaviva stayed in Fatehpur Sikri for three years. A second mission went to Lahore, the new capital, in 1591, and stayed a year. Father Jerome Xavier led the third mission to Akbar's court in 1594.[28]

In the *Commentary* of Father Monserrate, one of the three members of the first Jesuit Mission, we find many scattered, at times unrelated, entries on the women of Akbar's *haram*. In an initial discussion of the activities of the missionary Fathers, he says, for instance, that an atlas, which was brought on behalf of the archbishop of Goa as a present for Akbar, was also shown to the women in the "inner apartment."[29] There is nothing more than this passing reference to women here.

There are other, more detailed, references to the royal women in the *Commentary*. Monserrate speaks of the time when Akbar marched to Kabul in the late 1570s to suppress a conspiracy involving several rebels to install Mirza Hakim, his half-brother, as the ruler of Hindustan. On this occasion, he tells us, the emperor's mother, Hamideh Banu Begum, acted as

[26] The dates given in brackets refer to the dates of travel of subsequent visitors to India.

[27] John Correia-Afonso (ed.), *Letters from the Mughal Court* (Bombay, 1980), p. 5.

[28] Arnulf Camps, *An Unpublished Letter of Father Christoval Ce Vega, S. J. Its Importance for the History of the Second Mission to the Mughal Court and for the Knowledge of the Religion of Emperor Akbar* (Cairo, 1956), p. 7.

[29] J. S. Hoyland (trans.) and S. N. Banerjee (ed.), *The Commentary of Father Monserrate, S. J. On his Journey to the Court of Akbar* (London, 1922), p. 28; hereafter cited as Monserrate, *Commentary*.

the head of the province of Delhi, and provides extensive comments on the arrangements made by Akbar before his departure.[30]

Monserrate also refers to the pilgrimage to Mecca undertaken by the women of Akbar's *haram* in 1578, organized by the emperor's aunt Gulbadan Banu Begum.[31] The handing over of the province of Delhi to the charge of Akbar's mother, and the record of Gulbadan's *hajj*, are striking projections of the power of the senior Mughal women.

Gulbadan's enterprise was noteworthy because of its unusual character. The event does not easily fit with existing accounts of the place of royal women. In addition, Monserrate was aware of the hazards that the journey involved. Several court chroniclers discuss it. He himself comments on Gulbadan's negotiations with the Portuguese. In such circumstances, the event of the pilgrimage by the elder women of the imperial *haram* could not have been short of a curious moment for the Jesuit visitor.

Let us put the above information in Monserrate's *Commentary* by the side of another observation he makes on Akbar. Here he betrays a singular lack of sympathy with Islamic law and the intricate circumstances in which Akbar's empire was coming into being:

He [Akbar] also invented and introduced amongst the Musalmans [Muslims] two forms of marriage, first that with regular consorts, who may number four: and second that with those who are merely called wives, and who may be as numerous as a man's resources allow. Musalman kings employ this sanction and license of the foulest immorality in order to ratify peace and to create friendly relationships with their vassal princes or neighbouring monarchs. For they marry the daughters and sisters of such rulers. Hence Zelaldinus [Akbar] has more than 300 wives, dwelling in ... a very large palace. Yet when the priests were at the court he had only three sons and two daughters.[32]

Monserrate seems to have been struck by what he constructs as the near-infertility of the emperor: five children out of more than three hundred wives. Lane-Poole makes a similar statement in his writing on Akbar's *haram*, in which the question of the number of women is given overbearing importance without a remark upon the significance of the number. Akbar "took other women, Hindu, Persian, Moghul, and even an Armenian, until his harim formed a parliament of religions, though no rumour of their probable debates ever reached the outside world."[33]

Both Monserrate and Lane-Poole completely miss the point that most of Akbar's marital alliances took place in the early part of his reign when the need to cement his power was greatest: his kingdom was not yet a dominant imperial entity, and its general circumstances were fluid. The purpose of this

---

[30] *Ibid.*, pp. 74–75.   [31] I discuss these episodes in detail in chapter 7.

[32] Monserrate, *Commentary*, p. 202.

[33] Stanley Lane-Poole, *Medieval India under Mohammedan Rule A.D. 712–1764* (London, 1903), pp. 251–252.

large number of marriages was not to produce a huge number of children, but rather to stabilize a new and still unstable ruling power. Even if this were to be seen as a self-consciously Muslim polity that was seeking legitimacy as a "Muslim" kingdom, the rules that should govern marital alliances were not strictly laid down, either in the *Shari'a* or in the laws of the illustrious forefathers. A great deal of negotiation went into the making of the empire, and many new traditions arose in consequence.[34]

In Monserrate's text, the projection of the responsibilities (and the unusual visibility) of a number of senior women on the one hand, and his commentary about the "unnatural" character of much that went on in Akbar's court constitute, what Peter Burke, referring to the usage of Pierre Macherey, calls "fractures" – meaning a certain fluctuation in writing.[35] Fractures are perhaps to be expected in these accounts for their authors were continuously encountering new places and spaces. Their experiences of their own contexts and activities will have led to some rethinking and rearticulation.[36] It would be prudent to take what might seem to us "apparent contradictions" in these texts, Peter Burke suggests, "as invitations to explore further, to identify the author's aims and strategies and – in particular – his views of his own culture, from politics to religion."[37]

The missionaries at the court of Akbar seemed – metaphorically – to have stumbled upon the Mughal domestic world. Monserrate had no first-person contact with the *haram* residents. His inquisitiveness perhaps began when the gifted atlas was shown to the women of the "inner apartment." The author built upon this first indirect encounter in his *Commentary*, adding that in a Muslim court where women were not commonly visible, the emperor had left a woman in charge of the central province of the empire. While the details of the appointment of the emperor's mother as the governor of Delhi are likely to have been a matter of common knowledge in the court and the *haram*, the missionary's curiosity produced a record of a fascinating episode that is not mentioned anywhere else. Mughal chroniclers – like their contemporaries, the Ottomans and the Safavids – privilege senior royal women; their few and scattered references to women's lives are mostly about senior women wielding "political" power. Given this emphasis in the records, it is all the more surprising that the event of Hamideh's supremacy goes unacknowledged.[38]

---

[34] For the detail of the processes of the making of Mughal monarchy under Akbar, see chapter 6.

[35] Peter Burke, "The Philosopher as Traveller: Bernier's Orient," in Jaś Elsner and Joan-Pau Rubies (eds.), *Voyages and Visions: Towards a Cultural History of Travel* (London, 1999), pp. 131–132.

[36] Rubies discusses the question of the wider context of the European travelers to India in detail: Joan-Pau Rubies, *Travel and Ethnology in the Renaissance: South India through European Eyes, 1250–1625* (Cambridge, 2000).

[37] Burke, "Philosopher," p. 132.

[38] Peirce's *Imperial Harem* is a fine study of the Ottoman women and questions of sovereignty. Similarly, Maria Szuppe's exploratory article entitled, "The Jewels of Wonder: Learned Ladies and Princess Politicians in the Provinces of Early Safavid Iran" also makes the point about

The Jesuit fathers also wrote several letters home to their mission head-quarters. Most of this correspondence relates to missionary activity at the court, and hinges around the question of converting the emperor to Christianity. In two of these letters, we find a passing mention to imperial women. The first, dated 18 July 1580, written by Rudolf Aquaviva from Fatehpur-Sikri, is addressed to Father Everard Mercurian. Here Aquaviva expresses "doubt about the conversion of this king." He mentions several reasons for this, one being that "he has so many hobbies and at least a hundred wives."[39]

In the second letter, dated 20 July 1580, Rudolf Aquaviva writes to Father Rui Vicente Provincial that an obstacle to Akbar's conversion to Christianity was that he kept himself "greatly occupied" in watching the deer, pigeons, elephants, camels. Moreover, "part of the time he spends with the numerous women he keeps in his house, so that he has no time available to care for what is of consequence to him ... ." In addition, he says, "the opposition of his own people ... is rather great, for on the one side he has his mother, wives and friends to importune him, and on the other are those who wish him ill ... ."[40]

The obstacles to Akbar's conversion (women, deer, etc.) thus become a comment on poverty of character. Because the principal frame of reference for the missionaries was religion, other comments in their letters, such as the ones on women, appear stray, and indiscriminate. Even though some of the particulars in relation to imperial women and the issue of the emperor's conversion might have been important to Monserrate and his companions, their concern was clearly not to detail them in any careful way.

Ralph Fitch (1583–91), a merchant from London, provides us with a rather different kind of detail.[41] His account belongs to a period anterior to the establishment of the East India Company, a time when English merchants (together with the Dutch and the Portuguese) were striving to secure a share in the trade with the "East." Fitch is supposed to have carried a letter regarding commercial possibilities from Queen Elizabeth I for Akbar, though it is not known whether it was actually presented.[42] In any case, Fitch says precious little about the Mughal domestic world. He discusses the cities and court of Akbar: "the great Mogor." He describes the court at Fatehpur Sikri

---

royal women's visibility in records and contemporary activities (in Hambly (ed.), *Women in the Medieval Islamic World*). For the Mughal world, early biographical sketches of "powerful" imperial women were written precisely to make the point about their participation in contemporary politics. See Misra, *Women in Mughal India*; and Nath, *Notable Mughal and Hindu Women*.

[39] Correia-Afonso, *Letters*, p. 59; the English translation for the last Latin sentence is given by the editor as follows: "When the seed of the word has grown, the thorns grown at the same time choke it."

[40] Correia-Afonso, *Letters*, pp. 64–65.

[41] E. F. Oaten, *European Travellers in India during the 15th, 16th and 17th Centuries* (1909; rpt. Lucknow, 1973), p. 68.

[42] William Foster (ed.), *Early Travels in India 1583–1619* (New Delhi, 1985), pp. 2–5.

and mentions that "the King hath in Agra and Fatepore, as they doe credibly report, one thousand elephants, thirtie thousand horses, one thousand and foure hundred tame Deere, eight hundred concubines . . . ." He adds, "Agra and Fatepore are two very great Cities, either of them much greater then [*sic*] London, and very populous . . . ."[43]

Hearsay appears to have been the basis of Fitch's observations. In addition, Fitch seems to have copied substantial sections from an earlier narrative by an Italian called Caesar Frederici.[44] What purpose was this account meant to serve?

To make sense of the assemblage of detail in Fitch's text, let us situate Fitch's views on Akbar and his concubines by the side of some other extracts from his chronicle. He writes about the Brahmins in the following terms:

The Bramenes marke themselves in the foreheads, eares, and throats, with a kind of yellow geare which they grind, and every morning they doe it. . . . And their wives doe come by ten, twentie, and thirtie together, to the water side singing, and there doe wash themselves, and then use their Ceremonies, and marke themselves in their foreheads and faces, and carrie some with them, and so depart singing. Their Daughters bee married, at, or before the age of ten yeeres. The men may have seven wives. They be a kind of craftie people, worse then [*sic*] the Jewes.[45]

Or take his description of the women of Daman (on the west coast of India): "Here the Women weare upon their armes infinite numbers of rings made of Elephants teeth, wherein they take so much delight, that they had rather bee without their meat then without their Bracelets."[46] Consider also this early comment on *sati*, which becomes a common theme with the travelers later on: "The Wives here doe burne with their Husbands when they die, if they will not, their heads be shaven, and never account is made of them afterward."[47]

How do we understand Fitch's writings, and others of this genre? Fitch wrote at a time when there was no real conception of what we today think of as "society": an autonomous sphere of human existence possessing its own recognizable rules. Walther von Wartburg's definition of the late Middle Ages *société*, "communication, union, alliance, or partnership . . . as in a business association or religious order,"[48] might be more applicable to how Fitch and the travelers of his time conceptualized other societies and their conditions. Fitch would be better understood as having produced a picture of Indian *société* in somewhat European terms: recording "societies," to use

[43] Samuel Purchas, *Hakluytus Posthumus or Purchas His Pilgrims: Contayning a History of the World in Sea Voyages and Lande Travells by Englishmen and others*, vol. X (Glasgow, 1905), p. 174; cf. Foster (ed.), *Early Travels*, pp. 17–18.
[44] Kate Teltscher, *India Inscribed: European and British Writing on India 1600–1800* (Delhi, 1995), p. 15.
[45] Purchas, *Hakluytus*, pp. 175–176.   [46] *Ibid.*, p. 169.
[47] *Ibid.*, p. 178; cf. Foster (ed.), *Early Travels*, p. 14.
[48] Cited in Daniel Gordon, *Citizens without Sovereignty: Equality and Sociability in French Thought, 1670–1789* (Princeton, 1994), p. 51, n. 30.

Daniel Gordon's phrase, as "small associations" and the "convivial life that took place within them."[49]

Pietro della Valle – the "most insatiate in curiosity, the most intelligent in apprehension, the fullest and most accurate in description" among the travelers of his age[50] – remarked on several particulars of what he saw in India: the presence of the Dutch in Surat, the absolute freedom of religion extended to all in Gujarat, idol worship, Hindu marriages, and slavery. Born in Rome in 1586, he began his travels in 1615, and arrived in India in February 1623 (during the reign of emperor Jahangir).

Della Valle was a new type of pilgrim, a "secularized one," and the peregrination becomes a way of describing and interpreting.[51] He represented a moment in the "ethnological debate," as Rubies would have it, that made a move from an "essentially theological language towards a fully secular understanding of nature and history."[52] Hugo Plotius, in his *Tabula Peregrinationis continens capita Politica* (1569–70), presents a list of 117 questions to be answered by the traveler, and these distinctions can be associated with some of the divisions of the texts of the European travelers, including Della Valle. These are different "ways of looking" for precise aspects of reality the traveler encounters, which also appear in the German *De Arte Peregrinandi* (published in Nürnberg in 1591).[53] There is an education of the senses or, as these European travelers noted, a "prudential peregrinandi" stressing precisely the importance of interpreting and structuring through writing what the traveler observes.[54] In that sense, Della Valle was a "counter-figure to the armchair cosmographer, Protestant or Catholic."[55]

Della Valle remarks on the differences between "Mahometan Women" and on the "Indian Gentile Women."[56] The "Mahometan Women" in India "go clad" all in white, although "their clothes are oftentimes red . . . ." The "Indian Gentile Women" on the other hand, "use no other colour but red, or certain linnen stamp'd with the works of sundry colours . . . but all upon red, or wherein red is more conspicuous then the rest, whence their attire seems onely red at a distance . . . ."[57]

And then follows his portrayal of Nur Jahan, the wife of emperor Jahangir. The emperor, writes Della Valle, "esteems and favours" her "above all other

---

[49] *Ibid.*, p. 51.   [50] Oaten, *European Travellers*, p. 82.
[51] Rubies, *Travel and Ethnology*, p. 389. For a recent detailed and critical account of Della Valle's writing see, *ibid.*, ch. 10.
[52] *Ibid.*, p. 353.
[53] Justin Stagl, "The Methodising of Travel in the Sixteenth Century: A Tale of Three Cities," *History and Anthropology*, 4 (1990), pp. 306–308.
[54] Stagl, "Methodising," p. 316. I am grateful to Rita Costa-Gomes for these references.
[55] Rubies, *Travel and Ethnology*, p. 353.
[56] Edward Grey (ed.), *The Travels of Pietro Della Valle in India: From the English Translation of 1664, by G. Havers: In Two Volumes* (London, 1892), pp. 44–46; hereafter cited as *Pietro Della Valle*.
[57] *Pietro Della Valle*, pp. 44–46.

women; and his whole empire is govern'd at this day by her counsel." then he gives details of where the queen was born (Persia), and how the king came to marry her. In this connection he produces Nur Jahan's argument against being just another woman in the king's *haram*. According to him, Nur Jahan refused to go to the *haram* saying, "she had been the Wife of an Honourable Captain and Daughter of an Honourable Father, and should never wrong her own Honour, nor that of her Father and Husband, and that to go to the King's *Haram*, and live like other Female-slaves there, was unsuitable to her noble condition." So if the king "had a fancy to her he might take her for his lawful Wife, whereby His Honour would be not onely not injur'd, but highly enlarg'd, and on this condition she was at his service . . . ."[58]

Della Valle was probably following European conventions in writings on royal women. He had connections with the Roman court and his other European referents, the Papacy and the Spanish monarchy,[59] are likely to have affected how he interpreted what he saw of the Mughal queen in India.

Mill reproduced Nur Jahan's story with similar effect as that of Della Valle,[60] although the former's tenor was somewhat more measured than the latter's. For example, in the midst of his observation on Nur Jahan, Della Valle makes an incisive comment about the ethics of courtly behavior: the "honorable" place of the queen as a daughter and an ex-wife – both of noblemen – and what was suitable therefore to her "noble" condition if she were to be in the *haram* of the Mughal emperor.

Other parts of Della Valle's account too are marked by ambiguity and uncertainty. His narrative makes no final judgments on this "strange" life. In that sense, he is what Rubies calls him, "the recorder and interpreter of the East."[61] So when he sees a widow burning on her funeral pyre, Giaccama, the Telegu *sati* of Ekkeri, he articulates the entire experience in a reflective mode, drawing comparisons with similar ancient practices in the West: "a thing which anciently not onely the Indian Women did, according to what *Strabo* writes from the Relation of *Onesicritus* ... as appears by *Julius Solinus*."[62]

I shall now consider the journals of William Hawkins, a sailor, and Sir Thomas Roe, a diplomat, both of whom were sent to India by King James I of England to acquire trading privileges from the Mughal emperor. Hawkins succeeded in getting permission to establish an English factory in Surat. He left Agra in 1611. Then came Thomas Roe, a more prominent representative of the English court.[63] The concern with trading rights looms large in the

---

[58] *Ibid.*, pp. 52–55.   [59] Rubies, *Travel and Ethnology*, pp. 355, 359.

[60] As did Thomas Roe who is discussed below. Mill, *History*, cites Roe on many occasions; see, for example, vol. II, pp. 523, 366, n. 1.

[61] Rubies, *Travel and Ethnology*, p. 356.

[62] *Pietro Della Valle*, pp. 83–84. Cf. Fitch's remark on *Sati* cited above, "The Wives here doe burne with their Husbands when they die, if they will not, their heads be shaven, and never account is made of them afterward."

[63] Oaten, *European Travellers*, pp. 90–94.

writings of both men. The Mughal *haram* – sedate, controlled, and temperate sharply in contrast to the extravagance with which it is depicted in later accounts – appears tangentially in their journals.

Hawkins had devoted many pages of his record to Jahangir. He wrote about the Mughal court, the emperor's routine, his curiosity with regard to objects and issues, his treasure and wealth, his cruelty.[64] Hawkins comments on Jahangir's daily routine: the emperor would pray at daybreak, make a public appearance, this done, he would sleep for two hours and pass his time with his women. At noon, he would show himself to the people again. Here the author mentions the daily hearing of cases. Then he would go back to praying, followed by dinner, and "then he cometh forth into a priuate room ... (for two yeers I was one of his attendants here). In this place he drinketh other fiue cupfuls ... he eateth opium." Hawkins adds, the king "doth many idle things: and whatsoever he doeth, either without or within, drunken or sober, he hath writers, who by turnes set downe euery thing in writing which he doth [including] ... how often he lieth with his women, and with whom ...."[65]

In these accounts that are effectively focused on the emperor, one finds occasional references to women: for instance, "how often he [the king] lieth with his women." At one point in his journal where Hawkins recounts several feasts at the court, the sports and pastimes in the palace, precious metals and jewels that were being presented to courtiers, he inserts a paragraph on *sati*. There is no explanation for clubbing together what might seem to us quite unrelated matters; Hawkins returns after this to discussing the "entertainment of the Grandees."[66]

Thomas Roe's journal too provides extensive descriptions of Jahangir's court and his own meetings with the emperor. He pays close attention to the code of conduct in the court: the manner of seating of the nobles, the decorations, and the manner of personal presentation.[67] There are some quite unusual observations, such as that Jahangir, a Muslim emperor, was never circumcised.[68] (No other historical source records this "fact." Sometime after Roe, Thomas Coryat also discussed the issue of the circumcision of Jahangir. It remains unclear however whether he borrowed this information from Roe.)

Despite his accessibility to the court and the king, Roe seems to misread various ceremonial gestures. So when he is presented with a robe of honor, Roe misinterprets it, in Bernard Cohn's words, "as a sign of debasement, rather than an act of incorporation ... which made him a companion to the

---

[64] Clements R. Markham (ed.), *The Hawkins' Voyages during the reigns of Henry VIII, Queen Elizabeth, and James I* (London, 1878), pp. 93, 436–441. See also Oaten, *European Travellers*, pp. 82, 87–94, 101–104, 108–109, 111, 112, 114–116.

[65] *Hawkins' Voyages*, pp. 436–437.   [66] *Ibid.*, pp. 440–441.

[67] William Foster (ed.), *The Embassy of Sir Thomas Roe to the Court of the Great Mogul 1615–1619*, vols. I–II (London, 1899), I, pp. 108–109; hereafter cited as *Thomas Roe*.

[68] *Ibid.*, I, pp. 313–314.

ruler."[69] Indeed, as Stanley Tambiah suggests, Roe's excerpts on the territorial expansion of the Mughal empire, the incredible wealth of the emperor and his "decadent court life," the lack of an independent nobility and private property in land, the servile condition of the populace "wallowing in a lush of heathenism and presided over by an ungodly emperor" are likely to have contributed to the European construction of an "oriental despotism."[70]

As regards women: in a detailed comment on the king's routine in the court, Roe says "the king hath no man but Eunuchs that Comes within the lodgings or retyring roomes of his house: His weomen watch within, and guard him with manly weapons."[71] Likewise, in a letter to the East India Company advising them on the kind of presents that might be best made to the Mughal court, he refers to Nur Jahan's tastes: "Ther is nothing more welcome here, nor euer saw I man soe enamord of drincke as both the King and Prince are of redd wyne. . . . I thinck 4 or 5 handsome cases of that wyne wilbe more welcome than the richest Iewell in Cheapesyde. . . . If the Queen must be presented . . . fine needle woorke toyes, fayre bone lace, cuttworke, and some handsome wrought wastcote, sweetbagges or Cabinetts, wilbe most Convenient."[72] He also notes Nur Jahan's present to him of "a basquett of Muske-Millons,"[73] and an instance of her taking over of all the English goods under her protection.[74]

These stray allusions to women in Hawkins's and Roe's accounts in fact form a pattern. When women appear in their narratives, they are incidental to the larger discourse on the imperium: they appear only as a small part of the routine of the emperor. Indeed this is the mold that Elphinstone, Lane-Poole and others seem to have borrowed.[75]

Now consider William Finch (1608–11) who came to India on the same ship as Hawkins. He also provides a good deal of information on Jahangir: his kingdom, his court, his palaces, and the ways of his life.[76] In these descriptions there are some scattered references to women. At times, an unexpected detail appears, like the first record of the story of Anarkali, which was to be a feature of later films, fiction, and popular writing on the Mughals.[77] Finch refers to "Immacque Kelle" or "Pomgranate kernell . . . with

[69] Bernard S. Cohn, "The Command of Language and the Language of Command," *Subaltern Studies IV* (Delhi, 1985), p. 279. See also Teltscher, *India Inscribed*, p. 21.

[70] Stanley J. Tambiah, "What did Bernier Actually Say? Profiling the Mogul Empire," in Veena Das *et al.* (eds.), *Tradition, Pluralism, and Identity: Essays in Honour of T. N. Madan* (New Delhi, 1999), p. 221.

[71] *Thomas Roe*, I, p. 106.   [72] *Ibid.*, I, p. 119.   [73] *Ibid.*, I, p. 170.   [74] *Ibid.*, I, p. 436.

[75] Elphinstone's account of Jahangir, to take one example, is hardly different in tone from that of Pelsaert or Thomas Roe: "He was still capricious and tyrannical, but he was no longer guilty of such barbarous cruelties as before; and although he still carried his excess in wine to the lowest stage of inebriety, yet it was at night, and in his private apartments." Elphinstone, *History*, II, p. 319. Or to take an example from Lane-Poole, see *Aurangzib*, p. 12.

[76] See, as examples, Oaten, *European Travellers*, pp. 99–100; and Foster (ed.), *Early Travels*, pp. 148–149, 164, 165, 167–179.

[77] Note the classic Indian film hits: *Anarkali* and *Mughal-e Azam*.

who it is said Sha Selim [Jahangir] had to do [had an affair]; upon notice of which King [Akbar] caused her to be enclosed quicke within a wall in his moholl, where shee dyed ... "[78] We find no mention of Anarkali before Finch's reference.

The texts of the early European travelers do not deal with the Mughal *haram* in any focused way. What we have are snippets on "private" life, and these appear in an array of writings with miscellaneous agendas. People centrally concerned with public affairs, such as trade or conversion, wrote most of these accounts. For them, the domestic affairs of the Mughals were a peripheral matter, thus the extracts on the *haram* remain marginal to the texts. When they appear, they do so in the form of sketchy observation, in fragments – a line here and a line there, sometimes stories too.

These texts are varied, and the writers' chance discussions of different aspects of the activities of Mughal men and women produce a mix of unusual data (Hamideh Banu Begum's important role; that Jahangir was never circumcised; the story of Anarkali by Finch), curious tales (the Brahmins of Fitch), and attention-grabbing details (courtly ethics in the Nur Jahan story of Della Valle).[79] Because these chronicles are so assorted, they are susceptible to being read in many different ways. They do not describe a predictable "Eastern" or "Islamic" system. But they do have the occasional eye-catching fragments, precisely the kind that seem to have invited the attention of colonial writers who ended up using them as part of an authoritative statement about a court society.

Extravagant descriptions to detailed reflections

From the time of Jahangir, there is a considerable body of rather more extravagant writing on the *haram*, and on women more generally. In several of these accounts, the Mughal *haram* moves from the meager sketches of the earlier records to a relatively substantial presence. Scandal-mongering increases. It is the exaggerated extracts from some of these writings that become the classics to be cited in the colonial histories of the nineteenth and twentieth centuries.

I shall discuss the work of Francisco Pelsaert (1618–25) of Antwerp, who sailed for the East in 1618 in the commercial service of the Dutch East India Company, and the commercial account of Johannes De Laet (1593–1649), and then consider the more detailed reflections on the *haram* found in the writings of François Bernier (1656–68) and Nicolao Manucci (1653–1708).

---

[78] Foster (ed.), *Early Travels*, p. 166.
[79] Many of these reports are borrowed in subsequent writings, such as Thomas Coryat's (1612–17) collected letters, and Edward Terry's (1616–19) account of India.

Let us begin with the works of two employees of the Dutch East India Company: Johannes De Laet's *De Imperio Magni Mogolis*, and Francisco Pelsaert's *Remonstrantie*.[80] Scholars have suggested that De Laet may well have incorporated substantial parts of Pelsaert's work into his own.[81] In consequence of this interaction and borrowing, the texts of Pelsaert and De Laet are closely interwoven with each other, yet varied in style, and differing in their approach and projections.

Consider the following passages from Pelsaert, dealing with the lives of the nobility. "The *mahals* [palaces] are adorned internally with lascivious sensuality, wanton and reckless festivity, superfluous pomp, inflated pride, and ornamental daintiness." "While the servants of the lords may justly be described as a generation of iniquity, greed and oppression, for, like their masters, they make hay while the sun shines . . . ." He notes that the noblemen and their wives ("as a rule," three to four) live together in the "enclosure surrounded by high walls, which is called the *mahal*." He explains to us that each wife has separate apartments for herself and her slaves, "of whom there may be 10, or 20, or 100, according to her fortune . . . Jewels and clothes are provided by the husband according to the extent of his affection." Their food comes from one kitchen, but each wife takes it in her own quarters "for they hate each other secretly . . . ."

He adds that each night the noble visits a particular wife in her *mahal*, and "receives a very warm welcome from her and from the slaves, who, dressed specially for the occasion, seem to fly, rather than run, about their duties . . . ." In the cool of the evening, he tells the reader, they drink "a great deal of wine . . . drinking has become very fashionable in the last few years." Thus, the privileged nobleman sits like "a golden cock among the gilded hens" until midnight, or until passion or drink, send him to bed. "Then if one of the pretty slave girls takes his fancy, he calls her to him and enjoys her, his wife not daring to show any signs of displeasure, but dissembling, though she will take it out of [*sic*] the slave-girl later on."[82]

Compare De Laet: The nobles live in "indescribable luxury and extravagance," indulging themselves in every kind of pleasure. "Their greatest magnificence is in their women's quarters (or Mahal)." Like Pelsaert, he adds that the noblemen marry three or four wives and that each of these wives lives separately in her own quarters with her handmaids or slaves, "of whom she has often a large number according to the dignity or wealth of the household . . . ." He also explains the rules of visitation, the modesty and politeness of conversation, and then comments, "they do not use napkins, and eat with their fingers only: it is considered bad manners to use the left hand or to lick

---

[80] J. S. Hoyland (trans.), *The Empire of the Great Mogol: A Translation of De Laet's "Description of India and Fragment of Indian History"* (Bombay, 1928); hereafter cited as *De Laet*; W. H. Moreland and P. Geyl (trans.), *Jahangir's India: The Remonstrantie of Francisco Pelsaert* (Cambridge, 1925); hereafter cited as *Pelsaert*.
[81] *Pelsaert*, Introduction, p. xv.   [82] *Pelsaert*, pp. 64–65.

the fingers. They drink nothing till they have finished eating." This description, included in a chapter entitled "The Character, Customs, Institutions and Superstitions of the Inhabitants" (and according to De Laet, the "most usual method of life in India"[83]) appears in a different spirit in the hands of later, colonial historians.

The narratives of De Laet and Pelsaert stand out for their detailed descriptions of the living quarters, as also of the everyday life of the nobility, and the common-folk. These accounts are not entirely novel in terms of the themes that they take up. Monserrate provides one of the earliest descriptions of the palace of Akbar.[84] Pietro della Valle writes about the four main cities and the palaces there of the *Grand Moghol*.[85] In the texts of De Laet and Pelsaert, as in earlier writings, we find several references to administrative institutions, religious beliefs and practices. The difference that marks the texts of De Laet and Pelsaert lies in providing substantive information on the subjects they select. Their descriptions are no longer erratic, occasional lines and paragraphs, but more detailed accounts of the life of "the people of India."

The more elaborate descriptions do not prevent major mistakes. Pelsaert refers to Maryam Makani (the title of Hamideh Banu Begum, mother of Akbar) as the wife of Akbar.[86] Moreover, a lot of the well-organized detail takes the form of bazaar gossip. Thus: "Jahangir, disregarding his own person and position, has surrendered himself to a crafty wife of humble lineage, as the result either of her arts or of her persuasive tongue." Nur Jahan "enriched herself with superabundant treasures, and has secured a more than royal position." Accordingly, her former and present supporters had been well rewarded, "so that now most of the men who are near the King owe their promotion to her, and are consequently under such obligations to her." Meanwhile, Pelsaert adds, the queen "erects very expensive buildings in all directions ... intending thereby to establish an enduring reputation."[87]

The portrayal of Jahangir's routine provides another example. When the king returns from hunting in the evening, we are told all the nobles present themselves. As soon as they leave, the queen comes with the female slaves, and "they undress him [the king], chafing and fondling him as if he were a little child; for his three cups have made him so 'happy' that he is more disposed to rest than to keep awake." This is the time when his wife, according to Pelsaert, "obtains whatever she asks for or desires, gets always 'yes', and hardly ever 'no', in reply."[88]

Pelsaert's descriptions are not very different from Ralph Fitch's, and his depiction of Nur Jahan ("that crafty wife of humble lineage") parallels Pietro della Valle's "very cunning and ambitious Woman." Yet, the subjects that he

---

[83] *De Laet*, pp. 90–92. De Laet's translator says in a footnote that the materials for this chapter were taken from Pelsaert and Edward Terry, and that the author gives a "bowdlerized version" of Pelsaert's "The Manner of Life" from which my first passage comes: p. 80 n.
[84] Monserrate, *Commentary*, pp. 199–201.   [85] *Pietro Della Valle*, pp. 97–98.
[86] *Pelsaert*, pp. 2–5.   [87] *Ibid.*, p. 50.   [88] *Ibid.*, p. 53.

and De Laet write about are more effectively put in order now. In this context, the Mughal *haram*, and its various facets, begins to come into focus, moving in from the periphery, as it were. Never before Pelsaert do we have what the author himself calls a "record" of certain subjects he wishes to observe.[89] Texts such as Pelsaert's are no longer scattered reminiscences and observations but broad and careful reports in which the world gets structured into domestic and public, sociocultural and political. Exclusive chapters on women and domestic life appear for the first time.

This development has to do with the nature of these texts. Moreland notes that Van den Broecke (a Dutch commercial representative) and Pelsaert were simultaneously engaged in writing a history of the Mughal domain.[90] De Laet, in his turn, produced a systematic general survey of the empire. These texts attempted to provide comprehensive statements in which a recognizable systematization of themes and contents became essential. Therefore, one finds neatly classified chapters on "The Royal Court and Citadel of Agra" or "The Wealth of this Prince" in De Laet's book; or "The Administration of the Country," "The City of Agra," "The Manner of Life," and "Moslem Marriages in Agra" in Pelsaert's account.

In the writings of the late seventeenth-century Europeans, the *haram* moves from the wings to center-stage. The most detailed and systematized images of the Mughal *haram* appear in the accounts of François Bernier and Nicolao Manuccci. François Bernier, a French doctor, whose chief interest was political and speculative philosophy, spent twelve years at the court of Aurangzeb, out of his thirteen in India (1655–68).[91] He traveled widely (he was the first European to visit Kashmir) and spoke Persian, the *lingua franca* of the Mughals. Bernier arrived in Delhi when Aurangzeb, the third son of Shah Jahan, had dethroned his father and crowned himself emperor. Bernier's *History of the Late Revolution of the Empire of the Great Mogol*, based upon this visit, has "particular value as a more-or-less eyewitness account."[92]

"Bernier's various accounts of his travels," Peter Burke has noted, "if occasionally inaccurate, are among the fullest, the most vivid and the most philosophical descriptions of seventeenth-century India under Western eyes at a time when such descriptions were becoming increasingly common."[93] It is a well-organized account, which also contains several appended letters written to intellectual friends in France on varied subjects concerning the Mughals. Indeed, as Burke notes, his observations on Indian customs are often "systematic rather than casual," and more interesting than his eyewitness political accounts.[94]

[89] *Ibid.*, p. 2.   [90] *Ibid.*, Introduction, p. xv.
[91] Archibald Constable (ed.), *Travels in the Mogol Empire AD 1656–1668 by François Bernier* (1891; rpt. Delhi, 1968); hereafter cited as *Bernier*.
[92] Burke, "Philosopher," p. 127.   [93] *Ibid.*, p. 126.
[94] *Ibid.*, p. 127. The information on Bernier in the next page or so is taken from Burke "Philosopher."

What made for the mixture of sympathy and sense of inquiry found in Bernier was his scholarly milieu: he had "learnt something from Montaigne and taught Montesquieu something, but, unlike either of them, lived for some years in Asia." He had read about India from books. He cites the German Jesuit missionary Heinrich Roth, who produced a Latin description of the Mughal Empire with special reference to religion; and the Dutch Calvinist minister Abraham Rogier, who worked in south India on the Coromandel coast, and wrote on the customs of the Brahmins.[95]

Besides, his friends often sent him books and news from Europe, and "plied him with questions about the Orient"; Jean Chapelain (poet, critic, and literary adviser to Louis XIV's minister Jean-Baptiste Colbert), for instance, asked him about the position of women.[96] Scholars have argued that Bernier's experiences in India allowed him to make a subtle, but systematic, critique of the regime of Louis XIV, and of Europe; and that there is in his writing, therefore, a systematic thinking through of how monarchies and societies functioned.[97]

Like the chronicles of some of his predecessors (De Laet, Pelsaert), Bernier's "history" is comprehensive, and tidily divided into themes and chapters.[98] Let me summarize the substantial information on Mughal women and how it is placed in Bernier's text. This example should help to bring out the manner of his disquisition.

Bernier's first reference to Mughal women appears in a chapter entitled "History of the States of the Great Mughal," and fits in with the larger argument of the chapter, in which the author lists the names of, and gives information about, the sons and daughters of the then-ruling emperor Shah Jahan. In Bernier's words: "It is usual in this country to give similar names to the members of the reigning family. Thus the wife of Chah-Jehan [Shah Jahan] – so renowned for her beauty, and whose splendid mausoleum is more worthy of a place among the wonders of the world . . . was named Tage Mahall [Mumtaz Mahal], or the crown of the Seraglio."[99]

Later in the chapter, Bernier writes about Jahanara Begum (also called Begum Sahib), the daughter of Shah Jahan, "passionately beloved by her father."[100] He adds, "Rumour has it that his attachment reached a point which is difficult to believe . . . [and that] *Chah-Jehan* reposed unbounded confidence in this his favourite child. . . . It is not surprising, therefore, that her ascendancy in the court of the *Mogol* should have been nearly unlimited."[101]

---

[95] *Ibid.*, p. 126.   [96] *Ibid.*, p. 130.
[97] See, for example, Burke, "Philosopher"; Teltscher, *India Inscribed*, pp. 28–34; and Tambiah, "What did Bernier Actually Say?"
[98] And perhaps benefits from his training as a physician "to observe small details as symptoms of general states of affairs" (Burke, "Philosopher," p. 128).
[99] *Bernier*, p. 5.   [100] *Ibid.*, p. 11.   [101] *Ibid.*

There is a larger agenda in which Bernier's statement might be placed. In order to be able to discuss the two factions that were formed within the family when Aurangzeb rebelled against Shah Jahan, Bernier provided the details of each member of the royal family. "I have thought of a slight sketch of *Chah-Jehan* and his sons [as] a proper introduction to this history, and necessary to the right understanding of what is to follow. Nor could I avoid adding a few particulars concerning his two daughters, who play so prominent a part in the tragedy."[102] He tells us about Jahanara's lovers, who on two separate occasions were secretly led into the *haram*. When Shah Jahan discovered the occurrences, he masterfully conducted what Bernier calls the "tragic termination" of the princess's lovers.[103]

In the same chapter, the physician introduces Roshanara Begum, Shah Jahan's younger daughter, "less beautiful than her sister. ... She was nevertheless possessed of the same vivacity." She became the political partisan of Aurangzeb, he informs us, and her sister allied with the party of the other brother, Dara Shukoh.[104] The rest of the chapter focuses on the events that finally led to the crowning of Aurangzeb and the defeat of Dara Shukoh. In the course of relating these events, the reader is given some unusual details: after the defeat of Dara Shukoh, for example, his wife committed suicide in Lahore, his daughter was left in the care of Jahanara Begum at the latter's insistence, and when Dara's son Siphir Shukoh was brought to the court, "the principal ladies of the court had permission to be present, concealed behind a lattice work."[105]

The activities in the *haram* are central to many of Bernier's chapters. He details carefully the rules of the *haram*: how the inmates lived, who came and went, the activities of the people, their manners, codes of conduct, travel arrangements, and so on. He also provides an elaborate description of the physical qualities of the *haram*, and of the royal tents.[106]

"The citadel contains the *Seraglio* and other royal edifices; but you are not to imagine that they are such buildings as the *Louvre* or the *Escurial*."[107] He also cites the sources of his information: "I have sometimes gone into it [the *haram* or the Seraglio] when the king was absent from Delhi ... [to attend to] the case of a great lady so extremely ill that she could not be moved to the outward gate ...." Again, the eunuchs informed him that "the *Seraglio* contains beautiful apartments, separated, and more or less spacious and splendid, according to the rank and income of the females." And that "nearly every chamber has a reservoir of running water at the door; on every side are gardens, delightful alleys, shady retreats, streams, fountains ...."[108] Bernier's narrative on the Mughal *haram* is consistently recorded,

[102] *Ibid.*, p. 16.   [103] *Ibid.*, pp. 12–13.   [104] *Ibid.*, p. 14.
[105] *Ibid.*, pp. 102–106. There are other interesting reports of activities in the *haram* on pp. 126–131.
[106] *Ibid.*, pp. 358–368.   [107] *Ibid.*, p. 256.   [108] *Ibid.*, p. 267.

thoughtfully deployed and documented. It is one that struggles to convey a "true" picture of what he saw (and heard).

The *Storia Do Mogor* of Nicolao Manucci (written in Italian, Portuguese, and French), another history of Mughal India, is in some ways an amplification of Bernier's account.[109] A native of Venice, at the age of fourteen in 1653, Manucci ran away from home, entered the service of a certain Viscount Bellemont, and arrived in India in January 1656. There, he spent nearly seventy years of his life, in a chequered and adventurous career. Starting as an artilleryman in Mughal prince Dara's services, he subsequently succeeded in attaching himself in disguise to Aurangzeb's army. He then became a physician to a provincial governor, and afterwards a plenipotentiary of a Portuguese viceroy. Manucci then gained fame as a (quack) "doctor," and the wife of Prince Shah Alam became his patient in Delhi. Later on, he found formal service with this Mughal prince, before he retired to Salsette. He also worked as a foreign correspondent to a British Governor at Madras.[110] Eventually he began writing, and the product was the *Storia Do Mogor*.

There are two kinds of description of the Mughal *haram* in the *Storia*. First there are stories of royal women and men, which form sections of more general chapters. Second, there is a full chapter on the royal household that includes details of the physical structure of the *haram*.

Manucci also takes up the instances cited in Bernier and others, of Jahanara Begum's authority, her activities, and her pomp.[111] He includes descriptions of her sister Roshanara Begum, who was, "not very good-looking, but very clever, capable of dissimulation, bright, mirthful, fond of jokes and amusement, much more so than her sister Begam Sahib."[112] Even if a copy, Manucci's retelling is often fresh and evocative. In fact, within the general repetition, there are numerous additions. Note the following comment on Jahanara Begum:

> This princess [Jahanara] treated herself to many entertainments, such as music, dancing, and other pastimes. It happens one night while engaged in such-like dances that the thin raiment steeped in perfumed oils of the princess's favourite dancing-woman caught fire, and from the great love she bore to her, the princess came to her aid, and thus was burnt herself on the chest. From this arose great disturbance in the court, but what caused the greatest sorrow to the princess was that the dancing-woman died.[113]

Several other pieces by Manucci are new and instructive, for example, his chapter on Aurangzeb,[114] especially the discussion of the measures that the king took against wine and drugs, and the so-called "Burial of Music." A later

---

[109] William Irvine (trans.), *Storia Do Mogor or Mogul India 1653–1708 by Niccolao Manucci Venetian* (London, 1907), vols. I–IV; hereafter cited as *Manucci*.

[110] Oaten, *European Travellers*, p. 139. For details of Manucci's life, see *Manucci*, Introduction; Oaten, *European Travellers*, pp. 137–141.

[111] *Manucci*, I, see pp. 218–238, for example.   [112] *Ibid.*, I, p. 239.   [113] *Ibid.*, I, p. 219.

[114] *Ibid.*, II, ch. 1.

discussion in the chapter, "Begam Sahib gives wine to the wives of the learned doctors," is noteworthy:

It was in this year that the learned, or the *Mullas*, of the faith ... wanted him [the king] to make a rule against women drinking, or eating *bhang*, nutmeg, opium, or other drugs. The women had paid no heed to the orders he had given at the beginning of his reign, saying those orders did not apply to them, but to men only. ... When Padshah Begam ... learnt of this new rule, she invited the wives of the *qazi* and the other learned men to her mansion, and gave them wine until they were drunk. Aurangzeb came to her palace and referred to the restrictions under which he had placed women. ... Aurangzeb [also] told her that such was the opinion of all the learned. Thereupon Padshah Begam invited the king within the *pardah* [secluded area], where he saw the wives of the said learned men all lying drunk and in disorder. ... [115]

What is unusual in both these fragments is what they tell us about the homosocial communities in the *haram*. The close relationship between the dancer and the princess is one instance of the intensity of non-familial relationships, expressed both in the "greatest ... sorrow" of the princess, as well as in the "great disturbance" at the court.

In the second instance we learn how a "political" alliance came to be formed between noble women: between Padshah Begum and the wives of the *qazi* and of other learned men. More importantly, in Padshah Begum's having these women "lying drunk and in disorder" we encounter contestation and negotiation that went on in the *haram* in relation to issues at the court. In addition, this fragment clearly indexes the place of senior Mughal women. At the same time, it dispels any idea we might have about a neat compartmentalization of "public" and "private" affairs being conducted exclusively in the court and the *haram*.

Manucci's stories too are often accompanied by the sources of his information. "I say this because I was admitted on familiar terms to this house, and I was deep in the confidence of the principal ladies and eunuchs in her service."[116] Or, at another point: "These and other reports about the royal palace were given to me by a Portuguese woman called Thomazia Martins. ... She had charge of the royal table, and was much liked by Roshan Ara Begam ... through the affection she had for me, in addition to various presents that she made to me, she informed me of what passed inside the palace."[117]

Alongside the information on the *haram*, Manucci puts before the reader a description of the "Customs of the Royal Household, and the Way of dealing with the People living in the Palace, commonly called the Mahal, or Seraglio."[118] I cannot discuss this fascinating thirty-page treatise in any detail. Let me simply list the main themes that Manucci takes up, and illustrate the nature of his data through a few excerpts. The following are

---

[115] *Ibid.*, II, pp. 149–150.   [116] *Ibid.*, I, p. 220.   [117] *Ibid.*, II, p. 35.   [118] *Ibid.*, II, pp. 330 ff.

Manucci's subjects: the number of women, their living arrangements, sources of income, the officers of the palace (including the spies), King's routine, and his expenses.[119] He gives lists of the principal names given by the kings to the queens and princesses, and the meanings of those names (for example: "Farsana Begam, Liberality of Good Things"[120]), including separately the names of the mistresses and concubines, matrons, superintendents of the dancers and singers, and principal slaves in the "seraglio."[121] Manucci talks about the general expenses, allowances of Queens, details of celebrations and festivities, the titles of the Mughal emperor, and the manner of visiting the *haram*;[122] and specifically mentions the arrangements with regard to the visits of physicians.[123]

Now consider two very different descriptions of the "royal household." The first is as follows:

These queens and princesses have pay or pensions according to their birth or the rank they hold. In addition, they often receive from the king special presents in cash, under the pretext that it is to buy betel, or perfumes, or shoes. They live in this way, with no cares or anxieties, occupying themselves with nothing beyond displaying great show and magnificence, an imposing and majestuous bearing, or making themselves attractive, getting talked about in the world, and pleasing the king. For, in spite of there being among them many jealousies, they conceal this as a matter of policy.[124]

A second:

The king sits up till midnight, and is unceasingly occupied with the above sort of [meeting secret news-writers of the empire etc.] business. He sleeps for three hours only, and on awakening offers up his usual prayers, which occupy an hour and a half. Every year he goes into penitential retirement for forty days, during which he sleeps on the ground, he fasts, he gives alms – the whole to secure from God continuance of victory and the accomplishment of his designs. But, nowadays, being old and his enemies hindering him from undertaking anything, he must perforce remain at rest. Not withstanding, he never fails every morning to consider and give orders as to what should be done. Thus in the twenty-four hours his rule is to eat once and sleep three hours. During sleep he is guarded by women slaves, very brave, and highly skilled in the management of the bow and other arms.[125]

On the one hand, Manucci draws a thoughtful picture of the king's routine in the *haram*. On the other, he presents flat images of royal women. In the second description, he seems to be reproducing the embellished accounts that were likely available to him (compare Pietro della Valle's account of Nur Jahan, and Pelsaert's description of the lives of the nobility). Thus we get tired and trite descriptions of domestic life even in the midst of what is an unusual chapter on the royal household.

---

[119] *Ibid.*, II, pp. 330–332.   [120] *Ibid.*, II, p. 333.   [121] *Ibid.*, II, pp. 333–338.
[122] *Ibid.*, II, pp. 338–355.   [123] *Ibid.*, II, pp. 354–357.   [124] *Ibid.*, II, pp. 241–242.
[125] *Ibid.*, II, p. 332.

Clearly, both Bernier and Manucci consider the Mughal *haram* extensively in their "histories." The point to note about both is that they remain richly layered and allow for different kinds of readings. The *haram* in these accounts remains "a field of entangled and confused parchments."[126] There are no simple configurations in the texts that tell of one final meaning.

Two differences also stand out between Bernier and Manucci's narratives. First, Manucci's memoir is a very personal one, and the author's own presence continually marks his text. Bernier brought an intellectual distance to his writing, thus putting it in a more analytic mode. The second difference between the two texts lies in the far more exhaustive nature of chronicling that Manucci undertakes. The third part of his *Storia*, which covers the royal household, is exceptional in this regard. Never before do we encounter such detail.

Concluding thoughts

What is particularly arresting about the early European reports on the Mughals and their domestic world is their hesitation and tentativeness, their fluidity, and their self-contradictory character. While the authors struggled to make sense of this "strange" Eastern society and polity, the very course of seeking to examine or critique their own courts and institutions, meant that many of their representations were marked by a sense of exploration, undecidedness, even confusion, a quality that contributes to the making of rich and fairly "open" texts: texts that allow the recording of the quite striking exercise of power by Mughal women such as Hamideh Banu Begum and Gulbadan Begum.

A substantial picture of Mughal domestic life begins to appear for the first time in the "histories" that I have discussed in the previous section. The structure of these texts requires a delineation of the domestic arrangements among other facets of empire. Hence a description of the *haram* becomes necessary, and it gains a certain kind of visibility. It does not follow that these descriptions of the domestic world of another society or culture must be uniform, standardized, caricatured, and derogatory. To some extent, however, these latter tendencies were written into the travelers' encounters, which were dependent on repetition (of what they had already heard or read) and otherwise chancy, ephemeral, "titillating" and alien. The standardization and homogenization occurred later on, when the Orient had become a part of the West's domain – a subordinated Other. And then De Laet, Bernier, and Manucci would re-emerge as classic texts on the Orient.

When the more developed colonial caricature comes into place, nothing remains of this rich, layered, surprising character of the Mughal *haram* as represented in the earlier accounts. What we get instead is an increasingly

---

[126] James D. Faubion (ed.), *Michel Foucault: Aesthetics, Method, and Epistemology*, vols. I–II (London, 1998), II, p. 367.

coherent picture of a decadent, already-known and feminized East, and the *haram* emerges as one of its preeminent symbols, rather than as simply another object of observation. Mughal women, with the honorable exception of Nur Jahan (who turns out to be no exception at all because she is an honorary male), now appear as the hundreds of wives and mistresses of various Mughal monarchs – faceless, submissive, licentious and intriguing, all at the same time.

CHAPTER 3

The question of the archive: the challenge of a princess's memoir

The received image of the Mughal *haram* has been powerful in blinding historians to the density and variation of domestic life projected in the contemporary records. Consider a couple of extracts from one of these records, Gulbadan Banu Begum's *Ahval-i Humayun Badshah*, which I use as my central counterpoint here. After the battle of Panipat in 1526, which gave Babur a foothold in India, his close friend, Khvajeh Kilan, expressed a desire to return to Kabul. As Babur (reluctantly) gave him permission to go, he asked him to carry "valuable presents and curiosities [*tuhfeh va hadyeh*] of Hind" to his relations and other people in Kabul.[1]

Two generations later, when asked to record her memories of the Mughal forefathers towards the imperial history, the *Akbarnama*, Babur's daughter, Gulbadan Banu Begum, reconstructed Babur's conversation with Khvajeh Kilan as follows:

I shall write a list, and you will distribute them [the gifts] according to it. ... "To each begam is to be delivered as follows: one special dancing-girl of the dancing-girls of Sultan Ibrahim [Ibrahim Lodi, the king Babur defeated at Panipat], with one gold plate full of jewels – ruby and pearl, cornelian and diamond, emerald and turquoise, topaz and cat's-eye – and two small mother-o'-pearl trays full of *ashrafis*, and on two other trays *shahrukhis*, and all sorts of stuffs by nines – that is, four trays and one plate. Take a dancing-girl and another plate of jewels, and one each of *ashrafis* and *shahrukhis*, and present, in accordance with my directions, to my elder relations the very plate of jewels and the self-same dancing-girl which I have given for them [*sic*]. I have made other gifts; convey these afterwards. Let them divide and present jewels and *ashrafis* and *shahrukhis* and stuffs to my sisters and children and the *harams* and kinsmen, and to the begams and aghas and nurses and foster-brethren and ladies, and to all who pray for me."[2]

---

[1] Gulbadan Banu Begum, *Ahval-i Humayun Badshah*, British Library MS Or. 166; Annette Susannah Beveridge (trans.), *The History of Humayun: Humayun Nama* (2nd edn, 1902; rpt. Delhi, 1994); hereafter cited as Gulbadan, *Ahval*, and Beveridge, *Humayun*, respectively. Beveridge, *Humayun*, p. 94; cf. Gulbadan, *Ahval*, fol. 9b.
[2] Beveridge, *Humayun*, pp. 95–96; cf. Gulbadan, *Ahval*, fols. 9b–10b.

Gulbadan's record of her father's inventory is striking for several reasons. It brings to life questions of correct deportment in the preparation of gifts and the manner of presenting (and accepting) them – so central to the sensibilities of the Timurid-Mughal world.[3] It is particularly notable for depicting Babur's domestic life. In setting these out, the Begum also gives us glimpses of the range of Babur's domestic relationships and associations, with the old as well as the young. The list of gifts is a pointer to the centrality, and the hierarchical character, of these relationships. Babur gave clear instructions about what should be given to whom, and in what order. So the elder relations (*vali-u-ni'matan*) were to be given the following presents first: a dancing-girl, a plate of jewels, and a plate each of *ashrafis* and *shahrukhis* (designation for coins), to be followed by "other gifts" that Babur had listed for them. Similarly, his sisters, kinsmen and their wives, heads of households, nurses, and children were to receive presents later in accordance with Babur's list.

The Begum's memoir pays a great deal of attention to such illustrative inventories. In Gulbadan's elucidation, the details of presents and invitations serve not merely as a descriptive catalog, but as symbols of the privileges of seniority. They index the creation and maintenance of hierarchical relationships, as also the importance of building alliances and reinforcing kinship solidarities.

At another point in her memoir, Gulbadan discusses the time Humayun spent with the royal women when his court was settled for a while in Agra:

On court days, which were Sundays and Tuesdays, he used to go to the other side of the river. During his stay in the garden, *ajam* (Dil-dar Begam) and my sisters and the ladies (*haraman*) were often in his company. Of all the tents, Ma"suma Sultan Begam's was at the top of the row. Next came Gul-rang Begam's, and *ajam*'s was in the same place. Then the tent of my mother, Gul-barg Begam and of Bega Begam and the others. They set up the offices (*kar-khanaha*) and got them into order. When they had put up the pavilions (*khaima*) and tents (*khar-gah*) and the audience tent (*bar-gah*), the Emperor came to see the camp and the splendid set-out, and visited the begams and his sisters. As he dismounted somewhat near Ma"suma Begam's (tent), he honoured her with a visit. All of us, the begams and my sisters, were in his society. When he went to any begam's or sister's quarters, all the begams and all his sisters used to go with him.[4]

Note the careful attention paid to precise rules: designated days to go to the other side of the river, the careful arrangement of the tents of women, the *padshah* himself coming to see the arrangement, the manner and timing of his visits, and the deportment required of those who accompanied him.

---

[3] Whenever I use the word Timurid-Mughal (not just Mughal) it is to underline Babur's concern, which he continuously expresses in his memoir, to retain the link with his paternal forefather, Timur. He does not entirely do away with his familial connection with his maternal forefather, Chingiz Khan, yet his rivalry with his Uzbik clansmen (direct descendants of Chingiz Khan) perhaps required that he make a powerful declaration of his Timurid identity. For details, see chapter 4.

[4] Beveridge, *Humayun*, pp. 129–130; Gulbadan, *Ahval*, fols. 29b–30a.

These extracts, which could be set by the side of many others in Gulbadan's text, reveal a *haram* far different from that commonly presented to us. The complexity of relationships, and the sense of a multifaceted and intimate community that emerges here, is notable. By contrast, academic accounts of the *haram* that are available to us appear devoid of any historical depth, and unaware of the complex web and intricacy of relationships and activities found in the Mughal domestic world.

As noted in the introduction, historians have claimed that part of the reason for the absence of particular kinds of social history – specifically the history of the Mughal domestic life – lies in the inadequacy of available source material. I shall demonstrate here that the sources exist for very different kinds of histories as long as "different" kinds of questions are asked.

In thinking about early Mughal domestic life, I have not unearthed any new sources. Instead, I have returned to sources that have been available all along (imperial chronicles, ethical digests, visual representations, and architectural remains). This revisiting has involved listening to peripheral stories and voices, "drowned in the noise of statist commands."[5] It has also meant looking at well-known but neglected sources[6] – such as Gulbadan's memoir – and using them more centrally. The return to the mainstream official chronicles in the light of these "peripheral" sources is no less instructive for the many new "insights" it allows. On the basis of this "rediscovered" archive, then, I suggest a number of ways in which another history may be brought into view. I hope that this will be a gendered and more self-consciously political history that cannot simply be hived off as "supplementary," and that accounts such as the one I put forward here will serve to reopen other questions of central importance to Mughal history.

The question of sources

The first thing to do is to challenge the received wisdom that surviving sources are inadequate. The term "inadequacy" itself requires some unpacking. Are the sources scarce in the sense of being absent, or insufficient in quantity to provide an answer to specific questions? Are there not other important, though related, questions of inadequacy? How have the most "important" Mughal sources become available to us? In translation? What happens to these sources in translation? How much are the content and context transformed in the very process of translation? How do particular ways of

---

[5] Ranajit Guha, "The Small Voice of History," in *Subaltern Studies IX* (Delhi, 1996), p. 3.

[6] Sanjay Subrahmanyam has also made the point that many different dimensions of Mughal history could be more fully explored through an examination of a wider range of known but, in all sorts of ways, neglected sources; Subrahmanyam, "The Mughal State – Structure or Process? Reflections on Recent Western Historiography," *Indian Economic and Social History Review*, 29, 3 (1992).

collating, editing, translating, and analyzing affect the way in which a text is "situated" and "received"?

The discussion that follows, centering on the question of the archive in the time of the first three Mughal kings – Babur, Humayun, and Akbar – should help to show that the inadequacy of source materials is only part – and perhaps a small part – of the problem. Let us begin with an examination of the records that make up the accepted archive for early Mughal times. For Babur, his memoir, the *Baburnama*,[7] and the *Tarikh-i Rashidi* of his cousin Muhammad Haydar Dughlat,[8] have remained the most popular texts for scholars. Babur wrote the *Baburnama* mainly between 1526 and 1529 in his native Turkic language, known today as Chaghatay. The text was translated into Persian in the court of Babur's grandson Akbar. Babur's "unadorned prose," Stephen Dale says, "seems closer in style to the freshness and informality of the diary or court memoir than to any standard literary or historical format."[9]

Muhammad Haydar Dughlat spent some part of his career in Kabul. He was in close contact with Babur during this period, and his work (composed in 1545–46) is valuable as it highlights the political-cultural intricacies of those parts of Central Asia and Afghanistan that Babur was dealing with at the time. Details of religious scholars, poets, calligraphers, painters, singers, geographical descriptions of countries, and the associations and networks of diverse tribes are sprinkled through Dughlat's account; in that sense, it is a close accompaniment to the *Baburnama*.

Among the chronicles most extensively used for information on Humayun's reign is the *Qanun-i Humayuni* (also called *Humayun-nama*), composed in 1534 under Humayun's patronage by one of his officials, Khvandamir. The author spent time at the court of 'Abdul Ghazi Sultan Husain bin Mansur bin Bayqura, the ruler of Herat (1468–1505), and in Khurasan and Persia, before joining Babur in 1528. His last days were spent in the court of Humayun. Khvandamir's memoir is, by his own claim, an eyewitness's account of the rules and ordinances of Humayun's reign, accompanied by descriptions of court festivities and of buildings erected by the *padshah* (king).[10] The *Tazkirat-ul-Vaqi'at* (also called the *Tarikh-i*

---

[7] W. M. Thackston (trans. and ed.), *Zahiruddin Muhammad Babur Mirza: Baburnama*, Parts I–III, Turkish transcription, Persian edition, and English translation (Cambridge, Mass., 1993); and Annette Susannah Beveridge (trans.), *Babur-nama (Memoirs of Babur) of Zahiru'd-din Muhammad Babur Padshah Ghazi* (1921; rpt. Delhi, 1997); hereafter cited as Thackston, *Baburnama*; Beveridge, *Baburnama*. Cf. Dale, *Eight Paradises*, Introduction.

[8] Sir E. Denison Ross (trans.) and N. Elias (ed.), *The Tarikh-i Rashidi of Muhammad Haidar Dughlat: A History of the Moguls of Central Asia* (London, 1895).

[9] Dale, "Steppe Humanism," p. 41. For an extensive discussion of Babur's poetry and autobiography, see Dale, *Eight Paradises*, ch. V.

[10] M. Hidayat Hosain (ed.), *The Qanun-i Humayuni of Khwandamir*, Bibliotheca Indica Series 260, no. 1488 (Calcutta, 1940). Persian edition; hereafter cited as Hosain, *Qanun-i Humayuni*; see the preface to the text.

Humayun or the *Humayun Shahi*) was put together in 1587 by Jawhar Aftabchi, Humayun's ewer-bearer. Composed in a "shaky and rustic" Persian, the text was subsequently revised by Ilahdad Fayzi Sarhindi.[11] This contemporary and rather candid account by a servant has been one of the major source books for the reconstruction of the life and times of the second Mughal, although it has not been adequately explored in some respects.[12]

Next in the corpus of well-known sources, the *Tazkireh-i Humayun va Akbar* by Bayazid Bayat, which was completed in 1590–91, is a history of the reigns of Humayun and Akbar from 1542 to 1591. The author was a native of Tabriz who later joined the army of Humayun. He was apparently suffering from paralysis when he wrote the memoir, and therefore dictated it to a scribe.[13] The biographies by Jawhar and Bayazid owe their origins to the time when materials were being collected for an official history during Akbar's reign. It was in this same context that Gulbadan Banu Begum, the aunt of the emperor, wrote the *Ahval-i Humayun Badshah* upon which I focus in the next section.

The first official history of the Mughal court was commissioned by Akbar. The *Akbarnama* (completed in 1596) – a history of Akbar's life and times – and its official and equally voluminous appendix, the *A'in-i Akbari* – an administrative and statistical report on Akbar's government in all its branches, written by a close friend and minister of the emperor, Abu-l Fazl 'Allami – have remained the most important sources for all histories of his reign.[14] Apart from the imperial history, 'Abd al-Qadir Badauni's three-volume *Muntakhab-ut-Tavarikh* has also been very important.[15] Badauni, a severe critic of Akbar's policies, wrote his history in secret. The text was hidden, and was copied and circulated after the death of Akbar. Historians have found this chronicle a useful counter to the panegyric account of the court chronicler, Abu-l Fazl, and have used it to crosscheck Abu-l Fazl's "facts" and to get a "fuller picture" of the political and religious issues of the time. In the same vein, of obtaining a more "objective" picture, students of

---

[11] Hermann Ethé, *Catalogue of Persian Manuscripts in the Library of the India Office*, vol. 1 (Oxford, 1903), p. 222.

[12] Major Charles Stewart (trans.), *The Tezkereh al Vakiat or Private Memoirs of the Moghul Emperor Humayun* (1832; rpt. Lucknow, 1971); hereafter cited as Jouher-Stewart, *Tezkereh*.

[13] B. P. Saxena, "Baizid Biyat and His Work – 'Mukhtasar,'" *Journal of Indian History*, 4, 1–3 (1925–26), p. 43. Other Persian and English editions of Bayazid Bayat that I have used here are as follows: M. Hidayat Hosain (ed.), *Tadhkira-i Humayun wa Akbar of Bayazid Biyat*, Bibliotheca Indica Series 264, no. 1546 Persian text (Calcutta, 1941); B. P. Saksena, "Memoirs of Baizid," *Allahabad University Studies*, 6, 1 (1930), pp. 71–148; H. Beveridge, "The Memoirs of Bayazid (Bajazet) Biyat," *Journal of the Asiatic Society of Bengal*, 62, 1–4 (1898), pp. 296–316. These editions are hereafter cited as Saxena, *Mukhtasar*; Hosain, *Tadhkira*; Saksena, *Memoirs*; and Beveridge, *Biyat*.

[14] The following translations are most widely used by scholars: H. Beveridge (trans.), *The Akbar Nama of Abu-l-Fazl*, vols. I–III (1902–39; rpt. Delhi, 1993); H. Blochmann and H. S. Jarrett (trans.), *The A-in-I Akbari*, vols. I–III (1873, 1894; rpt. Calcutta, 1993).

[15] George S. A. Ranking, W. H. Lowe, and Sir Wolseley Haig (trans. and eds.), *Muntakhabu-t-tawarikh*, vols. I–III (1884–1925; rpt. Delhi, 1986).

Akbar's reign have found a neutral middle ground in the cautious, even-handed manner of description of the *Tabaqat-i Akbari*, written by another member of Akbar's court, Nizam al-Din Ahmad.[16]

For a long time now, a canonical position has been ascribed to these kinds of sources. The choice of certain sources as basic and central has in turn tended to perpetuate certain kinds of histories. The interest in agrarian-administrative-institutional histories for example has made chronicles like the *Akbarnama* and the *A'in-i Akbari* appear essential to any undertaking in Mughal history. Relying on texts like the *Akbarnama*, historians have often uncritically reproduced the primary sources themselves, and therefore duplicated one or another chronicler's assessments of the empire, imperial relations, and other related matters. In this way, many of our modern histories have turned out to be not very different from the primary text (or texts) out of which they are constructed.

One has to ask why it is that the *Akbarnama* and the *A'in-i Akbari* immediately capture the historians' attention when they turn to a reconstruction of the history of Akbar. Why is it that the Mughal miniatures found in museums across the globe, and the architectural sites of the time, located in Afghanistan, Central Asia, India, and Pakistan, do not figure in our minds in the same way? Akbar and his successors had the existing royal biographies, and other important volumes of histories and legends, including the *Baburnama* and the *Akbarnama*, illustrated – so that miniature paintings form a striking and important part of the historians' most prized sources. However, these other sources – visual materials, architectural remains, the anecdotal and poetic accounts of women and servants – have been marginalized by modern historiography, which allots them to separate, more specialized disciplines, or dismisses their concerns as "trivial."

The *Akbarnama* and the *A'in-i Akbari* have been singled out as "foundational" sources in this way, not only because of their supposed "accuracy" and "objectivity," but because they are official compilations dealing directly with political-administrative matters – and closest in that sense to a modern state's archive. Hence Ishtiaq Husain Qureshi: "The foundations of any historical study of Akbar must rest solidly upon Abu-l-Fadl's *Akbarnamah*. It is full, detailed and mainly authentic, because it was written by a man who was fully familiar with the official policies and actions of the government and enjoyed not only the confidence but actually the friendship of the emperor."[17]

Harbans Mukhia's well-known study entitled *Historians and Historiography During the Reign of Akbar* serves to illustrate my point about the pivotal position ascribed to certain Mughal sources.[18] The arrangement of this book is

---

[16] B. De and Baini Prasad (trans.), *The Tabaqat-i Akbari of Khwajah Nizammudin Ahmad*, vols. I–III (1936; rpt. Delhi, 1992).

[17] Ishtiaq Husain Qureshi, *Akbar: The Architect of the Mughul Empire* (1978; rpt. Delhi, 1987), pp. 2, 6.

[18] Harbans Mukhia, *Historians and Historiography During the Reign of Akbar* (New Delhi, 1976).

telling. In the three central chapters of the book, the author discusses the three "major" historians of Akbar's empire: Abu-l Fazl, 'Abd al-Qadir Badauni, and Nizam al-Din Ahmad. After a detailed discussion of the texts of these chroniclers, Mukhia, in his penultimate chapter, goes on to discuss "Some Minor Historical Works Written During Akbar's Reign."[19] Here he refers, among others, to the memoirs of Jawhar Aftabchi and Bayazid Bayat. While reading this chapter, I expected to find Gulbadan's text among the "minor historical works." Instead, all we find is a footnote in which the author says, "I have not included a study of the *Humayun Nama* of Gulbadan Begam in this chapter though it falls in the same class of ['Minor Historical'] works as the three mentioned above. The reason is that I feel I have practically nothing to add to what its translator, Mrs. Beveridge, has said in her introduction to the translation."[20]

It is striking that Mukhia provides no more than a single footnote on Gulbadan's text, and his comment that he has nothing to add to what its translator said in 1902 invites some reflection. Two suggestions might be made in this connection. Mukhia's reasons for not including the Begum's memoir in his monograph stems partly from the fact that the author distinguishes between major (political-administrative, and emperor-centered) and minor (of royal women, servants, and so forth), privileging the "hard politics" of the former against the "soft society" of the latter, thus neglecting to see the power-relations that go into the making of such categories. The presumption of the supposedly central character of some sources, as opposed to the peripheral (or minor) status of others, derives in this case from a belief that despite limitations, certain texts like the *Akbarnama* are authentic because they were based upon "official documents as well as memoirs of persons involved in, or witness to, the events."[21] As I have noted, Mukhia is not alone in this belief in the "authenticity," and hence "reliability," of these sources.

In addition, however, Mukhia is possibly aware of the challenges posed by feminist perspectives and questions in history writing; he does not know what to do with Gulbadan's unusual memoir – or those challenges. Therefore in his writing, the Begum's text becomes even more peripheral than the other so-called minor historical works. What this amounts to is a refusal to take on the task of looking anew at sources, and to acknowledge major developments that had occurred in history writing even before his book was published in 1976.

It is in this context of a rather simple (transparent) reading of the Mughal archive that I wish to explore the "minor" text, the *Ahval-i Humayun Badshah*, left to us by Gulbadan Banu Begum, and to show by a critical engagement with it, how many hidden dimensions of Mughal history may yet be probed.

---

[19] *Ibid.*, p. xvi.   [20] *Ibid.*, p. 154, n. 1.   [21] *Ibid.*, p. 71.

The challenge of a princess's memoir

Gulbadan was the daughter of Babur, sister of Humayun, and aunt of Akbar. She was born in 1523 in Afghanistan, and traveled to Hindustan (to Agra) at the age of six-and-a-half (1529), after Babur had made some substantial conquests in that region. Her mother was Dildar Begum, but Maham Begum, the senior wife of Babur, took charge of her.[22] As her memoir reveals, Gulbadan witnessed the early turmoil of Babur's and Humayun's reigns. She and her husband, Khizr Khvajeh Khan, seem to have spent much of their time wandering with what may be described as her peripatetic Mughal family home. "She spent her childhood under her father's rule in Kabul and Hindustan; her girlhood and young wifehood shared the fall and exile of Humayun; and her maturity and failing years slipped past under the protection of Akbar," as her translator, Annette Beveridge, put it in 1902.[23]

Gulbadan was thus a close witness to the making of the Mughal monarchy, seeing it through many vicissitudes – from the inception of the Mughal kingdom in the early conquests of Babur to its established splendor in Akbar's reign. She came to write about all this at the behest of her nephew, Akbar, whose efforts to consolidate and institutionalize Mughal power included the command that a comprehensive and authoritative official history be written of its early stages and of his reign.

Around 1587, when Akbar commissioned an official history of his empire, several "servants of the State" and "old members of the Mughal family" were requested to write down or relate their impressions of earlier times.[24] Gulbadan herself notes: "There had been an order issued, 'Write down whatever you know of the doings of *Firdaus-makani* [posthumous title for Babur meaning "dwelling in paradise"] and *Jannat-ashyani* [posthumous title for Humayun meaning "nestling in paradise"].' "[25] It was in accordance with this instruction that Bayazid Bayat, Jawhar, and Gulbadan Banu Begum produced their memoirs.[26]

What Gulbadan wrote, however, was no panegyric. Her writing was markedly different from anything that other official chroniclers or servants of the king produced at the time, as the list of the sources used for the compilation of the *Akbarnama* shows.[27] Other memoirists tended to favor genres that have been labeled as *tarikh*, a word referring to annals, history, or chronological narrative; *tazkireh*, written in the form of biographies and memoirs; *name*, included biographies and exemplary accounts, aside from histories, epistles, and accounts of exemplary deeds; *qanun*, written in the mode of normative accounts or legal texts; and *vaqi'at* meaning a narrative of happenings, events,

---

[22] Beveridge, *Humayun*, pp. 1, 8–9.   [23] *Ibid.*, p. 2.   [24] *Akbarnama*, I, p. 29.
[25] Beveridge, *Humayun*, p. 83, and n. 1; cf. Gulbadan, *Ahval*, fol. 2b.
[26] Beveridge, *Biyat*, p. 296.   [27] *Akbarnama*, I, see Introduction, especially pp. 29–33 and notes.

and occurrences.[28] Interestingly, the genre title that Gulbadan chose was different from all of these: it was *Ahval*, a word meaning conditions, state, circumstances, or situations.[29] Does this title index a different conception of what a "history" of the times should be?

It is not possible to give a straightforward answer to this question. One disadvantage is that only one copy of Gulbadan's *Ahval* survives today. This manuscript, now held at the British Library, is incomplete, ending abruptly some three years before Akbar's accession. Annette Beveridge, the translator of the *Ahval*, noted in 1925 that her search for a second copy of the *Ahval* that began in 1902 was unsuccessful.[30]

Turki was Gulbadan's native language, and one can trace many Turki words in the Persian manuscript. Yet we do not know if she wrote both in Turki and in Persian. From Humayun's time on, the influence of Persian had clearly increased in the Mughal court.[31] Gulbadan Begum, his sister, is almost certain to have learnt the language as she grew up in these surroundings. Indeed, two lines of poetry by her in Persian are preserved in the work of Mir Mahdi Shirazi.[32] By the time Gulbadan wrote her memoir, Persian had already been declared the language of administration at all levels. As Muzaffar Alam puts it, it had emerged as "*the language* of the king, the royal household and the high Mughal elite."[33] The nomination of Gulbadan to write a memoir of the times, as well as the Persian verse attributed to her, indicates her standing as a "learned" person.[34]

For all that, we know little about Gulbadan's total literary output, her education, or the circumstances of the composition of her memoir. We cannot know, therefore, what models Gulbadan drew upon to write her own text. It certainly does not show adherence to any available format, differing markedly in this respect from most court chronicles of the time. It is without any didactic purpose, and lies outside the "mirror for princes" genre, which seems to have been prevalent then. Gulbadan read some contemporary memoirs and chronicles of kings, including her father's memoir,[35] but the *Baburnama*

---

[28] For the meanings of the words, see the following: S. Haim (ed.), *Dictionary English–Persian Persian–English* rev. edn; F. Steingass, *A Comprehensive Persian–English Dictionary*, 2nd edn; and S. Haim, *Shorter Persian English Dictionary*, 3rd edn, s. v. "tarikh," "tazkireh," "name," "qanun," "vaqi'at."

[29] Steingass, *Persian*; Haim, *Shorter Dictionary*, s. v. "ahval."

[30] British Library, MSS Eur C176/ 221, 1–2; M. A. Scherer, "Woman to Woman: Annette, the Princess, and the Bibi," *Journal of Royal Asiatic Society*, Series 3, 6, 2 (1996), pp. 208–209.

[31] For the importance of Persian among the Muslim elite in India even in the pre-Mughal period, and its remarkable growth under the Mughals, see Alam, "The Pursuit of Persian," pp. 317–350. The observations of the Jesuit fathers in the time of Akbar tell us a great deal about the everyday usage and popularity of the language. See, Monserrate, *Commentary*, and Correia-Afonso, *Letters*.

[32] Beveridge, *Humayun*, p. 76.

[33] Alam, "The Pursuit of Persian," pp. 324, 325 (emphasis Alam's).

[34] For an early comment on Gulbadan's life, see Annette Susannah Beveridge, "Life and Writings of Gulbadan Begam (Lady Rosebody)," *Calcutta Review*, 106 (1892), pp. 346–347. Hereafter cited as *Gulbadan Begam*.

[35] Beveridge, *Humayun*, p. 83; cf. Gulbadan, *Ahval*, fol. 2b.

was clearly not the literary model for her *Ahval*. Annette Beveridge tells us
that the Begum had a copy of Bayazid Bayat's *Tazkireh-i Humayun va Akbar*
in her library, and that she found a copy of Khvandamir's *Qanun-i Humayuni*
inscribed with the Begum's name.[36] Yet Gulbadan did not imitate the styles of
either of these accounts, which were in any case contemporaneous with her
own, and thus perhaps unavailable at the time of her writing. The *Ahval-i
Humayun Badshah* might thus be classed as an "open" text belonging to no
recognized genre.

Whatever we may conclude about the problems of authorship, and of
personal memory, given the uncertainties surrounding the Begum's memoir,
one thing is clear. If most chronicles of the age aimed to be authoritative
histories in the manner of the generic (panegyric) histories of rulers,
Gulbadan moved away from this genre to produce an account of far more
"modest" incidents in the lives of Babur and Humayun. Her account of the
everyday lives of this royal family in peripatetic circumstances is a unique
piece of writing. Gulbadan creates an unusual space in her writing to compose
a picture of many areas of Mughal life very different from that provided in
other sources.

Even a brief description of the contents and the organization of *Ahval*
serves to illustrate this point. The surviving copy of the memoir is divided
into two parts. In the first part, Gulbadan discusses the period of the life of
her father, Babur. This includes detail quite similar to that contained in
Babur's memoir, about his wanderings in parts of Afghanistan, and
Hindustan, his wars and victories at the time, and the early years of his
establishment of Mughal rule in Hindustan. The specialness of the Begum's
memoir, however, is to be found in the images she provides of her father's
"home" life: extensive information about his marriages, his wives and
children, his relationships with his kith and kin, especially the senior
women of the Mughal lineage. The memoir is remarkable not only for this
rare account of domestic life, but also for the complexity that the author
brings out in those episodes that are discussed in other chronicles of the time.
Consider the inventory of gifts and instructions for their presentation that I
mentioned at the beginning of this chapter. In his own brief discussion of the
same event, Babur makes only a casual, and far less interesting, mention of
the presents.[37]

Gulbadan begins a substantial discussion of the reign of Humayun, her
brother, from the nineteenth folio. Alongside a discussion of the king's
expeditions and reconquest of Hindustan, the memoir provides here, too,
other kinds of fascinating information. We learn of Mughal women lost
during wars, as well as of Akbar's birth in the harsh circumstances of the
itinerant life of Humayun and his wife, Hamideh Banu Begum. Gulbadan's

---

[36] Beveridge, *Humayun*, pp. 76 and 78.
[37] Thackston, *Baburnama*, pp. 634–635; and Beveridge, *Baburnama*, pp. 525–526.

record of royal women's articulations about how they should marry is telling. So is her elaboration of Humayun's frequent visits to the senior women of the family, and the tension that arose between him and his wives as a result of these visits. Add to these the impressive detail provided of the celebrations and feasts held by the senior women on occasions such as Humayun's accession, and at the time of the wedding of his stepbrother, Mirza Hindal, and we have a lost world of the court in camp brought to life in a way that no other chronicle of the time even approaches.

Gulbadan lists all sorts of people, and details substantially the activities of several Mughal women – in moments of marriage, childbirth, and "adoption," in the celebration of feasts, on occasions of death, in times of intimacy, strategy, and planning – thus illuminating the practices involved in the making of early Mughal monarchy. In her memoir, we hear of forbidden feelings, hierarchical but intimate relationships, and acts contrary to the logic of imperial power. In this way, we are reminded of the flesh and blood of historical figures, wellknown and not so wellknown, as well as the limitations and inventiveness of their lives. What the text provides is a rich, inflected sense of the domestic lives of the early Mughals.

The two extracts from the *Ahval-i Humayun Badshah* cited in the first section of this chapter are enough to indicate the kinds of questions that the text immediately raises, and that it is necessary for us to ask about the imbrication of the Mughal domestic world in the everyday life of the courts and kings, or equally, the imbrication of courts and kings in the everyday life of the domestic world. Let me point to one more episode to delineate further the potential of Gulbadan's memoir. The event concerns the participation of the *haraman* (women of the *haram*) in relation to matters of kingship. Gulbadan sets this episode during the period when Humayun was on the run owing to the challenge of the Afghan ruler Sher Shah. Humayun's movements through various parts of Hindustan and Central Asia at this time were complicated by the struggle for power with his own stepbrothers, Mirza Kamran and Mirza 'Askari, who were often accomplices.

At one point during this struggle, Mirza Kamran suggested to 'Askari that they should work together to take Qandahar from Mirza Hindal, the third stepbrother of Humayun. On hearing of this, Humayun approached Khanzadeh Begum, his paternal aunt (elder sister of Babur), and requested her to go to Qandahar to advise Mirza Hindal and Mirza Kamran that since the threat of their rival clansmen was immense, it was best to be friends among themselves. Khanzadeh Begum traveled from Jun to Qandahar, and Kamran arrived there from Kabul. Mirza Kamran urged Khanzadeh Begum to have the *khutba* read in his name. As regards the matter of *khutba*, he also wrote to Hindal's mother (and his stepmother), Dildar Begum, who suggested he asked Khanzadeh Begum, their elder kinswoman, "the truth about the *khutba* [*haqiqate khutbeh*]." When Kamran finally spoke with Khanzadeh Begum, she advised him as follows: "as his Majesty *Firdaus-makani* [Babur] decided it and gave his throne to the Emperor Humayun, and as you, all of you, have read the *khutba* in his name till now, so now regard him as your superior and remain in obedience to him."[38] This extract focuses upon an influential aunt playing a key role in the reading of the *khutba* – the decree for the proclamation of kingship. I shall deal with this episode in greater detail in a later chapter; I cite it here only to ask whether we could have a more striking statement of how senior women collaborated in the process of the promotion of kings.

Questions of translation

The colonial scholar Annette Beveridge accomplished the truly commendable task of unearthing, translating and presenting to the scholarly world the *Ahval-i Humayun Badshah*. Yet it would be surprising if, a hundred years on, we did not have some questions about the way in which that work was done. The process by which Gulbadan's memoir was made available to us, and the mutations that took place in the course of that process, need to be borne in mind by the modern historian. Much would be gained from considering carefully what happens to the content and context of sources in the process of collation and translation.[39] While this will have to be the subject for larger investigation, a brief discussion of it here, in relation to the *Ahval-i Humayun Badshah*, should indicate further the existing possibilities of rethinking Mughal social history.

As a first step, it will help to keep in mind Annette Beveridge's own social and intellectual context. She was born Annette Akroyd (1842–1929) in Stourbridge, a small town just west of Birmingham. A daughter of "a self-made man of England's rising middle class,"[40] she was brought up as a Unitarian in religion and "radical" in politics. In 1861, she enrolled at the Unitarian supported Bedford College in London. Her education was premised on the notion of "evolution" and "progress" alongside a Victorian grooming with an emphasis on domestic and personal life, and the ideology of nineteenth-century scientism with its constituent components.[41] She also shared the nineteenth century's unquestioned belief in science's objectivity

---

[38] Beveridge, *Humayun*, p. 161; cf. Gulbadan, *Ahval*, fol. 51b.

[39] My concern is not only with accuracy in the translation of individual words and phrases, which is, of course, important; cf. Shahpurshah Hormasji Hodivala, *Studies in Indo-Muslim History: A Critical Commentary on Elliot and Dowson's History of India as Told by its Own Historians*, vols. I–II (Lahore, 1979).

[40] Scherer, "Woman to Woman," p. 198.

[41] Pat Barr, *The Memsahibs: The Women of Victorian India* (London, 1976), pp. 188–189; see Scherer, "Woman to Woman," p. 197, for a discussion of what she calls Annette Beveridge's "sturdy Victorian temperament." Scherer also refers to Beveridge's interest in Christian Science during the years of her translation of the *Ahval*; "Woman to Woman," p. 209; also, Scherer, "Annette Akroyd Beveridge: Victorian Reformer, Oriental Scholar" (unpublished Ph.D. diss., The Ohio State University, 1995), ch. II, especially, pp. 96–99, 118–122.

and its ability to "represent" reality. In this triumphalist vision, the institutions, practices, traditions and belief-systems of the West were rational, and those of other (non-Western) parts of the world were presented as being backward, if not uncivilized. Annette Beveridge's public opposition to the Ilbert Bill of 1883, seeking to empower Indian civil servants with criminal jurisdiction over European subjects in country stations, was very much in accord with these views.[42]

How does this self-confident colonial context affect Beveridge's translation of the *Ahval-i Humayun Badshah*? The first point to note is that the Victorian translator's fixed frame of knowledge also "fixes" the stories she reads in the *Ahval*. As a result, numerous interesting nuances are lost and what appears before the reader is a flattened picture of early Mughal domestic life. This may be witnessed in many instances of Beveridge's literal paraphrasing and in her attempt to find exact English equivalents of Persian words that have complex histories and associations. It may also be seen in the "aristocratic" (yet colonial bourgeois) sensibility with which she regards the characters of the memoir.

Consider the following passage, which evokes marriage practices in the time of Humayun. In the memoir, the conversation between Maham Begum and others is placed two years after Babur's death (1532) when Humayun was trying to retain and expand his father's territories in India. Gulbadan writes:

My lady, who was Maham Begam, had a great longing and desire to see a son of Humayun. Wherever there was a good-looking and nice girl, she used to bring her into his service. Maywa-jan, a daughter of Khadang (? Khazang), the chamberlain (*yasawal*), was in my employ. One day (after) the death of his Majesty *Firdaus-makani*, my lady said: "Humayun, Maywa-jan is not bad. Why do you not take her into your service?" So, at her word, Humayun married and took her that very night.

Three days later Bega Begam came from Kabul. She became in the family way. In due time she had a daughter, whom they named 'Aqiqa. Maywa-jan said to Lady (*Aka*) Maham Begam, "I am in the family way, too." Then my lady got ready two sets of weapons, and said: "Whichever of you bears a son, I will give him good arms." ... [She] was very happy, and kept saying: "Perhaps one of them will have a son." She kept watch till Bega Begam's 'Aqiqa was born. Then she kept an eye on Maywa-jan. Ten months went by. The eleventh also passed. Maywa-jan said: "My maternal aunt was in Mirza Ulugh Beg's *haram*. She had a son in the twelfth month; perhaps I am like her." So they sewed tents and filled pillows. But in the end everyone knew she was a fraud.[43]

"My lady Maham Begam, had a great longing and desire to see a son of Humayun," Gulbadan tells us. In this world, as elsewhere, it was the role of the younger wives to produce heirs: in their turn, at a later stage, they themselves instructed younger wives about such responsibilities. This duty

---

[42] Mrinalini Sinha, *Colonial Masculinity: The "Manly Englishman" and the "Effeminate Bengali" in the Late Nineteenth Century* (Manchester, 1995), pp. 58–60; cf. Scherer, "Annette Akroyd Beveridge," ch. V.

[43] Beveridge, *Humayun*, pp. 112–113; cf. Gulbadan, *Ahval*, fols. 21b–22a.

of elder women to advise the young, and of the young to carry forward the name of the family through reproduction, was of no small moment in the Timurid-Mughal world. Miveh-jan and her "services" would fit this tradition. The production of royal children was a much-desired event: for such an esteemed birth meant the perpetuation of the eminent Timurid-Mughal family. The task was especially crucial in the time of Babur and Humayun when the risk of the disappearance of the family was very real, on account of the Uzbik threat that Babur faced in Central Asia, and later because of the Afghan challenge encountered by Humayun in Hindustan. It was an urgent requirement in these circumstances to preserve the lineage, and to achieve that, marriages and the birth of children were essential. It was in this context that Maham Begum made the point about male heirs. She looked for wives for Humayun for the momentous task of producing heirs to the throne.[44]

In a separate article on Gulbadan Begum's life and writings, the revised version of which was to later become the Introduction to her translation, Annette Beveridge drew the following picture of Maham Begum while discussing the episode described above:

Maham Begam was a clever woman, and both as wife and as widow made herself felt in her home. Lady Rosebody [Gulbadan Begum] lifts the *parda* and shows us the Empress-mother busied in duties not often thus disclosed to the outside eye. In telling the story, which for the sake of its many special points we quote in full, she has no air of being indiscreet, and is, as may be seen, quite matter-of-fact.[45]

Beveridge sees in Maham's activities more "a clever ... Empress-mother" than a senior woman with wisdom, status and authority, who would have seen it her duty to advise and guide her younger kinsfolk, and to sustain the name and honor of her family. She elevates this "elder" to a rarefied and singular position that is far removed from the projection of plural, and sometimes overlapping, circles of intimates and authorities in the peripatetic Mughal world of Gulbadan's memoir.

Gulbadan describes many different kinds of royal women, and marks the different ways in which they worked to preserve the lineage and its practices. The senior women helped make dynastic linkages through marriages by which the name of the Timurid-Mughals was carried forward. Younger wives produced heirs. The function of senior women was neither sexual nor reproductive, although as young mothers, they too had been expected to give birth to children. Tradition was preserved (and perpetuated) by their bodily, reproductive functions in their youth, but also by their role as elders and advisers. They were inheritors and transmitters of tradition, in both roles.

There were, within the intimate circles of the Mughal kings, nurses, servants, and grooms, with their respective commitments to Mughal royalty.

---

[44] Beveridge, *Humayun*, pp. 111–112 and nn. 1, 2; Gulbadan, *Ahval*, fol. 21b.
[45] Beveridge, "Gulbadan Begam," pp. 353–354.

Take the example of nurses who fed, fostered, and cared for Akbar. Many of them were tied to the family of Humayun, not by birth or kinship but by acts of loyalty. Jiji Anageh, for instance, was married to "the nobly-born" Shams al-Din Muhammad of Ghazni who had helped Humayun up the steep banks of the Ganges when Sher Shah defeated him.[46] Fakhr-un-Nisa Begum, who also fed Akbar, seems to have been Humayun's attendant from his childhood. Gulbadan Begum lists her as one of those who attended the wedding feast of Hindal Mirza.[47] Likewise, another nurse who fed Akbar was Kuki Anageh, the wife of Tuq Begi, who is referred to as *Tuq Begi Saqi*, i.e., page or cup-bearer by Bayazid Bayat.[48]

In this context of highly open and variegated domestic relations, the attribution of "cleverness" and "singularity" to Maham Begum by Beveridge is perhaps too hasty. One example of this kind of slanting, which is accompanied by an assimilation of early Mughal society and mores into something more recognizably Victorian, is the use of the honorific "My Lady" for *Akam*, and other cognate terms. This form of address is found dispersed throughout the translation, as also in the first line of the extract from Gulbadan that we have been considering here. Beveridge ponders over the meaning of "*Akam*" at one point. She writes: "the Turki Aka is used as a title of respect from a junior to a senior. It has also the sense 'elder brother,' which makes application to a woman doubtful. Babar uses the word ... and Mr. Erskine [a contemporary scholar of Annette Beveridge, known for the first English translation of the memoir of Babur] suggests to read 'my Lady' [*sic*]."[49]

Beveridge declares it hard to apply the connotation of respect embedded in the word *akam* to a woman, and instead chooses "My Lady" – with its implications of elevation and romance in the likeness of late medieval European (knightly) traditions, which are not readily instantiated in the Timurid-Mughal world. Gulbadan, in fact, uses the word *akam* with a great sense of affection and respect in her descriptions: *akam*, or "my *aka*." *Aka*, a Turki word (used for men), is very close in essence to *khanum* or *begum*. Reverence, privileged status, and deference (that came with enhanced age) are marked characteristics of all of these words.

In a similar way, we might ask questions about the word *havasak*, in the translation cited above. In the last line of the passage, the word "fraud" is used for the Persian word *havasak*. The latter, which is not found as such in Persian dictionaries, is an affective diminutive of *havas*, meaning desire, caprice. While Beveridge interprets *havasak* as a pejorative, Miveh-jan's craving for a child is hardly unexpected, given the Timurid-Mughal context of the politics of marriage and reproduction, and the quick dismissal of her

---

[46] *Akbarnama*, I, p. 130, n. 1; Beveridge, *Humayun*, p. 142, and n. 4; Gulbadan, *Ahval*, fol. 37b.
[47] Beveridge, *Humayun*, pp. 122, 185; cf. Gulbadan, *Ahval*, fols. 26a, 71a.
[48] *Akbarnama*, I, p. 130, n. 1.   [49] Beveridge, *Humayun*, pp. 89–90, n. 4.

state as "fraudulent" – rather than, say, as a case of hysterical pregnancy – amounts to a reduction of the ambivalence and tension that marks Gulbadan's text.[50]

Despite the evident problems of translation, it is not difficult to see the memoir's rich potential in helping us comprehend the processes at work in the making of the Mughal monarchy and its domestic world. Against the background of fragments from the *Ahval-i Humayun Badshah*, it is therefore possible to consider the conditions and ways of domestic life under the early Mughals. Gulbadan's documentation of the roles and positions of Mughal men and women allows us to explore the meanings of relationships among them: the extremely varied, and mostly hierarchical, nature of these relationships, the kinds of conflict, and the solidarities making for diverse forms of community. Different kinds of relationships are indexed in the participation of women and men, in the making of marriages, in festivities and other celebrations, and in the observance of customs and rituals at births and deaths and more everyday occasions. It is through an excavation of these relationships and events that we are likely to be able to delineate forms of Mughal sociability as well as think through other concepts, those of motherhood and wifehood, for instance, the ways in which marriages were effected (and why in those ways), or the prevailing notions of duty, loyalty, and love.

Concluding thoughts

If the multiplex character of Gulbadan's memoir opens some fascinating arenas for us, it also helps us to read other Mughal chronicles very differently, for these too are richer in meaning and content than the historians have made them out to be.

In histories of the Mughals, there is a sharp focus on the personality and politics of the Mughal kings and their most prominent lieutenants. The emperor, his nobles and their political-administrative-military exploits are explored over and over again; other worlds are hardly even noticed. There are two problems that flow from this. First, as feminist writings have shown in so many other contexts, a large part of the human experience falls outside

---

[50] The context of Timurid-Mughal reproductive politics might allow us to read *havasak* as a condition applicable to women who become desirous of having children and begin to have symptoms of pregnancy (swelling breasts and stomach and milk) without any biological conception of a child (termed hysterical pregnancy in current medical terminology). This condition, which occurs due to a keen desire for motherhood, can change. Of course, hysterical pregnancy, medically speaking, is a fairly complex phenomenon. There are several realms in the spectrum of hysteria, thus acquiring many forms and conditions. *Couvade* or "hysteria by proxy" is one such form: a factitious disorder since there is some awareness on the part of the agent that they are not really pregnant. "Malingering" is "deliberate faking" of pregnancy. *Pseudocyesis* falls in the third realm of this scale: compulsive disorder where the patient completely believes that her condition of pregnancy is true. I am thankful to Dr. Ajay Wasan (research fellow at the Harvard Medical School) and Simone Taubenberger for these details.

history. (This happens partly because ordinary, everyday, "domestic" events are not neatly documented by the state, or institutionalized in public archives.) As a consequence, the account of the great historical changes and developments also fails to come to life. Few Mughal histories have been histories of people building lives, relationships, or domestic worlds; and even the description of the momentous and the extraordinary sometimes becomes empty.

Gulbadan Begum's *Ahval-i Humayun Badshah* draws our attention to the importance of the quotidian at the very moment of extraordinary, momentous events. The challenge of her memoir may be summed up in a number of ways. Perhaps the easiest point to note is that she raises important questions about life and activities in the household of the early Mughals. Gulbadan's text poses a second, and less obvious, challenge too. The Begum shows us the Mughal empire in a very different light from that of the official histories and much of its subsequent historiography. Her empire is not yet fully institutionalized. Though Gulbadan's text was actually used as a source for the official chronicle of Akbar's empire, interestingly it is her text, and not the imperial history, that tells us about the *making of the empire*. What the *Akbarnama* (and the *A'in-i Akbari*) provides is an institutionalized history of an empire already in place – fully formed, so to speak. Gulbadan's text, by contrast, shows us the empire (and its history) *being formed*.

Thus her *Ahval* appears important in at least three ways. First, chronologically speaking, it evokes a powerful impression of an empire that is not already known or made, a political formation taking unsteady steps from infancy to maturity. Secondly, in terms of domestic manners and emotional life, the text provides much food for thought on the less tangible (and less documentable) aspects of Mughal history. Finally, on the question of history (and empire) itself, the text serves as a symbol of how official "history" came to be written as part of the construction of an empire; of course, the Begum's memoir ended up as historiographical flotsam, suggesting both the entrenched politics and the machinations involved in the construction of historical archives.

Once we have been alerted to some of these hidden dimensions of Mughal history by a text like Gulbadan's, we discover that the canonical, mainstream sources long used by Mughal historians themselves yield information on many "hidden" matters when we go to them with new questions: unusual and unexpected evidence on the rough and tumble of social life, on everyday struggles, fears and pleasures, on the construction of new subjectivities and new historical conditions.

It is interesting in this context to refer once more to Abu-l Fazl's grand compendium, the *Akbarnama*, the place where we find detailed reference to a women's *hajj* (pilgrimage) led by Gulbadan Begum herself. The exceptional character of this event – a *hajj* of women, initiated by a woman, and to a large extent organized by women – remains an unusual happening in the annals of high Mughal history. The *hajj* is remarkable precisely because it is a *women's hajj*; it tells us something about the process of the consolidation of a Muslim empire in South Asia. The women's *hajj* seems to be one of the major pietistic activities that Akbar supported during his reign, part of a whole series of moves that he and others in his court and household perhaps saw as reinforcing the Islamic face of the empire. We never hear of such an incident again in the reigns of Akbar's well-established successors. Is this because they were already so well established? Or because the royal women, now better "incarcerated," had far less opportunity to take exceptional initiatives and set off on such a pilgrimage?

It was a bold and significant adventure, given the constraints of the passage, and other restrictive circumstances, and one that was largely initiated and planned by the elder women. Like the seeking of Khanzadeh Begum's opinion in the matter of kingship (the reading of the *khutba*), this collective women's *hajj* remains an unparalleled example in the annals of the Mughals. Indeed, the royal women's *hajj* led by Gulbadan comes as a startling discovery because, while the *Akbarnama* provides considerable detail about the *hajj*, historians writing on the Mughals in general or the history of the *hajj* from India in particular have paid little or no attention to it.[51]

Once such challenging complexities are noted in one set of materials, it is to be hoped that the historian will look at other texts with a different eye. European travelers' accounts are, as we saw in the last chapter, another major source of information for historians of Mughal India, which contain unusual and valuable details on several aspects of Mughal social life and hierarchy. The point is to attend to them carefully because they depict social visions and contests in interesting ways. Recall only one example, that of Father Monserrate, one of the three members of the first Jesuit Mission that arrived at Akbar's court in 1580. His account of Akbar's court is, like that of other travelers, full of scandalous stories and hasty generalizations. Recall too his not so subtle observation that Akbar had "more than 300" wives and yet "only five" children.[52] At the same time, Monserrate records that Akbar's mother, Hamideh Banu Begum, acted as the head of the province of Delhi, when he marched to Kabul in the late 1570s to suppress a conspiracy involving several rebels to install Mirza Hakim, the emperor's half-brother, as the ruler of Hindustan.[53] Add to this, his reference to the pilgrimage to Mecca undertaken by the women of Akbar's *haram* in 1578.[54] Both these episodes

---

[51] The single mention of Gulbadan Begum in Richards, *Mughal Empire*, appears in a reference to the women's *hajj*. However, the whole pilgrimage is represented as the initiative of the emperor Akbar, and completely misses the initiative of the Begum. A similar review of Gulbadan's *hajj*, hinging upon the enterprise and centrality of the emperor, may be seen in Michael N. Pearson, *Pilgrimage to Mecca: The Indian Experience 1500–1800* (Princeton, 1996), especially the chapter, "The Mughals and the *Hajj*." I consider Gulbadan Begum's *hajj* extensively in chapter 7.

[52] Monserrate, *Commentary*, p. 205.   [53] *Ibid.*, pp. 74–75.

[54] *Ibid.*, p. 166 and nn. 255, 167, and 205.

are remarkable examples of the high profile of the senior Mughal women and their wielding of authority – instances that are rarely detailed in other court chronicles of the time. This, in itself, should serve as sufficient invitation for us to explore further why European travelers' accounts carry such details, and how they might contribute to a better understanding of Mughal society and culture.

In a similar way, a concern with "domestic" affairs and changing relationships could lead to new readings of some of the miniature paintings made in Akbar's atelier (and subsequently, on an even larger scale). Mughal miniatures are among the few documents that provide us with a rich body of materials for the study of the Mughal court and society. Yet, even where their importance as sources has been recognized, the questions asked have been chiefly about processes of production, and about authorship and dates.[55]

Thus, the easily available but neglected memoir of a Mughal princess enables us to raise questions about a Mughal "becoming" that Mughal historians have all too often skirted. This relates both to the coming into being of an empire, and to the simultaneous institution of an archive. By making it possible for us to see how one of the most vaunted Mughal sources (the *Akbarnama*) came into being, rendering its own "sources" peripheral as it did so, the memoir opens up the question of the *making* of sources, even as it raises questions about the assigned limits of Mughal history.

The Begum's text challenges some of Mughal historiography's most beloved propositions, such as the one that the sources are simply not available for this or that inquiry. Sensitized by the Begum's account of the struggles involved in the establishment of a new royal life and culture, one also learns what other ("central," official) frequently mined sources are capable of telling us about these processes. For what Gulbadan's *Ahval-i Humayun Badshah* suggests very clearly indeed is the fact of the fluidity and contestation that went into the founding of this new polity in its new setting – not only its new power and grandeur, but also its new regulations and accommodations, its traditions and its hierarchies. Her writing points to the history of a subjectivity and a culture, of political power and of social relationships, struggling to be born. Historians wishing to extend the frontiers of Mughal history cannot but ask, as part of this endeavor, for a more sustained history of everyday lives and associations based on sources like Gulbadan's memoir, but hardly on that alone.

---

[55] Cf. Juneja, *Architecture.*

CHAPTER 4

The making of Mughal court society

The first Mughal *padshah*, Babur, was born on 14 February 1483. He descended from Chingiz Khan (1167–1227) on his mother's (Qutlugh Nigar Khanum) side and from Amir Timur (1336–1405) on his father's ('Umar Shaykh Mirza). In keeping with the prevalent practice amongst his clan, Babur's paternal grandfather, Sultan Abu Sayyid Mirza, parceled out his empire to his sons: Samarqand and Bukhara to Sultan Ahmad Mirza, Farghaneh to 'Umar Shaykh Mirza, Kabul to Ulugh Beg Mirza, and Garmsir-Qandahar to Sultan Murad Mirza. It was over these possessions, provinces controlled by uncles, or cousins of varying degrees, that Babur fought with close and distant relatives for much of his life. Particularly notable among Babur's long drawn-out conflicts was a fight over Samarqand, Timur's capital, coveted alike by Babur and his rival clansmen, the Uzbiks. During a protracted struggle for the city, Babur lost Farghaneh, bequeathed to him by his father. By about 1504, he was driven to Kabul, and eventually to Hindustan.

In recounting the trajectory of Babur's eventual arrival in Hindustan, what historians have failed to dwell upon is the detail of this peripatetic life and the homosocial character of the early Mughal world. The texts of the time do not speak of splendid permanent domestic spaces (palaces and the like), but of a camp – fellow-nobles, retainers, women, wives, children, and household – on the move. There was little in the way of fixed territories to govern: indeed, as all histories of Babur tell us, he spent most of his life desiring to recover territory in his "homeland." There were no regular taxes to collect, no permanent administrative staff, no well-established bureaucratic structures. Yet, a sense of a courtly life comes through Babur's memoir and his well-documented claims to kingship. It is not insignificant that in 1508 he declared himself a *padshah*, discarding the "lesser" title of Mirza as unsatisfactory.

Warfare remained an important part of Humayun's life too. But whereas for Babur this was a matter of "incessant conflict among cousins," for Humayun, it was primarily against one major outside rival, the Afghan ruler Sher Shah, and a number of rival insiders – his own stepbrothers, Kamran, 'Askari, and Hindal. Humayun was more recognizably a "king" than his father. He had his capital at Agra and lived, at least for some time, in grand stone buildings. Overall, his life may be described as that of a king and an exile, as Babur's had been that of an adventurer and a poet (as well as a "king" and an exile). No longer was the camp or court a widely dispersed line of cousins and clansmen competing with one another for scarce resources and temporary military advantage. While it was still in part like that, it was also a tighter-knit royal entourage in which hierarchies and positions were more clearly defined than before.

Much of this "background" is well known. Yet, it is rarely asked how one might conceptualize a court that was peripatetic yet courtly (that of Babur), and another (Humayun's) that was organized in the midst of a transition from a peripatetic to an increasingly settled life: what one might describe as "courts in camps." Part of the inquiry in this chapter is to explore the character of the court at this time, and with that to consider the fluidity, shifting locations, and "unsettled" character of the domestic life of these early Mughals.

Two aspects of the early Mughal peripatetic landscape stand out. The first is the perennial state of warfare, which often involved the complete movement of *ahl va 'ayal* – of wives, other women, men, children, servants, nurses, and goods. We know little about how this movement affected the texture of the domestic life and its relationships. While these battles occurred, other activities did not cease: births, celebrations, festivities, domestic and factional alliances, all continued. Scholars have not asked what the fact of perpetual war and mobility, and the simultaneous continuation of production, consumption, and reproduction, meant for Babur, Humayun and their people.

Another aspect of early Mughal life was its marked homosocial character. Striking descriptions of parallel communities of men and women abound in the chronicles of the reigns of Babur and Humayun. In what follows, I examine events and activities that project the links, the emotions and relationships that flowered in this world of multiple communities: of men and men, of women and women, of men, women and children, and of other intimate circles of people around the royalty. I look at the ways (and the conditions) in which these communities worked with each other, engaging and enhancing lives, building relationships and kingdoms. It is within the context of these communities that Mughal domestic life finds its meaning.

In tracing the activities of the people in the Mughal world, we find that hierarchies are reinforced, conflicts as well as solidarities arise, and the meanings and significance of diverse relationships begin to unfold. It is through a close investigation of such interactions and developments that we may be able to delineate forms of Mughal sociality.[1] In this chapter and the next I examine

---

[1] I take Norbert Elias's concept of "figuration" in his book *Court Society* as an entry point for discussion here (Norbert Elias, *The Court Society*, trans. Edmund Jephcott, Oxford, 1983). For Elias, figuration is intended to cover a range of things. Human beings are interdependent and are best understood in this way because their lives are significantly shaped by the social

early Mughal notions of motherhood and wifehood, or what made for an "ideal" mother or wife. I point to the political clout of senior women. I also delineate the activities of several Mughal women and men in moments of intimacy, childbirth, and "adoption," in incidents of death, and celebrations of feasts, and in strategic debates and planning. This indicates the complex web of processes, as well as the intimate circles of people, involved in the early Mughal monarchical formation.

Here, as in the following chapters, I shall insistently, and in many different ways, ask the question: where are the women in the narratives handed down to us? Women lived in their own homosocial circles but obviously interacted with others as well. By posing the question, "where are the women?", I do not simply wish to make them "visible." While that exercise still needs to be pursued in Mughal and related historiographies, I want to take it further. I ask what is the place of women in these narrative structures. Where are they in the pathways that Babur and Humayun traverse? Where are they in the (homosocial) communities that the kings inhabit and describe? What is their place in the camps and the courts – which are not always like the camps and the courts we know in other contexts?

What I do, in effect, is to mark and delineate women's present/absence – for women are not clearly "visible" either way. Paradoxically, whenever they appear in the records of the time, they seem to be constructed in a rather narrowly defined manner: as producers of much coveted heirs to the throne and as carriers of tradition – not surprisingly; also as skilful participants in the preservation of the imperial and genealogical traditions. Sometimes individual women make an appearance too when they do not fit into any of the modes prescribed for them. Through the fragmentary evidence that there is, I want to be able to think of ways of constructing these women's voices and their subjectivity in a historical and historiographical context of this kind.

Court and society in Babur's commentary

As we noted in chapter 3, the most important source for a reconstruction of Babur's court and society is his memoir, written in the form of a diary. By this, I do not refer to a modernist sense of an individual's diary. Yet, Babur's memoir is one in which the exposure or opening of the human self is very

---

figurations they form with each other. The figurations are "continually in flux, undergoing changes of different orders – some quick and ephemeral, others slower but more profound." Norbert Elias, "The Concept of Figurations," in Johan Goudsblom and Stephen Mennell (eds.), *The Norbert Elias Reader* (Oxford, 1998), pp. 130–131. What the concept of figuration does is to take us away from the figure of the monarch – the endless monographs on the "life and times" of Babur and Humayun – "contrasting it with the notion of a royalty which is 'constructed' through concrete, social mechanisms that can be analysed"; Rita Costa-Gomes, *The Making of a Court Society: Kings and Nobles in Late Medieval Portugal*, trans. Alison Aiken (Cambridge, 2003), p. 2.

noticeable. This allows a certain accessibility to a world that in other texts does not "surface" in the same way.

Stephen Dale has noted the uniqueness of Babur's memoir: its "freshness and informality"; its depiction of intimate details; its record of fascinating drinking moments; Babur's thorough consideration of human failures and successes, faults, and fragility; and, above all, his representation of the human-ness of a king, a "sense of his humanity in a manner that is scarcely encountered in Islamic or Indian literature."[2] In this section, I use the *Baburnama* to think about the court and society that Babur conjures up.

Gulbadan Banu Begum, Babur's daughter, underlines the non-stop war-fare of the times: "For eleven full years his [Babur's] wars and struggles against the Chaghatai and Timurid and Uzbeg princes in Mawara'u-n-nahr (Transoxiana) were such that the tongue of the pen is too feeble and weak to recount them."[3] His plight in 1497, when Babur had ridden out for Samarqand, may be described in his own words: "During the period of siege letters arrived constantly from my mother and her people and Khwaja Qazi saying, 'They have us under siege. If you do not come help us, it will be all over. Samarkand was taken through the strength of Andizhan. If Andizhan is held, and God wills, Samarkand can be taken.'"[4]

In March 1505 Babur was conducting early forays into towns around Kabul and into those bordering Hindustan. While returning to Kabul, Babur writes in an entry on 7 March in the *Baburnama* that the river Gumal, which they were to cross, was very tempestuous. The water was so high that he had to "hold deliberations on horseback as to which road to take." It was also the day of 'Id-ul Fitr, so he offered the prayers on the banks of the Gumal. He notes that that year Nawruz was only two or three days away from 'Id. He composed a poem to mark the occasion of Nawruz.[5] This is not an untypical entry for the *Baburnama*.

After a substantial break in his memoir (1508–19), Babur tells us in 1519 that he had begun a campaign against Bajaur.[6] He had taken two forts, crossed into Sind, and captured Bhira, Khushab, and Chinab. In the midst of this campaign, Babur took Bibi Mubarika, the Yusufzay, as his wife. Gulbadan says: "on the same day the father of Afghani *aghacha*, Malik

---

[2] Dale, "Steppe Humanism," p. 41; Dale, "Poetry," p. 637; cf. Dale, *Eight Paradises*, ch. V.

[3] Beveridge, *Humayun*, p. 84; cf. Gulbadan, *Ahval*, fol. 3a.

[4] Since Thackston's translation of the *Baburnama* is without the cumbersome diacritical marks, I have in the main preferred to use his edition. I continue, of course, to refer to Beveridge's extremely erudite translation, and often point to the differences between the two. At some places I also use complete extracts from Beveridge because they seem to be more sensitively rendered than Thackston's. The reader will notice that the Persian edition is used simulta-neously alongside the translations. I should add that at places, I also modify the translations. Thackston, *Baburnama*, pp. 107–108; cf. Beveridge, *Baburnama*, p. 88.

[5] Thackston, *Baburnama*, pp. 309–310.

[6] I am referring to only some details of the year 1519 from the *Baburnama*. See the relevant pages from the two editions used here under the broad heading 1519.

Mansur Yusufzai, came in and paid his respects. His Majesty took his daughter in marriage and then gave him leave to depart."[7] Or in the words of Babur, "While we were at this camp word came that Shah Mansur's daughter was coming with the Yusufzai tribute. That night there was a wine party ... Shah Mansur's younger brother brought his niece to this camp."[8] At the time of his marriage with Bibi Mubarika, Babur's other wife Dildar Begum was pregnant. Maham Begum, Babur's senior wife and mother of Humayun, wrote to Babur saying it did not matter whether a girl or a boy was born to Dildar Begum, she would take the "chance" and raise it as her own.[9]

There are no sharply distinct war times;[10] no emergency situations in which war might be said to create a special circumstance – except in the sense that there were repeated, even constant, "emergencies." Wars (and movement) acquire an altered character and significance in this light. Peripatetic communities did not take wars to be completely cut off from other things – after which, "normal" life resumed. This *is* a life of warriors, of peripatetic kings, and of communities on the move. As Babur struggles to gain territories, he continues to marry and have children. He promotes a close follower to the rank of royal taster,[11] and writes poetry to celebrate Nawruz. He gains and loses possessions, but carries on writing about the beauty of the harvest crops of Koh Daman (north of Kabul), and its wondrous autumnal trees. He finishes copying Mir 'Ali Sher's *divan* and sends his *divan* to Pulad Uzbik in Samarqand.[12]

To understand this condition of constant mobility better, it is important to consider the community and companions of the king at different times. The *Baburnama* is populated with many different kinds of people. The first section, on Farghaneh and Transoxiana, has detailed portraits of the maternal and paternal male relations of Babur's distinguished lineage: of grandfathers, of his father, his uncles, cousins, and other younger male relations. He details the birth and lineage of each of these illustrious clansmen, their country,

---

[7] Beveridge, *Humayun*, p. 91; cf. Gulbadan, *Ahval*, fols. 7b–8a; *aghacheh* (written *aghacha*, above) here means "the Afghan Lady."

[8] Thackston, *Baburnama*, p. 468; Beveridge, *Baburnama*, p. 375. There is another version of this story that enables a different reading; I shall come to it in the next chapter. For the time being I shall continue to evoke something of the spirit of Babur's wandering life as it appears in the *Baburnama*.

[9] Thackston, *Baburnama*, p. 467; Beveridge, *Baburnama*, p. 374.

[10] So different from the medieval European situation where war was often a seasonal activity of kings and royal retinues. This is discussed by Philippe Contamine, *War in the Middle Ages*, trans. Michael Jones (New York, 1984).

[11] Thackston, *Baburnama*, pp. 312–313; Beveridge, *Baburnama*, pp. 236–238.

[12] Pulad (literally, steel) was a son of Kuchum the Khaqan of the Uzbiks and Mihr-ban, whom Annette Beveridge thinks was a half-sister of Babur. She was captured on one of the occasions when Babur lost to the Uzbiks. The *divan* that he sent to Pulad contained a verse on its back that looks to be addressed to his sister through her son. (Beveridge, *Baburnama*, p. 402, nn. 2, 3, and p. 632, n. 3).

appearance, qualities and habits, battles and careers. He lists their noblemen – and *their* qualities, children, ladies, and mistresses.

Babur pays attention even to the mundane characteristics of these men. ʿUmar Shaykh Mirza, his father, "was short in stature, had a round beard and a fleshy face and was fat. He wore his tunic so tight that in order to fasten the ties he had to hold his stomach in. ... He was unceremonious [*bitakalluf*] in both dress and speech."[13] A paternal uncle, Mahmud Mirza

never missed his prayers. ... His assemblies, table and divan were very good [*majlis va bakhshish va divan va shilan*]. Everything was done according to rule and with military precision. ... [but] He was addicted to vice and debauchery. He drank wine continually. He kept a lot of catamites, and in his realm wherever there was a comely beardless youth he did everything he could to turn him into a catamite. He turned his begs' sons and his sons' begs and *kukaldashes* [milk-brothers] into catamites – he even demanded this service of his own *kukaldashes* sons. [14]

Babur also draws close sketches of men other than his kith and kin. Shaykh Mazid Beg, one of the *amirs* of his father, and Babur's first guardian, was "a vicious man who kept catamites."[15] The retainers of ʿAbdul ʿAli Tarkhan, an *amir* of Babur's paternal uncle Sultan Ahmad Mirza, "numbered three thousand, and he kept them splendidly," Babur says. "His liberality, concern for his realm, his court and accoutrements, table and assembly were regal, but he was a harsh, tyrannical, vicious and conceited man."[16]

In Babur's commentary, a certain social order and spirit is projected. Detailing the society of men is the life force of the *Baburnama*. That he spent his time primarily in male company is displayed conspicuously. His detailed account symbolizes the vigor of his male company; he noticed how the men around him dressed, how much they drank, how they carved a roasted fowl, and more generally their social skills, virtues, and qualities, particularly their points of temptation.

This is not the case for women. In the section on Babur's lineage, women creep into the narrative, but only as the appendages to men: as daughters, wives, or mothers, and, importantly, as the makers of children. Babur provides very brief, bland descriptions of the ladies and mistresses of various male relatives. The references that stand out are to senior women, and to what appear as bizarre characters. Consider the sketch of Qataq Begum in Babur's delineation of Sultan Ahmad Mirza's women: "Sultan Ahmad Mirza married her for love [*biʿashiqi*]. He adored her passionately, but she was utterly domineering. She also drank wine [*sharab mikhurd*]. During her lifetime Sultan-Ahmad Mirza did not go to any other wives. In the end he had her killed and obtained release from disgrace."[17]

[13] Thackston, *Baburnama*, p. 13.
[14] *Ibid.*, pp. 50–51. Thackston translates catamite from the Persian phrase *chihreh nigah dashtan*.
[15] *Ibid.*, p. 26.   [16] *Ibid.*, p. 43.   [17] *Ibid.*, p. 40.

It is Qataq Begum's unusual demeanor and actions that are noted. Babur's entry on her is more elaborate than his references to most other women. His amazement with Qataq Begum stems partly at least from a lack of continual contact and association with women, and from an insistence that no women should dominate a man's life. Hence the notion of "release" through the murder of a forceful wife.

Homosociality

The homosocial character of Babur's life on the move is very well illustrated in his detailing of the time he spent with various men, and the range of their activities together. We may begin by considering the intricacies of this homo-social world through the diverse errands that the *aichkildar*, the close circle of the *padshah*, ran for him.

Two features of the activities of these associates are conspicuous. First, there were no clear demarcations of their tasks, no caste divisions whereby particular errands, jobs, and responsibilities were confined to some, and denied to others. A water-carrier could (and did) write a memoir, a foster nurse could serve as a diplomat, and a swordsman could be a storyteller, however strict the codes of conduct to be followed in the carrying out of each of these responsibilities. Second, given the personal character of kingly power, people who were not of the Timurid-Mughal lineage were often extremely important in Babur's circle. The activities of these people provide an incisive comment on the character of early Mughal courtly life, and some attention to their place is called for.

Several different kinds of men appear among Babur's closest associates. One is ʿAbdul Karim Ashrit, whom Babur describes as "a brave and generous man."[18] He served Sultan Ahmad Mirza, a paternal uncle of Babur.[19] ʿAbdul Vahhab *shiqavul* (chief scribe[20]) was in the service of ʿUmar Shaykh Mirza (Babur's father) as well as of Sultan Ahmad Mirza. Sayyidim ʿAli *darban* (the gatekeeper) was a retainer of Badiʿ-uz-zaman Mirza (son of Sultan Mirza Husain Bayqura), Babur's cousin. Babur says Sayyidim ʿAli "was of excellent nature and manners, a bold swordsman, a singularly competent and methodical man. His house was never without company and assembly; he was greatly generous, had wit and charm, a variety of talk and story, and was a sweet-natured, good-humoured, ingenious, fun-loving person."[21]

---

[18] Beveridge uses two spellings of the last name for ʿAbdul Karim: Ushrit, and Ishrit. She thinks that this is a clan-name; see Beveridge, *Baburnama*, p. 40, and Index, p. 718.

[19] Beveridge, *Baburnama*, p. 718.

[20] See also Beveridge's comments on the meaning of *shiqavul* ("*shaghaval* as chief scribe") at many places in the *Baburnama*; Beveridge, *Baburnama*, p. 25, n. 1. Her comment at another place is that "Shaw's vocabulary explains the word as meaning also a 'high official of Central Asian sovereigns, who is supreme over all *qazis* and *mullas*,'" p. 463, n. 2.

[21] *Ibid.*, p. 307.

There were many other men of the *khasa-tabin*, or the "elite royal contingent," to use Thackston's English translation of Babur's phrase.[22] The *khasa-tabin* were in Babur's immediate command, close in physical proximity to him during his numerous battles.[23] These soldiers or "guards" surrounded and protected the king. Beveridge's translation of the *khasa-tabin* as "corps of braves" and her reference to "household brave[s]"[24] who fought by Babur's side, suggests something of a "wild West frontier," where prospectors and entrepreneurs might demonstrate their masculinity in the pursuit of property and profit. Yet the bravery, courage, and sensibility of Babur's followers was not primarily concerned with individualism, that is, with a sense of individual selfhood, and desire for accumulation of wealth and individual profit. What one needs to set against particular individual desires and ambitions is a society that is governed by collective consciousness, where people live as part of a multiplicity of communities, several of which they may belong to at any one time. This is a society in which notions of honor and shame (individual and collective) are central. Hence, when individuals act, they act not only for themselves but also on behalf of values and concerns larger than themselves.

The following *khasa-tabin* are listed in Babur's memoir:[25] Baba Chuhra, Baba Jan *akhtaji* (an equerry or groom), Bujka, Karimberdi, Mir Khurd *bakavul* (an overseer of the kitchen, who was also made Hindal's guardian[26]), Sultan Muhammad Duldai (a Barlas Turk who was at the right wing of the army in the battle of Panipat), Muhammad Sultan *bakhshi* (secretaries or scribes; in this instance, the paymaster who took custody of the cook who poisoned Babur), Yakka Khvajeh, Yarim Beg, Yusuf ʿAli *bakavul* (an overseer of the kitchen) and Zard-rui. Besides, there was Darvish ʿAli *piyadeh* (footman, foot-soldier), later *tufang-andaz* (matchlock man) who took the news of Hindal's birth to Babur; Yusuf ʿAli *rikabdar* (a stirrup-holder, groom, attendant, cup-bearer) who conveyed a letter concerning Hindal's pre-natal adoption to Babur; and Yusuf ʿAli, Khvajeh Yusuf Andijani, and Yusuf ʿAli Kukaldash who were musicians. Babur especially commented on Kukuldash's dancing: "[he] danced in the drunken time, and being, as he was, a master in music, danced well."[27] Babur also mentions Nurullah, a drummer, who often played before him.[28] All the men mentioned here, whether a drummer, guardian of the kitchen, or cup-bearer, were fighters.

---

[22] Thackston, *Baburnama*, III, p. 904.

[23] For an example of the arrangements of the *khasa-tabin*, see the description of the battle of Panipat in 1526, Thackston, *Baburnama*, pp. 568–572. See also the example of Babur's victory over Qandahar in 1508, Beveridge, *Baburnama*, pp. 333–337.

[24] Beveridge, *Baburnama*, p. 474, n. 2; *Ibid.*, Index I, p. 736.

[25] For the entire list of Babur's associates cited above, see Beveridge, *Baburnama*, pp. 717–825. The meanings of the designations alongside the names have been derived from Steingass, *Persian*.

[26] Beveridge, *Baburnama*, p. 408.   [27] *Ibid.*, p. 303.

[28] *Tamburachi* has several meanings: lutenist, guitarist, drummer. Babur uses the term variably, here as a drummer. Beveridge, *Baburnama*, p. 247, n. 3.

Ahmad *Yasavul*, the messenger, and Qara Ahmad *Yurtchi* (a repairing tailor) figure as confidants who took messages across to Babur's allies during his raids on the Turkman *hazara* in 1507.[29] Babur writes about Qul-i Bayazid, the taster, and paymasters Muhammad *bakhshi* (mentioned above) and Taghayi Shah *bakhshi* who were put in charge of Shah Beg's treasury after Babur took the spoils of Qandahar (1507).[30]

At one point in the *Baburnama*, Babur regrets the loss of some men of his *khasa tabin*, who left him in despair at Andijan during his attempts to gain Samarqand (1497–98). The names that Babur includes are 'Ali Darvish Beg, 'Ali Mazid Qawchin, Muhammad Baqir Beg, Shaykh Abdullah (also "Lord of the Gate"), and Mirim Laghari. He adds: "of men choosing exile and hardship with me, there may have been, of good and bad, between 200 and 300."[31] Among these were: Qasim Qawchin Beg, Ways Laghari Beg, Ibrahim Saru Mingligh Beg, Shirim Taghayi, Sidi Qara Beg and, "of my household," Babur puts in, Mir Shah Qawchin, Sayyid Qasim Eshik-aqa Jalayir (also "Lord of the Gate"), Qasim Ajab, 'Ali Dust Taghayi's son, Muhammad Dust, Muhammad 'Ali Mubashshir (messenger of good tidings), Khudaberdi Tughchi Mughul, Yarak Taghayi, Baba 'Ali's son, Baba Quli, Pir Ways, Shaykh Ways, Yar 'Ali Balal (great-grandfather of 'Abdur Rahim *Khan-i Khanan*, the Persian translator of the *Baburnama* at the court of Akbar), Qasim Mirakhvur (chief equerry), and Haidar *Rikabadar* (stirrup-holder).[32]

The Mughal king records the qualities of each of these men. According to him, 'Abdul Karim Ashrit and 'Abdul Vahhab *shiqavul* stand out as exceptional men who served the Timurid-Mughal forefathers. Sayyidim 'Ali was brave, dignified, and sociable. Muhammad Sultan *bakhshi* was very reliable. Yusuf 'Ali *rikabdar* was trustworthy enough to carry a significant piece of news. Yusuf 'Ali Kukaldash was remembered for his extraordinary dancing talent. Likewise, Mir Khurd *bakavul*, an overseer of the kitchen and Hindal's guardian, and Darvish 'Ali *piyadeh*, the footman who brought the news of Hindal's birth, were especially remembered.

The term "servants" has sometimes been used as a generic one to describe many in this intimate circle. Yet, the term hardly serves, for complicated gradations of rank and the appended notions of honor were fundamental to the being and demeanor of these men. No doubt, some servants also formed a part of this intimate community.

Service is a complex notion, relating not only to the "domestic" side of life. Thus, the ewer-bearer Jawhar was both a servant and an "officer" whose function (or "office") was well defined. From the point of view of the

---

[29] Beveridge, *Baburnama*, p. 314, n. 3. Beveridge refers to Qara Ahmad's title as Yurunchi. She explains: "as yurun is a patch, the bearer of the sobriquet might be Black Ahmad the repairing-tailor."

[30] Beveridge, *Baburnama*, pp. 237, 338.

[31] Beveridge, *Baburnama*, p. 91; Thackston, *Baburnama*, p. 112.   [32] *Ibid.*

individual, as Elias reminds us, different roles and offices can be accumulated (for instance, ewer-bearer and "historian"), but from the point of view of configurations, we need to look at the designated roles independently from the vicissitudes of individual lives, that is typical associations that might be reproduced in successive generations, like those of the king or the ewer-bearer. These assigned roles are regulated by norms, even legal norms, so that they appear as normative in the texts.

Kingly associates of this kind, performing manifold tasks alongside their nominated responsibilities, were essential in the life of this peripatetic court society. These men fought at Babur's side, they tested his food and bore his cup, they groomed him and danced for him, they guarded his sons. They carried news of birth and adoption to royal males. (The information of births and deaths had to be carried quickly for these were matters of immense political importance.) When the occasion arose, they carried messages across to Babur's allies. They offered solace and support in times of exile and hardship. What is so striking here is the multifaceted character of the performance of these people: a *bakavul* is not just a *bakavul*, a *rikabdar* not only a *rikabdar*.

Drinking parties

Nothing refracts the homosocial ethos of the times as effectively as the *Baburnama*'s accounts of drinking rituals and parties. Equally, these gatherings are material manifestations (time/space/events) of court configurations. Drinking rituals were a common feature of pre-Islamic Iranian aristocratic society, of Perso-Islamic courts such as the Ghaznavids, as well as of ancient Near Eastern societies.[33] Scholars have remarked on drinking as a "social event" in these societies, a time of conviviality, and festivity, sometimes ending in decadent behavior.[34]

The numerous reports of drinking parties, the *majlis-i sharab*, in the *Baburnama* indicate that the conduct at parties was strictly regulated. Rules preceded chaos. Yet when chaotic moments came, it often meant bawdy, irrepressible conduct. Through all this, Babur projects his closeness with his associates, his delight in these moments, the conversations, the drinks and the poetry – above all a sense of camaraderie. Dale reminds us that the comradeship of these social gatherings was very important to Babur for it generated social cohesion, very crucial in a society where "kinship bonds were notoriously fragile."[35] These gatherings speak of Babur's community. In many ways, these *are* his communities.

Babur's first statement on drinking is recorded for 12 January 1519 when a party was organized at the house of Khvajeh Kilan, a long-time confidant

---

[33] See, for example, Lucio Milano (ed.), *Drinking in Ancient Societies: History and Culture of Drinks in the Ancient Near East* (Padua, 1994).
[34] Dale, *Eight Paradises*, p. 181.   [35] *Ibid.*, p. 182.

whom Babur refers to as a *musahib*, or companion.[36] This is a brief entry. Babur moves on to elaborate accounts of the revelries that appear to be central in everything he does. Given the constraints of space, it would be hard to reproduce many of these colorful descriptions of Babur's drinking gatherings. Let me take a few examples from one year, which was an unusual one for Babur.

In 1519, Babur had turned thirty-nine. At forty, he had vowed to give up drinking completely. "With only one year left to my fortieth year I was drinking to excess out of anxiety."[37] This may be one reason why entries on Babur's drinking bouts are so frequent in 1519. This is also the time he had just entered into Hindustan, the first of Babur's five expeditions, hence a demanding time in terms of strategic thinking about capturing a new domain. Dale suggests that the prominence Babur gives to drinking narratives in 1519 and early 1520, "reflects in part at least the powerful nostalgia he felt for his social life in Kabul as he struggled in the enervating Indian climate to subdue the panoply of Muslim and Hindu rulers he encountered in northern India."[38] What stands out also in these entries, as in those from other years, is the meticulous depiction of the social sensibility of the time; these fragments are clearly more than a simple record of conviviality.

Let us reflect on what these entries illuminate and what kind of worlds they help us configure. After the gathering on 12 January, Babur mentions another party at Khvajeh Kilan's house, on 5 February. Then on 4 March 1519, just before entering Hindustan, Babur gets the news from his matchlockman, Darvish 'Ali, that a son had been born to him. Babur took that news "as a good omen" and named his son Hindal ("taking of Hind").[39] The next morning, Babur reports, "we mounted for an excursion, got on a boat and drank spirits." There were fourteen other men with him. He says, "we drank until the late afternoon, and then, disgusted by the bad taste of the spirits, we at our end [they sat at two ends of the boat] agreed to switch to *ma'jun* [a mild narcotic concoction made into a chewable pellet]. Those at the other end of the boat did not know we were having *ma'jun* and kept on drinking spirits."[40] Babur goes on to explain that wine parties and *ma'jun* parties were never mixed, and when people found out what was happening, "they got very angry." However, "for a time the party continued in strained politeness." The party-makers invited Baba Jan, the *qopuz* (a lute-like musical instrument) player. Baba Jan also drank and "talked a lot of nonsense." "No matter how we tried to get the party under control, nothing worked," Babur adds, "It turned into an uproar."[41]

---

[36] Thackston, *Baburnama*, p. 534.   [37] *Ibid.*, p. 532.   [38] Dale, *Eight Paradises*, p. 311.
[39] Thackston, *Baburnama*, p. 481; cf. Beveridge, *Baburnama*, p. 385
[40] Thackston, *Baburnama*, pp. 481–482. For translation of *ma'jun*, see p. 902.
[41] *Ibid.*, pp. 482–483.

On 11 and 12 March, Babur writes again about a party on a boat. "We drank on the boat until late that night, left the boat roaring drunk and got on our horses." Babur declares, "I must have been really drunk." The next day, the party rode out on a boat again. They consumed *ma'jun* and *'araq* (fermented juice of rice or of date-palm). The musicians sang too. On the whole, this gathering seemed to have gone off well, except that one of the men, Minuchir Khan, became very drunk.[42] On 24 March, Babur records that *ma'jun* was eaten. He also speaks about its influence on him: "There were nothing but purple flowers blooming in some places, and nothing but yellow flowers blossoming in other places. In other spots there were yellow and purple flowers blossoming together like gold fleck. ... As far as the eye could see there were fields of flowers."[43]

The accounts of festive consumption of drink and *ma'jun* sit by the side of Babur's descriptions of campaign-planning in Hindustan. Babur and his men crossed rivers, wandered into unknown fields, found out about new mountains, flora, and fauna. He comments upon the tribes he saw on the way, their practices, and their pronunciations. He even gives a history of Bhera, on the border of Hindustan. Babur was a keen spectator and his skills of observation carry over to a whole variety of matters.[44] Babur's recounting of the drinking parties is especially striking: who came to the parties and how they behaved, how much they drank, who was drunk, who composed quatrains, how much Babur himself drank – as if nothing is missed in the *padshah*'s narration.

I have cited but a few examples of the parties recorded in the year 1519. It is hardly an exaggeration to say that at this time Babur celebrates each step of his movement with his men. He drinks with them on boats, at the confluence of rivers, in the houses of people, on the roofs of pigeon-houses, whenever they arrive in new towns – in the morning, at mid-day, during the afternoons, and at night. What is significant for my purposes is the sense this account gives of Babur's close engagement with his men.

The continual togetherness of these men on the move does not seem to leave a great deal of time or space for the company of women. Babur was constantly on the move, spending much more of his time in the company of his men than he ever suggests doing with the women. "Retiring to women's quarters" is hardly a common motif here. No wonder the appearance of Qataq Begum in Babur's diary seems out of the ordinary, as does Hulhul Anika who comes to drink in Babur's party on 14 November 1519. Babur was about thirty-three miles north-northwest of Kabul at this time.[45] He asked Turdi Beg, who was in his service, to "make ready wine and implements [*sharab va asbab tyar bikun*]." Turdi Beg went off towards Bihzadi (in the

[42] *Ibid.*, pp. 484–485. For the meaning of *'araq*, see Beveridge, *Baburnama*, p. 385, n. 1.

[43] Thackston, *Baburnama*, pp. 492–493; see also Beveridge, *Baburnama*, p. 393 and n. 1.

[44] Dale has noted the quality of an unusually explicit, though complex, narration in Babur's memoir; see *Eight Paradises*, ch. V

[45] Dale, *Eight Paradises*, p. 299.

direction of Kabul). He returned with wine and Babur records, "we started drinking, just the two of us."[46] Gradually two other men, Muhammad Qasim Barlas and Shahzada, joined them. At this point, Turdi Beg also said to Babur that a woman named Hulhul Anika wanted to drink with him.

Babur, it appears, told Turdi Beg, "I've never seen a woman drink ... Invite her to the party." They also invited a dervish named Shahi and a couple of other men who played the rebeck. They all drank until nightfall and then went to Turdi Beg's house and continued to drink by candlelight. "It was a really relaxed party," Babur says. In a while everyone, except Babur, went off to "another" (unnamed) house to drink. Hulhul Anika "came" (whether from the house where others were, remains unclear in the text) and behaved in what Babur describes as an excessively loose and importunate way.[47] In the end Babur escaped by pretending he was drunk.

The particularity of court life that Babur speaks into being is best registered in the homosocial collective imagining portrayed by him. As I have said before, the *Baburnama* is filled with rich descriptions of men – political rivals, military experts, litterateurs, servants, and confidants. In Babur's envisioning, the figuration of the communities of men, and their intersecting zones of activities, are significant. These communities are the pathways that he traverses. He longs for them when they are missing, and feels ecstatic in remembering them. Indeed, the image of these communities stayed with Babur throughout his life. Much later in Kabul and Hindustan he revealed his homesickness, and spoke of the fruits and gardens of Central Asia with great longing. Towards the end of his life Babur became, as Dale puts it, "a refugee, a stranger in a strange land. He desired to return once more to the mountain gardens near Kabul or to the Ferghana valley of his youth."[48] He expressly criticized Hindustan's lack of gardens, and especially melons. But melons and gardens were, I suggest, only a metaphor for the communities he lived with, for community life, and for his particular court society.

Women and the genealogy of the king

Where are the women in these memories? How is domestic life conceived of in these communities? To probe this subject, let us turn to Babur's construction of his illustrious genealogical connection. The one thing that seems to have remained stable for Babur in the midst of his constant mobility is reference to his distinguished lineage. One way of strengthening and legitimizing a ruler's

---

[46] Thackston, *Baburnama*, pp. 526–527.

[47] Thackston, *Baburnama*, p. 527. Neither Thackston's translation of *bisyar shilainha* as "talked a blue streak," nor Beveridge's translation as "made me [Babur] much disturbance" (Beveridge, *Baburnama*, p. 417) captures the quality of this description. Dale translates this last sentence from Turki as follows: "Hulhul Anika came and made offensive requests"; *Eight Paradises*, p. 312.

[48] Dale, "Steppe Humanism," p. 48.

position is through the construction of a distinguished genealogy. It is such an enterprise that may be seen at work in Babur's construction of a lineage tying him to the great Timur.[49] Yet there is more to be said about the way in which Babur constructs his heritage. Of two possible great ancestors, Chingiz Khan and Timur, he chooses to emphasize one, Timur. This is an integral step in the legitimation of his own kingship, something that marks him as distinct from other nobles or pretenders around him. He repeatedly invokes the set of rules given by his ancestors, which the king, his relatives and kinsfolk, and other associates, all must abide by – in times of war, in celebration and festivity, in marriages, in births and deaths.[50] While invoking the Chingizid-Timurid tradition, Babur draws more heavily from the Timurid side than from the Chingizid.[51] The *Baburnama* itself enhances the genealogical connection with the Timurid line. Babur provides a detailed account of all the *mirza*s – the descendants of Amir Timur – while he mentions the Chaghtayid *khan*s briefly. And there is a special tenderness and sense of glory in his "evocative portrayals"[52] of the Timurid side of his family tree (*nasl-i Timur*).

Incessant conflict between the Timurid-Mughals and Uzbiks may have been one reason for the stronger Timurid identity that Babur professed, perhaps responding to the Uzbiks' strong Chingizid and mildly Timurid assertion. As Babur put it in the context of the events of 1498–99, when Andijan was recovered:

My mother had fifteen hundred to two thousand of the Mughul nation [*sic*] with her. An equal number of the Mughuls had come from Hissar with Hamza Sultan, Mahdi Sultan and Muhammad Dughlat. (Havoc and destruction have always emanated from the Mughul nation. Up to the present date they have rebelled against me [Babur] five

---

[49] The importance of an exalted genealogy may be seen in the history of Timur himself, for whom "a legitimation through association" was crucially needed in his search for support among the nomads over whom he ruled; Beatrice Forbes Manz, *The Rise and Rule of Tamerlane* (Cambridge, 1989), pp. 14–18; John E. Woods, "Timur's Genealogy," in Michael Mazzouni and Vera Moreen (eds.), *Intellectual Studies on Islam* (Salt Lake City, 1990); and Soucek, "Timurid Women." Likewise, Chingiz Khan rose to prominence through matrimonial alliances with important dynasties; Mansura Haider, "The Mongol Traditions and Their Survival in Central Asia (XIV–XV Centuries)," *Central Asiatic Journal*, 28, 1–2 (1984), p. 64, n. 26.

[50] Each successor after Timur seems to have worked out the connection differently for himself. For details, see Lentz and Lowry, *Timur and the Princely Vision*. Manuscripts were produced in almost all "Timurid lands" illustrating the importance of maintaining genealogical links. See, for example, the illustrated *Zafarnameh*, MS Add. 7635 (Shiraz/Safavid period, 1523), at the Oriental and India Office collections, British Library, and the MS Or.1359, British Library *Zafarnameh* (Shiraz/Safavid period, 1552). A large number of such depictions were also undertaken during the reign of Akbar. The epitome of this spectacular miniature grandeur under Akbar is the *Tarikh-i-Khandan-i Timuriyyan*, now at the Khuda Bakhsh Oriental Public Library, Patna, India. These manuscripts continued to be produced in India as late as the nineteenth century.

[51] Maria Eva Subtelny also makes this observation for Timurids at large, saying their connection with Chingiz Khan was "somewhat more tenuous" than with Timur (Maria Eva Subtelny, "Art and Politics in Early 16th Century Central Asia," *Central Asiatic Journal*, 27, 1–2 (1983), pp. 131–132). This issue requires more research than the subject of my book allows.

[52] Dale, "Poetry," p. 637.

times – not from any particular impropriety on my part, for they have often done the same with their own khans.) Sultan-Quli Chanaq, whose late father, Khudaberdi Buqaq, I had favored among the Mughuls, was with the Mughuls and did well to bring me the news. (However, later he did such a heinous thing, as will be related, that it could not be made up for by a hundred such good deeds, and that deed was the direct result of his being a Mughul.)[53]

The Chingizids here are referred to as "Mughuls" to differentiate them from the Timurids, the patrilineal identity of Babur. The following is another example of Babur's anti-Mughul (and anti-Uzbik) sentiment. When Sultan Husain Mirza resolved to repel Shaybani Khan, he summoned all his sons, and also invited Babur. "There were several reasons why we felt it necessary to go to Khurasan," explains Babur. "One was that when a great padishah like Sultan Husayn Mirza, who sat on Timur Beg's throne, sent out a summons to all parts to his sons and begs and was mounting a campaign against a foe like Shaybani Khan, if others were going on foot, we would go on our heads, and if others were going armed with clubs, we would go armed with rocks."[54]

Such statements are found scattered through Babur's diary. When Babur provides details of Mughul ways, whether in his description of the Mughul Yak-Tail Ceremony or in meeting Kichik Khan,[55] his Chingizid uncle, when the latter came to Tashkant, there is a perceptible aloofness in his narration. At these points the narrative voice is devoid of the emotion with which Babur discusses matters connected with his Timurid descent. The implications of Babur's emphasis on this Timurid heritage, and its meaning for the character of Mughal rule in India, require greater study.

Babur constructs the place of women in his genealogy in a very precise manner. There are two interrelated yet distinct ways in which the women are invoked: there are "women who remember" and "women who are remembered."[56] The women who were remembered in the *Baburnama* were ancestors of exceptional quality. Babur's exemplary women all belonged to important lines of descent, or were married to a member of a distinguished

---

[53] Thackston, *Baburnama*, pp. 131–132; Beveridge's first line of this extract is translated as: "In my mother's service were 1500 to 2000 Mughuls from the horde," a more sensitive rendering than Thackston; Beveridge, *Baburnama*, p. 105. Note there is no Persian word for "nation" in the manuscript. As far as the Uzbik acknowledgment of a Chingizid declaration is concerned, it is more complicated than it appears to be, as Subtelny herself shows through the entire length of her article. The inadequacy of the Uzbiks' Chingizid assertion, and their gradual absorption of the Timurid cultural tradition, is not within the purview of this chapter; for details, see Subtelny, "Art and Politics."

[54] Thackston, *Baburnama*, pp. 336–337; Beveridge, *Baburnama*, p. 255.

[55] Thackston, *Baburnama*, pp. 201–202, 206–209, and 220–221; Beveridge, *Baburnama*, pp. 154–156 and 157–161. Illustrations of the Yak-Tail ceremony are available in British Library, MS. Or. 3714, fol. 128b. The main part of the ceremony was the standard styled like those of Turkish sovereigns: a white banner with nine pendants or yaks' tails that hung from the head (Mansura Haider, *The Mongol Traditions*, p. 68). For a detailed discussion of the Yak-Tail ceremony, see also Dale, *Eight Paradises*, pp. 171, 221, 295.

[56] Patrick J. Geary, *Phantoms of Remembrance: Memory and Oblivion at the End of the First Millennium* (Princeton, 1994), p. 52.

family. One citation from the *Baburnama* serves to show the qualities of these commendable women that Babur wished to keep alive: "Few amongst women will have been my grandmother's equals for judgement and counsel," Babur writes.[57] Or as an alternative rendering has it: "For tactics and strategy there were few women like my grandmother Esan Dawlat Begim. She was very intelligent and a good planner. Most affairs were done by her counsel."[58]

Yet what Babur recalled no less insistently were women who fulfilled a reproductive role. To continue with Babur's discussion of his maternal grandmother Isan Dawlat Begum, it is not her "judgement and counsel" or wisdom alone that gains her a place in the *padshah*'s memoir. The entry on her emphasizes the fact of her marriage to Yunis Khan, Babur's maternal grandfather, and her three daughters by him: Mihr Nigar Khanum, Qutluq Nigar Khanum, and Khub Nigar Khanum. Her role was central in keeping alive the line of the Khans. By the time Babur wrote his memoir, the place of Isan Dawlat's children had been rendered even more important, since Babur was the son of her second daughter, Qutluq Nigar Khanum.

Isan Dawlat Begum and other women are hardly ever mentioned by contemporary chroniclers in any of the major discussions of genealogical descent, no doubt because political power was transmitted through the male line. However, their memories survive as daughters of dynasts, married into memorable families, carrying forward famous names through their sons. The description of the daughters of Isan Dawlat Begum in Babur's account is instructive:

The eldest was Mihr Nigar Khanim, who *was married* to Sultan Abu-Sa'id Mirza's eldest son, Sultan Ahmad Mirza. She *had no sons or daughters* by the mirza. ... The second daughter *was my mother*, Qutlugh Nigar Khanim. ... The third daughter was Khub Nigar Khanim. *She was given in marriage to* Muhammad Husayn Kuragan Dughlat, *by whom she had a daughter and a son*.[59]

Another wife of Yunis Khan mentioned is Shah Begum. Babur says, "although he [Yunis Khan] had other wives, the mothers of the sons and daughters were these two" – Isan Dawlat Begum and Shah Begum. Babur emphasizes Shah Begum's lineage, going back to Alexander of Macedon, and the fact that she had two sons and two daughters with the Khan.[60] The details of Shah Begum's daughters likewise center around whom they were married to and how many children they bore. Her sons, keeping in line with the typical male characterization in the *Baburnama*, were remembered, above all, for their military prowess.

---

[57] Beveridge, *Baburnama*, p. 43.   [58] Thackston, *Baburnama*, p. 49.
[59] Thackston, *Baburnama*, pp. 20–21 (my emphases). The *Baburnama* is full of such details. See especially the description of the women, wives, and concubines of both sides of Babur's family (cf. Beveridge, *Baburnama*, pp. 1–42, Section 1, "Farghana").
[60] Thackston, *Baburnama*, p. 22; Beveridge, *Baburnama*, p. 22.

The first part of the *Baburnama*, which lists the "illustrious" wives, mistresses, and concubines of Babur's male relatives, is illuminating. The wives were exalted for their keeping alive of the prestigious Chingizid-Timurid line. Theirs was a vital social function. The birth of noble children (like Babur), although a routine act, (still) produced extraordinary effect: the perpetuation of the eminent Timurid family.

Concubines and mistresses too were praised for their reproductive capacity. Referring to the many concubines and mistresses of Sultan Mahmud Mirza, his paternal uncle, Babur notes: "The chief concubine was Zuhra Begi Agha, an Uzbek. ... She had one son and one daughter. He had many mistresses. By two of them he had the two daughters ... [Rajab Sultan and Muhibb Sultan]."[61] Babur's comment on the consorts and children of Sultan Husain Mirza of Herat is even more noteworthy in this regard: "there were many other concubines and mistresses of no consequence. The important wives and concubines are those who have been mentioned."[62] The valuable concubines and mistresses produced children; the rest were of "no consequence."

Women could be "sent out"[63] if they failed to live up to this reproductive norm. This was seen in the example of Ulus Agha, a wife of Babur's father, ʿUmar Shaykh Mirza. Ulus Agha had a daughter who died in infancy. Babur reports that approximately a year and a half later (presumably after the death of the daughter) Ulus Agha was "sent out of the harem."[64]

Scholars have written about the prominence of imperial women, their exercise of power, and talked about their "considerable personal freedom," particularly in the context of nomadic Mongol and Turkic groups of eastern and Central Asia.[65] Mughal women – the successors of Timurid-Mongols – were significant partners too in the making of Babur's and Humayun's courts. As we shall see in the next chapter, the senior women were promoters of "tradition," maintainers of lineage, and organizers of successors. By dint of their seniority, they controlled marriages and assigned marital duties, shepherding younger women in the production and training of children. In the maintenance of "hallowed" traditions, however, the royal women's own presence tended to be erased. Such women's lives were not for themselves, but for creating other lives: they were required to keep intact the illustrious past, and secure the future of the generations to come by working upon the present ones. "The feminine is produced and erased at the same time."[66]

[61] Thackston, *Baburnama*, p. 56; Beveridge, *Baburnama*, p. 49.
[62] Thackston, *Baburnama*, p. 352.   [63] *Ibid.*, p. 24.
[64] Thackston, *Baburnama*, p. 24; Beveridge, *Baburnama*, p. 24.
[65] Soucek, "Timurid Women," p. 200.
[66] Judith Butler, "Against Proper Objects," *Differences*, 6, 2–3 (1994), p. 18.

Humayun's court and society: the peripatetic life continued

I wish now to move on to a discussion of how the genealogical connection, the place of women, and the homosocial world of the court appears in the chronicles dealing with the time of Humayun. As we have noted earlier, the archive for Humayun's reign consists of the chronicle of his contemporary courtier Khvandamir, as well as the memoirs of Bayazid Bayat, Gulbadan Begum, Jawhar, and Abu-l Fazl, recorded in Akbar's time, in which royal life is depicted as being more ritualized and elaborated. Although memoirists Bayazid Bayat, Gulbadan, and Jawhar wrote in Akbar's time, they were contemporaries and witnesses of the courtly and domestic life of Humayun. Of course, we have nothing like the diary of Babur available to us for this time, indeed nothing in writing by Humayun himself. The historian must examine the different kinds of texts available here to see what kind of ethos they seek to depict, or end up depicting, in relation to Humayun's society, court, and domestic life.

It is through these texts that we have access to Humayun's world. This world continues to be peripatetic. Without doubt, it is homosocial. But social interaction now appears to be regulated by more firmly enforced courtly norms. The very decorous and reverential character of the texts, chiefly Akbari, already provides evidence of this more regulated society.

Humayun's life was not altogether different from Babur's. It was more settled for longer periods of time. Babur took his people, their wives and children with him when he set out for Samarqand. Children were born and feasts held, Babur's title was changed from *mirza* to *padshah*, and the *padshah* married again in this very turbulent period when the extent, and even the existence, of his kingdom was in doubt. Likewise, during his wanderings in search of help to repel the challenge of Sher Shah and of his stepbrothers, Humayun married Hamideh Banu Begum at Pat, while on his way to Bikaner; in Amarkot, nine months later, she delivered a son (the future emperor Akbar); and in Sabzvar, she delivered a daughter.

Gulbadan provides several extracts that point to Humayun's life on the move, often deprived, difficult, and challenging – not very different from Babur's. It should be borne in mind that Gulbadan was with Kamran from 1540 to 1545, hence was not a direct witness of Humayun's wanderings. She acknowledges Khvajeh Kasak (from Turki *kisik*, meaning a guard) for the help she derived from his writings in relation to the early part of Humayun's reign.[67] In addition, more than once she says, "Hamideh Banu says ...," another note of acknowledgment to the immediate witness of the events she was recording.

---

[67] Beveridge, *Humayun*, p. 162; Gulbadan, *Ahval*, fol. 52b.

Yet, the Begum's account is instructive for its projection of the king's itinerant life and its harsh circumstances. Humayun, along with several associates, and the then pregnant Hamideh Banu Begum, was on his way to Amarkot. It was extremely hot, according to our memoirist, and "on they went, thirsty and hungry." For three days the horses had not drunk any water. Meanwhile they were being threatened by the troops of Maldeo of Jodhpur. They went on through the night. At dawn some water was found. Just then a man came in shouting. Gulbadan puts these words into the mouth of the informant: "The Hindus are coming up in numbers, mounted on horses and camels." Humayun sent Shaykh 'Ali Beg Jalayir, Rawshan Kukeh, Nadim Kukeh (all to become important officials under Akbar) and several others to fight. He rode on with the camp and a few followers.[68]

Eventually Humayun's men won a victory and water was found, but only after marching on for another three days. This is the picture that Gulbadan draws of the moment when men and women at last quenched their thirst: "As each bucket came out of the wells [sic] into reach, people flung themselves on it; the ropes broke and five or six persons fell into the wells with the buckets. Many perished from thirst. When the Emperor saw men flinging themselves into the wells from thirst, he let anyone drink from his own water-bottle."[69]

If Babur's court on the move was a band of notables, chiefly clansmen, with a distinguished leader (Babur himself), Humayun's situation was slightly different. There is a sense of grounded-ness now, a regularity in life so to speak, displayed especially in the beginnings of the construction of imperial dwellings,[70] in greater formality, and in the prescription and writing down of elaborate rituals of comportment. There is also a sense of greater distance between the *padshah* and other individuals, and a more accentuated projection of asymmetrical relations in which Humayun is the center of power and privilege – no longer the numerous one-to-one exchanges of the *Baburnama*. We are given no glimpse of Humayun drinking with his men, or of any direct deliberations of strategy with them. Now, as the records have it, Humayun confers with other monarchs. His men await his decisions, and abide by them.

Nonetheless, it is important to note that a peripatetic element remains in Humayun's monarchy. The shift from peripatetic to settled structures was partial for the early Mughal kings, although the life of the emperors in the splendid courts and palaces of Agra and Fatehpur-Sikri was obviously unlike the perpetually wandering lifestyle of their predecessors. Even for the period

---

[68] Beveridge, *Humayun*, pp. 154–155; Gulbadan, *Ahval*, fol. 46a–46b.

[69] Beveridge, *Humayun*, pp. 156–157; Gulbadan, *Ahval*, fol. 47b.

[70] It should be added that with the exception of the discussion of the building of Dinpanah in Delhi in Khvandamir's *Qanun-i Humayuni*, and a brief mention of the beginnings of the construction of buildings in Agra and Gwalior by Gulbadan, there is no reference to the buildings constructed by Humayun. Jawhar, Bayazid, Abu'l Fazl, Nizam al-Din Ahmad, and Badaoni are all silent on this matter. For a brief discussion of this issue, see also B. Prasad, "A Note on the Buildings of Humayun," *Journal of the Royal Asiatic Society of Bengal: Letters*, 5 (1939).

of Akbar and his successors, 1556–1739, Stephen Blake suggests, "an emperor would leave the capital and begin a tour for one or more of the following reasons: to hunt, to put down a rebellion, to check the administration of a province, to conquer new areas, to reconquer old ones, to visit a shrine, to attend a festival or to escape the midsummer heat of northern India."[71] The Mughal emperors, therefore, continued to spend a good part of their time in tents. Indeed, Aurangzeb (1658–1707), "the most peripatetic of the seven emperors" according to Blake, emphasized the significance of repeated movement.[72]

Humayun remained a political exile for much of his life. But he was, even in exile, recognized as a king. His wanderings in Persia, Sind, and Afghanistan between 1540 and 1550 after his tussles with Sher Shah in Hindustan, and the frequent claims, counter-claims, and conflicts with his stepbrothers, Kamran and Hindal, and other Timurid-Chaghtayid distant cousins, demonstrate this amply. It took Humayun some time to wipe out the opposition of his step-brothers, and of Sher Shah, and to emerge as the dominant ruler of northern India, but he was never treated as anything but a king.

Some details of Humayun's activities during his exile, and the responses of other rulers towards the dispossessed *padshah*, underline the circumstances of deprivation that he faced, but they also show the authority of the person of a king. During these wanderings, Humayun possessed no fixed, physically palpable court. Yet the court seems to have existed in Humayun's presence. When Humayun first went to Garmsir, its governor, Mir 'Abdul Hai, is said not to have paid much attention to him.[73] According to the *Akbarnama*, however, Mir 'Abdul Hai informed Humayun that it was rumored that Mirza 'Askari had dispatched a large force towards Garmsir. Hence it was in Humayun's best interests to move to Sistan, which belonged to the king of Persia, and where he would be protected.

According to Jawhar and Bayazid, Humayun proceeded to Sistan where Ahmad Sultan Shamlu, the governor, gave him a "kind reception."[74] In the *Akbarnama*'s flowery rendering, Ahmad Sultan Shamlu recognized Humayun's arrival "as an unexpected blessing and tendered acceptable ser-vice and showed alacrity in offering hospitality." Humayun spent some time "in that pleasant country, the arena of the cavaliers of fortune's plain [refer-ring to Sistan as Rustam's country, the Persian epic hero], in the sport of catching waterfowl [*shikar-i qashqaldagh*] ...."[75] Among other gestures of hospitality, Jawhar, Bayazid Bayat, and Abu-l Fazl note, Ahmad Sultan

[71] Blake, "Patrimonial-Bureaucratic," p. 300.   [72] *Ibid.*, p. 301.
[73] Sukumar Ray, *Humayun in Persia* (Kolkata, 2002), p. 5. At several places in this section, I have considered the detailed and scholarly work of Sukumar Ray about Humayun's wanderings between 1540 and 1550. Ray's reconstruction of this period of Humayuni history, based upon comparison of several editions of each of the sources discussed above in the text, is very useful.
[74] Ray, *Humayun in Persia*, p. 7.   [75] *Akbarnama*, I, p. 415, nn. 2, 3.

Shamlu sent his mother and his wives to "wait on" Hamideh Banu Begum, and "tendered all the revenues (*amwal*) of his district as a present."[76]

We are told that Ahmad Sultan Shamlu also sent a messenger to Sultan Muhammad Mirza, the son of Shah Tahmasb of Persia, and Muhammad Khan Sharaf al-Din Ughli Taklu, governor of Herat, informing them of Humayun's arrival.[77] Grandees and people of Herat, Khurasan, and of other towns welcomed Humayun. The inhabitants of towns like Jam, Turbat, Sarakhs, and Isfarain came to Herat for what Abu-l Fazl calls the "sublime advent."[78] The *Afzal-ut-tavarikh*, by an anonymous writer, records that the governor of Mashdad gave entertainments in honor of Humayun, where one thousand cups gilded in Khurasan, full of soup, were served at dinner.[79] According to the *Akbarnama*, stately feasts were given at all the places where Humayun stopped. He spent a New Year festival at Herat. Plans were made for him to visit several gardens, shrines of the great saints, and places of recreation and amusements, such as the *shikar-i qamargha* (hunting-drive), were organized for him.[80]

Jawhar discusses three steps of how Humayun was received at the Safavid court of Shah Tahmasb. In the first stage, the Shah attempted to convert Humayun to the Shi'a faith. At the second, there was complete cessation of any communication between the two kings. In the third, the Shah changed his mind and made preparations to aid Humayun in the recovery of his dominion.[81] Sharaf Khan, the author of the *History of Kurdistan*, confirms Jawhar's statements, while the Shah "boasts" in his own writings of the "excellent treatment" he accorded to Humayun.[82]

Abu-l Fazl records that Shah Tahmasb wrote letters to the governors of every city or halting place that Humayun and his cortege passed by, "the leading men and the inhabitants, high and low, should keep the occasion as the *fête* ... and should go out to welcome his Majesty and should engage in royal feastings."[83] A *farman* of Shah Tahmasb to the governor of Khurasan, introduced Humayun as follows:

greatest and best of the khaqans, the lord of majesty high-born sovereign of supremacy's throne, exalted king of kingdom of the dispensation of justice ... lord of diadem and throne (*taj u takht*), Sahib-qiran [same title as Timur, Lord of Conjunction] of the world of fortune and prestige, crowning diadem of famous khaqans, the aided by God, defender of the faith (Nasir-ud-din Muhammad) Humayun Padshah.[84]

As we can see, the most ornate version of the Humayuni progress comes from the *Akbarnama*. Abu-l Fazl devoted the first part of the *Akbarnama* to the events and happenings of the time of Babur and Humayun, in order to

[76] Ray, *Humayun in Persia*, p. 7; *Akbarnama*, I, p. 415.
[77] Ray, *Humayun in Persia*, p. 8.   [78] *Akbarnama*, I, p. 432, nn. 2–5.
[79] Ray, *Humayun in Persia*, pp. 19–20.   [80] *Akbarnama*, I, pp. 433–445.
[81] Ray, *Humayun in Persia*, p. 27.   [82] *Ibid.*, p. 25.   [83] *Akbarnama*, I, p. 417.
[84] *Ibid.*, p. 419.

emphasize the genealogical connection of Akbar – the splendid monarch around whom he was writing a voluminous imperial history. Gulbadan's memoir to some extent shares the language of Akbar's majestic court, and casts that on to the time of Humayun. The Begum's report of Humayun's time in the dominions of the Persian Shah is close in character to that of Abu-l Fazl's (or, more likely, Abu-l Fazl drew his sketch from the Begum's commentary): full of gaiety, celebration and what she calls, "sociable festivity [*ma'rakeh va majlis*]."[85] She discusses the receptions by nobles and grandees, high and low, to welcome Humayun. She speaks of "the friendship and concord of those high-placed pashas [Humayun and Shah Tahmasb]." She mentions the hunting expeditions, which Hamideh Banu Begum used to enjoy "from a distance either on camel or a horse litter." She speaks favorably of the valiant Shahzadeh Sultanam, Shah Tahmasb's sister, who "used to ride on horseback, and take her stand behind her brother." "In short," according to Gulbadan, "the Shah showed the Emperor much hospitality and courtesy, and laid a charge (on his sister) to show motherly and sisterly [*madaraneh va khvaharaneh*] hospitality and sympathy (to Hamideh Banu Begum)."[86]

The traditions of Humayun's court

The traditions and the sociopolitical structures of Humayun's time seem to be carefully organized, not to say rigid, according to the contemporary record. Consider marriages. It is notable that as compared to Timur's eighteen wives,[87] and Babur's sixteen, no more than four or five of Humayun's are mentioned in the contemporary writings. Even though the homosocial character of his world remains marked, Humayun's visits to women are more carefully recorded. Likewise, the extensive kinsfolk and structures of affinity that Babur evokes – his *khanivadeh* that included great-grandmothers and -grandfathers, grandmothers and grandfathers, mothers and fathers, uncles, aunts, and cousins of several generations and degrees, most of them of the illustrious Timurid ancestry[88] – seem to be altering in the texts of Humayun's time. Greater attention is now paid to what might be called a more condensed Mughal domestic unit. A focus on the close relationships by blood and by marriage did not negate the presence of distant cousins and relatives who came from the wider Timurid community. However, the significance of the latter's presence was considerably reduced in courtly and domestic activities.[89]

[85] Beveridge, *Humayun*, p. 171; Gulbadan, *Ahval*, fol. 59a.
[86] Beveridge, *Humayun*, pp. 168–170; Gulbadan, *Ahval*, fols. 57b–58b.
[87] Soucek, "Timurid Women," p. 202.
[88] *Khanivadeh* is a compound noun meaning *khandan* or "household." It also carries the following meanings: *dudman* or *dudeh* or "genealogy," *tabar* or "extraction." For these meanings, see Aliakbar Dehkhoda, *Loghatname, 1879–1955, Encyclopedic Dictionary*, vols. I–XIV, ed. Mohammad Mo'in and Ja'far Shahidi (Tehran, 1993–94), I, pp. 82–98.
[89] I discuss the structure of the domestic relations of Babur and Humayun in greater detail in the next chapter.

During the campaign of Balkh, Humayun visited the fountain of Band Kusha near Ishkamish. There he ordered some blacksmiths to prepare an iron pen, saying that when Babur had returned from Samarqand he had written the date and the number of his companions and that it was proper that Humayun too should make a similar gesture. Abu-l Fazl also records this event, adding that Babur had put up the inscription because his brothers Khan Mirza and Jahangir had just then made their submission.[90] Humayun was following the precedent: his brothers Kamran and 'Askari had reconciled with him and paid their homage at this point. Soon afterwards, Humayun went to Parian; here, he repaired the fort constructed by Timur,[91] another "symbol" of the old Timurid association.

While the chronicles of his reign document Humayun's obeisance to his ancestors, they also attend to other appropriate procedures and practices. Khvandamir's *Qanun-i Humayuni* shows the beginnings of the settlement of Humayun's court: its increased organization, of peoples, of relationships, of duties, of designation of roles. Alongside the orderliness comes a clearer sense of courtly hierarchies, now more clearly delineated and structured than before.

According to Khvandamir, the inhabitants of Humayun's domains and the officers of his state were divided into the *ahl-i Dawlat* (people [men] of the state or dominion), the *ahl-i Sa'adat* (literally propitious people), and the *ahl-i Murad* (people of pleasure or joy).[92] The first category included – apart from the officers – holy persons, religious men, the literati, the law officers, scientific persons, and poets. The second category included "honorable men," in whose association eternal prosperity could be secured, which might enable men to rise in dignity and rank.[93] The *ahl-i Murad* were so called because of their beauty and elegance; they were gentle and full of goodness, clever musicians, singers, and composers.[94]

Certain days of the week were assigned to these peoples. *Ahl-i Sa'adat* were allocated Saturdays and Thursdays as their days. Saturday was especially significant because it was ascribed to Saturn, "the instructor of mashaikhs, the learned men." Similarly, Thursday was related to Jupiter, the protector of religious men and persons of old respectable families, and of the followers of the *Shari'a*.[95] Sundays and Tuesdays were fixed for state officers; Sunday

---

[90] Beveridge, "Biyat," p. 303.
[91] *Ibid.*, pp. 302–303. Richard Foltz notes that both Jahangir and Aurangzeb sent money and manpower to Samarqand for the restoration of *Gur-i Amir* (the tomb of Timur); Richard C. Foltz, *Mughal India and Central Asia* (Karachi, 1998), p. xxviii.
[92] Hosain, *Qanun-i Humayuni*, pp. 34–35. The *Akbarnama* translates *Ahl-i Sa'adat* as "learned or literary men," *Akbarnama*, I, p. 610; and on p. 643, the translation of the three words is given as follows: *murad* (joy), *dawlat* (dominion), and *sa'adat* (auspiciousness). See also Gulbadan's discussion of the *ahl-i Dawlat*, the *ahl-i Sa'adat*, and the *ahl-i Murad* at the time of the feast organized by Khanzadeh Begum; Beveridge, *Humayun*, pp. 123–126; Gulbadan, *Ahval*, fols. 26b–28a.
[93] Hosain, *Qanun-i Humayuni*, p. 35.   [94] *Ibid.*   [95] *Ibid.*, p. 36.

belonged to the Sun on who rested the destiny of rulers and kings. Similarly Tuesday was the day of Mars, the God of war and the patron of warriors and brave men. Mondays and Wednesdays were allotted for pleasure parties. Monday, the day of the Moon, and Wednesday of Mercury, both days for men as beautiful as the Moon, were reserved for hearing sweet, delightful songs.[96]

Khvandamir also records other regulations and practices. Three arrows were made after the name of the three above-mentioned groups. These were given to the *padshah*'s closest confidants who were supposed to manage the affairs of that group, and their salaries were fixed accordingly. If they lost the trust of the *padshah* through laxity or arrogance, they were removed from office. Likewise, the affairs of the government were divided into four groups according to the four elements: fire, earth, water, and air. In dress and clothing, the approved colors were based on the traditions of the Prophet. Again, Humayun was weighed with gold on his birthday, and the gold was distributed to the people.[97] Distribution of money, a polysemic activity, underlined a passage to kingship (the election of the new king) in many cultures. Roman kings, for instance, had coins with their images distributed, an activity attributed to Persian influence.[98] In Humayun's reign, the annual distribution of gold acts as a reaffirmation of his kingship.

Humayun represents an interesting new stage in the organization, rule, conduct and being of Mughal royalty in India. The texts stress the fact that the practices of his reign derived from several authorities: the traditions of the Prophet on dress and clothing, and rituals of scattering of money that may have come from Persia.[99] They indicate also a continued sense of attachment to the Chingizid-Timurid tradition and very clear emphasis on accurate codes of behavior and the correct comportment in every action.

The emphasis on courtly manners

Court etiquette is emphasized in Humayuni chronicles in a way it was not in the more mobile, fluid court of Babur – and certainly not in the *Baburnama*. As noted before, Humayun's kingly status was never an issue; the issue was its

---

[96] *Ibid.*, pp. 36–37. I should stress that the description appears in the form of a doctrinal construct. It is not how people were chosen to be a part of the three groups that the author discusses. What happened on the days that were scheduled for each of these groups?

[97] Hosain, *Qanun-i Humayuni*, pp. 33–34, 48–49, 71–78, and 102–109. See also, *Akbarnama*, I, ch. LXI.

[98] Sergio Bertelli, *Il corpo del re: sacralità del potere nell'Europa medievale e moderna* (Florence, 1990), p. 102.

[99] Hosain, *Qanun-i Humayuni*, pp. 71–100. Humayun may have learnt about a Persian practice like the *Qabaq-andazi* in Iran. It involved the shooting of a pumpkin (according to Khvandamir), or a golden ball (according to the *Akbarnama*). The pumpkin or the ball contained money, which was then distributed to the shooters. See also *Akbarnama*, I, pp. 448, 613, 614 and n. 2.

preservation. Unlike Babur, Humayun did not have to declare himself *padshah*. He was given the throne of Hindustan and confirmed as king by his father. Although the same law of patrilineal descent applied to Babur as well, it is to be noted that he declared himself *padshah* only in 1506, after taking Kabul. His clansmen had until then designated themselves either as *mirzas* (from Timur's side) or as *khans* (from Chingiz Khan's side). This was a sign of Babur's imperial ambitions and his supremacy, but he had to wait for the opportune time to make this declaration. Another great Timurid ruler, Mirza Husain Bayqura of Herat, whom Babur admired enormously, had just passed away. Babur was left unchallenged at the head of the Timurids. His Uzbik foes had been removed to a less ominous distance. Other clansmen had been defeated.[100]

Other points of difference between Babur and Humayun may also be noted. Consider genealogy. Although matters of genealogy remained crucial to Humayun, the narratives of his time do not indicate the insistence on the Timurid identity that we notice in the *Baburnama*. Strict adherence to an elaborate code of conduct may have seemed a part of a search for a new identity, an element of which was certainly Timurid. Yet an emphatic Timurid identity mattered less to Humayun. During the conquest of Balkh, Humayun sought the advice of some Uzbiks who had been captured. When asked by one of them, Khvajeh Beg Ataligh, as to why Humayun was seeking counsel from them, he responded "I have heard that the Uzbegs are righteous people, and amongst them you [Khvajeh Beg] are the best. I am now testing you."[101] Kamran had also approached the Uzbiks during his conflicts with Humayun. He had, in fact, married into an Uzbik family.[102] The rivalry with the Uzbiks, which had worried Babur a great deal, had clearly lost its intensity by the time of Humayun.

For Humayun, the incorporation of Chingizid-Timurid ways was of another order – part of a shared conception of nobility and good bearing. *Adab* is continuously referred to in the histories of his time. Khvandamir uses the word *adab* in a variety of ways in his *Qanun-i-Humayuni*. In a concluding *masnavi* to the history of the "inventions" of the *padshah*, he puts the following words in the mouth of Humayun: "I have inherited and acquired the lineage, knowledge and *adab* (*nasab va fazl va adab*)."[103] This is an appropriate concluding statement for the history of a *padshah* who demonstrates a keen concern, almost a fixation, with matters of comportment.

In the various Humayuni reports, questions of *adab* surface repeatedly, reflecting a continuous concern with the ways in which actions were to be

---

[100] Beveridge, *Baburnama*, p. 344, n. 2. Gulbadan emphasizes that Babur took the title *padshah* after the birth of Humayun. If we are to accept the Begum's version then it means that Babur was now declaring not only his supremacy, but of the Timurid-Mughals and their generations to come. Beveridge, *Humayun*, p. 90; cf. Gulbadan, *Ahval*, fol. 7a.

[101] Saxena, "Mukhtasar," p. 54.   [102] Beveridge, "Biyat," p. 302.

[103] Hosain, *Qanun-i-Humayuni*, p. 117.

carried out on specific occasions. "No, never, for the vanities of this perishable world, will I imbrue [sic] my hands in the blood of a brother,"[104] says Humayun. This was a part of the training that Babur gave to his son, a rule that Humayun seems to have followed meticulously. Babur had advised Humayun: "Live well with your younger brother. Elders must bear the burden [buzurgan bardasht mi-bayad kardand]" – an instruction aimed to incorporate virtues of magnanimity in relation to seniority and age.[105] He instructed Kamran not to choose his vakil-i mutlaq outside the circle of nobles belonging to a particular Mughal tribe, emphasizing the hereditary claims to certain offices.[106]

The importance of behavior is demonstrated again in the accounts of marriages of Humayun. The negotiation of Humayun's marriage with Shahzadeh Khanum, the daughter of Mirza Sulayman of Badakhshan, is discussed in Bayazid Bayat's Tazkireh-i Humayun va Akbar.[107] After his return from Iran, Humayun was in a relatively advantageous position, having gained possession of Qandahar from his half-brother 'Askari, and Kabul from his eldest half-brother, Kamran Mirza. His control of southern and eastern Afghanistan was still uncertain because of continued challenges from Mirza Kamran. Nonetheless, having taken the necessary set of precautions, he went ahead with an attempt to take Badakhshan from its ruler Sulayman Mirza, a formidable rival: "like Humayun himself, his bloodlines combined both Caghatayid and Timurid ancestry, making him a potential rallying-point for the disaffected."[108] Unfortunately Humayun fell ill, and his plans went awry.

Beset by new difficulties, especially with Mirza Kamran who had reoccupied Kabul, Humayun thought it best to patch up matters with Sulayman Mirza through a marriage alliance. Jalal al-Din Mahmud headed a matrimonial embassy to Sulayman's court. A revenue officer of Mirza 'Askari, Jalal al-Din had moved into Humayun's service as the mir-i saman (steward of the household). There were eighty people including Bibi Fatimeh and Bayazid Bayat in the convoy that went to Sulayman Mirza.[109] Some complications arose in forging this alliance, one being the Badakhshani family's engagements with Mirza Hindal, Humayun's stepbrother, who had promised to give Kunduz to them. This issue was resolved when Sulayman Mirza swore to remain faithful to Humayun.[110] There was another point of dispute, however.

[104] Jouher-Stewart, Tezkereh, p. 25

[105] I have taken the Persian sentence above from Annette Beveridge's reference to it in her translation of the Baburnama, p. 626, n. 1. Thackston does not give the Persian text of this letter that Babur wrote to Humayun; only the Chaghatay text is available in his Baburnama, pp. 740–744. See also W. M. Thackston, The Baburnama: Memoirs of Babur, Prince and Emperor (New York, 1996), p. 413.

[106] Letter of Babur to Kamran dated April–May 1526, cited in I. A. Khan, "The Turko-Mongol Theory of Kingship," in Medieval India: A Miscellany, vol. II (London, 1972), p. 16 and n. 2.

[107] Hosain, Tadhkira, pp. 141–142.

[108] Gavin Hambly, "Armed Women Retainers," in Hambly (ed.), Women in the Medieval Islamic World, p. 444.

[109] Hosain, Tadhkira, p. 137; cf. Hambly, "Armed Women Retainers," pp. 445–446.

[110] Hambly, "Armed Women Retainers," pp. 446–447.

Haram or Khanum Begum, the wife of Mirza Sulayman,[111] objected to Humayun's manner of putting forward the marriage proposal, saying to Bibi Fatimeh: "[Humayun] has appointed you in Kabul to seduce the daughters of others. Do you consider my daughter to be of the same type? Why did not some of the Begums and Aghachis come? . . . When people like you come to ask the hand of my daughter, how may I have given her away in marriage?"[112]

Haram Begum had expressed annoyance because persons of inferior rank were sent to demand the hand of her daughter.[113] Gavin Hambly comments on the "unusual choice" of Jalal al-Din Mahmud for this important mission; he was a man of no great social standing.[114] Haram's other argument was that Mirza Sulayman and Mirza Ibrahim, and she herself, had rendered important services, especially at the battle of Ishturgram against Kamran, when they had personally acted as stewards and sent their troops. The point that Haram was underlining related to her important familial standing and political position. She was contemptuous of the "bazaar clothes" that were sent for her. While she was willing to accept these for herself, she believed that Humayun should have sent a *khil'at* (a robe of honor, belonging to the *padshah* or to one of his close female relations[115]) for her daughter. Moreover, if he wanted her hand in marriage, he ought to have sent "more prestigious negotiators"; she named Khvajeh Dust Khvand *madarchi* (one of Babur's companions-at-arms and senior *beg* of Humayun's) and Mir Sayyid Birkah Tirmizi (the illustrious Sayyids of Tirmiz).[116]

According to Bayazid, "to accomplish this sacred business" of asking for the hand of Shahzadeh Khanum, Humayun sent Bibi Fatimeh with Khvajeh Dust Muhammad. All the requisites for the marriage ceremony were sent through Bibi Fatimeh.[117] So Humayun followed the necessary rules, but this marriage presumably never took place for there is no mention of it in the contemporary literature. Interestingly, Haram's son Ibrahim was later married to Humayun's daughter, Bakhshi Banu.[118]

There are many other instances in the Humayuni histories that indicate very close attention to rules of privilege, hierarchy, and correct behavior. An

---

[111] Annette Beveridge explains that Haram Begum may be a sobriquet after the bearer's character and dominance. The meaning of the name is, according to Beveridge, the Princess of the Haram. The Persian texts support Haram, and the editors of the Bibliotheca Indica have also adopted this name. Her name has also been transliterated as Khurram, "blossoming, cheerful," a more probable name. For details, see Beveridge, *Humayun*, p. 242.

[112] Hosain, *Tadhkira*, p. 141; cf. Saksena, "Memoirs," pp. 132–135; Beveridge, "Biyat," p. 306; and Saxena, "Mukhtasar," p. 57.

[113] Hosain, *Tadhkira*, p. 141.   [114] Hambly, "Armed Women Retainers," p. 446.

[115] *Ibid.*, p. 448.   [116] Hosain, *Tadhkira*, p. 141; Hambly, "Armed Women Retainers," p. 448.

[117] Hosain, *Tadhkira*, p. 137; Saksena, "Memoirs," p. 132.

[118] Beveridge, "Biyat," p. 306. One might note that Haram Begum's negotiations were complicated by the stressful political relationship between the family of Mirza Sulayman of Badakhshan and the Timurid-Mughals; Saxena, "Mukhtasar," p. 48, and Beveridge, "Biyat," p. 309.

important example is the trial in 1547 of Mirza Yadgar Nasir (a son of Babur's half-brother), on account of his violation of imperial rules. Bayazid reports that Humayun's officers drew up a list of thirty charges against Mirza Yadgar Nasir. Among these one was the following:

> After the capture of the Champaner fort when we were in the treasury, we ordered that none, without permission, should enter the palace; but you came in without orders [*bi-hukm*], and sent your compliments through the Bakawal who was serving the royal dinner. We sent you a plateful of various precious articles, but you in your audacity took one Muzaffari out of it, and gave away the rest to the bakawal. This conduct according to the royal etiquette was insolent [*bi-tureh*].[119]

Food symbolism was a crucial aspect of imperial organization. As Peirce explains in the context of the Ottoman empire, "refusing to attend [a ceremonial gathering for feasting] or rejecting food was a sign of withdrawal of allegiance to the ruler."[120] Since Mirza Yadgar Nasir did not conform to the required *adab*, he was *bi-adab*; and a punishment became inevitable.[121] This disrespect of royal etiquette based upon imperial conventions of conduct (*tureh*)[122] cost the Mirza his life.

To further illustrate the matter of *adab*, I shall consider two episodes cited by Jawhar that deal with the necessary conduct of a servant and a king in their association with each other. Jawhar's responses to Humayun and others closely related to the emperor display a deep sense of attachment, an emotion that is "very much like the emotion of awe, which is a blend of fear and love, a sense of inadequacy mingled with a sense of profound longing."[123] This emerges clearly at several points in his memoir. During the battle of Kipchak in 1550, Humayun was seriously wounded. He rode on to Purwan where a small canopy (*shamiyaneh*) was procured for him to sleep under. Jawhar, who was with the emperor, woke him up at the hour of his morning prayer. Humayun said to Jawhar that he could not bear to purify himself with cold water. Jawhar arranged some warm water for him. Humayun then performed ablutions and mounted his horse to go; he had not ridden far when he complained that the clotted blood on his clothes hurt him. He asked the servants if they had any coat (*jameh*) to lend to him: Bahadur Khan, one of the *padshah*'s men accompanying him at the time, gave him a *jameh* that the emperor had earlier given him. Humayun took the *jameh*, gave his blood-stained clothes to his ewer-bearer, Jawhar, and instructed him to "take care" of the clothes and to wear them only on "holy days."[124]

[119] Hosain, *Tadhkira*, pp. 61–62; Saksena, "Memoirs," p. 92.
[120] Peirce, *Imperial Harem*, p. 175.
[121] For a fine discussion of the question of *adab*, see Mohammad Ajmal, "A Note on Adab in the Murshid-Murid Relationship," in Metcalf, *Moral Conduct and Authority*.
[122] Beveridge, "Biyat," p. 301. Beveridge translates *tureh* as "Imperial constitution."
[123] Ajmal, "A Note on Adab in the Murshid-Murid Relationship," p. 246.
[124] Jouher-Stewart, *Tezkereh*, p. 103.

Let me summarize another conversation as reported by Jawhar before thinking further about questions of comportment contained in these accounts. This conversation is said to have taken place between Jawhar and Mirza Kamran just before the latter was blinded. Jawhar describes the exchange vividly:

"What is your name?" ... He [Kamran] asked, "how long have you been in the king's service?" I [Jawhar] replied, "I have been nineteen years in his Majesty's employ"; he said, "you are an old servant" ... He then said, "I have fasted six days, during this Holy month of Ramzan; can you be my deputy for the remainder of the month?" I replied, "I can, but your highness will do it yourself; keep up your courage; do not allow melancholy anticipations [*sic*] to take possession of your heart"; he then said, "do you think they will kill me?" I replied, "princes only understand the motives or intentions of princes; ... and I know that his Majesty [Humayun] is a very compassionate personage." ... The night passed in this kind of melancholy discourse.[125]

In the previous example, the king gave Jawhar his blood-stained dress to be worn on "holy days" – the *jameh* becoming symbolic of honor, carrying as it did the blood of the monarch. To have the *padshah*'s own garment was a sign of honor, as we have seen earlier in Haram Begum's demand during the marriage negotiations for her daughter. Humayun's demand that it be worn on holy days attributes to it even greater significance, and makes the gesture towards Jawhar very special. In the second instance, Kamran initially conducted what might be seen as a ceremonial conversation with Jawhar. However, when he realized that Jawhar was an "old servant," the complexion of the conversation changed: thereafter, "the melancholic discourse." His demeanor, even – perhaps especially – when some intimacy developed between master and servant is striking (only "princes understand the motives or intentions of princes"). His deep pain at Kamran's state is poured out not in the Mirza's presence, but in the pages of his memoir. Recounting this moment while writing for Akbar's imperial history, he notes, "the author of these pages seeing the prince in such pain and distress, could no longer remain with him; I therefore went to my own tent, and sat down in a very melancholy mood ...."[126]

Through reports like these, one sees something of the multifaceted courtly world. The dynamics of this world come through in the language employed by the actors. Humayun and Kamran, as well as Jawhar, are distinct historical agents here who make choices colored by expectations and notions of self-regard, yet share a wide range of collective values. In his dialogue and actions, both with Humayun and Kamran, Jawhar displays sensitivity to the rules of proximity – to what was appropriate to his masters' (and his) status – and a full recognition of the importance of courtesy and self-esteem. The rituals and symbols of communication deployed in these two examples bring out a certain

[125] *Ibid.*, p. 113.   [126] *Ibid.*, p. 114.

hierarchy, but also the autonomy – and the limits – that may be seen in the reticent yet close relationship of the *padshah* and his brother with Jawhar.

Elsewhere, Jawhar describes how the duty of the *aftabchi*, the official bottle-carrier of the king, came to be assigned to him, and discusses the required bearing of the ewer-bearer. Following his wanderings in parts of Central Asia and Iran, Humayun was returning to Hindustan. From Kabul via Jalalabad, through Peshawar, the royal troops reached the western banks of the Indus. They then marched towards the river Chenab (1554–55). On arriving in its vicinity, Humayun directed some of his officers to proceed to Lahore and make preparations for his arrival there. At this time a water-carrier named Herbay expressed his wish to proceed to Lahore – that was his birthplace, his kinsfolk were there, and he wished to make inquiries about them. Jawhar was at that point given charge of the royal bottle.

When Herbay had gone some distance, he developed some doubts about whether he would ever get back the position of the royal ewer-bearer. He therefore returned and asked for the royal bottle. Jawhar, however, decided to ask Humayun: "is it your royal pleasure, that I shall continue in the *Abdar Khaneh* (water house), or in the *Ewry*?"[127] Humayun asked him to continue the job and ordered him as follows:

remember you are always to keep a china cup, a jug with a lid, and the water bottle in your possession; you are not to allow any other person to offer me water to drink without your seal being affixed; don't permit the water to remain empty during the night; when you give me to drink, pour water into the china cup, and on the march have the bottle on the horse with you.[128]

The rules of etiquette were well laid out. Whatever the reason, Jawhar seems to have been pressurized into handing over the bottle to Herbay soon afterwards. When Humayun saw the bottle in Herbay's hand, he alighted, gave Jawhar two blows on the side of his head, and said, "Whenever I again [*sic*] confer an employment on you, beware not to resign it to anybody."[129] Death by poisoning was an ever-present danger, and the duty of the water-carrier was an important one. Scholars have suggested that fluids (including water) also came to be associated with magical spells. So the control of the king's water was possibly meant to prevent witchcraft being enacted upon the king.[130] At any rate, the matter of who could be the *padshah*'s *aftabchi* (ewer-bearer) was of much consequence. Humayun's warning to Jawhar in this

---

[127] *Ibid.*, p. 120.   [128] *Ibid.*, pp. 119–120.   [129] *Ibid.*

[130] For a discussion of magical spells and fluids, see A. M. Hocart, *Kingship* (Oxford, 1969), especially the chapter "Ambrosia." The taboos on the manner of drinking are also discussed in a very early work by James George Frazer, *The Golden Bough: A Study in Magic and Religion* (London, 1933), see ch. XIX, "Tabooed Acts." See also Evon Z. Vogt, "Water Watching: An Interpretation of Ritual Pattern in a Rural American Community," in William A. Lessa and Evon Z. Vogt (eds.), *Reader in Comparative Religion* (3rd edn, New York, 1972). As a founding text for witchcraft and magic, see E. E. Evans-Pritchard, *Witchcraft, Oracle and Magic among the Azande* (Oxford, 1937).

connection is an example of the stringent regulations that governed the conduct of close associates.

Women's presence/absence in the Humayuni chronicles

Where are the women in all this, in the matter of correct comportment, and in the elaboration of hierarchies and appropriate behavior? To a large extent they are simply absent from the narratives. But the absence of the women's voice does not mean that women were voiceless. We need to ask whether women's absence stems from the nature of the record (produced mainly by men), or because women were simply without agency.

Consider the community that surrounds Humayun during his wanderings into Afghanistan and Iran in search of help in the years 1540–50. The estimates of men and women that accompanied him vary between 22 and 560 in different sources.[131] Jawhar, who traveled with Humayun, says that the royal party consisted of 40 men and 2 women; according to one scholar, this is perhaps the most reliable figure.[132] Of the 2 women mentioned in both Gulbadan's and Jawhar's accounts, one was Hamideh Banu Begum, Humayun's wife, and the other was "the wife of Hasan 'Ali, the chamberlain."[133]

The women who are named in the Humayuni records are chiefly senior women, acting as arbitrators, elders, and guides. However, Gulbadan fills out the picture in interesting ways. Let me elaborate this point by citing another episode relating to another marriage of Humayun.

In the midst of a protracted war between Humayun (the second Mughal *padshah*) and his stepbrother Kamran, there was a brief settlement when Humayun permitted Kamran to march to Kabul and he himself left for Bikaner (1541). At Pat, Humayun's stepmother Dildar Begum organized an entertainment at which, as Jawhar puts it, "all the ladies of the court were present." The author does not give the names of the women but notes that amongst those present was Hamideh Banu Begum, the daughter of the preceptor of another of Humayun's stepbrothers, Mirza Hindal. Gulbadan is more specific about the women present at this moment. She mentions "mirza [Hindal]'s *haram*," Hamideh Banu Begum who according to Gulbadan "was often in the mirza's [Hindal's] residence (*mahall*)," and her [Gulbadan's] mother Dildar Begum.[134]

According to both Jawhar and Gulbadan, Humayun made inquiries about Hamideh Banu Begum. Jawhar goes on to say that Humayun asked if Hamideh Banu had been "betrothed." He was informed that while she had

[131] Ray, *Humayun in Persia*, p. 3. According to Gulbadan's source, the number was thirty, and there were two women. Whether the two women were included in the lot of thirty is unclear; Beveridge, *Humayun*, p. 166; Gulbadan, *Ahval*, fol. 55b.

[132] Ray, *Humayun in Persia*, p. 3.   [133] Beveridge, *Humayun*, p. 166; Gulbadan, *Ahval*, fol. 55b.

[134] Beveridge, *Humayun*, p. 149; Gulbadan, *Ahval*, fol. 42a–42b.

been asked for in marriage, the ceremony had not yet taken place. In response, Humayun asserted: "I will marry her." On hearing this, Jawhar records, Hindal objected, saying "I thought you came here to do me honour, not to look out for a young bride . . . ." This displeased Humayun, and he left. Dildar Begum then patched up matters: "you [Hindal] are speaking very improperly to his Majesty, whom you ought to consider as the representative of your late father." The Begum gave "a nuptial banquet" the next day, "after which she delivered the young lady to his Majesty, and gave them her blessing." Humayun and Hamideh then proceeded to Bhakkar.[135]

Mirza Hindal's response to Humayun's expressed desire to marry Hamideh Banu, and Dildar Begum's firm chiding of Hindal, are both statements about the necessity and importance of correct behavior in the matter of seeking brides and making marriages, as also in interaction between a younger and older brother. Gulbadan provides us with other telling details. By her account, Humayun was told that Hamideh Banu was Mir Baba Dost's daughter, referred to as a *suchi*, water-bearer, by Babur.[136] Humayun is reported to have said to Dildar Begum: "Mir Baba Dost is related to us. It is fitting that you should give me his daughter in marriage." Hindal in his turn is supposed to have objected to Humayun's demands on the grounds that he saw Hamideh Banu as a "sister and child of my own. Heaven forbid there should not be proper alimony [*ma'ash*], and that so a cause of annoyance should arise."[137]

Ma'ash, translated as "alimony" by Beveridge, is an interesting word here. The word means livelihood, subsistence, living, means of living, a place where one lives, victuals, viands, wages, income, sufficient for subsistence, or landed property.[138] To be able fully to grasp the implications of the use of the word *ma'ash*, we need to bear in mind the context of the long-drawn-out wanderings of Humayun that brought about the question of the proper maintenance of Hamideh Banu Begum if they married. At this moment of the king's life, Hindal's objection as portrayed by Gulbadan seems apt.

Other differences of detail between Jawhar and Gulbadan Begum's memoirs may also be noted. Jawhar does not mention an exchange between Hamideh and Dildar Begum that Gulbadan reports. According to Gulbadan, Hamideh initially refused to marry Humayun. When invited to Dildar's quarters on Humayun's insistence, she is reported to have said: "If it is to pay my respects, I was exalted by paying my respects the other day. Why should I come again?" Dildar Begum advised her, "After all you will marry someone. Better than a king who is there?" Hamideh's reported response was:

[135] Jouher-Stewart, *Tezkereh*, p. 31. Gulbadan says Dildar Begum *majlis-i dadand*, "gave a party"; Gulbadan, *Ahval*, fol. 42b.
[136] Beveridge, *Baburnama*, p. 551, and Index I, p. 749, n. 1.
[137] Beveridge, *Humayun*, pp. 149–150; Gulbadan, *Ahval*, fol. 42b.
[138] Haim, *Shorter Dictionary*, p. 691; Steingass, *Persian*, p. 1265.

"Oh yes, I shall marry someone; but he shall be a man whose collar my hand can touch, and not one whose skirt it does not reach."[139]

What is important is not the facticity (or literal veracity) of this exchange between Dildar Begum and Hamideh Banu Begum, but the fact that Gulbadan was willing to put such a conversation into her text. This is a part of her representation of the cultural practices of the time. One may thus see Gulbadan's account of Hamideh's reluctance as a statement about frequent debate, and tension, in matters of appropriate behavior in the lives of people at the court. During the same encounter, in one of her communications Hamideh is supposed to have said to the emperor: "To see kings once is lawful [*jayiz ast*]; a second time it is forbidden [*na-mahram ast*]. I shall not come." It is precisely a question about proper conduct to which she draws Humayun's attention, for "proper" conduct was always being worked out even as it was prescribed. Humayun responds to the concern implicit in Hamideh's refusal to visit him a second time: "If she is not a consort [*na-mahram-and*], we will make her a consort [*mahram misazim*]."[140] Their marriage follows.

In the marriage of Humayun and Hamideh Banu, we have an interesting depiction of the issue of organization and "control" in marriages. Women's choice in matrimonial matters illustrates a concern about whom they married and, importantly, their attention to genealogy and dynasty. In this instance, the details of the negotiation of marriage are especially striking for the careful attention paid to tradition, protocol and legality, and to the minute rules of social interaction – the number of times it was legitimate (*jayiz*) to visit a king, the equal status that had to be sought in marriages, as well as the importance of getting married (*mahram misazim*, in the words of Humayun) when a king desired to enter into a relationship with a noble woman.

Gulbadan gives life to Mughal women, who might otherwise be lifeless in the chronicles. More importantly, her characterization points to the negotiated character of the regulations that had to be enforced, as also to the negotiated fiber of domestic life. It is this negotiation and construction of a newly contested court society and its attendant domestic life that I now take up.

In examining the multifaceted set of relations in which imperial women of the nobility negotiated their everyday life, and the public-political affairs that were conducted in the (intersecting) "inner" lodgings as well as in the "outer" courts, the assumptions that have been made about the existence of separate "public" and "private" domains in the Mughal world are immediately challenged. So is the sexualized image of the *haram* – that secluded feminine domain in which a crude principle of sensual pleasure regulated the "private"

---

[139] Beveridge, *Humayun*, pp. 150–151; cf. Gulbadan, *Ahval*, fol. 43a–43b.
[140] Beveridge, *Humayun*, p. 151; cf. Gulbadan, *Ahval*, fol. 43a. The following is a neatly summed-up definition of *mahram*: "Mahrem literally refers to intimacy, domesticity, secrecy, women's space, what is forbidden to a foreigner's gaze; it also means a man's family." See Gole, *The Forbidden Modern*, p. 7.

lives of imperial men and women. In the light of the above findings, the question before us is: "Where was the *haram* in a peripatetic world?" I turn to this subject in the next chapter, where I focus directly on the issue of the presence/absence of women. By paying close attention to sketches of "domestic" activities and debates scattered in the records, I consider how women participate in the making of a dynamic, vulnerable, "human" domestic life.

CHAPTER 5

Where was the *haram* in a peripatetic world?

In the absence of clear-cut and detailed descriptions on the subject of the domestic life of the Mughals, I have argued, two sets of historiographical positions have emerged. First, historians who claim that sources are not available find it unfeasible to think about a history of domestic life. And second, in the work of those who have written on Mughal women or the *haram*, the history of domestic life gets folded into, and is completely encompassed by, the *haram*, presented as a segregated domain where women live in seclusion awaiting the pleasure of men. Thus, the *haram* becomes a field of lust and sensuality, and paradoxically also of beauty and serenity, designed for the comfort and ease of men.

It is remarkable how differently the term *haram* is conjured up, when invoked in the chronicles of Babur and Humayun, from Mughal historians' envisioning of it. In the *Baburnama*, the *haram* is never discussed as an institutionalized entity, a well-regulated physical set-up. The term almost always refers to the women. This begins to change in the texts from Humayun's time, where the *haram* is more regularly alluded to, but still in relation to the imperial women, the *haraman-i padshah*. As to the romantic and lustful associations of the *haram*, there is very little of it projected in the records. To the extent that romantic allusions occur, these are more often made in relation to young adolescents, met by the *padshah* in the bazaars, than they are to women in the *haram*. Where then are the women? And where was the *haram* in this peripatetic world?

Norbert Elias's first comprehensive chapter in his *Court Society* is about the internal disposition of royal dwellings as an "indicator of social structure."[1] According to Elias, the court of the *ancien régime* was a "highly differentiated descendant of the patriarchal form of rule whose embryo is to be sought in the authority of the master of the house within a domestic community."[2] To make his point, Elias gives detailed descriptions of the accommodations of the court people in the time of Louis XIV of France, providing through graphic detail an unusual access to understand certain social relationships

[1] Elias, *Court Society*, p. 41.   [2] *Ibid.*

characteristic of court society. He particularly emphasizes the construction of
appartement privé, private apartments, one for the lord and the other for the
lady of a house of nobility. Both apartments were built identically: "the
position of man and wife in this society could scarcely be more succinctly or
clearly characterized than by this equal but wholly separate disposition of
their private apartments,"[3] Elias notes.

It is not surprising that no such architectural parallelism is found in the
records of the peripatetic Mughal kings. There are scattered references to
women's tents, and their *khaneh* (quarters, houses) are often mentioned, but
hardly ever in detail – not until the time of Akbar in whose reign an extensive
codification occurs of all courtly arrangements, including separate quarters
for women. Even then, women's quarters can hardly be described as equal
and separate. How are we to investigate the figurations of women and men in
this more fluid court society? The answer, it seems to me, is to be found in the
language of the texts of the time.

The present chapter is divided into two parts. The first part is an exploration
of the language through which Babur and Humayun conjure up their domestic
world. I examine their power to name, to describe, and to evoke this world.
The vocabulary of the chroniclers (and its variability) is crucial in the projection
of the domestic lives of the early Mughals: in terms of its location, strategies,
degrees of association, experiences, and expectations; its virtues of generosity,
loyalty, and accountability; the concentric circles of homosociality; and the
place of love and longing in different kinds of relations, "homosexual" as well
as "heterosexual."

This Persian terminology of the early Mughal chronicles deserves close
attention. Part of the exercise in the following pages is to give it just that.
Certain expressions found in the literature refer to the pointedly hierarchical
nature of consanguineous relationships. Then there are references to large
numbers of people in the different camps or resting places of the Mughal
kings. The texts evoke numerous domestic communities, and allude to the
importance of race, tribe, locality, fealty, generation, and age. What we have
in the chronicles of the early Mughals are numerous concepts that are not a
part of modern vocabulary. These index a domestic world that is very different
from current representations of the Mughal *haram*, or private life or familial
situation.

The second part of the chapter investigates how the denizens of this
domestic world, in their turn, "conjure up" a Mughal world of their own.
This world where royal women are major actors is deeply homosocial in
character – in this respect, differing little from that of men – building upon
and deriving sustenance from communities of women. Relationships here,
however, are not entirely cemented in the service, friendship, love and longing
of home and hearth. Mughal women are intensely invested in the construction

[3] *Ibid.*, p. 49.

of monarchy and imagine themselves through the figure of the monarch. Women's involvements in matters of succession, arrangement of marriages, brokering of peace, indeed even offering themselves for peace, tell us a great deal about how they occupy scripted roles in the interests of the monarchy, yet bring themselves forward as distinctive agents in the production and circulation of power.

What we can infer from the evidence is the existence of coeval communities (of men and women) and distinct orders of prescribed norms, desires, and interests. Yet the traces of these highly variegated, open, and multiplex communities undermine any attempt to suggest a separate and independent "domestic" sphere. Our task is to recognize the invocation of such communities as part of the domestic core of camp life, while seeing how their entanglement in the making of the monarchy works against reducing this domestic life to any segregated or circumscribed domain.

The power of utterance: speaking a world into being

What is the terminology employed to describe kith and kin, intimate circles, and other domestic relationships, in different narrative contexts in the early Mughal chronicles? One expression frequently used by Babur in the *Baburnama* is *ahl va 'ayal*.[4] *Ahl* means companion or relative, persons, people of distinction, servants, and attendants: and in the plural (*kasan*), kinsmen (*khvishavand*), relatives of men, race or tribe (*qawm*), friends (*payruvan, yaran, ashab*), or wife and children of someone (*ahl-i-bayt-i kisi* or *zan va farzand-i kisi*). *Ayal* carries with it the connotation of dependence (*muhtaj*). It is used for one who lives with a man, and who bears his/her expenses, such as a servant, wife, or small child. It is used, for example, for *ghulam*, a slave, and servant.[5] *Ahl va 'ayal* thus encompasses the sense of an entourage covering several generations. Babur uses the term to incorporate mothers, grandmothers, great-grandmothers (and the paternal equivalents), wives, and kinsmen. He also includes in this expression the wives of his men, and dependants like children and servants.

The place of Babur's own relatives, and of those of his supporters, emerge well in his emotional recording of the siege of Andijan – a painful recounting of his desperation, helplessness, and need for support at the time. In 1497–98,

---

[4] The meanings of terms that follow are derived mainly from the *Loghatname*, the encyclopedic dictionary. Its compiler, Aliakbar Dehkhoda, lists several meanings for each term based on readings from varied authorities. These include Quranic, legal, customary, and more general philosophical treatises. Moreover, Dehkhoda shows the variable meanings of words over time and in different contexts. What I have highlighted here are the meanings of words that best fit contemporary description portrayed in histories of Babur and Humayun. Other meanings are cited synoptically to provide a broader sense of the resonance of these terms.

[5] *Loghatname*, III, p. 3149, and X, p. 14517. For the meanings of the terms *kisan* and *khvishavand*, also see Steingass, *Persian*, and Haim, *Shorter Dictionary*, s.v. "kisan" and "khvishavand."

Babur had ridden out to capture Samarqand. Meanwhile, his base at Andijan was threatened. He continually received letters from his mother and his "master and guide" Khvajeh Mawlana Qazi, with pleas such as the following: "They have us under siege. If you do not come help us, it will be all over. Samarqand was taken through the strength of Andizhan. If Andizhan is held, and God wills, Samarkand can be taken."[6] Babur went back, but by that time Andijan had been captured, and Khvajeh Mawlana Qazi hanged on the citadel gate of Andijan. Many Begs deserted Babur. "It was very difficult for me. I wept involuntarily. From there I went to Khodzhend, where my mother and grandmother were sent to me with the families [*ahl va 'ayal*] of those who remained with me."[7]

Similarly in 1501–02, after Babur had lost both Samarqand and his sister Khanzadeh Begum to Shiybani Khan Uzbik, he moved to Dzhizak where "from fear and hardship we found release – new life, a new world we found"[8] (a life plentiful with good grapes, melons, and fine flour!). From there, Babur and others moved to Pishagar, where he received the news that his mother's younger sister, Khub Nigar Khanum, as well as his father's mother had passed away. Moreover, he records, "My mother had not seen her stepmother Shah Begim or her younger brothers and sisters, Sultan-Mahmud Khan, Sultan Nigar Khanim and Dawlat Sultan Khanim since my grandfather the khan had died. Their separation had lasted for thirteen or fourteen years. She set out for Tashkent in order to see her family."[9] Babur too decided, in 1501–02, to leave his "family" [*oruk*] in Dakhkat and set out for Tashkant to see Shah Begim, his uncle the Khan, and his kinsmen (*khvishan va 'azizan*).[10]

The terms, *ahl va 'ayal*, *oruk*, *khvishan va 'azizan*, indicate the wide-ranging pattern of linkages. *Ahl va 'ayal* in the context of turmoil in Andijan suggests the participation and importance of a large network encompassing several generations. A similar "multi-generational sense" may be witnessed again in the events of 1501–02, when Babur left his *oruk* and followed his mother to Tashkant. He joined her in visiting her stepmother, younger brothers and sisters, as well as their kinsmen. The *khvishan va 'azizan* of Babur's uncle too suggests an extended range of relatives and kinsfolk.

The words and phrases discussed above are obviously far from being synonymous. Different terms are used in different contexts to invoke diverse conceptions of the Mughal community. A strong genealogical component is woven into Babur's conception of his kinsfolk. In Babur's comment – "For nearly a hundred and forty years the capital Samarkand had been in our

---

[6] Thackston, *Baburnama*, pp. 107–108; Beveridge, *Baburnama*, p. 88. In line with other chapters, I have kept Thackston's English translation of the extracts, inserting required Persian words whenever necessary. I discuss these words in detail after every citation.

[7] Thackston, *Baburnama*, p. 112; Beveridge, *Baburnama*, pp. 91–92.

[8] Thackston, *Baburnama*, p. 192; Beveridge, *Baburnama*, p. 148.

[9] Thackston, *Baburnama*, p. 193; Beveridge, *Baburnama*, pp. 148–149.

[10] Thackston, *Baburnama*, p. 193; Beveridge, *Baburnama*, p. 149.

family [*khanivadeh*]"[11] – we come across the term, *khanivadeh*. This word is close in meaning to *khandan*, carrying with it the sense of "pertaining to an illustrious family," "familial" or *khanivadigi*.[12]

These terms are particularly striking for Babur's construction of a noble selfhood. Both *khanivadeh* and *ahl va 'ayal* seem to carry the sense of an eminent genealogical connection and suggest the participation and engagement of several generations of that house. *Khanivadeh* is evidently used for what we might roughly translate as a "large kin set-up."[13] This connotation is present also in Babur's application of another term, *nasab*, used frequently in the *Baburnama*.[14] *Nasab*, entailing race, genealogy (*nasl*), line of descent (*rag va risheh*), origin, also relatives (*khvish*), was used to describe the birth and lineage of several distinguished ancestors of the Timurid and Chingizid lines of Babur. There are two other derivatives of *nasab*, both of which seem relevant to Babur's construction above: first, *nasab-i tuli* or a vertical descent, of father, son, grandson, and so on, and second, *nasab-i 'arzi* or horizontal descent, of nephews, and cousins on the paternal side.[15]

The following citation from the *Baburnama* on the "birth and lineage" of ʿUmar Shaykh Mirza and Qutluq Nigar Khanum (Babur's father and mother) typifies the construction of the Chingizid-Timurid *nasab* in Babur's narrative:

He was Sultan Abu-Saʿid Mirza's fourth son, younger than Sultan Ahmad-Mirza, Sultan-Muhammad Mirza and Sultan Mahmud Mirza. Sultan Abu Saʿid Mirza was Sultan Muhammad Mirza's son. Sultan Muhammad Mirza was the son of Miranshah Mirza, Timur Beg's third son, who was younger than Umar Shaikh Mirza and Jahangir Mirza, and older than Shahrukh Mirza. ... Yunus Khan and Esan Buka Khan were sons of Ways Khan. Yunas Khan's mother was the daughter or grand-daughter of Shaykh Nuruddin Beg, a Qipchaq beg of Turkistan who was patronised by Timur Beg. ... The second daughter [of Yunus Khan] was my mother, Qutlugh Nigar Khanim.[16]

In this way, by situating all his *khvishan va 'azizan* (relatives and kinsfolk) in a complex network, Babur engrosses the reader in the details about himself:

The eldest of all the sons was I, Zahiruddin Muhammad Babur. My mother was Qutlugh Nigar Khanim. Another son [of ʿUmar Shaykh Mirza] was Jahangir Mirza. ... His mother was from the tuman begs of the Mughuls, Fatima Sultan by name. The third son was Nasir Mirza. His mother was from Andizhan a concubine

---

[11] Thackston, *Baburnama*, p. 171; Beveridge, *Baburnama*, p. 134. [12] *Loghatname*, I, pp. 82–98.

[13] The word *khanivadeh* is not restricted to his reputed *khandan* only by Babur. It was also used, to take an example, for the prestigious line of ʿAbdul ʿAli Tarkhan, who was one of the eminent officers of Sultan Ahmad Mirza, Babur's paternal uncle. A similar glorious connection emerges again in a description of Mawlana Qazi, the master and guide of Babur, who guarded Andijan whilst the *padshah* was on a campaign to Samarqand.

[14] Thackston translates *nasab* as lineage throughout his translation of the *Baburnama*.

[15] *Loghatname*, XIII, pp. 19848–19849.

[16] Thackston, *Baburnama*, pp. 12, 18, 21; Beveridge, *Baburnama*, pp. 13, 14.

named Umed. ... The eldest of the daughters was Khanzada Begim, who was my sibling. ... Another daughter was Mihr Banu Begim ... a sibling to Nasir Mirza. ... Another was Shahr Banu Begim ... a sibling to Nasir Mirza. Another was Yadgar Sultan Begim, whose mother was Agha Sultan, a concubine. Another was Ruqayya Sultan Begim. Her mother was Makhdum Sultan Begim, who was called Qara Koz (Black Eyes) Begim ...[17]

It was the credence of his privileged ancestry of Timur and Chingiz Khan that he tried to convey to Humayun on his death-bed, "Moreover, Humayun, I commit to God's keeping you and your brothers [*tura va biradaran-i tura*] and all my kinsfolk and your people and my people [*khvishan va mardum*]; and all of these I confide to you."[18]

The *Baburnama* resonates throughout with references to illustrious antecedents. This is not a mere literary flourish. Rather, it makes tangible Babur's belief of what constituted his ancestral line; note his continual stress on setting out several generations of the lineage to which he belonged. Conceptually, as well as in practice, Babur's domestic life hinged on his Timurid-Chingizid ancestry: the *khandan* of Timur and Chingiz Khan were the focus of almost all his arrangements and plans. Thus, two rebels, Mirza Khan and Mirza Muhammad Husain Gurakan, were forgiven in the name of the senior women of the prestigious Chingizid-Timurid lineage. Or to take a different instance, of Babur's early marriages: 'Ayisheh Sultan Begum, Ma'sumeh Sultan Begum, and Ziynab Sultan Begum were all daughters of his paternal uncles, from the great Timurid line.

In keeping with this ancestral emphasis, Babur laid stress, in the battles against the Uzbiks, and later in Hindustan, on the support of the members of this multigenerational lineage: the aunts, great-grand-aunts, and sisters. Those of the "*nasl*" of Timur and Chingiz Khan were all invited to share in the prosperity of Hindustan.[19] Gulbadan quotes Babur as saying, "Whoever there may be of the families [*nasl*] of Sahib-qiran and Chingiz Khan [*az nasl-i Sahib Qiran*], let them turn towards our court."[20] The *nasl* of Sahib Qiran incorporated children (*awlad, bachcheh*), descendants (*akhlaf*), and great-grandchildren (*nabireh*). It implied the *khandan, dudman, dudeh*, and *pusht* (several generations).[21] A strong genealogical component is woven into Babur's narrative here. Likewise, the first set of presents from Hindustan, the "valuable presents and curiosities of Hind," were sent by Babur for the Begums, sisters, children, kinsmen, heads of households, nurses, and foster-brethren.[22]

Consider also the people from Babur's distinguished ancestral line who went to Hindustan and became influential presences in his court: Babur's

---

[17] Thackston, *Baburnama*, pp. 16–17; Beveridge, *Baburnama*, pp. 17–18.
[18] Beveridge, *Humayun*, p. 109; Gulbadan, *Ahval*, fol. 19b.
[19] Beveridge, *Humayun*, p. 97; Gulbadan, *Ahval*, fol. 11a.
[20] Beveridge, *Humayun*, p. 97; Gulbadan, *Ahval*, fol. 11a.   [21] *Loghatname*, XIII, p. 19860.
[22] Beveridge, *Humayun*, p. 94; Gulbadan, *Ahval*, fol. 9b.

sister Khanzadeh Begum, distinctly involved in the crucial Uzbik affair and then in critical situations of Humayun's life; the grandsons of Sultan Husain Mirza Bayqura (Babur's cousin), all of whom were in India; and two Timurid women, Fakhr-jahan Begum and Khadijeh Begum, both paternal aunts of Babur who went to Hindustan as early as 1527[23] (several of these connections will be considered in more detail later in this chapter).

Several references in the *Baburnama* focus on other, non-kin links, which are also very closely associated with the king. The following statement is from the time when Baqi Chaghaniyani, a Turkistani Qipchaq, joined Babur in 1504–05, when the latter left Ferghaneh.[24] Babur says: "In three or four marches we came to Kahmard and left the household [*khaneh va mardum*] at Ajar fortress."[25] The meanings of *khaneh* and *mardum* separately are as follows: *khaneh*, somewhere where people live, that which is carried with a king or *amir* during a journey, or the court of the king (*darbar-i-padshah va saray-i-saltanat*). It also means friend (*yar, rafiq*), husband (*shawhar*) and wife (*zan*).[26] The other term, *mardum*, designates other people, servants, or workers. The word's meaning, as understood in the light of its usage in the *Baburnama*, is *digaran* or others,[27] but those in close proximity.

"That which is carried with the king or *amir* during a journey" is the meaning of *khaneh va mardum*, as it emerges in this context. The events are of the year 1504–05, when Babur had left Ferghaneh for Khurasan, and when Baqi Chaghaniyani had offered his fealty. Babur was on the move, accompanied by a small entourage. *Khaneh va mardum* here refers to a small number of people, those involved at this crucial juncture.

There is another word that Babur uses, *kuch*, usually for his followers. *Kuch* means a man's wife and children.[28] So, for Shirim Taghayi, Babur says that he was "the greatest of my men ... he had sent his family [*kuch*] off and stayed by himself to command the fort." Similarly, the *padshah* records his gratitude for Baqi Chaghaniyani, "who sent his family [*kuch*] across [*sic*] and joined" Babur.[29] These comments were made in the context of the events of 1505 when Babur had left Farghaneh. There were other loyal men and their people too: Qambar 'Ali Sallakh, for instance, who was Babur's "greatly favoured Beg and had received such patronage but who at such a time refused to co-operate and took his family [*kuch*] out of Samarkand" (in 1500–01 just before Babur was besieged in Samarqand).[30]

---

[23] Beveridge, *Humayun*, Introduction, p. 19.
[24] Baqi Chaghaniyani was half-brother of Khusraw Shah, the chief Beg of Sultan Mahmud Mirza, Babur's uncle.
[25] Thackston, *Baburnama*, p. 248; Beveridge, *Baburnama*, p. 189.
[26] *Loghatname*, VI, pp. 8299–8304.   [27] *Ibid.*, XII, p. 18224.   [28] Steingass, *Persian*, p. 1059.
[29] Thackston, *Baburnama*, pp. 247–248; Beveridge, *Baburnama*, pp. 188–189.
[30] Thackston, *Baburnama*, p. 182; Beveridge, *Baburnama*, p. 141. Beveridge does not mention the name of Qambar 'Ali Sallakh in her translation of this particular paragraph from the *Baburnama*.

Babur uses *kuch* in an unhindered manner for his men and their women and children. At a few places Babur even writes *kuch* for his own unit, but usually together with *oruk*, the Turkish word for women and children, or household, thus invoking a slightly more extended set of relationships. The following description from the *Baburnama*, of the problems in Andijan and Samarqand in 1501, is a good example of the usage of *kuch* strung along with another term: "Some days after that my grandmother, Esan Dawlat Begim, who had remained behind when I left Samarkand, arrived with the hungry and lean family members [*ba kuch va oruk*] who had stayed in Samarkand."[31]

if Babur's notion of intimate circle and kinship is predicated upon a sense of the unity of several generations, the *ahl va ʿayal* of Humayun's time begins to focus on a somewhat more contemporary set of relationships. At any rate, there is a reduced invocation of the weight of many generations. It is the people and relations directly around Humayun that become the points of discussion in chronicles of the time: most importantly, his mother, stepmothers, stepbrothers, and some kinsmen, servants, and followers. A description from Gulbadan Begum's *Ahval*, about the time of the battle of Chawsa between Humayun and Sher Shah, serves to make the point. The Begum informs us that many people were lost during this battle. ʿAyisheh Sultan Begum, the daughter of Sultan Husain Mirza Bayqura (her husband was the governor of Patna), Bachaka, a Khalifa from Babur's time,[32] as well as others from Humayun's *haram*. "Of many who were in that rout," Gulbadan says, "there was never heard, in any way so ever, news or sign" of Bigeh-jan kukeh, ʿAqiqeh Begum, and Chand Bibi, "who was seven months with child," and Shad Bibi, all of whom were *haraman-i padshah*, women of Humayun's *haram*.[33]

Consider another incident from Gulbadan's memoir, again emphasizing the contemporary generation of the Timurid *khandan*. In Amarkot, just before Akbar was born, Humayun left his people and relations (*ahl va ʿayal*), and also Khvajeh Muʿazzam in charge of his *haram*.[34] Hamideh Banu Begum (Humayun's wife) was pregnant at this point, so she was also left in Amarkot. Gulbadan's entire description centers around Hamideh Banu who gave birth to Akbar three days after Humayun had departed. Humayun then went to Jun, and thereafter to Thatta. It was in Thatta that he brought his *ahl-i haram* (people of the *haram*) and the whole Amarkot group there.[35]

---

[31] Thackston, *Baburnama*, p. 196; Beveridge, *Baburnama*, p. 151. Note the inaccuracy of the translation of *ba kuch va oruk* by Thackston.

[32] Khalifa as applied to a woman, Beveridge explains, denotes a servant or slave "who exercises surveillance over other women-servants, and has charge of rooms – an upper maid-servant." Bachaka had escaped along with Babur from Samarqand in 1501, nearly thirty-eight years before the Chawsa incident. Beveridge, *Humayun*, p. 136, n. 2.

[33] Beveridge, *Humayun*, p. 137; Gulbadan, *Ahval*, fol. 33b.

[34] Beveridge, *Humayun*, p. 157; Gulbadan, *Ahval*, fol. 48b.

[35] Beveridge, *Humayun*, p. 158; Gulbadan, *Ahval*, fol. 49a.

Two clarifications are in order here. First, the change in the manner of allusion to the Timurid-Mughal *khandan* between the time of Babur and that of Humayun can hardly be said to constitute a radical break. As we may see in the episodes from Gulbadan, simultaneous referencing to earlier generations comes alongside invocations of the more immediate ones; no doubt, the latter are more frequently discussed in the Humayuni chronicles. Take again, the focus on Hamideh Banu in the citation above. The comment from Gulbadan Banu indicates that the *haram* that Humayun left behind at Amarkot did not include a very wide range of relatives and kinsfolk. Instead, she focuses upon a few people and a pregnant wife. It is known through other chronicles, like Jawhar's, that it was Hamideh Begum who accompanied Humayun in all his wanderings.[36] Such condensed networks are often foregrounded in the Humayuni histories. The emphasis that the *Baburnama* places on ancestral connections is now largely missing. In its place, smaller kin groups gain greater force and, as noted already, the term *haram* also appears more regularly (however, several different terms still continue to be used inter-changeably, as in the *Baburnama*).

The second clarification: a reminder about the language of the memoirs. Words such as the *ahl-i haram* are taken from Gulbadan's memoir, which as we know, is a later reconstruction of the Baburi and Humayuni times. The language of this memoir exudes a context of the sacred associations that went into the making of the traditions of Akbar's empire. Gulbadan's text, how-ever, is not the only example of this linguistic quality. Many other Akbari chronicles partake of such evocations that rendered Akbar's empire extra-ordinary.[37] What is important, therefore, is to underline how Gulbadan deploys the language used in Akbari chronicles to project it back to Humayun's domestic world. So, for example, the common expression for Akbar's institutionalized *Shabistan-i Iqbal*, the *haram*, is transferred to a presentation of Humayun's reign as well.

Babur's marriages

One thing is certain from an examination of the terms that conjure up the domestic life of the early Mughals: no single term serves to project its variability. What we have is a multiplicity of terms that index networks or communities, which intersect, interconnect, and overlap. Quite who belonged to which communities was a matter that changed over time, and depended on speaker and context. The ancestors of generations past were part of the Mughal community, but not always equally insistently. Servants and lack-eys, male and female, were part of it, and yet by no means uniformly. This

---

[36] For a discussion of men and women who accompanied Humayun in Persia, see also Ray, *Humayun in Persia*, p. 3, n. 3.
[37] For details, see chapter 6.

rich and changing language of the chronicles does at least one other thing: it dispels any simple belief we may have in a bounded familial unit within which conjugal and filial relationships were worked out by the early Mughals.

To engage with the "inflections and complexities" of this "multiform social order,"[38] let me undertake a quick review of Babur's marriages. Babur mentions several of his marriages and wives in the *Baburnama*; Gulbadan provides a more complete list of the women and their children.[39] This information is important in considering how multiform relationships were established between men and women: in marriages, in associations between parents and children, in bonds of duty and affection. Most importantly, the analysis of the extracts that follow further serves to indicate the place the women occupy in the narrative structures of the time. In addition, the analysis in this section also begins to demonstrate that one does not hear as much of a play of individual lives and emotions (romance in the *harams*!) as one would in modern times. What is prominent here is the placement of individuals in collectivities, which are governed by honor, shame, duty, and deeply embedded monarchical concerns; and in these, it is mostly males that are made visible, as are senior or elder females. The place for younger women and their activities is scant in the records of the time.

The records often speak of the actions and achievements of individual men and women. However, as they are presented here, these individuals do not speak only for themselves. In an uncanny way, they seem to represent some greater collectivity, a larger tradition, or established practice. Take the example of Khanzadeh Begum, elder sister of Babur who was "captured" by his ardent foe, Shiybani Khan. We do not hear Khanzadeh's version of the event, but most histories of the time depict this occurrence as special. Khanzadeh was not the only Mughal woman who was taken over in times of conflict. The question is why do records place significance on Khanzadeh's captivity. Khanzadeh was "taken," we are told, after a direct and clear conversation between Babur and Shiybani Khan: the latter told Babur if Khanzadeh would marry him, there would be peace between the two. Thus, the monarchical interest had to be protected and, if required, "sacrifices" had to be made towards it. "At length it had to be done": Gulbadan constructs Babur speaking these words.[40] Her construction demonstrates that it was not the individuality of individuals that mattered so much: rather these descriptions of individual actions are better seen as statements reflective of the spirit of the times.

[38] I take this phrase from Natalie Zemon Davis, *Society and Culture in Early Modern France* (Stanford, 1975), p. xviii.

[39] The list of Babur's marriages is derived from the *Ahval-i Humayun Badshah* and Annette Beveridge's translation of the *Baburnama*. The Index of Mughal women at the back of the *Ahval* as well as Beveridge's note, "Babur's wives and children" in the *Baburnama* are very informative (pp. 711–713). I list other references where necessary.

[40] Beveridge, *Humayun*, p. 85; Gulbadan, *Ahval*, fol. 3b.

These propositions are further borne out by what we know about Babur's marriages. In 1488–89, when Babur was five, he was betrothed to ʿAyisheh Sultan Begum, daughter of Sultan Ahmad Mirza Miranshahi (Babur's paternal uncle). She gave birth to Fakhr-un-nisa, who died about a month later. ʿAyisheh Sultan Begum left Babur before 1503. Babur and Zainab Sultan Begum, daughter of Sultan Mahmud Mirza (Babur's paternal uncle), were married in 1504 or 1505. Zainab Sultan Begum died childless two or three years after this. Maham Begum, whose parentage is not mentioned in any of the contemporary chronicles, is recorded as having married Babur in 1506. She gave birth to Barbul Mirza, Mihr-jan Begum, Aisan Dawlat Begum, and Faruq Mirza, all of whom died in their infancy. Her only surviving son was Humayun. Babur was also married to Maʿsumeh Begum, another daughter of Sultan Ahmad Mirza Miranshahi, in 1507. She gave birth to Maʿsumeh (same name as the mother) and died in childbirth.[41]

Gulrukh Begum, again whose background is not mentioned in the contemporary records, was married to Babur sometime between 1508 and 1519 (these years of the *Baburnama* are missing from the manuscripts). She bore Shahrukh, Ahmad, Gulʿizar (all three died young), and Kamran and ʿAskari. Like Gulrukh and Maham, Dildar Begum's ancestry is not discussed in the contemporary records. She married Babur in the same unaccounted period and gave birth to Gulrang, Gulchihra, Hindal, Gulbadan, and Alwar (the last of the five children died in childhood). Bibi Mubarika Yusufzay, whom Gulbadan describes as "Afghani *Aghacheh*," was married to Babur in 1519. She died childless.[42]

In Niyaz Muhammad Khukandi's *Tarikh-i Shahrukhi* and Nalivkine's *Khanate of Khokand*, it is mentioned that when Babur left Samarqand in 1512 after his defeat by the Uzbiks, one of his wives, Sayyida Afaq, accompanied him in his flight, and gave birth to a son in the desert between Khujand and Kand-i badam.[43] During the nomadic circumstances and the hazardous journeys of Babur, we are told, the king left his newly born son under some bushes, his own girdle around him with numerous things of value in it. The child was found by local people and in allusion to the valuable materials in which the infant lay, he was called Altun Bishik (golden cradle). He is said to have spent most of his life in Akhsi, and to have died in 1545.

Two other women, Gulnar *agacheh* and Nargul *agacheh*, became important in Babur and Humayun's intimate circle.[44] Gulnar and Nargul were Circassian slaves and were gifted by Shah Tahmasb to Babur in 1526.

[41] Beveridge, *Baburnama*, p. 711; Beveridge, *Humayun*, pp. 89–90.
[42] Beveridge, *Baburnama*, p. 712; Beveridge, *Humayun*, p. 90.
[43] Beveridge, *Baburnama*, p. 358. Annette Beveridge suggests with some uncertainty that Maham who belonged to a religious family might have been styled Sayyida (*ibid.*, p. 358, n. 2).
[44] Beveridge's insightful comment that *agacheh*, which means "a lady" as opposed to a begum or a woman of noble birth, is often inaccurately translated as concubine should be kept in mind when discussing these pre-modern women bearing this title. The translation of *agacheh* as "lady" has problems of a certain Victorian sensibility being transported to the reading of pre-modern Indo-Persian texts. I have discussed this issue in chapter 2 (Beveridge, *Humayun*, pp. 2, 3, 91n).

Gulbadan mentions Gulnar in her discussion of the wedding feast of her brother, Hindal. Gulnar was also one of the women who accompanied Gulbadan in the royal women's pilgrimage to Mecca in 1575.[45]

It may be useful to elaborate a little on Babur's first four marriages and the poetic narration of his *avan-i mihr va muhabbat* (time of love and affection) with a bazaar youth which occurs in the same period. These moments are recorded in the first section of the *Baburnama* and tell us a great deal about the meanings and politics of marriage at a time when Babur was embroiled in struggles against his Timurid and non-Timurid kinsmen. Babur writes that 'Ayisheh Sultan Begum was "affianced" to him when both their fathers were still alive. They were married in August 1499. Babur adds:

> Although my affection for her was not lacking still it was my first marriage, and I was so bashful that I went to her only once every ten, fifteen, or twenty days. Later on I lost my affection altogether, but I was still very bashful. Once every month or forty days my mother the khanim drove me to her with all the severity of a quartermaster.[46]

At this time Babur had also developed a keen desire for an adolescent (*pisar*) named Baburi, who lived in the camp market (*urdu bazaar*).[47] Babur emphasizes that he regarded his initial feeling as "a strange inclination" but gradually realized that "before this I had never felt a desire for anyone, and neither [*sic*] did I listen to talk of love and affection nor did I speak of such things."[48] These stirrings prompted him to compose, what Dale calls, "a trite poem ... using Persian, the lingua franca of Turco-Mongol aristocrats in heavily Iranized Mawarannahr."[49]

> May no one be so distraught and devastated by love as I;
> May no beloved be so pitiless and careless as you.[50]

He says more: "In the throes of love, in the foment [*sic*] of youth and madness, I wandered bareheaded and barefoot around the lanes and streets and through the gardens and orchards, paying no attention to acquaintances or strangers, oblivious to self and others."[51]

---

[45] Beveridge, *Humayun*, pp. 232, 269; Beveridge, *Baburnama*, p. 712.

[46] Thackston, *Baburnama*, p. 152; Beveridge, *Baburnama*, p. 120.

[47] Thackston, *Baburnama*, p. 152. In the context of her work on Qajar Iran (1785–1925), Afsaneh Najmabadi refuses to accept the use of the word "boy" or "boy-love" as an explanation for *amradparasti* (loving *amrads*, *amrad* meaning a young male) because of modern connotations of pedophilia and of the "boy" as a child (Afsaneh Najmabadi, "Gender and the Sexual Politics of Public Visibility in Iranian Modernity," in Joan W. Scott and Debra Keats (eds.), *Going Public* (Illinois, 2004), p. 3. The same argument should apply to the pre-modern Mughal homosocial context where Baburi is better characterized as a young adolescent rather than as a boy.

[48] Thackston, *Baburnama*, p. 152; Beveridge, *Baburnama*, p. 120. For a discussion of Babur's "love" and "marriages," see, Dale, *Eight Paradises*, pp. 106–110.

[49] Dale, *Eight Paradises*, p. 108.

[50] Thackston, *Baburnama*, p. 153; Beveridge, *Baburnama*, p. 120.

[51] Thackston, *Baburnama*, pp. 153–154; Beveridge, *Baburnama*, p. 121.

A little before "the throneless times,"[52] as Beveridge describes these, i.e., after the losses of Samarqand and Andijan, we learn that Sultan Ahmad Mirza's wife Habibeh Begum (Babur's paternal uncle and aunt) brought their daughter Ma'sumeh Begum to Heri. One day when Babur was visiting his relatives, Ma'sumeh Begum happened to be there with her mother. As Babur records it, "upon first seeing me she felt a great inclination towards me."[53] It was then arranged between Payandeh Sultan Begum and Habibeh Sultan Begum that the latter should bring her daughter to Kabul. According to the arrangement they all met later in Ghazni. Babur also married Zainab Sultan Begum (1504), the daughter of Sultan Mahmud Mirza, his other paternal uncle "through the good offices of my mother," says Babur, adding that, "she [Zainab Sultan Begum] was not very congenial, and two or three years later she died of small-pox."[54]

What is indexed in the statements above is the condition of Babur's peripatetic life: in flux, and not easily described. The continually changing social and political circumstances, the context of the long absences of the wandering king, and the instability that ensued necessitated strong political alliances. In this pre-modern world, as in other times, matrimonies were a common way of establishing political networks. The list of Babur's marriages provides ample demonstration of this.

In addition, there is something about the presence of (the desire for) multiple attachments in this context of perpetual movement. Extracts from Babur's marriages as well as his homoerotic articulations, placed next to each other, make us wonder what it meant to marry, or to love, in circumstances of constant physical movement, especially when Babur had no secure territorial base and he was continually engaged in battle to retain or extend what land he controlled.

How is one to grasp Babur's experience of Ma'sumeh's "great inclination" towards him, his "bashfulness" and his "modesty"[55] towards 'Ayisheh Sultan Begum, and his distraught and devastated feelings in relation to Baburi? One difficulty is that our contemporary experience of sexuality asks us to visit these extracts with an opposition between homosexual and heterosexual roles, or at best, to investigate these extracts with the possibility of transgression of sexual roles. However such oppositions are not necessarily at work here. As Afsaneh Najmabadi has argued, a homoerotic genre is not exclusively premised upon same-sex practices that define the Western notion of homosexuality.[56] Hence the proposition of a "latent homosexuality" is not required here.[57]

[52] Beveridge, *Baburnama*, p. 306.
[53] Thackston, *Baburnama*, p. 402; Beveridge, *Baburnama*, p. 306.
[54] Thackston, *Baburnama*, p. 54; Beveridge, *Baburnama*, p. 48.
[55] Beveridge's translation is powerfully rendered here. According to her, Babur says of his marriage with 'Ayisheh Sultan Begum: "Though I was not ill-disposed towards her, yet, this being my first marriage, out of *modesty*, and *bashfulness*, I used to see her once in 10, 15 or 20 days" (Beveridge, *Baburnama*, p. 120, emphasis mine).
[56] Najmabadi, "Gender and Sexual Politics," p. 4.
[57] Michel Foucault, *The Use of Pleasure: The History of Sexuality*, vol. II (New York, 1990), p. 85.

From the foregoing accounts, it is possible to suggest that in the *Baburnama*, love for male company could sit by the desire, and recognition of the need, for marriages, especially the necessity of having children that would enhance the name of the distinguished Timurid line. The problem is not one of "loving" both sexes, but rather of a regimen that was widely accepted in society, and that may have been especially fitting for a peripatetic life and its demands. It still remains the case, however, that in a memoir where marriages, *avan-i mihr va muhabbat*, and the communities of men and women are projected as sitting beside each other, where none of these was privileged over others, there is still a moment when the king's affection for a bazaar boy is elevated to poetic grandeur.

There is a further point to be made about Babur's prose and poetry in relation to Baburi. Since there does not appear to have been very much room in Babur's life on the run for the nurturing of constant (or long-lasting) affections, one might see his *mihr va muhabbat* for Baburi as an idealizing strand in his poetry, an almost inaccessible love expressed in a homoerotic literary genre. The passages describing this experience are, however, more than an indicator of Babur's literary ambitions and his effort to master the art of poetry writing. His narration here is significant also in the light of the fact that a few decades later any such celebratory statement, and even the notion of "homosexuality," would come to be regarded as transgressive. Such a display of affection between men was severely criticized by Babur's grandson, Akbar; it was in fundamental contradiction with his model of masculinity. As O'Hanlon says, "It blurred the proper boundaries between emotions and generated forms of desire and pleasure which sapped male moral strength at its most sensitive point. It could derive only from disordered worlds ... where men tolerated base and bestial forms of sexual expression, and where the path to male virtue was closed."[58]

Similar expressions of inaccessible love (for males and females) may, of course, be imagined in a lifestyle where the *padshah*'s camp was perpetually on the move. Unfortunately, no record of such yearning for a woman is available to us until much later in Hindustan, where Gulbadan Banu Begum's memoir seems to suggest a very close relationship between Babur and his wife Maham Begum.

Let me return to Babur's marriages and reiterate the particularity of the context in which his wives were named in the *Baburnama*. What is perhaps most striking in all the examples of the *padshah*'s early matrimonial alliances is that they take place at crucial junctures of his life, mostly in turbulent circumstances when the extent, and even the existence, of his kingdom was quite uncertain. The Uzbiks posed the biggest challenge to Babur's ambitions in Central Asia, and more precisely in Samarqand – a threat potent enough to extinguish Timurid rule over Transoxiana. Babur's marriages with the

---

[58] O'Hanlon, "Kingdom, Household and Body," p. 19.

Timurids were, at one level, an answer to the Uzbik challenge. The ongoing Timurid–Uzbik conflict was one reason that may have contributed to a stronger articulation of Timurid identity, which as we saw in the last chapter, was consistently underlined by Babur. Marrying in Babur's own line of descent ('Ayisheh Sultan Begum, Ma'sumeh Begum, and Zainab Sultan Begum, were all daughters of the paternal uncles of Babur) was yet another way of reinforcing this identity.

Thus the wives named in the *Baburnama* were daughters of important dynasts who upon marriage with Babur were expected to beget noble progeny. The years after these early marriages were a time when Babur was all-powerful in Kabul. Eighteen children were born to him and in 1508, after Humayun's birth, he styled himself *padshah*. Babur tried once more to return to his ancestral land when his formidable foe Shahi Beg Khan was defeated by Shah Isma'il, the ruler of Persia. But the Uzbiks defeated Babur. In these circumstances, he entrusted Kabul to Nasir Mirza, his half-brother, and set out for Samarqand, "taking with him his people and wives and children," that is, Humayun Mirza, Mihr-jahan Begum, Barbul Mirza, Ma'sumeh Begum, and Kamran Mirza.[59] He took Samarqand in October 1511 with the help of Shah Isma'il and for a while the whole of Transoxiana was in his power. In the same year Babur was vanquished yet again by the Uzbiks and he set out for Badakhshan and Kabul. In the midst of this turbulence, Babur took Bibi Mubarika, the Yusufzay, as his wife.

Babur's marriage with Bibi Mubarika is an obvious example of the political character of marriages, widely practiced in these ruling circles of society. This marriage took place in Afghanistan, in the context of a new set of pressures on Babur. He had lost hold of his Central Asian domain, and Kabul was his last foothold for a new Timurid Empire. Yusufzay, the clan of Bibi Mubarika, was Babur's enemy. Before Babur's marriage with Bibi Mubarika, there had been one earlier attempt at conciliation between the Yusufzays and the *padshah*.[60] Based on a review of two manuscripts dealing with the Yusufzay clan, Annette Beveridge writes of a meeting between Ahmad Yusufzay and Babur where equal, honorable, and friendly exchanges took place between the two. However, when Babur invited Ahmad Yusufzay to Kabul a second time, he declined the offer. He sent his brother Shah Mansur (father of Bibi Mubarika) instead. Babur was displeased, and Shah Mansur returned to his tribe. Babur followed him backed by an army.[61]

Later on, while Babur was near Mahura hills, the stronghold of the Yusufzay, Shah Mansur held a feast at his house for 'Id. We are told that Babur went in disguise to the back of the house and stood there among the crowd in the courtyard. The daughter of the chieftain, seeing a stranger,

[59] Beveridge, *Humayun*, p. 91; Gulbadan, *Ahval*, fol. 7a.
[60] Beveridge, *Baburnama*, Index K, "An Afghan Legend."   [61] *Ibid.*, pp. xxxviii–xxxix.

courteously sent him some food. Babur was apparently much struck by her beauty, and inquired about her.[62]

According to Gulbadan, the father of Afghani *aghacheh* (or "Afghan Lady"), Malik Mansur Yusufzay, "came in and paid his respects," and Babur married his daughter.[63] According to Beveridge, on the other hand, Malik Mansur still had some reservation about his daughter's marriage to Babur because of the ongoing rivalry between them. He agreed to the marriage, however, "for the good of the tribe."[64] As the story goes, after the marriage, Babur cemented his relations with the Yusufzay on Afghani *aghacheh*'s insistence. Here is the report of the conversation between Babur and Afghani *aghacheh*. Bibi Mubarika's words first: "I have a petition to make. If an order be given, I will make it." She took up her dress in both hands and said, "Think that the whole Yusuf-zai tribe is enfolded in my skirt, and pardon their offences for my sake." Babur is reported to have said, "I forgive the Yusuf-zai all their offences in thy presence, and cast them all into thy skirt. Hereafter I shall have no ill-feeling to the Yusuf-zai."[65]

In the accounts of both Gulbadan and Annette Beveridge, the politics of alliance are clearly foregrounded: the political links that the marriages were intended to forge appear unequivocally in the case of Afghani *aghacheh*.[66] Afghani *aghacheh*, like many of her contemporaries, is thus a normative figure performing the ideals of domesticity, for her father as well as for her husband. As one might expect in the lives of pre-modern chieftains and political adventurers, marriages were not meant purely to serve the modern ideals of domesticity. Given that, one can hardly search for the pull of home and hearth, the secure routines of homely life, or a single (or for that matter, a series of) heterosexual or homosexual relationship that can be elevated to the status of "love."

The social event of marriage continued to have considerable political importance among the Mughals – as among their royal contemporaries the world over. The order of marriage changed somewhat in the altered conditions of Babur's Hindustan. This may be noted particularly in images of Babur's relationship with Maham Begum (the "wife of Babur's affection," as Beveridge describes her[67]) in Gulbadan's account. The recently acquired territory of a prosperous Hindustan and a relatively less peripatetic lifestyle constituted the new, more sedentary context of the *padshah*'s later years.

---

[62] *Ibid.*, p. xxxix.   [63] Beveridge, *Humayun*, p. 91; Gulbadan, *Ahval*, fol. 7b.
[64] Beveridge, "An Afghan Legend," p. xl.
[65] *Ibid.*, p. xli.
[66] The story is certainly far removed from the "pure romance" of the situation, as portrayed by Rumer Godden: "the charming Mubarika who came to the emperor in a romantic way." Rumer Godden, *Gulbadan: Portrait of a Rose Princess at the Mughal Court* (London, 1980), p. 28.
[67] Beveridge, *Humayun*, Introduction, p. 2.

Babur invited members of the lineage of Timur and Chingiz Khan to share the benefits of his "sovereignty [*dawlat*] in Hindustan."[68]

A year after this invitation, Maham Begum and her six-year-old daughter Gulbadan (whose charge Maham had taken from Dildar Begum) also arrived from Kabul. Several decades later, Gulbadan provided an intimate portrayal of Maham's arrival. She writes that at evening-prayer time some-one went and informed Babur that he had just passed Maham Begum on the road, four miles out. "My Royal father did not wait for a horse to be saddled but set out on foot," Gulbadan reconstructs the moment: "he met her near the house of Maham's *nanacha* [*nanahcheh*]. She wished to alight, but he would not wait, and fell into her train and walked to his own house."[69] Note the keenness expressed by the *padshah* at Maham's arrival in the Begum's rendering. Is the depiction of Babur's reaction somewhat akin to his longing for Baburi, and the author's elevation of this moment to a special one?

The depiction of Babur's haste, rushing out "on foot" to receive Maham, is significant for several reasons. A record of such open behavior is unusual. Much more is to be found on the intimate relationship between Babur and Maham Begum in Gulbadan's *Ahval*. Interestingly, Gulbadan's account finds no place for a description of any such affection of the *padshah* for his other wives. These wives find a place in many contemporary writings, but merely as a statistical presence. In Gulbadan's memoir, there is considerable discussion of their emotional entanglements with other younger and older Mughal men and women. There is no indication at all, however, of the nature of the emotional bond between the rest of them and Babur. It is all the more notable therefore that Gulbadan has so much to say about Babur's special affection for Maham.

When Maham arrived in Hindustan, she was not a newly wedded wife of Babur.[70] At this time, Babur was forty-five years old, which may be con-sidered an advanced age, given both the average life expectancy at the time, and the fact that he had become the ruler of the principality of Farghaneh at the age of eleven-and-a-half. Note that Babur's first marriage took place in 1499 when he was sixteen. Other matrimonial alliances followed in quick succession. Maham and Babur were married in 1506 when Babur visited Herat. Therefore in 1527, when Babur rushed to receive Maham – at the age of forty-five – his emotional display has to be recognized as being quite

---

[68] *Ibid.*, p. 97; Gulbadan, *Ahval*, fol. 11a. *Dawlat* has many other connotations: felicity, victory, and wealth, and dominion (Steingass, *Persian*, s.v. "dawlat").

[69] Beveridge, *Humayun*, pp. 100–101; Gulbadan, *Ahval*, fol. 14a. *Nanahcheh* is a diminutive form of *naneh*, meaning an elderly female here. It is also suggestive of a person of the innermost circle or one of close affection (Beveridge, *Humayun*, p. 101, n. 1). The word *nanahcheh* occurs thrice in the *Ahval-i Humayun Badshah*, on fols. 14a, 18b, and 26a.

[70] For details of Maham Begum, see Beveridge, *Humayun*, Appendix A, "Maham Begam: *aka* and *akam* (lady and my lady)," pp. 256–258.

special. Gulbadan may be expected to depict the exalted status and influence of her "adoptive" mother, about whom she writes in an admiring fashion throughout. At the same time, Gulbadan's adulation of Maham Begum has to be seen as the honoring of a respected, senior wife. Likewise, her deferential writing about her father indexes her respect and honor for him, but her narrative also struggles to underline the context of his loneliness in Hindustan (which Babur himself alludes to repeatedly in the *Baburnama*). It is significant nonetheless that she constructs her appreciation of Babur in part through this valorizing of his reception of Maham.

The domestic speaks back: motherhood and wifehood

The preceding two sections have begun to trace the contours of the domestic life of the peripatetic Mughal kings, Babur and Humayun. Tracking the terms of address used by Babur and Humayun and their contemporaries, their descriptions, and their evocations, tells us a great deal about the domestic life they experienced and expected. The section on Babur's marriages provides instances to understand the degrees of association and assemblages of relationships in the king's domestic world. This section takes forward something about love, loyalty, and accountability, embodied by men and women. In all of this, women are projected as deeply entangled in the construction of the monarchy. This is a timely moment to think how the Mughal women were invested in the kings' construction of their world and their domestic life. Let us consider the "reply of the domestic," as it were.

Since senior women, especially mothers, are the most ubiquitous figures in the early Mughal chronicles, it is appropriate to begin by probing what constitutes the notion of Mughal motherhood, as well as the attendant notion of female seniority (including the frequent attribution of senior and junior statuses to royal women in the texts), and how senior status was projected in the records. What was involved in being a senior member of the domestic world – an "elder," with wisdom, status, and, importantly, authority? Considering these questions should allow us to witness how, alongside inhabiting scripted roles, women charted their own paths – even if these were largely mediated through the figure of the monarch.

A striking figure in the records is Maham Begum, wife of Babur and mother of Humayun. The narratives on Maham Begum enable us to explore a mother's engagement in the politics of marriage and reproduction, and through these her interests in monarchy. Encouraging younger women to produce children and endorsing birth was a central aspect of senior women's responsibility. The issue of births itself, as we have seen earlier, was tremendously vital to the Mughal world. But a mother's tasks did not stop at that.

Maham had taken charge of Gulbadan Banu Begum and Mirza Hindal from Dildar Begum, another wife of Babur. As a young mother, Maham Begum had worried about the loss of several of her children, who died in infancy. Her only surviving son was Humayun: this may explain her taking over of Gulbadan Banu Begum and Mirza Hindal from Dildar Begum. All this perhaps reinforced her urge to see that Humayun was not left without sons.[71]

But the production or the taking charge of (male) children was only a first step in a wife's ascendancy. The chronicles demonstrate that if the mother of a royal son had high status, the mother of the heir to the throne was even more privileged. We can see the concern for this high standing in Maham Begum's responses during the events of the summer of 1529, as Gulbadan Banu Begum reports these.

Humayun, who was in charge of Badakhshan at the time, heard that Babur was seriously ill. Humayun went to Kabul, met and conferred with his stepbrother, Mirza Kamran, and left the government of Badakhshan in charge of their other (ten-year-old) stepbrother, Mirza Hindal. Humayun then journeyed to Agra without informing his father. Babur was annoyed at Humayun's desertion of Badakhshan, for he felt this had put the city at risk. He wished Humayun to return; the latter argued, "he must go if ordered," but he "was not willing to leave his people again."[72] Whilst in Agra, Humayun was attacked by a serious illness, which led to Babur's "self-sacrifice" – as histories of the time portray it – to restore his son's life.[73]

Maham's statements at the time of Humayun's illness are indicative of her concerns, both as a mother and as the mother of the potential heir to the throne. According to Gulbadan, she said to Babur, "Do not be troubled about my son. You are a king. . . . You have other sons. I sorrow because I have only this one." To this, Babur replied: "Maham! although I have other sons, I love none as I love your Humayun. I crave that this cherished child may have his heart's desire and live long, and I desire the kingdom for him and not for the others, because he has not his equal in distinction."[74] It was consequent upon this, in Gulbadan's rendering, that Humayun became the *padshah* at Babur's death. According to other chroniclers, however, a lot more transpired in relation to the succession before Humayun's nomination.

[71] Beveridge, *Humayun*, pp. 112–113; Gulbadan, *Ahval*, fols. 21b–22a.
[72] Beveridge, *Humayun*, p. 23. Badakhshan was then restored to Sulayman Mirza, the heir to its throne. Sulayman Mirza's father, Mirza Khan, had died ten years ago, in 1519, just after Babur had taken Bajaur. The threat of the Uzbiks was imminent at the time, and Sulayman was too young and inexperienced to rule. Sulayman's grandmother Sultan Nigar Khanum, the maternal aunt of Babur, escorted the young *mirza* to Kabul. It was under these circumstances that Badakhshan was given to Humayun.
[73] See, for example, Gulbadan's discussion of this episode: Beveridge, *Humayun*, pp. 104–105 and p. 105n. Gulbadan, *Ahval*, fols. 16b–17b.
[74] Beveridge, *Humayun*, pp. 104–105; Gulbadan, *Ahval*, fol. 17a.

Nizam al-Din Ahmad writes in the *Tabaqat-i Akbari* that there were two other strong contenders to the throne of Hindustan at the death of Babur. One was a man called Khalifa or Nizam al-Din Barlas. His brother Junayd Barlas was married to Babur's half-sister Shahr Banu (daughter of his father 'Umar Shaykh Mirza and Umid *Aghacheh*). Khalifa and Babur were friends of long standing. The other man was Muhammad Mahdi Khvajeh, husband of Khanzadeh Begum, Babur's sister. According to Nizam al-Din Ahmad, Khalifa had plans of getting Muhammad Mahdi Khvajeh to supersede Humayun.[75] It is interesting to note that Babur had not sent for Humayun during his illness. Despite his alleged communication to Maham, it may be that he was still not confident that Humayun deserved the kingship. A letter written by Babur to Humayun in November 1528–29 is informative: "God willing, this is your time to risk your life and wield your sword. Do not fail to make the most of an opportunity that presents itself. Indolence and luxury do not suit kingship."[76]

As Babur lay dying, we are told how fretfully anxious he was for Hindal's coming,[77] perhaps because he was uncertain as to whom should succeed him? It is likely that Maham, a respectable senior mother, would have been aware of the jostling for position that took place while Babur lay ill. Maham's concern about Humayun's succession is clear. Humayun arrived "just when," as Beveridge puts it, "by a coincidence which Maham may have helped to bring about, his parents were talking of him."[78] What is hard to establish, in this instance, is the extent of her intervention and influence.

The succession of a son was an exceptional – and wonderful – dream. Long before that the first step on the ladder of success for a wife was the birth of a son. On the birth of children rested the future status of any wife. The concern with Mughal children is put to us in many ways in the records, but perhaps most fittingly in the listing of childless women, and dead children. Take a few examples that haunt the chronicles of the time: Barbul, Mihr-jan, Ishan Dawlat, and Faruq, all of whom died in infancy (children of Maham Begum and Babur); Ma'sumeh (same name as her mother) died at the time of her birth (daughter of Ma'sumeh Begum and Babur); Dildar Begum (wife of Babur) lost Alvar, the last of her five children who died in childhood; Bibi Mubarika Yusufzay and Zainab Sultan Begum (wives of Babur) died childless. Gulbadan reports that 'Aqiqeh Begum (daughter of Humayun and Bigeh Begum) died at the age of eight during the war of Chawsa between Humayun

---

[75] *Tabaqat-i Akbari*, II, pp. 41–44; see also Annette Beveridge's discussion of this tussle for succession in her notes in the *Baburnama*: Beveridge, *Baburnama*, pp. 702–711.

[76] Thackston, *Baburnama*, p. 741. This text is in Chaghatay Turki only; it is not available in Persian in Thackston's edition.

[77] Beveridge, *Humayun*, p. 106; Gulbadan, *Ahval*, fols. 17b–18a.

[78] Beveridge, *Humayun*, p. 23.

and Sher Shah.[79] Chand Bibi of Humayun's *haram*, seven months pregnant at the time, was also killed in Chawsa.[80]

The chronicling of the names of dead children, and childless women, is a potentially rich area for investigating the intricacies of attitudes towards children, and questions of kinship within the domain of the family. The place of the (dead) children in the construction of Mughal monarchy is clearly crucial. The few factual indications here are intended to invite reflections on this subject.[81]

Motherhood marked the inauguration of a new – senior – status, and with that the promise of a new life. Motherhood was a frequent attribute of the beneficent "seniors [*vali-ni 'matan*]" – indeed, the two notions appear closely related in many of the records. Yet they were obviously not exact equivalents. The different implications of motherhood and of seniority require examination. Besides motherhood, we need to look at age and experience, the status of mother of the heir to the throne, and the position of the favorite wife, as factors in the making of respected elders. Needless to say, these factors and their relative weight were far from being constant.

Maham's custody of the two children of Dildar Begum provides a rather unusual case of "adoption," and requires further reflection. I feel some hesitation in using the word "adoption" here: "taking charge" seems more fitting for a context where the biological and the guardian mothers were members of the same domestic community. In this context, moreover, it is also important to dispel ideas such as absolute dispossession for a mother who handed over her child. Nonetheless, there will sometimes have been indecision or even reluctance in this arrangement. This is not recorded in the instance under discussion. What we do know from Gulbadan is that Dildar lived with her son Hindal when she became a widow, and that Gulbadan herself was sent back to her at the age of ten.[82]

It is difficult to locate the grounds on which Maham justified the guardianship of the two children of Dildar Begum. Maham's especially elevated status

---

[79] Beveridge, *Humayun*, p. 136 and n. 3; Gulbadan, *Ahval*, fol. 33b. In the introduction to the translation of the *Ahval*, Beveridge says that 'Aqiqeh will have been about six at the time of her death. That seems incorrect. A little after Babur's death, Bigeh Begum came from Kabul and joined Humayun in Hindustan. Gulbadan reports that in a year's time (*ba'd az yek sal*), she had a daughter who was named 'Aqiqeh (Beveridge, *Humayun*, p. 112; Gulbadan, *Ahval*, fol. 22a). The rout at Chawsa took place in 1539. That should make 'Aqiqeh about eight at the time.

[80] Chand Bibi is mentioned as a "wife of low degree" by Annette Beveridge. Beveridge, *Humayun*, p. 31. I have found no other details of Chand Bibi.

[81] Veena Das has recently argued that although concern with childhood is not entirely absent in early anthropological literature, ethnographies of children and their agency have been rather scant. (Veena Das, "Wittgenstein and Anthropology," *Annual Review of Anthropology*, 27 (1998), pp. 171–185). Das's call to study the making of children and their subjectivities is important for historians as well, especially those thinking about kinship networks and the making of families.

[82] Beveridge, *Humayun*, pp. 10, 116; Gulbadan, *Ahval*, fol. 23b.

might provide part of the answer. I should stress that this high status can only be inferred from subsequent writing, primarily Gulbadan's memoir. In the *Ahval-i Humayun Badshah*, there are several indications of Maham and Babur's close relationship, demonstrable straightaway in Maham's engagement in different activities and questions that ostensibly concerned only the *padshah*. Her intervention in the matter of Humayun's succession points to her privileged position. Gulbadan records a more joyful moment of sharing between Maham and Babur at the time when Badakhshan was conferred on Humayun. Maham and Babur followed Humayun there, and "spent several days together."[83] In other affairs too, her participation and influence is projected as far more consequential than that of Babur's other wives.

Most of our inferences about Maham's status must remain speculative. Gulbadan's memoir, from where we obtain these unusual traces of intimacy and domestic politics, was written in Akbar's reign. Clearly Gulbadan wrote with the knowledge (hindsight) that Maham was the wife whose son succeeded to the throne. However that might be, it is important to see how exceptionally detailed and subtle Gulbadan's sketching is of Maham.

The relative positions of Dildar Begum and Maham Begum, as narrated in the contemporary accounts, tell us a great deal about the requirements for seniority and status in the early Mughal household. As regards Dildar Begum, Gulbadan suggests that it was only late in life that any of the privileges or prerogatives of seniority come to be associated with her. At one point in his conflict with Humayun, Kamran sought her out as an elder to be consulted, asking her advice on whether he should have the *khutba* read in his name. In that instance, according to Gulbadan, Dildar Begum referred him to Khanzadeh Begum on the premise that she was their "elder kinswoman, and oldest and highest" of them all.[84]

Khanzadeh Begum, sister of Babur, was "given" to Shiybani Khan Uzbik (although, as we have seen, some histories say she was "demanded" by the Khan) in an attempt to establish peace between the two great enemies. Her personal history, such as a first marriage with Shiybani Khan, and the fact of a son, Khurram Shah Sultan, from that marriage make her case aberrant. Her other two marriages, one to a Sayyid Hada, "a man of inferior rank," according to Beveridge, and then to one Mahdi Khvajeh, of Timurid lineage, acquire a rather impersonal color in the narratives.[85] Even in Gulbadan's detailed and varied account, Khanzadeh is consistently remembered in a solemn way: as a wise elder who continued to aid and support the Timurid-Mughals with her trusted wisdom, born of age. No suggestion of her frailties is ever made. I shall return to other details of Khanzadeh's story in the next section.

---

[83] Beveridge, *Humayun*, p. 92; Gulbadan, *Ahval*, fol. 8b.

[84] Beveridge, *Humayun*, p. 161; Gulbadan, *Ahval*, fol. 51b. The *khutba* was read in the name of a *padshah*; in this instance, the implication of the *khutba* would be the declaration of kingship in the name of Kamran.

[85] Beveridge, *Humayun*, Appendix A, "Khan-zada Begam *Miran-shahi*," p. 250.

The respect that Dildar and Khanzadeh acquired was one that came with age. This is a point that emerges repeatedly in the narratives. It was the senior generation that was revered, especially influential mothers, not the "favorite" wives. In this hierarchy of wise seniors, those who stand out are the sisters, aunts, as well as the older wives of the monarchs, and the mothers of their children: not so much the favorites or paramours.

Entailed in articulations of the modes of authority of the senior women are clear traces of an emphatically hierarchical domestic life. This is not to say that such relationships are out of the ordinary in the case of the Mughals: they might be said to be characteristic of nearly all pre-modern Islamic societies. The particularity of the peripatetic Mughal times is that alongside its fluid circumstances and shifting locations, its hierarchical structures were deeply ritualized. The various dimensions of such hierarchical relationships may be extrapolated from the chronicles of the time.

The following example comes from Gulbadan's description of Babur and Maham's stay in Agra. In addition to accentuating the agency of the mothers, it points to the place of other senior women. At the time, Gulbadan reports, Babur used to go and see his paternal aunts every Friday. On one of the days, it was very hot and Maham suggested to Babur, "the wind is very hot, indeed; how would it be if you did not go this one Friday? The begams would not be vexed." Babur replied: "Maham! It is astonishing that you should say such things! The daughters of Abu-sa'id Sultan Mirza, who have been deprived of father and brothers! If I do not cheer them, how will it be done?"[86]

It is noted in Gulbadan's account that, a few years later, Bigeh Begum made a similar complaint to Humayun. "For several days now," she said to Humayun, "you have been paying visits in this garden, and on no one day have you been to our house. Thorns have not been planted in the way to it. ... How long will you think it right to show all these disfavours to us helpless ones? We too have hearts...." Humayun later sent for the women. "We all went," says Gulbadan:

He said not a word, so everyone knew he was angry. Then after a little while he began: "Bibi [addressing Bigeh Begum], what ill-treatment at my hands did you complain of this morning? ... That was not the place to make a complaint. You all ... know that I have been to the quarters of the elder relations (*wali-u-n-ni 'matan*) of you all. ... It is a necessity laid on me to make them happy. Nevertheless, I am ashamed before them because I see them so rarely. ... I am an opium-eater. If there should be delay in my comings and goings, do not be angry with me. Rather, write me a letter, and say: 'Whether it please you to come or whether it please you not to come, we are content and are thankful to you'."[87]

---

[86] Beveridge, *Humayun*, p. 97; Gulbadan, *Ahval*, fol. 11b.
[87] Beveridge, *Humayun*, pp. 130–131; Gulbadan, *Ahval*, fol. 30a–30b.

There is a lot to be noted about the pecking order in the discussion over the question of Babur's and Humayun's visits to their senior relatives. In the hierarchical relationships that are refracted through the conversations above, senior women (mothers, aunts, and sisters) are shown to have exercised considerable control over younger women as well as men in the family. The management of both sexes is one of the important registers of the superior status of the older women in the texts of the time. The reported comments of Maham Begum, Babur, Bigeh Begum, and Humayun point to the complicated sets of relationships that had to be negotiated. The competing responsibilities of Babur and Humayun, on the one hand, and the (conflicting) desires of their wives, on the other, bring out remarkably well the tension that would have prevailed at many times. In reading these conversations, and the unease they embody, the reader also begins to grapple with the conception of wifehood in the Mughal world. The example of Maham Begum pointedly illustrates the two hierarchical levels of a mother and a wife: as Babur's preferred wife, Maham had expressed a desire to break his routine of visiting the elder relations each Friday; as a mother she exercised considerable control over the personal life of her son.[88]

The influential position of senior women manifests itself in other ways too in Gulbadan's fine description of their everyday activities. *Ahval-i Humayun Badshah* contains a small note on the activities of Maham Begum after the death of Babur – her allowance of daily food, and her part in the organization of feasts. Gulbadan takes care to record a number of specific occasions when big feasts occurred.[89]

Here is a note from Gulbadan on the arrangements of one feast given by Maham Begum:

a jewelled throne, ascended by four steps, and above it gold-embroidered hangings, and laid on it a cushion and pillows embroidered in gold. The covering of the pavilions and of the large audience tent was, inside, European brocade, and outside, Portuguese cloth. The tent-poles were gilded; that was very ornamental. (My Lady) had prepared a tent-lining and a *kannat* and *sar-i-kannat* of Gujrati cloth-of-gold, and a ewer for rose-water, and candlesticks, and drinking-vessels, and rose-water sprinklers – all of jewelled gold.[90]

During the preparations for this feast, Maham Begum ordered that common people (*mardum adami*) and soldiers (*sipahi*) also decorate their houses and make their quarters beautiful. Gulbadan says this was "an excellent and splendid feast."[91]

Both Maham Begum and Khanzadeh Begum planned feasts on numerous occasions. Khanzadeh Begum "gave everything she had collected" and

[88] Beveridge, *Humayun*, pp. 112–113; Gulbadan, *Ahval*, fols. 21b–22b.
[89] Beveridge, *Humayun*, pp. 117–129; Gulbadan, *Ahval*, fols. 24a–29b.
[90] Beveridge, *Humayun*, p. 113; Gulbadan, *Ahval*, fol. 22b.
[91] Beveridge, *Humayun*, p. 113; Gulbadan, *Ahval*, fol. 22b.

arranged a feast, Gulbadan notes, "such as had not been made for any other child of my royal father." This was to celebrate Mirza Hindal's wedding. "She planned it all and carried it all out," according to the memoirist.[92]

Alongside Mirza Hindal's wedding feast was also held the so-called feast in the *'Imarat-i tilasm* which commemorated Humayun's accession to the throne.[93] The latter was celebrated first; Khanzadeh Begum said: "the things for the Mystic Feast are also ready. Let us first celebrate this, and afterwards Mirza Hindal's."[94] Great attention was paid to every detail and to appropriate order; the order of presents, the seating arrangements, all formed crucial elements of the plan, indicating the importance of correct ways. "First there was a large octagonal room with an octagonal tank in the centre, and again, in the middle of the reservoir, an octagonal platform on which were spread Persian (*wilayati*) carpets."[95] A jeweled throne was given by Khanzadeh Begum and was placed in the forecourt of the house. A gold-embroidered *divan* was laid in front of it, upon which Humayun and Khanzadeh Begum sat together.[96] On Khanzadeh Begum's right sat her paternal aunts, the daughters of Sultan Abu Sayyid Mirza; on another cushion, the sisters of Babur.

On the day of the feast at the *'Imarat-i tilasm*, Humayun asked all the Begums and Mirzas to bring gifts. He made three lots from these. The first lot, called the share of the dominion (*hissiyeh dawlat*), went to the *mirza*s, chiefs, *vazir*s, and soldiers. The second heap, the share of good fortune (*hissiyeh sa'adat*) went to eminent and respectable theologians, religious men, ascetics, dervishes, and devotees. The last part was called the portion of pleasure (*hissiyeh murad*). This apportioning, very much in keeping with the division of the peoples of the kingdom that Khvandamir talks about, suggests the ritual importance of different groups of people in the feasts. Some of these gifts were also taken to the Begums, the *ashrafi*s out of which were scattered before the beneficent seniors (the *vali-ni 'matan*), and then among the others present at the entertainment. After this feast, came Mirza Hindal's wedding feast. Some of the Begums went away. Some of them now sat on the *padshah*'s left, on the embroidered *divan*s, Gulbadan Begum among them. Other women, the wives of various *amir*s, were also present at the marriage feast.[97]

Gulbadan's descriptions point to the significance of the organization of these feasts by the older women. The arrangements and execution of

[92] Beveridge, *Humayun*, p. 128; Gulbadan, *Ahval*, fol. 29a. For details of these feasts, see Beveridge, *Humayun*, pp. 117–126; Gulbadan, *Ahval*, fols. 24a–28b.

[93] *'Imarat-i tilasm*, Beveridge explains, is an epithet from astrological phraseology. See Beveridge, *Humayun*, p. 118, n. 1. Khvandamir in his *Qanun-i Humayuni* also discusses the building *'imarat-i tilasm*.

[94] Beveridge, *Humayun*, p. 118; Gulbadan, *Ahval*, fol. 24a.

[95] Beveridge, *Humayun*, p. 118; Gulbadan, *Ahval*, fol. 24a.

[96] Humayun's mother, Maham Begum, had passed away some time before the feast. This feast was organized at the end of the mourning. Beveridge, *Humayun*, p. 116; Gulbadan, *Ahval*, fol. 23b.

[97] Beveridge, *Humayun*, p. 121; Gulbadan, *Ahval*, fol. 25b.

celebrations by senior Mughal women is yet another demonstration of the ritualized hierarchy as *the* principle of the Mughal domestic universe. Other aspects of these feasts are illuminating as well. The ritual aspect is significant: who organizes feasts, who sits where during the festivity, who comes, who goes, the sensuous symbols associated with the arrangements, and so on. What is crucial in relation to these feasts, as Geertz noted in another context, is "the whole structure ... of which they are a part and in terms of which they get their meaning."[98]

In the above descriptions, the sensuous symbols that Gulbadan lists are notable: tent-linings, Gujarati cloth-of-gold, ewers for rose-water, candle-sticks, drinking-vessels, and rose-water sprinklers – "all of jewelled gold" – in the first feast. A jeweled throne, a gold-embroidered *divan*, and cushions in the other two. These are very explicit choices of material for discussion. The continual reference to materials of gold has its own logic; it is a signaling of the prosperity of the monarchy. Note especially the splendor of the octagonal room in Gulbadan's description: the jeweled throne, the wonderful strings of pearls, glass globes, all speaking of the rich materiality of the court in Hindustan. More importantly, here is an icon through which ideas about seniority itself might be anticipated: use of special kinds of stuff to be confined to senior people – so the king (senior by dint of his majesty) and the senior lady (senior by dint of her generation) sat together on the special *divan*. For the paternal aunts of Khanzadeh Begum, who sat on her right, cushions were brought.

It was only the senior women of means that organized the feasts. Even kings were not privy to this activity. And since the seniors were the spokes-women for correct deportment more generally, in this instance too, they determined in what order the feasts would take place (Humayun's to be celebrated before Hindal's), and what might be the most proper contribution at the time of the festivity (for example, a jeweled throne). In this order of hierarchical relationships, other symbols are also worthy of notice. Particularly in the examples above, the moment of the *ashrafis* being scattered before the beneficent seniors (the *vali-ni 'matan*) before the gifts were taken to other Begums is a significant one. However, there were other aspects to seniority and the privileges that it brought, which I shall consider below.

Brokering peace: senior women and contemporary politics

There is one area in which senior Mughal women are recorded ubiquitously as having played a central part: in the affairs of peace-making. In spite of a great deal of interest in the wars of the period, this concomitant politics of con-ciliation has attracted little attention. In the narratives of the time, moments

---

[98] Clifford Geertz, *Negara: The Theatre State in Nineteenth-Century Bali* (Princeton, 1980), p. 103.

of brokering peace by senior Mughal women suggest their complex engagement in the circulation of power, as agents by virtue of age/generation (and
their supposedly accompanying virtues of wisdom) or through a nomination to
the position of intermediary (or broker or peace-maker) by a royal male or
another senior woman. Sometimes the politics of peace-making also worked
in the names of the senior women – "for their sake" as it were – but such
episodes are not very common in the records.

An early example of this kind comes from Babur's Kabul period. Babur
was on his way back to Kabul from Khurasan (1506) after paying condolences to the sons of Sultan Husain Mirza who had recently passed away.
While on his way, he heard that Mirza Khan (a son of Babur's paternal uncle,
Mahmud, and his maternal aunt, Sultan Nigar Khanum) and Mirza
Muhammad Husain Gurakan (married to Khub Nigar, sister of Babur's
mother) had rebelled. Babur sent comforting notes to his friends holding
the fort in Kabul and told them he would be with them soon. He organized the
details of an attack on the rebels that was to be launched jointly with his
kinsmen in Kabul. However, Babur got to Kabul earlier than expected, and
fought and defeated the rebels even before his kinsmen came out to join him.
Subsequently, "Mirza Khan hid himself in his mother's house," Gulbadan
reports (the mirza's mother was Babur's maternal aunt). And Mirza
Muhammad Husain went to his wife's house (she was Babur's younger
maternal aunt). "He [Muhammad Husain] flung himself down on a carpet,
and in fear of his life cried to a servant, 'Fasten it up!'" The *padshah*'s people
heard of this. They took Muhammad Husain out of the carpet and brought
him to Babur. In the end, Gulbadan tells us, Babur forgave the mirzas their
offences, "for the sake of his aunts [*bikhatir-i khalhaye*]."[99]

The direct intervention of Babur's aunts is not reported in this episode. But
even rebels, it is suggested, could be forgiven in the name of the senior
females: "for the sake of the aunts." Babur says in the *Baburnama*, "If I had
had him ripped to pieces for undertaking such heinous and shameful
actions ... it would have been proper." He adds, however, "since there were
family connections, his sons and daughters being my own aunt Khub Nigar
Khanim's children, I kept these claims in mind and let him go free."[100]

Although the dissension of Mirza Khan and Mirza Muhammad Husain
was a threat to Babur's unsteady position, both he and Gulbadan suggest
how kinship solidarity and respect for elders had its place in the king's
decisions. Harmonious relations in this instance were established largely

---

[99] Beveridge, *Humayun*, p. 89; cf. Gulbadan, *Ahval*, fol. 6a; *Akbarnama*, I, pp. 230–233; British
Library, MS Or. 3714, fol. 279b: "Muhammad Husain Mirza brought before Babur and
laughing courtiers in the bedroll in which he tried to hide." (Description of the illustration as
given in Norah M. Titley, *Miniatures from Persian Manuscripts: A Catalogue and Subject
Index of Paintings from Persia, India, and Turkey in the British Library and the British
Museum*; London, 1977, p. 123.)
[100] Thackston, *Baburnama*, p. 423; Beveridge, *Baburnama*, p. 319.

through the reference to the revered status of senior women in both Babur's and Gulbadan's accounts. Although the names of the elder women clearly carried great authority, we cannot discount the possibility that the invocation of the names of the seniors was in fact a political judgment about the safest policy at this time.

There is another dimension of brokering peace in the records of the time: women offering themselves or being offered for political reconciliation. The following instance, referred to briefly earlier, comes from 1500–01 when the conflict between Babur and the Uzbiks was at its most intense. For six months Shiybani Khan Uzbik besieged Babur in Samarqand. None of his powerful relatives, such as his paternal uncles, Sultan Husain Mirza Bayqura, the ruler of Khurasan nor Sultan Mahmud Khan, his maternal uncle who ruled in Kashghar, sent him help (Babur especially complains against these two men). This was the time when Shiybani Khan sent a message to Babur, "If you would marry your sister Khanzada Begam to me, there might be peace and a lasting alliance between us." According to Gulbadan, "at length it had to be done; he gave the begam to the khan, and came out himself (from Samarqand) . . . in this plight, unarmed, and relying on God, he went towards the lands of Badakhshan . . . and Kabul."[101]

This is the Begum's version of the event. The *Baburnama* has a slightly different rendition of the affair. According to Babur, "The second time I took Samarkand . . . I went and held the fortress for five months. The padishahs and begs from the surrounding territories gave me no aid or assistance whatsoever. . . . During that interregnum Khanzada Begim fell captive to Muhammad Shaybani Khan."[102] Babur's words, especially *tushti* (fell), imply that Khanzadeh became part of Shiybani's share of the division of captives.[103] In a footnote in volume I of the *Akbaranama*, Henry Beveridge writes that according to the *Shiybani-nama*, Khanzadeh's marriage with Shiybani Khan was a "love-match." He also suggests the probability that "Babur has not mentioned the whole of the circumstances and that her [Khanzadeh] being left behind was a part of Babur's agreement with Shaibani."[104]

This episode is laden with poignant meaning, whatever version we accept. The "sacrifice" of Khanzadeh in Gulbadan's memoir, and in other contemporary literature, is a striking example of how a sister and a city were both relinquished to gain peace in a situation of incessant warfare. In Babur's rendition, the loss of a city and sister is narrated simultaneously, so entwined with each other that it might not be an exaggeration to say that they are experienced as one. The mutuality of this loss (of sister and the city) makes for a despondent moment in the *Baburnama*.

[101] Beveridge, *Humayun*, p. 85; Gulbadan, *Ahval*, fol. 3b.
[102] Thackston, *Baburnama*, p. 16; Beveridge, *Baburnama*, pp. 17–18.
[103] Beveridge, *Baburnama*, p. 18, n. 2.   [104] *Akbarnama*, I, pp. 221–222, n. 3.

Such capture and bartering away in warfare was the fate of many other women in the warfare of the times. Babur's half-sister Yadgar Sultan Begum (daughter of ʿUmar Shaykh Mirza and Agha Sultan Agacheh) had "fallen to the share of" Hamzeh Sultan Uzbik's son ʿAbdul Latif when Shiybani Khan had defeated her kinsmen near Akhsi.[105] Then Babur's maternal aunt Mihr Nigar Khanum also "fell" to Shiybani Khan.[106] Mihr-ban, half-sister of Babur, was also captured on one of the occasions when Babur lost to the Uzbiks.[107] Also Kabuli Begum, a Miranshahi Timurid, was abandoned by her husband Badiʿ-uz-zaman Bayqura (nephew of Babur), and later captured by Shiybani Khan.[108] Bigeh Begum, Humayun's wife, was captured by Sher Shah at the battle of Chawsa. It was here that she lost her infant daughter ʿAqiqeh.[109]

As far as Khanzadeh Begum is concerned, any agency that she might have displayed in this negotiation (if negotiation occurred) is not documented. Yet the eminent position that Khanzadeh Begum acquired subsequently is clear from the mode of address adopted for her, as well as several later comments and references in the contemporary texts. Khanzadeh Begum came back from Shiybani Khan ten years after the marriage, when the Khan was defeated by Shah Ismaʿil Safavid in 1510. Yadgar Sultan Begum also returned to the Mughal camp at this time. Khanzadeh was thereafter held in high esteem. Gulbadan's constant style of address to Khanzadeh – "my dearest lady (*aka-janam*)", "my oldest paternal aunt and my royal father's eldest sister"[110] – is one sign of the affection and the respect she commanded. Interestingly, the records do not indicate anything like such a high status for Yadgar Sultan Begum.

The privileged status of Khanzadeh Begum, despite something of a similarity in her and Yadgar Sultan Begum's captivity, may have to do with the difference in their ages. In 1501 when Khanzadeh fell to Shiybani's horde of captives, she was twenty-three. She came back ten years later, now advanced in years, "elderly" given the life expectancy of the time. Yadgar Sultan, on the other hand, was captured at the age of ten (in 1503). She came back eight years later (1511), at the same time as Khanzadeh, after Babur's successes at Khutlan and Hissar.[111] However, she was young compared to Khanzadeh Begum, and the episode of her capture may for this reason perhaps not have figured so centrally in the recall of her life.

---

[105] Beveridge, *Baburnama*, p. 356. The above details are taken from the translator's notes on the study of the sources that help reconstruct the missing years, 1508–19 in the *Baburnama*.

[106] Thackston, *Baburnama*, p. 20; Beveridge, *Baburnama*, p. 21.

[107] Babur later sent a *divan* to Mihr-ban's son Pulad that contained a verse on its back that seemed to have been addressed to his sister through her son. This is one of the premises for Annette Beveridge to speak of the relationship between Babur and Mihr-ban; Beveridge, *Baburnama*, p. 402, nn. 2 and 3, p. 632, n. 3.

[108] Beveridge, *Baburnama*, Index I, p. 767.

[109] Beveridge, *Humayun*, p. 112, n. 5; Appendix XXXV, p. 218, "Bega [*Haji*] Begam (?) *Begchik* Mughal." Bigeh Begum was returned later in safety to Humayun, escorted by Sher Shah's general Khvas Khan.

[110] Beveridge, *Humayun*, p. 103; Gulbadan, *Ahval*, fol. 15b.

[111] Beveridge, *Humayun*, Appendix A, p. 294, "Yadgar-sultan Begam *Miran-shahi*."

There is another point that needs to be borne in mind in relation to the captured women. It may be that captured, and then "recovered," women were not stigmatized in the way they have been in more recent times. The eventual return of Khanzadeh Begum and Yadgar Sultan Begum provide extraordinary examples of the ready acceptance, and in Khanzadeh's case even elevation, of "recovered" women who had made a sacrifice – or been sacrificed – for the Mughal cause. The difference from the (predominant) response to a woman's rape, loss of chastity or honor in our own age is remarkable.[112] When Khanzadeh Begum and Yadgar Begum returned, they probably came back to what was relatively easily reestablished as their "home." Once back, it is recorded, they went about doing tasks and taking on responsibilities suitable to their age and status. And Khanzadeh's seniority may be the reason why her activities were more readily recorded by contemporary chroniclers. This is not unusual, since we find continual deference to such senior women in the records of the time.

With Khanzadeh Begum's return came renewed hope of friendship and support from the Persian Shah. Khanzadeh came to Qunduz under the protection of Shah Isma'il Safavid, after the death in the battle of Marv of her successive husbands, Shiybani Khan as well as Sayyid Hada. The events of the years 1508–19 are missing in the Baburnama. Based upon other contemporary sources, Annette Beveridge remarks that Khanzadeh Begum came back with "an envoy from Isma'il proffering friendship, [and] civilities calculated to arouse a hope of Persian help in Babur. To acknowledge his courtesies, Babur sent Mirza Khan with thanks and gifts ... that Mirza also conveyed protestations of good faith and a request for military assistance. He was well received and his request for help was granted."[113] Note the tying together of an anticipation of the restoration of lost territory to the homecoming of a sister, akin to the structures of loss – loss of a sister and a city (land and people) – remarked upon earlier.

A symbolic representation of Khanzadeh's power and the respect that she commanded as a senior woman may be seen in an illustration from the British Library Baburnama, "Babur Reunited with his Sister after a Ten-Year Separation" (1493) (Plate 1).[114] Though drawn up much later, in the atelier

---

[112] For a recent discussion of the question of captured women during one example of "modern" political strife, see Gyanendra Pandey, Remembering Partition: Violence, Nationalism and History in India (Cambridge, 2001); Urvashi Butalia, The Other Side of Silence: Voices from the Partition of India (Delhi, 1998); Ritu Menon and Kamla Bhasin, Borders and Boundaries: Women in India's Partition (Delhi, 1998); Veena Das, Critical Events: An Anthropological Perspective on Contemporary India (New Delhi, 1995), especially ch. 3.

[113] Beveridge, Baburnama, p. 352. Information taken from Beveridge's notes in relation to the ten missing years in the Baburnama.

[114] British Library, MS Or. 3714. fol. 13b; Titley, Miniatures, p. 122. The date of the folio, as given in Titley's description is 1493. This is incorrect because Babur and Khanzadeh met after a ten-year separation in 1510 (Beveridge, Baburnama, pp. 18 and 352). For a similar representation of women in position of authority, compare, "Babur visiting the Begams at Herat in Sultan Husain Baikara Mirza's college at his mausoleum (1506)," British Library, MS Or. 3714, fol. 256b; Titley, Miniatures, p. 123.

Plate 1: "Babur Reunited with his Sister after a Ten-Year Separation"

of Akbar in 1590, the folio is significant for its depiction of Khanzadeh Begum. The interesting point about this miniature, which portrays a time when Khanzadeh Begum returned to Qunduz and joined Babur after a ten-year separation,[115] is that it shows Khanzadeh Begum in a clear mode of authority. The gesture of her hand is royal and imperious. Far from any stigma, or question mark attaching to the status of this returned relative, she is the main focus of the cast and is represented in a commanding position.

If Khanzadeh Begum's episode looks like a case of circuitous and indirect arbitration in Mughal matters, there are other examples of what might be called express arbitration by Mughal women. One is Sultan Nigar Khanum, Babur's maternal aunt's ushering of Mirza Sulayman, her grandson, to Kabul during a crisis precipitated by the death of his father.

In 1519, Babur had taken Bajur, and then set out for Kabul. He received a letter from Badakhshan saying, "Mirza Khan is dead; Mirza Sulaiman is young; the Uzbegs are near; take thought for this kingdom lest (which God forbid) Badakhshan should be lost."[116] The young Mirza Sulayman's grandmother, Sultan Nigar Khanum, brought Sulayman to Kabul immediately after this. Gulbadan adds cryptically, "Agreeably to this petition and their wish, the Emperor assigned to Mirza Sulaiman the lands and inheritance which had been his father's, and he gave Badakhshan to Mirza Humayun."[117]

The activities of senior women are reported even more frequently in the time of Humayun.[118] The chronicles of his time are full of matters of dissension between the stepbrothers of the *padshah* and examples of the four brothers soliciting advice from their women elders.[119] Here is an example from a difficult moment in Humayun's life. After the death of Babur, Humayun allotted Kabul and Qandahar to Mirza Kamran, Sambhal to Mirza 'Askari, and Alwar to Mirza Hindal. However, the squabble for territory and conspiratorial infighting continued between the brothers. This tussle was complicated by Sher Shah's threatening presence in Hindustan. The situation became very much worse around the autumn of 1541 when Humayun was almost driven out of Hindustan. At this time, Mirza Hindal received a letter from one Qaracheh Khan, governor of Qandahar, stating that he had long

---

[115] For a description of this meeting, see Beveridge, *Baburnama*, p. 352.

[116] Beveridge, *Humayun*, p. 92; Gulbadan, *Ahval*, fol. 8a.

[117] Beveridge, *Humayun*, p. 92; Gulbadan, *Ahval*, fol. 8a–8b. On p. 92, n. 6, of *Humayun*, Sultan Nigar-Khanum is referred to as Mirza Sulayman's mother. This is corrected by Beveridge in *Baburnama*, p. 433, n. 1.

[118] Annette Beveridge calls these senior women "ambassadors of peace," a phrase that hardly captures the contemporary sensibilities. "Ambassadors of peace" as a title accords these women a clear-cut position of power, which as we have seen, is not likely to be feasible in the Timurid-Mughal context of multiple layers of authority (Beveridge, *Humayun*, p. 20).

[119] See a discussion of Khanzadeh Begum's intervention on behalf of Mirza Kamran, in Saksena, "Memoirs," p. 84. Bayazid also records Khanzadeh Begum's counsel to Mirza 'Askari; Saksena, "Memoirs," p. 86. The role of Khanzadeh Begum is discussed by Abu-l Fazl as well; *Akbarnama*, I, pp. 462, 467–468.

been near Bhakkar and during the whole time Shah Husain Mirza had displayed no good will. The letter requested Humayun to go to Qandahar: if this could not be done, Hindal should go. As Humayun's arrival was delayed, Hindal went and Qaracheh Khan gave him the town of Qandahar.[120] According to Gulbadan, Kamran now urged 'Askari to work with him to take Qandahar away from Hindal. Through all of this Humayun's position grew weaker.

On hearing of these happenings, Humayun approached Khanzadeh Begum, and requested her to go to Qandahar to advise Mirza Hindal and Mirza Kamran that since the threat of the Uzbiks and Turkmans was great, it was necessary to maintain unity among themselves. Khanzadeh Begum traveled from Jun to Qandahar, and Kamran arrived there from Kabul. Mirza Kamran urged Khanzadeh Begum to have the *khutba* read in his name. He had earlier written to Hindal's mother (and his stepmother) Dildar Begum, who suggested he asked Khanzadeh Begum, their elder kinswoman, "the truth about the *khutba* [*haqiqat-i khutbeh*]." When Kamran finally spoke with Khanzadeh Begum, she advised him thus: "as his Majesty *Firdaus-makani* [Babur] decided it and gave his throne to the Emperor Humayun, and as you, all of you, have read the *khutba* in his name till now, so now regard him as your superior and remain in obedience to him."[121] A telling instance of the centrality of women in the process of negotiation and promotion of Mughal kings.

To return to the question of the *khutba*, it is reported that Mirza Kamran insisted on having the *khutba* read in his name. He tried to resolve the issue by saying that the king was far away. "Read the *khutba* in my name and when he comes back, read it in his."[122] The *khutba* was read, whether with Khanzadeh's approval or not, we are not told. Kamran promised to give Qandahar to Mirza 'Askari and Ghazni to Mirza Hindal as part of the new arrangement. The conflict between Humayun and Kamran, however, was not resolved until much later when Humayun came back from Persia after gaining support from Shah Tahmasb.

I shall take one more example from Gulbadan to consider the projection of the power of senior women in the Mughal domestic world. This too comes from the unstable period in Humayun's life immediately before the rout at Chawsa, the battle where Bigeh (or Haji) Begum was captured. The episode is instructive for its portrayal of the constantly shifting familial alliances

---

[120] Beveridge, *Humayun*, p. 160; Gulbadan, *Ahval*, fol. 50b. Among the many reasons why Shah Husain Arghun was ill-disposed towards Humayun, one was of long standing: Babur had dispossessed the Arghuns from Kabul and Qandahar. He had also given in marriage to his foster brother Qasim, an Arghun woman, Mah-chuchak, the daughter of Muqim Mirza. This was a misalliance according to the Arghuns because it was forced and the bride was part of the "spoil[s] of battle"; Beveridge, *Humayun*, p. 36; see *Ibid.* for more details on the rivalry between the Timurids and the Arghuns.

[121] Beveridge, *Humayun*, p. 161; Gulbadan, *Ahval*, fol. 51b; see also *Akbarnama*, I, pp. 463–470.

[122] Beveridge, *Humayun*, p. 162; Gulbadan, *Ahval*, fol. 51b.

amongst the four brothers. Around 1537, just before the rout at Chawsa, Hindal rebelled and had the *khutba* read in his name.[123] Then on his behalf, Nur al-Din Muhammad, a son-in-law of Babur and grandson of Sultan Husain Bayqura, murdered Shaykh Bahlul, a close associate of Humayun's. Annette Beveridge comments on the motive of this murder saying this was an attempt to "place the death as an impassable barrier between the royal brothers."[124]

Humayun, then at Gaur, promptly set out for Agra. It was on his way back that the battle of Chawsa took place in which Humayun lost many of his kith and kin, including some of the women in his entourage and a little daughter, 'Aqiqeh. Gulbadan records an important discussion that took place between Humayun and Dildar Begum after the episode. There were apparently others present at the time of this conversation, including Gulbadan, Afghani Aghacheh, Gulnar Aghacheh, Nargul Aghacheh and an unnamed nurse of Gulbadan. Humayun, it seems, said to Dildar Begum that there was no anger in his heart, adding that Hindal was his strength and the might of his arm: "What was to be has been!"[125] He discussed with her the next step that he might take. Then he told Gulbadan to fetch her brother. Dildar Begum intervened at this point and suggested that she herself would go to get Hindal, instead of Gulbadan, who was very young. (In 1578, a prince of six was designated to escort a group of royal women, led by Gulbadan Begum, up the shore before they set off for the *hajj*! I shall return to this episode in the chapter on Akbar's *haram*.) Dildar Begum went and escorted Hindal back from Alwar and the latter paid his respects to Humayun.[126]

It is reported in the *Akbarnama* that after Shaykh Bahlul was murdered, and Hindal had had the *khutba* read in his name, he also went to see his mother, Dildar Begum. The reported exchange between the two is worth citing. On his arrival, Hindal found that Dildar Begum had a blue cloth over her breast. He asked her, "What kind of dress is that [which] you have donned at such a time of rejoicing?" She replied: "Why do you regard me? I am wearing mourning for you [*Kabud*, the blue cloth, a sign of mourning]; you are young [nineteen] and have, from the instigation of irreflecting sedition-mongers, lost the true way; you have girded your loins for your own destruction."[127]

These "imagined" conversations are rich with inflections of the sensibilities of the time. They say something about the reinforcing of "correct" deportment. Be it in war or victory, let the victorious be one's son, hierarchies of kinship had their own rules. And the spirit of camaraderie was to be expressed in keeping with these rules. Indeed, sometimes even words were not necessary; *kabuds* would be enough.

[123] Beveridge, *Humayun*, pp. 136–137; Gulbadan, *Ahval*, fols. 33b–34a; *Akbarnama*, I, p. 338.
[124] Beveridge, *Humayun*, p. 30.   [125] Beveridge, *Humayun*, p. 139; Gulbadan, *Ahval*, fol. 35a.
[126] *Ibid.*   [127] *Akbarnama*, I, p. 339 and n. 1.

It might be useful to conclude this section by referring briefly to the contemporary Safavid example of Shahzadeh Sultanam, the sister of Shah Tahmasb. I pointed out in the previous chapter that after a long combat with Sher Shah, Humayun left Hindustan and journeyed to reach the dominion of the Persian Shah. According to Sukumar Ray, the interaction between Shah Tahmasb and Humayun was fairly contentious, to begin with, and several sources indicate that Shah Tahmasb even intended to put Humayun to death.[128] His sister Sultanam Begum apparently dissuaded him from doing so. She is said to have rebuked her brother, saying that he was already surrounded on all sides by enemies – Uzbiks, Circassians, Europeans. By injuring Humayun, she pointed out, he would only create more rivals. Some other chronicles depict Sultanam Begum pleading to her brother and imploring him "not to be guided by self-seeking persons" and to give whatever assistance he could to Humayun.[129] The chronicles suggest unanimously that much changed thereafter in the Shah's outlook towards Humayun: the famous hospitality and help that he then extended towards his peer is exuberantly recorded in almost all the histories of the time. As the *Akbarnama* puts it, the interview between Humayun and Shah Tahmasb in July 1544 was one in which "all conditions of reverence and veneration were fulfilled."[130] The story about his sister's advice as marking the turning point suggests at least that such examples were conceivable, if not always documented.[131]

Concluding thoughts

Where was the *haram* in a peripatetic world? In early Mughal domestic life, everyday activities were constructed in ways that make it difficult to tie them exclusively to any strict, well-defined domain such as the *haram*, the family, or private life – terms and descriptions that have been treated so far as substitutes for the entire world of domestic affairs in the Mughal context. The core of the domestic cannot be encircled at all. I should add that the limits of the domestic life in the context of Babur and Humayun's peripatetic lives are necessarily even more in flux, more fluid and indefinable, than in the later more settled times of an Akbar or a Jahangir.

Our understanding of family or private life today centers on a notion of a distinct private sphere where the state and the outside world have a minimal presence. These terms, and especially the notion of the family, suggesting kinship along exclusively reproductive lines, bring to mind ready-made ideas

---

[128] Ray, *Humayun in Persia*, p. 33.   [129] *Ibid.*, p. 34.   [130] *Akbarnama*, I, p. 437.

[131] For a detailed discussion of royal women in the Safavid times, see Babayan, "'Aqa'id al-Nisa," and Maria Szuppe, "The 'Jewels of Wonder': Learned Ladies and Princess Politicians in the Provinces of Early Safavid Iran," in Hambly (ed.), *Women in the Medieval Islamic World*. For questions of sovereignty in relation to imperial women in Ottoman Turkey, see Peirce, *Imperial Harem*. I turn to a comparative discussion of the domestic lives of the Mughal, Ottoman, and Safavid royalty in the conclusion to this book.

of home and intimate hearth, of a well-demarcated domain of comfort and retreat from the world, a secure cocoon for the protection of women, the satisfaction of men, and the upbringing of children – all suggesting small units of almost natural affinity, sharply separated from organized public affairs.

In the Mughal domestic world of the time of Babur and Humayun, everyday activities went hand in hand with "historic" events in ways that make it difficult to label them as matters of state, or of exclusive public activity or private interest. The domestic is present in many intersecting spaces, many intersecting activities, and not least in the intersecting participation of many different kinds of men and women. Women and men went to war, 'Aqiqeh Begum disappeared "in that first interregnum [*fitrat*]" to take an example;[132] Bigeh Begum was captured during the battle at Chawsa; Khanzadeh Begum extended her advice to Humayun and Mirza Kamran regarding matters of the declaration of kingship; and of course men and women rejoiced together in feasts and ceremonies, and mourned together at deaths and losses.

Early Mughal women were, like their male counterparts, highly homosocial in character. They lived in intricate and varied assemblages, usually comprising other women. They figure far less commonly in the communities of men that we have described in the previous chapter. The detail of the women's world is much harder to extricate from the records; predictably, there is a persistent silence in relation to their everyday life. Nonetheless, they appear every now and then in the (male) narratives. In the main, they are presented as being deeply invested in the kings' construction of an imperial vision, secondary players in the enhancement of genealogical connections.

In the projection of the homosocial communities of women, however, it is worth noting how frequently the men appear in the narratives; whether it is the king's visit to senior women, or the celebration of feasts, the king surfaces repeatedly. In that sense the early Mughal domestic world continually negotiates, and revolves around, the presence of the monarch. For heuristic purposes, I have marked out a domain of early Mughal domestic life, where women are visible as major actors, as if it were separate from the domain of the court. Yet, according to the records of the time, these women had to contend unceasingly with the figure of the king. Quite often in this process the king becomes larger than life, and the women – even seniors – are rendered "invisible."

Several other points about the domestic life of the peripatetic Mughals need to be underscored. In this world (as in any other) there were ambitions and tensions, solidarities and conflicts. But there were also assigned roles and duties, which all members, royal or not, had to learn. Strict notions of "service" went together with a strong memory of Chingizid-Timurid links. This was a domestic world with prescribed codes of conduct that were informed by a larger understanding of honor and duty, practiced by the

---

[132] Beveridge, *Humayun*, p. 143; Gulbadan, *Ahval*, fol. 38a.

*padshah*s and those around them. We have delineated in the previous chapter details of the ways and regulations of the forefathers (Chingiz Khan and Timur), expected methods of conduct and how these were enforced. The structures and relationships of the domestic life enforce this concern with tradition, as well as the practical conditions of early Mughal life.

A good deal of this would change as the Mughal empire in India came to be more firmly established. Stone palaces appeared; major princesses and queens came to have their own separate apartments. With all this, the sanctity and invisibility of the *haram* increased, and the women's quarters came to be more protected from the outside world. Yet the domestic world could never be fully domesticated, or deprived of its say in political affairs, as we shall see in a later chapter on Akbar's *haram*.

CHAPTER 6

Settled, sacred and all-powerful: the new regime under Akbar

In the received histories of the Mughal rule, Babur and Humayun are passed over rather quickly, although the institutions and symbolism of Mughal rule as it was developed in later times are read back even into their reigns. Yet the proposition that the Mughal "empire" as we know it today came into being in Akbar's time needs to be qualified in at least two ways. First: it could hardly be the case that the construction of Mughal institutions and practices was completed for all time in Akbar's reign (or that of any one ruler, however innovative). Second: it is important to stress the considerable element of uncertainty and experimentation that marks the making of regimes.[1] It is this latter qualification that I am concerned with in this chapter.

Mughal histories speak of Akbar the Great and his many accomplishments. Central to these accomplishments is his record of unbeaten military campaigns, which led to the establishment of a far-flung sovereignty, easily the most powerful kingdom on the Indian subcontinent.[2] Akbar's supreme military authority was based upon a great array of cannons, forts, and elephants, as well as trained armies now maintained as crucial arms of the empire, not gathered together when the need arose. He consolidated his political authority through the reorganization and expansion of the agrarian system that he inherited from Sher Shah, the Afghan chieftain who displaced Humayun for a while on "the throne" of Hindustan. Akbar's *mansabdari* system, and the accompanying panoply of *jagirs* and titles, has been much acclaimed.[3]

While emphasizing Akbar's military-political-administrative advances, historians have also taken note of the growing wealth and the grandeur of

---

[1] Alam and Subrahmanyam have made these points in their introduction to *The Mughal State*. See also, Subrahmanyam, "Structure or Process."

[2] For details of Akbar's military achievements, see the most current writing on the Mughal Empire: Richards, *Mughal Empire*, chs. 1 and 2.

[3] According to this system, the nobles were awarded ranks called *mansab* and, in keeping with their ranks, they were expected to provide horsemen for the emperor's use. The nobles had the right to collect assessed tax revenue of pieces of land called *jagirs* as their payment. W. H. Moreland describes the system as deriving from Mongol and Turkish practices, in his classic essay, "Rank (mansab) in the Mogul State Service," *Journal of the Royal Asiatic Society*

his empire: the grand stone establishment, especially the splendid courts and palaces of Agra and Fatehpur-Sikri, the marvelous royal hunts, and the fabled maestros (of music, of administrative genius, of philosophical depths) at the court. Mughal historians do not forget to add in this inventory of achievements the extensive maintenance of records and accounts of all imperial activities, the commissioned histories, the translation of epics, and their dazzling illustrations in the first Mughal atelier. This was a power that was splendidly displayed, and carefully sanctified.[4]

What remains undiscussed in these catalogs of the icons of regality under Akbar is what we might call the vision of empire-building that underlay this Mughal advance, and the narrative structures that emerged – in chronicles, in imperial rules and regulations, in architectural sites – to project the new imperium. We have little understanding of the processuality involved in the making of Akbar's empire – how its image, its colors, contours, and lines were conceived and constructed. What were the strains, the breaks, and the choices that were made in the creation of the new regime under Akbar: how this imperium was elaborated in the texts of the time, and how its particular prescriptions were negotiated and contested? The domestic life of the Mughals will appear in its fully historical character only in this light.

The sources (explored and unexplored) for Akbar's reign are extensive.[5] Contemporary chronicles, ethical digests, as well as pictorial and architectural remains form the empirical grounds for the arguments that I present in this and the next chapter. I read these sources to see how they project the formation of the structures and procedures of empire-building and kingship, in order to open up questions regarding the contemporary understanding of sovereignty and appropriate order. As I have argued in chapter 3, my goal is not to explore the entire Akbari canon, but to put forward through reading a few chronicles their complicated and nuanced character. In order to make my point, I turn to the most well known of these texts: the officially commissioned and meticulously detailed *Akbarnama* of Abu-l Fazl, along with its counterpart, the *A'in-i Akbari*; Badauni's *Muntakhab-ut-Tavarikh*, a counter to Abu-l Fazl's panegyric account; and the *Tabaqat-i Akbari* of Nizam al-Din Ahmad, which evokes (and shares) the larger context of Akbar's sacred empire, not dissimilar from the evocation in the *Akbarnama*. In thinking about the making of monarchy and a history *being constructed* under

---

of Great Britain and Ireland (1936), pp. 641–665. This view was subsequently revised by Irfan Habib, in his essay, "The Mansab System, 1595–1637," *Proceedings of the Indian History Congress, 29th Session, Patiala* (1967), pp. 221–242.

[4] The writings on these subjects are extensive. For excellent bibliographies, see Alam and Subrahmanyam, *The Mughal State*; Richards, *The Mughal Empire*; Barbara D. Metcalf and Thomas R. Metcalf, *A Concise History of India* (Cambridge, 2001).

[5] Alam and Subrahmanyam make this point in relation to the *Tarikh-i Alfi*, a chronicle related to Islam that Akbar had commissioned from about 1581; *The Mughal State*, p. 24. See also Subrahmanyam, "Structure or Process?," for a detailed discussion regarding the question of Mughal sources.

Akbar, Gulbadan Banu Begum's *Ahval-i Humayun Badshah* is crucial. Gulbadan and Badauni – as well as some of the European travel accounts – present us with materials that open up some of the cracks that Abu-l Fazl papered over in his narrative.

In exploring the process of empire-building, I note how Abu-l Fazl brings into play Nasir al-Din Tusi, the thirteenth-century Persian philosopher's idea of the monarch, household, and empire as homologous domains. The way in which Tusi's ideas are put to use by Abu-l Fazl tells us a great deal about the imagined structures and procedures of the Mughal imperium under Akbar. I examine three sites that may be said to exemplify Tusi's three realms. These are: the body of the emperor as sovereign and masculine; the elaborate set of women's quarters at Fatehpur-Sikri, the only ones surviving from the time;[6] and the network of the emperor's marriages. I read the narratives surrounding these three different "texts" to make an argument about the new imperial vision and the new relationships and hierarchies (not least among these, the hierarchies of gender) that it sought to set in place.

The sacred and sublime monarch

Abu-l Fazl constructs a unique place for Akbar as the center of the universe in his narrative on Akbar's genealogy, and through his use of a new vocabulary to project the power of the monarch. Both the genealogy and the language are well known and often cited in historical writings on Akbar. Historians have not, however, paid close attention to the manner in which this genealogy is constructed and how the new terms come to display the special place of Akbar. Through an examination of this genealogy and terminology, I shall explore the exalted place that Abu-l Fazl gives his monarch (positioning Akbar at the very center of the cosmos) – "the King of manifestation and reality, the leader of religion and realm (*din-u-dunya*)"[7] – the ways in which he builds up his luminous qualities, and the omnipotence he ascribes to the emperor.

Akbar is raised to this pedestal through repeated references to his extraordinary undertakings, political and familial; through lists of his "holy qualities"; through a language signifying a sacred milieu; and through a discourse

---

[6] Ebba Koch points out that we lack the means to compare the plan of the palace at Fatehpur-Sikri with earlier Mughal architecture of Akbar's period, because "no palace ensemble predating Fatehpur-Sikri has survived intact." Ebba Koch, "The Architectural Forms," in Michael Brand and Glenn D. Lowry (eds.), *Fatehpur Sikri* (Bombay, 1987), p. 126. The only "living" example of an Akbari palace is the Jahangiri Mahal in the Agra Fort; for an analysis, see William G. Klingelhofer, "The Jahangiri Mahal of the Agra Fort: Expression and Experience in Early Mughal Architecture," *Muqarnas*, 5 (1988), pp. 153–169.

[7] I use Maulawi 'Abd-ur-Rahim (ed.), *Akbarnamah by Abul-Fazl I Mubarak I 'Allami*, vols. I–III (Calcutta, 1873–86), Persian edition, along with Beveridge's English translation already cited; hereafter cited as Maulawi, *Akbarnamah* and *Akbarnama*. For the above quote, see *Akbarnama*, I, p. 25.

on the body of the emperor that is now constructed as the most appropriate
site for learning the rules of conduct, control, and ethics. It is in the extraordinary detail presented by the author, and in the recurrent glorification that
we begin to see the wondrous projections of the monarch.

Consider these remarks allegedly heard by Abu-l Fazl himself from the
"sacred lips of his Majesty":[8]

I perfectly remember [says Akbar] what happened when I was one year old, and
especially the time when his Majesty Jahanbani [Humayun] proceeded towards Iraq
and I was brought to Qandahar. I was then one year and three months old. One day
Maham Anaga, the mother of Adham Khan (who was always in charge of that nursling
of fortune), represented to M. ʿAskari, "It is a Turki custom that when a child begins to
walk, the father or grandfather or whoever represents them, takes off his turban and
strikes the child with it, as he is going along, so that the nursling of hope may come to the
ground. ... At present his Majesty Jahanbani is not here; you are in his room, and it is
fitting you should perform this spell which is like *sipand* [henna] against the evil eye. The
mirza immediately took off his turban and flung it at me, and I fell down.

" 'This striking and falling', his Majesty deigned to observe," Abu-l Fazl
goes on, " 'are visibly before me. Also at the same time they took me for good
luck to have my head shaved at the shrine of Baba Hasan Abdal. That journey
and the taking off my hair are present before me as in a mirror'."[9] Abu-l Fazl
begins here to construct the childhood of Akbar by documenting his incredible memory, "as in a mirror."

Another example of Akbar's "illuminated border of miracles (*karamat*)"
occurred when Akbar was eight months old.[10] There was a lot of contention
among the nurses who fed Akbar in his infancy. Jiji Anageh, in particular,
was opposed by others, especially by Maham Anageh. At one point, Abu-l
Fazl records, Jiji Anageh was disturbed to learn that the nurses had reported
to Humayun that "Mir Ghaznavi's wife (i.e. herself) was practising incantations" so that Akbar, "the prince of mankind, should not accept anyone's
milk but her own."[11] At this time, says the imperial chronicler, Akbar spoke
out to comfort Jiji Anageh. "Be of good cheer," Akbar apparently said to her,
"for the celestial light of *khilafat* shall abide in thy bosom and shall bestow on
the light of thy sorrow the effulgence of joy." But he warned her not to reveal
this secret of the "mystery of God's power" to anyone "for hidden designs and
great previsions are infolded therein."[12] The nobility of the emperor is highlighted by his speech in infancy, and a revelatory conversation with Jiji
Anageh, alongside a warning of confidentiality.[13]

Great marvels occur in Akbar's adulthood as well. According to Abu-l
Fazl, though Akbar "used his tender age as a veil and lived secluded," yet,
since God had willed that his greatness be made manifest, he involuntarily

---

[8] *Akbarnama*, I, p. 396.   [9] *Ibid.*, pp. 396–397.   [10] *Ibid.*, p. 384.   [11] *Ibid.*
[12] *Ibid.*, pp. 384–385.
[13] I probe the question of foster-care and foster community in detail in the next chapter.

performed unusual deeds, "each of which was a competent witness to his lofty nature."[14] The marvels of Akbar's childhood were only the beginning of the magical activities that the Great Mughal apparently embarked upon.

The *Akbarnama* brims with such "miraculous" episodes. Here is one instance. One day Akbar had gone from Delhi to hunt in Palam (near Delhi) when an enormous serpent appeared along the line of the road. On this occasion, Akbar "exhibited the miracle of Moses," we are told. He put forth his "white hand," an allusion to the white hand of Moses, and approached the serpent, "seized its tail with his holy hand and quelled it."[15]

Through such examples, Abu-l Fazl projects the luminosity of Akbar, and his near-divine qualities. He makes clear that God grants the gift of imperial power only when a very large number of accomplishments have been gathered in one individual. He then argues that Akbar visibly was the repository of these external and internal, physical and spiritual, qualities. At one place, Abu-l Fazl lists Akbar's virtues as follows:

It is clear to the wise that a few among the holy qualities (requisite) are, magnanimity, lofty benevolence, wide capacity, abundant endurance, exalted understanding, innate graciousness, natural courage, justice, rectitude, strenuous labour, proper conduct, profound thoughtfulness, laudable overlooking (of offences), and acceptance of excuses. ... The holy personality of the shahinshah is a fount of perfect qualities, and a mine of holy principles.[16]

Akbar possessed these qualities, therefore God granted him the kingship. Everything was written of as magical and divinely ordained. The following episode recorded by Nizam al-Din Ahmad in his *Tabaqat-i Akbari* reproduces the spirit of the *Akbarnama* in its description of the emperor's attributes. On 12 March 1579, Akbar traveled towards Agra, hunting along the way. According to the chronicler, at this time, people suffered great hardship from excessive rain. Akbar called for a mirror, breathed three times on it "with his auspicious breath," and then placed the mirror on fire. The rain immediately stopped, and the people escaped from the distress caused by it.[17]

Consider also the names used for the Mughal *padshahs* from Akbar's time. Akbar was "the spiritual and temporal khedive," *khidive-i surat va maʿni,*[18] "the khedive of the world," *khidive-i jahan,*[19] "the khedive of the age," *khidive-i jahan,*[20] and "the unique jewel of the Caliphate," *gawhar-i yekta-i khilafat.*[21] His "holy mind," *batin-i quddusi,*[22] and his "holy personality" were "pure and

[14] *Akbarnama*, I, p. 629.
[15] *Ibid.*, p. 385. The miracle of Moses referred to above seems to be the conversion of Moses's rod into a serpent (*ibid.*, n. 4).
[16] *Akbarnama*, II, p. 421.   [17] *Tabaqat*, II, pp. 510–511.
[18] *Akbarnama*, II, p. 156; Maulawi, *Akbarnamah*, II, p. 103.
[19] *Akbarnama*, II, p. 445; Maulawi, *Akbarnamah*, II, p. 304.
[20] *Akbarnama*, II, p. 537; Maulawi, *Akbarnamah*, II, p. 369.
[21] *Akbarnama*, III, p. 112; Maulawi, *Akbarnamah*, III, p. 80.
[22] *Akbarnama*, III, p. 365; Maulawi, *Akbarnamah*, III, p. 252.

chaste," *zat-i muqqadasi, 'afif va pak*.[23] He was even called "*Hazrat Shahinshah*," thus being honored with the honorific of the Prophet (*Hazrat*) himself. Similarly, Babur's posthumous title was *Giti-sitani-i Firdaws Makani* (Conqueror of the World Abiding in Paradise). *Ghufran-i qubab* (Cupola of Pardon or Absolution) and *Jahanbani Jannat-i Ashyani* (Guardian of the World whose Nest is Paradise) were used for Humayun. Hamideh Banu Begum was addressed as *Maryam-Makani*. There is some uncertainty about the date of Hamideh Banu's new name.[24] Maryam means Mary and the epithet may be rendered in various ways – she who dwells with Mary, is of the household of Mary, and who is of equal rank with Mary.

The point to be noted is the frequency with which these traditionally marked, and sacred, names are used in the accounts written in Akbar's time. Even in Gulbadan Banu Begum's memoir, the reader finds a continuous application of posthumous honorific names for Babur and Humayun. In the same way, Nizam al-Din Ahmad continuously refers to Akbar as *Khalifa-i Ilahi* (Divine Caliph), Babur as *Firdaws Makani*, Hamideh Banu Begum as *Hazrat Maryam Makani*, Humayun as *Jannat Ashyani*, and the royal consorts as *hazrat-i-sarapardeh-i-saltanat* (Majestic, Highnesses, Veiled Ones of the Kingdom).[25]

The language of the contemporary chronicles transfers the sacredness of the emperor to everything around him. Akbar's court came to be described as the "sublime court," *darbar-i mu'alla*,[26] a "sublime cortege," *mawqib-i mu'alla*, a "sublime threshold," *astan-i mu'alla, darbar-i izadi*, a "fortunate and prosperous court," *darbar-i dawlat va Iqbal*,[27] and/or "holy court," *darbar-i mu'alla*.[28] In the same way, the Shahinshah's family were a "sublime family," *dudman-i vala*,[29] his *haram*, the "*haram* of fortune," *Shabistan-i Iqbal*,[30] and his women, "the veiled ones of the curtains of fortune," *niqab guzin-i saradiq-i dawlat*,[31] "chaste secluded ladies," *pardeh giyan, 'Iffat-i qubab*,[32] and/or "cupola of chastity," *'Iffat-i qubab*.[33] (The word "fortunate" in these phrases has the implication of "blessed by God.")

---

[23] *Akbarnama*, II, p. 404; Maulawi, *Akbarnamah*, II, p. 271.

[24] Henry Beveridge suggests that Hamideh Banu's title must be translated as "rank" or "station," and not "household," for it was given to her in her lifetime. See *Akbarnama*, I, p. 33, n. 1. Annette Beveridge suggests that Hamideh Banu's other name was given posthumously (*Humayun*, p. 83, n. 1). According to S. A. I. Tirmizi, the title was bestowed upon Hamideh Banu after her marriage, Tirmizi, *Mughal Documents 1526–1627* (Delhi, 1989), p. 30. For a discussion on posthumous titles, see, W. M. Thackston (trans.), *The Jahangirnama: Memoirs of Jahangir, Emperor of India* (New York, 1999), p. xiii.

[25] *Tabaqat*, II, pp. 78, 96, 110 and 559.

[26] *Akbarnama*, II, p. 413; Maulawi, *Akbarnamah*, II, p. 278.

[27] All the terms from "sublime court" onwards may be found in *Akbarnama*, II, pp. 413–425; Maulawi, *Akbarnamah*, II, pp. 278, 281, 283, 284, and 285.

[28] *Akbarnama*, III, p. 116; Maulawi, *Akbarnamah*, III, p. 83.

[29] *Akbarnama*, II, p. 426; Maulawi, *Akbarnamah*, II, p. 289.

[30] *Akbarnama*, III, p. 205; Maulawi, *Akbarnamah*, III, p. 145.

[31] *Akbarnama*, III, p. 205; Maulawi, *Akbarnamah*, III, p. 145.

[32] *Akbarnama*, III, p. 569; Maulawi, *Akbarnamah*, III, p. 385.

[33] *Akbarnama*, III, p. 569; Maulawi, *Akbarnamah*, III, p. 385.

The texts reverberate a time, and a royal environment, of sacred-spiritual associations. The language of these chronicles and memoirs conveys the sense of omnipotence that came to surround the third Mughal ruler. This sacrosanct apex of the empire – the emperor – is cast on to everything around him in such a way that the entire environment is radiated with his halo, so to speak. The sacred underpinnings of the genealogy drawn up in the *Akbarnama*, like the sacred invocations of language commonly employed for Mughal men and women, glow with the same kind of effervescence.

Abu-l Fazl's construction of Akbar's genealogy

"The King of manifestation and reality, the leader of religion and realm," as Abu-l Fazl called Akbar, needed no ordinary genealogy. Such a king did not need to draw on vital, noble connections for legitimacy. He, who was divinely selected as the leader of the sacred and profane, was above such requirements. Thus the family tree was drawn to place at its center the all-important birth of Akbar: the center came at the end, as it were.

The chronicler explains that it is by the extraordinary weddings that take place after various planetary conjunctions that a unique child is born:

> The man of experience knows that many years must elapse before a ruby develop in the embryonic sac of the mine and arrive at maturity, so as to be fitted for a royal diadem ... it was after thousands of years had been spent, womb after womb, in the cradle of preparation, that the broidery of existence was bestowed on her Majesty Alanqua, so that she might become worthy of that world-illuminating Light.[34]

Abu-l Fazl presents here the notable Mongol ancestor of Akbar, Alanqoa, existing for a momentous purpose: that of the preparation for the birth of Akbar at the right time and place. He simultaneously alludes to the Timurid-Chingizid lines as well.

Genealogies are important legitimizing instruments. Royal families everywhere have constructed glorious genealogies for themselves.[35] We noted in chapter 4 how Babur took special care to delineate his noble ancestral connections in the *Baburnama*, suggesting a subtle inclination for the Timurid side, without, however, completely negating the Chingizid blood in his veins. Humayun followed suit, keeping his reverence for both lines, though for him the practice of the methods laid down by his forefathers was more crucial than the invocation of their names alone.

---

[34] *Akbarnama*, I, pp. 34, 36, 37.
[35] As illustrative examples of works on Western royalty and questions of genealogy, see Paul Magdalino (ed.), *The Perception of the Past in Twelfth-Century Europe* (London, 1992). Gabrielle M. Spiegel, *The Past as Text: The Theory and Practice of Medieval Historiography* (Baltimore, 1997).

A genealogy of this kind was not enough for Akbar's purposes. Babur and Humayun had to lay the foundations of kingship in a land and among peoples who were unknown to them, distant from their earlier stomping grounds in Central Asia and Afghanistan. Akbar, working in the context of new imperial formation, looked for more than such claims of high connections or inheritance. He needed a larger declaration of grandeur and uniqueness in the interests of imperial power.

What happens in Akbar's reign is the proclamation of empire in the form of a great, settled polity, whose fixed center – the provider of good, and the font of all power – is Akbar. This makes for a very different spirit from the evocations in the *Baburnama*, for instance, where several generations of the *khandan* of Timur and Chingiz Khan are called upon at every step.

A central feature of this increasingly stable Mughal polity was Akbar's own distinguished presence. This is displayed forthrightly in the claims made about the sublime nature of the monarchy. Though a distinguished genealogy may be seen at work in the creation of Akbar's empire, one has a sense of it being peculiarly inverted. It appears as if it is not Akbar who derives legitimacy from a distinguished lineage, but the lineage itself that derives legitimacy from him. In other words, the fact that the emperor is magnificent, and extraordinary, makes his predecessors look extraordinary too. He is the reason for the existence of that distinguished lineage, not the other way around. It is wondrous because of him.

The broad genealogical point made by Abu-l Fazl in the *Akbarnama* – that the ancestors were privileged and the genealogy awesome only because Akbar was the result of it – becomes the founding ground for the several strands that he entwines in this genealogical grid. Abu-l Fazl's construction of this genealogical background leading to Akbar's glorious birth is fascinating. The discussion of the virtues of Akbar's mother, for example, is not derived from the mother's lineage, status, or experience. It is rather a statement about a necessary honorable medium that becomes the vehicle for the birth of a perfect son. Since the son was so illustrious, the qualities attributed to the mother – the "auspicious ascension point"[36] for the heavenly birth of Akbar – could of course not be less than extraordinary. So Abu-l Fazl embodied her with perfection, chastity, modesty, honor, and greatness.[37]

In this context, Abu-l Fazl's chapter on the Mongol princess, Alanqoa, bears reflection for a moment. In Abu-l Fazl's family tree, Akbar's ancestors included Adam, then the biblical prophets, followed by Joseph and his son, Turk, who became the first Turco-Mongol figure in this genealogy. Thereafter, the genealogist lists the Mongol kings till the ninth generation, when the ruling house was defeated and dispersed by an enemy to find refuge in a mountain valley, Mughulistan. At this point Abu-l Fazl gives us a full chapter on the divine impregnation of a Mongol princess, Alanqoa. She was

---

[36] *Akbarnama*, I, p. 50.   [37] *Ibid.*, pp. 50–51.

married to the king of Mughulistan but became a childless widow owing to
the premature death of her husband.[38] As the princess lay sleeping one night,
a "Radiant Being" of Mongol mythology impregnated her.[39] Triplets were
born of this pristine conception: "that day [of Alanqoa's conception] ... was
the beginning of the manifestation of his Majesty [Akbar], the king of kings,
who after passing through divers stages was revealed to the world from the
holy womb of her Majesty Miryam-makani for the accomplishment of things
visible and invisible."[40]

Why is a whole chapter devoted to this little-known Mongol princess, "the
cupola of chastity [*'iffat-i qubab*]," as Abu-l Fazl calls her,[41] in the midst of this
detailing of Akbar's lineage? The possible explanations are suggestive, as are
the possible sources from which the story of Alanqoa's impregnation may
have been derived. Some of the features of Alanqoa's story closely resemble
the story of the virginal conception of Christ. Interaction with Jesuit missionaries could have contributed to this construction, and it may help to
recapitulate the circumstances of missionary interaction with Akbar's
court.[42]

The first Jesuit mission, under Rudolf Aquaviva, arrived at Akbar's court
in February 1580, and stayed in Fatehpur-Sikri for three years. A second
mission arrived in Lahore, the new capital, in 1591. Father Jerome Xavier led
a third mission to Akbar's court in 1594.[43] As already noted, Monserrate, a
member of the first mission, wrote a whole commentary on his visit to
Akbar's court. Several passages of this *Commentary* indicate the detailed
nature of many of the exchanges between Akbar and the Jesuit priests. On
one Christmas, when Akbar visited the fathers, Monserrate wrote: "They
[Jesuits] adorned their chapel with rich silken curtains. They made models of
the grotto where Christ was born, of the crib in which his mother laid him,
and of the mountain on which the shepherds watched. He [Akbar] examined
everything, and began to talk about the birth of Christ."[44]

Later in the *Commentary*, recounting the time when Akbar advanced into
Kabul to check the troubles with his half-brother Mirza Hakim, Monserrate
wrote that Akbar stayed "at the halting-place" until the entire army had
crossed the Indus. A Christian priest was called who addressed the king on
the importance of the Christian Law, the Psalms and the Gospel, "attributing
equal trustworthiness and authority to all three, as being given by God." The
priest apparently explained how Christians revered and worshiped the

[38] The details given above come from *Akbarnama*, I, pp. 143–180. For a detailed sketch of the
    ancestry of Akbar, see the initial sections of *Akbarnama*, I.
[39] Woods, "Timur's Genealogy," p. 87.
[40] *Akbarnama*, I, p. 180.   [41] *Ibid.*
[42] Abu-l Fazl started to collect materials for the *Akbarnama* in 1587, eight years after the Jesuit
    arrival. Beveridge, *Humayun*, p. 83, n. 1; *Akbarnama*, I, p. 29, n. 4.
[43] Camps, *An Unpublished Letter of Father Christoval Ce Vega*, p. 7.
[44] Monserrate, *Commentary*, p. 59.

"undivided Trinity of Father, Son and Holy Ghost – One God," and how they recognized that Jesus Christ alone, "the Son of God made through the Virgin Mary, as the giver of the Gospel law, to whom all other law-givers, though sent by God, even Moses and David and the other prophets, yield place in humble submission."[45]

Thus particular notions of the Christian miraculous – the conception of "the son of God made through the Virgin Mary," the birth of Christ, and the undivided Trinity – made their way into the discussions of Akbar with the Jesuit missionaries. The records of the Jesuit fathers suggest a remarkable openness of exchange between Akbar and his Christian guests.[46] One might also note the legend that appears on the tomb of Timur, associating Alanqoa with the Virgin Mary.[47] However, any hypothesis of a direct connection between Abu-l Fazl's genealogical sketch and "Jesuit inspiration" must remain tentative, for there were, at the same time, other equally probable sources and points of reference for the court chronicler.

The example of the *Mahabharata*, translated and illustrated in the Akbari atelier as the famous *Razmnama*, may be cited as a case in point. Kunti, one of the protagonists in the epic, conceives a son by way of an "immaculate conception," and here, precisely through the rays of the Sun. The possibility of Kunti's episode being the stimulus for Abu-l Fazl's writing is as large (or small) as the discussions with the missionaries at Akbar's court. It is worth referring in this context to the ancient Rajput practice of tracing aristocratic lineage alternatively from the Sun (*suryavamshi*) or the Moon (*chandravamshi*): recall that Ram himself, the great God/King of the religious epic, the *Ramayana*, belongs to a *suryavamshi* clan. Given the close marital and political relations that Akbar forged with a large number of Rajput principalities, it is not too far-fetched to suggest that Abu-l Fazl may have been trying to link the new regime of Akbar with the deeply rooted Rajput tradition by constructing an ancestry in which the Sun figures prominently.

Obviously, the inversion of the genealogical tree, as it appears in the *Akbarnama*, could not be a simple overturning. Abu-l Fazl underlined Akbar's centrality in terms of his extraordinary being. He deployed his information to point to the "divine" inheritance of the emperor. It is in this light that the story of Alanqoa's immaculate conception might best be understood. Yet the emperor's unique character could not be demonstrated in a void. Therefore the genealogist drew continuous connections between the emperor and his Timurid-Chingizid ancestors, as well as between the emperor and Quranic-mythical exemplars.

---

[45] Monserrate, *Commentary*, pp. 136–137. For further detail, see Correia-Afonso, *Letters*, pp. 34, 42–43.

[46] Correia-Afonso, *Letters*, p. 34. It has also been noted that there is a considerable influence of Abu-l Fazl in the accounts of Monserrate and other such visitors (Mansura Haider, *Muktabat-i-Allami (Insha'i Abu'l Fazl) Daftar I* (New Delhi, 1998), p. xvi.

[47] Woods, "Timur's Genealogy," p. 88.

If Akbar radiated divinity, he also shared the qualities of his lineage. So if "Amir Sahib Qaran [Timur] from his earliest years up to the flower of his youth, was occupied in practising the art of hunting and the methods of war and battles,"[48] it was recorded that Akbar too was engaged in very similar activities in the early part of his reign. Again, it has been suggested that the visual folios of the *Dastan-i Amir Hamza* (or the *Hamzanama*), which concerns the stories of Hamzeh, the uncle of the Prophet, and is the earliest major illustrated manuscript attributed to Akbar's patronage, tell us "something of his [Akbar's] personality at the time."[49]

According to the *Hamzanama*, Hamzeh "traveled throughout the world" to spread the doctrines of Islam. Milo Cleveland Beach suggests that the *Hamzanama* "obviously appealed enormously to the young and energetic emperor, himself occupied with extending Islamic control over a predominantly Hindu country."[50] How greatly Akbar was inspired to spread Islam by the escapades of Hamzeh is hard to establish, but the projected correspondence between the life of Hamzeh and that of the emperor is crucial for another reason. Akbar comes, in this record, to parallel – to be like – the uncle of the Prophet himself. "Divinity" is close at hand, one might say. Indeed, this claim to divinity or near-divinity is one feature of Akbar's kingship that was subjected to scathing attack in the history written in hiding by Badauni, one of his courtiers.

The invocation of earlier connections, Turco-Mongol, Quranic, Timurid, Chingizid, Baburi, Humayuni, and of the Sur kings, in a new combination is central to Abu-l Fazl's genealogy, which we might call an ideology for imperial governance. But that is not all there is to it. Perhaps one of the most significant aspects of the *Akbarnama* is the way in which it garners its information to point towards the unique power of the emperor. Just as Akbar gives rise to the greatness of his forefathers, so his mere presence will contribute – in this interpretation – to the prosperity of his subjects and his successors. The next section elaborates this point.

The structure of empire (i): the emperor's body

In the next three sections, I examine the body of the emperor, the new *haram* and court structures at Fatehpur-Sikri, and the network of marriages in which the emperor was centrally placed as the empire came to be consolidated, which, as I have indicated earlier, one may take as instances of Tusi's suggested homology between individual, household, and state. Abu-l Fazl underlines the importance of Tusi in his repeated recommendation of his works to Akbar.[51] Yet, the implications of the chronicler's appropriation of Tusi's philosophy do not appear to have been adequately appreciated.

---

[48] *Akbarnama*, I, p. 207.
[49] Milo Cleveland Beach, *Early Mughal Painting* (Cambridge, Mass., 1987), p. 60.   [50] *Ibid.*
[51] Muzaffar Alam, "Akhlaqi Norms and Mughal Governance," in Muzaffar Alam *et al.* (eds.), *The Making of Indo-Persian Culture: Indian and French Studies* (New Delhi, 2000), p. 84.

In his study on the religious and intellectual history of the Muslims in Akbar's reign, S. A. A. Rizvi discusses Abu-l Fazl's reliance upon Tusi's *Akhlaq-i Nasiri*.[52] The author, however, provides no extended analysis of the way in which Tusi's theory shaped the structure of the chronicler's account of Akbar's empire-building. Another major article, Muzaffar Alam's "Akhlaqi Norms and Mughal Governance," concerned with an investigation of the relationships between *akhlaqi* norms and codes of Mughal governance, does not consider the importance of the "emperor, household, empire" homology in Abu-l Fazl's construction of the new imperial order.[53]

Rosalind O'Hanlon carries this discussion of forms of governance a step further by focusing upon what she describes as the "manipulation of bodily and gender identity" in the explanation of norms and practices of imperial authority under Akbar.[54] O'Hanlon proposes that Akbar and his colleagues worked upon "the natural inner purity of the male body, and the possibilities for moral and human perfection" in all three worlds that men inhabited as governors – the individual body, the household, and the kingdom[55] – and combined these with some tenets of Brahmanic Hinduism in order to be able to appropriate an "eclectic range of norms for ideal manhood."[56] While the move that O'Hanlon makes is important, there is little demonstration of the elaborate working out of imperial masculinity and order in domains beyond the body of the emperor.[57]

Tusi's *Akhlaq-i Nasiri* begins with a proposition about the nature of equilibrium between the three elements of man's inner being. Among these, the first is the faculty of rationality ("*quwat-i nutq*"), the source of thought and judgment, which distinguishes between good and evil and is located in the brain. The second is the concupiscible faculty ("*quwat-i shahwi*"), the principle of attraction towards pleasures and gratification – foods, drinks, and women – and is placed in the liver. The third is the irascible faculty ("*quwat-i ghadabi*"), the principle for resisting injuries and for facing up to perils, and of yearning after authority and exaltation.[58] Just as a balance needs to be found between these different elements within the body, Tusi suggests, a similar balance is to be sought outside – in the social and political world.

Tusi's formulation was that the body was the active instrument of the soul's discipline, as well as the point from which harmony and balance with the

---

[52] Rizvi, *Religious and Intellectual History*, especially ch. 9, "Religious and Political Thinking of Abu'l Fazl."

[53] Alam, "Akhlaqi Norms and Mughal Governance."

[54] O'Hanlon, "Kingdom, Household and Body," p. 19.   [55] *Ibid.*, p. 2.   [56] *Ibid.*

[57] *Ibid.* The author herself notes in conclusion that her investigation is only a starting point and an invitation for the kind of work that needs to be done.

[58] G. M. Wickens (trans.), *The Nasirean Ethics by Nasir ad-Din Tusi* (London, 1964), p. 43, and nn. 89, 90, and 135.

other (social and political) domains had to be built. Since the king (his body), household and kingdom were homologous realms, well-being in each of these depended upon the others. What I wish to do here is to consider the overlap between these different domains, and the way in which the details of one directly related to or impinged upon those of the others.

As we have already observed, the *Akbarnama* placed Akbar on an awesome pedestal. In this construction, the king appeared inordinately controlled, righteous, and masculine. Indeed, the emperor's fortified masculinity may be seen as an organizing principle of the order and discipline that the empire was to expound. The description of the "untainted" body of the emperor, as model of masculinity and male virtue, in the *A'in-i Akbari* is particularly interesting. The first of the five books of the *A'in-i Akbari* speaks of the emperor himself, and then of his household and court. The spirit of regimen and restraint set up here in the discussion of the emperor's own comportment becomes the exemplar for the disciplining of other domains. Abu-l Fazl explains, the "success of the three branches of the government [those concerning the army, the household, and the empire[59]], and the fulfillment of the wishes of the subjects, whether great or small, depend upon the manner in which a king spends his time."[60] Thus the vision of empire starts with the emperor, and extends outwards to the household, and then on to the kingdom – Tusi's theory at work, in the imperial chronicle.

Abu-l Fazl's description of the "inward and outward austerities" of Akbar in his discussion of the "manner in which his Majesty spends his time" provides the spirit of the argument. Although there was "every inducement to lead a life of luxury and ease," every step that the emperor took in his daily routine, the chronicler argues, was dictated by an "allegiance to wisdom."

His Majesty abstains much from flesh, so that whole months pass away without his touching any animal food, which, though prized by most, is nothing thought of by the sage. His august nature cares but little for the pleasures of the world. In the course of twenty-four hours he never makes more than one meal. He takes a delight in spending his time in performing whatever is necessary and proper. He takes a little repose in the evening, and again for a short time in the morning; but his sleep looks more like waking.[61]

According to this account, the emperor retired to his private apartments only when "four *gharis* [moments]" were left till the morning, at which point he "launche[d] forth into the ocean of contemplation."[62] In all of this, it is really the matters of the soul that Abu-l Fazl calls attention to through the medium of the body of his virtuous monarch. Akbar's qualities, particularly his

---

[59] *A'in-i Akbari*, I, p. 9. I use Henry Blochmann (ed.), *The Ain I Akbari by Abul Fazl I 'Allami*, Persian text, vols. I–III (Calcutta, 1872–77), along with Blochmann and Jarrett's translation already cited, hereafter cited as *A'in-i Akbari* and *Persian Ain*.

[60] *A'in-i Akbari*, I, p. 162.   [61] *Ibid.*, p. 163.   [62] *Ibid.*, p. 164.

guarding of motives and control of emotions and forbearance, are listed along with his earnestness and his unmatched mental powers.

Badauni also notes (albeit with scathing overtone) the emperor's moderation and asceticism, his acute physical self-control and spiritual exercises, including the carefully chosen dietary habits, fasts, and preferred vegetarianism. The *Muntakhab* engages in a sustained critique of the emperor's dietary regime and his particular means of caring for the self. To take one example, the emperor had prohibited the eating of beef, which according to Badauni was the result of Akbar's company of the "rascally Hindus, and thence a reverence for the cow ... [which] became firmly fixed in his mind."[63] Again, Badauni notes that "in imitation of the usages of these Lamas [of Tibet]," Akbar limited the time he spent in the *haram*, curtailed his food and drink, "but especially abstained from meat."[64] Although Badauni makes the point in relation to the unusually long lives of the Lamas of Tibet that may have inspired the emperor to emulate their curative ways, the author's criticism of the emperor's new practices is clear.

Indexed in these records are proper forms of bodily and sexual behavior, and the comportment (restraint) of the monarch himself as the most outstanding model of the appropriate norms. In keeping with the display of kingly power and dignity, the Akbari records often project a very disciplined "use" of food, women, and sleep – all of these for higher purposes.

Abu-l Fazl's writing is particularly striking for his illustration of Akbar's controlled sexuality. The chronicler applauds the emperor's hetero-normativity, as well as the "obligatory" concentration upon marriages, primarily, if not exclusively, for reproduction. In this discussion of Akbar's virtues, the emperor's minimal display of emotion and his guarding of feelings is amplified. Monserrate, the Jesuit priest, was puzzled by Akbar's abstinence – "Zelaldinus [Akbar] has more than 300 wives, dwelling in separate suites of rooms in a very large palace. Yet when the priests were at the court he had only three sons and two daughters"[65] – but Akbar's very limited time in the *haram* is underlined and praised by Abu-l Fazl.

Imperial regulations on marriage provide one striking example of the simultaneous construction of a wider sexual regime that was to follow that of the emperor. Consider the rather provocative affair of the musician Gadai recorded in the *Akbarnama*. This man, who had twenty-five children from one wife, was once brought before Akbar. Akbar is reported to have said, "A Biluci had twenty children from one wife and he came to the court and petitioned ... this chaste matron [his wife] has become forbidden to me on account of the numerous births. 'What remedy have I, and what cure is there for my wretchedness?'" Abul-l Fazl says Akbar comforted the Biluchi by

---

[63] *Muntakhab*, II, p. 312.   [64] *Ibid.*, p. 335.
[65] Monserrate, *Commentary*, p. 202. The importance of the large number of wives is discussed below.

saying that wicked storytellers must have invented what was being said about his wife, and added, "If any matrimony (*kesh*) produced such a good result (as so large a progeny) it was an honour to the parties, and not a case for abstention (*hurmat*). Let him then go on to display his own virility, and the fertility of his spouse."[66]

This story needs to be read together with an extract from the regulations on marriages in the *A'in-i Akbari*:

Every care bestowed upon this wonderful tie between men is a means of preserving the stability of the human race, and ensuring the progress of the world; it is a preventive against the outbreak of evil passions, and leads to the establishment of homes. Hence His Majesty [Akbar], in as much as he is benign, watches over great and small, and imbues men with his notions of the spiritual union and the equality of essence which he sees in marriage. He abhors marriages which take place between man and woman before the age of puberty. They bring forth no fruit .... [67]

The point of an ideal marriage, Akbar counseled Gadai, was reproduction. The feelings of the woman, and the labor pain she goes through, count for nothing. The larger the number of children, the greater the glory of God and the family. The subtext of these two citations together is equally crucial. The institution of marriage and the reproduction of offspring now become the only appropriate, sanctioned form of sexual behavior. Anything that did not work along these lines was now represented as deviant.

Akbar's views in relation to the affair of 'Ali Quli Khan Zaman (an official) with the son of a camel-driver illustrates the point. When a report of this liaison was brought to Akbar, he prefaced his judgment with the following lines: "The man who by submitting himself to desire and the society of wicked flatters [*sic*] is overpowered by the lord of lust and passion becomes the mark of various disgraces." He added: "let nothing be said now of virility, truth, loyalty, devotion and sincerity, but take hold of the thread of prudence. ... " He asked 'Ali Quli Khan Zaman to repent his deeds and amend his "evil doings by good service" and directed him to send the camel-driver's son to the court, "so that we [Akbar] may regard your deeds as not done, and exalt you by royal favours."[68]

As part of this scheme of disciplining deviance, the prostitutes (we gather from Badauni) were made to live outside the city in a place called Shaitanpura, literally Devilsville![69] This is a comment on the imperial demand for regulated sexuality. In Abu-l Fazl's account of the making of a towering monarchy, the process started in the body of the emperor himself. The sexual/ethical norm of Akbar's new regime articulated through his body was deeply heterosocial and masculine. This context would not easily allow

---

[66] *Akbarnama*, III, p. 378.   [67] *A'in-i Akbari*, I, p. 287.
[68] *Akbarnama*, II, pp. 105–106. Also see two interesting orders of the emperor, as recorded by Badauni. They add well to the points we have been making above; *Muntakhab*, II, p. 405.
[69] *Muntakhab*, II, p. 311.

expressions of romantic love, or the chance of writing love poems for a bazaar boy, because both of these departed from the norm that was being established. The design is elaborated in relation to the past, as much as it looks ahead to the future.

It is useful in this context to compare Babur's discussion of marriages, love, and poetry which appear together in his memoir, and his delineation of an ethos where male and female love are both speakable, with Abu-l Fazl's (or Akbar's) institutionalization of marriages, and declared abhorrence of male–male love as intrinsically base and innately depraved.[70] In Babur's context of perpetual traveling, it was relatively difficult to maintain a very strict control over marital and other sexual or romantic relationships. The entire tendency of Akbari politics on the other hand, as it developed, was one of extending control for the maximization of power. There was little place in it for what might be called irrationality, or emotionalism – the emotionalism of love and poetry, for instance – in what was being set up as a disciplined sexuality. The large number of Akbar's own marriages, along with the absence of any known (declared) loved one or favorite wife, serve as icons of the need for the controlled virility and strength of the "base" body.

Once the emperor's body was disciplined, it was necessary to move on to other areas, which too would be aligned in accordance with the kingly example. In Tusi's proposition of homologous domains, the different domains converge and even stand in for one another. In Abu-l Fazl's account of the regulation of the empire, the emperor makes his appearance in all kinds of spheres and in all sorts of unexpected ways, suggesting something about the correspondence of these different domains and the emperor's centrality in all of them.

The structure of empire (ii): court and quarters

Modern scholarship has asked a variety of questions about Fatehpur-Sikri. Most of these have been concerned with the architectural layout, the material and splendor of the complex. Most recently, Ebba Koch has suggested the importance of detailed art historical studies that stress stylistic analysis and formal comparisons to be able to explore the functions and the meanings of the buildings.[71]

The forms and architectural intricacies are indeed significant. The Sikri complex was a part of the grand design of a new monarchy. Monica Juneja has argued that Fatehpur-Sikri "was conceived of as a microcosm of the

---

[70] *Akbarnama*, II, p. 104.
[71] Koch, "Architectural Forms," p. 123. For two excellent compilations on architectural history of Fatehpur-Sikri, see S. A. A. Rizvi and V. J. Flynn, *Fatehpur-Sikri* (Bombay, 1975); Brand and Lowry (eds.), *Fatehpur Sikri*; and by the same editors, see also *Akbar's India: Art from the Mughal City of Victory* (London, 1985–86). For a recent detailed bibliography on Fatehpur-Sikri, see Juneja, *Architecture*.

Mughal empire through uniting within its spaces a distillation of visual and structural forms that had once belonged to regions brought under the imperial umbrella."[72] In order to explore the vision of the world in which a grand complex such as Fatehpur-Sikri comes into being, what an historian needs to do is to work further through the implications of the discourses that developed around this complex.

Let us turn first to the popular account of the building of Fatehpur-Sikri. As the *Akbarnama* has it, Akbar built this city and the imperial complex as a thanksgiving to Shaykh Salim Chishti, owing to whose blessings a son was born to the emperor. The Shaykh lived outside the little town named Sikri; it was in his hospice that Prince Salim was born.[73] There are several scholarly interpretations about the founding of Fatehpur-Sikri. Attilio Petruccioli contends that any hypothesis to do with the "sovereign's whim" of building his residence so that it remained in contact with Shaykh Salim al-Din Chishti must be "shelved": Fatehpur-Sikri was a "political operation" to keep the nobility firmly under control by centralizing the court, and for controlling various groups of Rajputs, Turks, and Afghans who were continually at war with each other. Moreover, he adds, the notion that the whole city was constructed at once is highly untenable.[74] Glenn D. Lowry also adds that work on Fatehpur-Sikri did not begin until 1571, two years after Salim's birth, and continued well into the 1570s and 1580s.[75]

Brand and Lowry suggest that Fatehpur-Sikri was part of a 300-mile-long corridor running from Agra to Ajmer in western India. Because Ajmer was the destination for annual pilgrimages that the emperor made to the tomb of Khvajeh Muin al-Din Chishti, the new capital represented "a formal point of connection between the older political and spiritual poles of Agra and Ajmer." In the "ideologically linked" and "formally related" tomb of Shaykh Salim Chishti and Akbar's imperial palace, Akbar was making a statement about the spiritual, Islamic basis of his rule.[76]

John Richards's analysis of Fatehpur-Sikri is situated in the context of the elaboration of what he calls "imperial authority" under Akbar and Jahangir. He argues that Akbar spent the first two decades of his rule "establishing an infallible spiritual authority that would make his person the metaphor for empire: one could not exist without another." As part of this "ideological campaign," Richards argues, Akbar constructed Fatehpur-Sikri and made a break with the "Delhi-centered political tradition of Muslim India."[77]

---

[72] Juneja, *Architecture*, p. 43.   [73] *Akbarnama*, II, pp. 503, 530.
[74] Attilio Petruccioli, "The Geometry of Power: The City's Planning," in Brand and Lowry (eds.), *Fatehpur Sikri*, pp. 56–57.
[75] Glenn D. Lowry, "Urban Structures and Functions," in Brand and Lowry (eds.), *Fatehpur Sikri*, pp. 26–27.
[76] John F. Richards, "The Imperial Capital," in Brand and Lowry (eds.), *Fatehpur Sikri*, p. 66.
[77] *Ibid.*

I would argue, however, that the proclamation that Sikri makes is much larger than one guided by a desire for stability or legitimacy. Whether it was a "political operation" or a "formal point of connection between the older political and spiritual poles," there is a striking political statement about aspirations to permanence in the construction of the court and palaces at Fatehpur-Sikri. This is about kingship of exceptional luster and power, *made more lustrous and powerful by the birth of an heir*: a monarchy that is "here to stay."

The new construction at Sikri has a great deal to tell us about the changes that came with the shift from the peripatetic life of the earlier *padshah*s. Consider the architectural layout of the complex containing both official and non-official quarters, as indicated in the plan surveyed and drawn by Attilio Petruccioli (see Plans 1–3).[78] There are some isolated palaces that are outside the main palace complex. *Hada Mahal* (109) and *Todar Mal's Barahdari* (114), for instance, belong, to "the category of isolated pleasure pavilions of a compact kiosk type with a centralised plan placed in the context of garden or water architecture."[79] There are other buildings outside the main complex: *bazaar*s (markets, nos. 75, 77), and *caravansarai*s (travelers' lodgings, 103), which are in line with "established types of Islamic civic architecture." Then there are several towers, like the much discussed *Hiran Minar* (100), which is "studded with (imitation?) elephant tusks ... its decoration with elephant tusks was clearly meant to underline its special status, since it refers to the emperor as captor and dominator of elephants – his exclusive prey."[80]

The Imperial Complex is an "irregular agglomeration of courtyards enclosed by more or less fragmentary colonnades, of various groups of buildings ... arranged in echelon formation on the east-west axis."[81] It is possible that there were several "axes of significance," along which the entire structure was orientated. An "axis of imperial appearances"[82] runs through the entire complex, for example, connecting the *Divan-i Khas* (63), the roof pavilion and the *Khvabgah* (53), and the *Anup Talau* (56).

When entered from the State Hall, *Divankhana-i aam* (66), a rectangular courtyard, a water tank in the middle (referred to as *Anup Talau* in Akbar's contemporary texts, no. 56) will be seen. Several structures mentioned above are set around it. The *Daulatkhana-i Khas* or *Khvabgah* (53) is "usually identified as the private imperial living quarters. The small chamber at the top is traditionally accepted to be Akbar's bedroom."[83] This structure juts onto the rim of *Anup Talau*. According to Nadeem Rezavi, the *Daulatkhana-i Khas* appears to have been divided into two parts: the *daulatkhana* and the

---

[78] Taken from *Akbar's India*.
[79] Koch, "Architectural Forms," p. 123. The details of the buildings may be gathered from this article.
[80] *Ibid.*, p. 125. See the architectural details.
[81] Koch, "Architectural Forms," p. 125.   [82] *Ibid.*
[83] Glenn D. Lowry, "Urban Structures and Functions," p. 15.

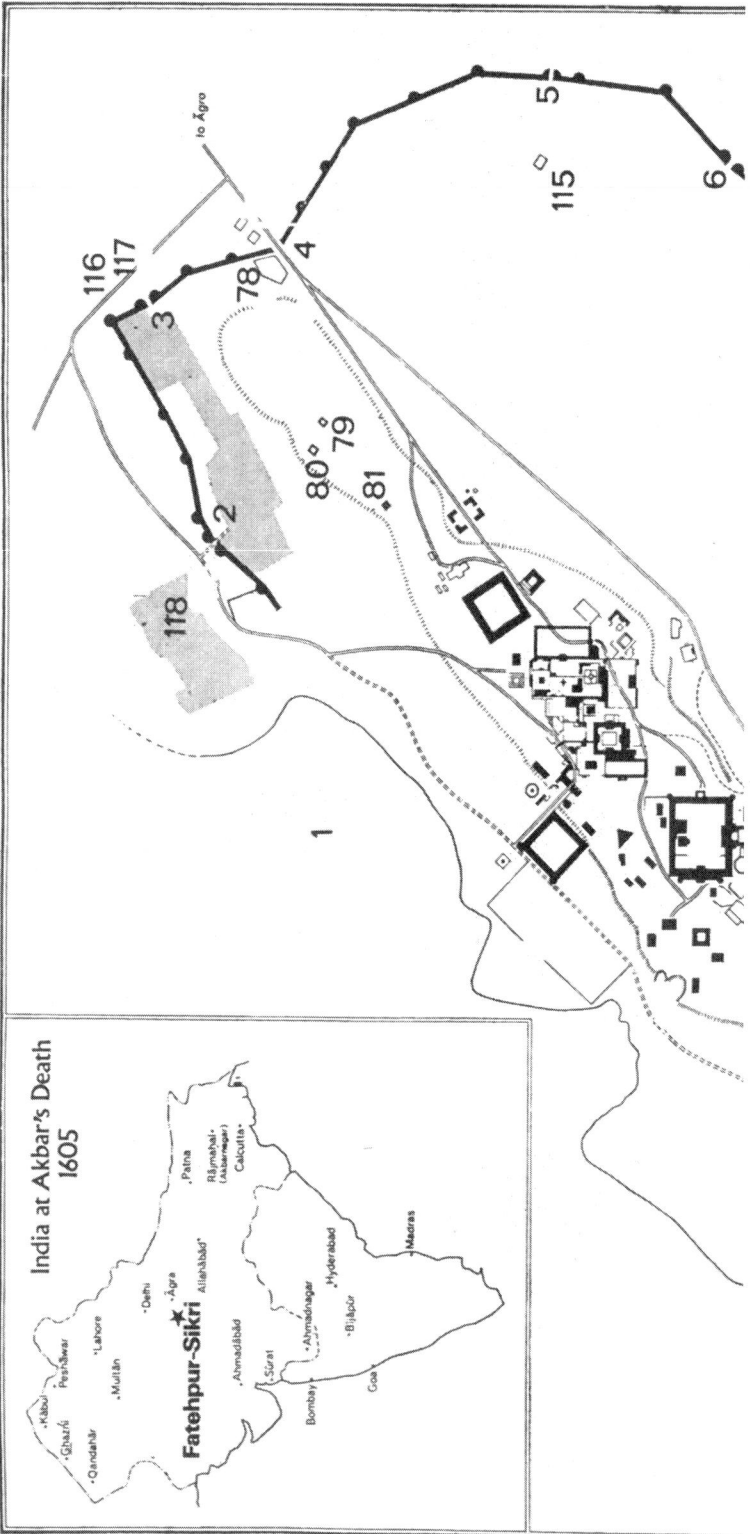

India at Akbar's Death
1605

Fatehpur-Sikri

·Kabul ·Peshāwar
·Ghazni
·Qandahār ·Multān
·Lahore
·Delhi
·Āgra
Allahābād· ·Patna Rājmahal·
(Akbarnagar)
Calcutta·

·Ahmadābād
·Sūrat ·Ahmadnagar
Bombay ·Hyderabad
Goa ·Bijāpur ·Madras

To Āgra

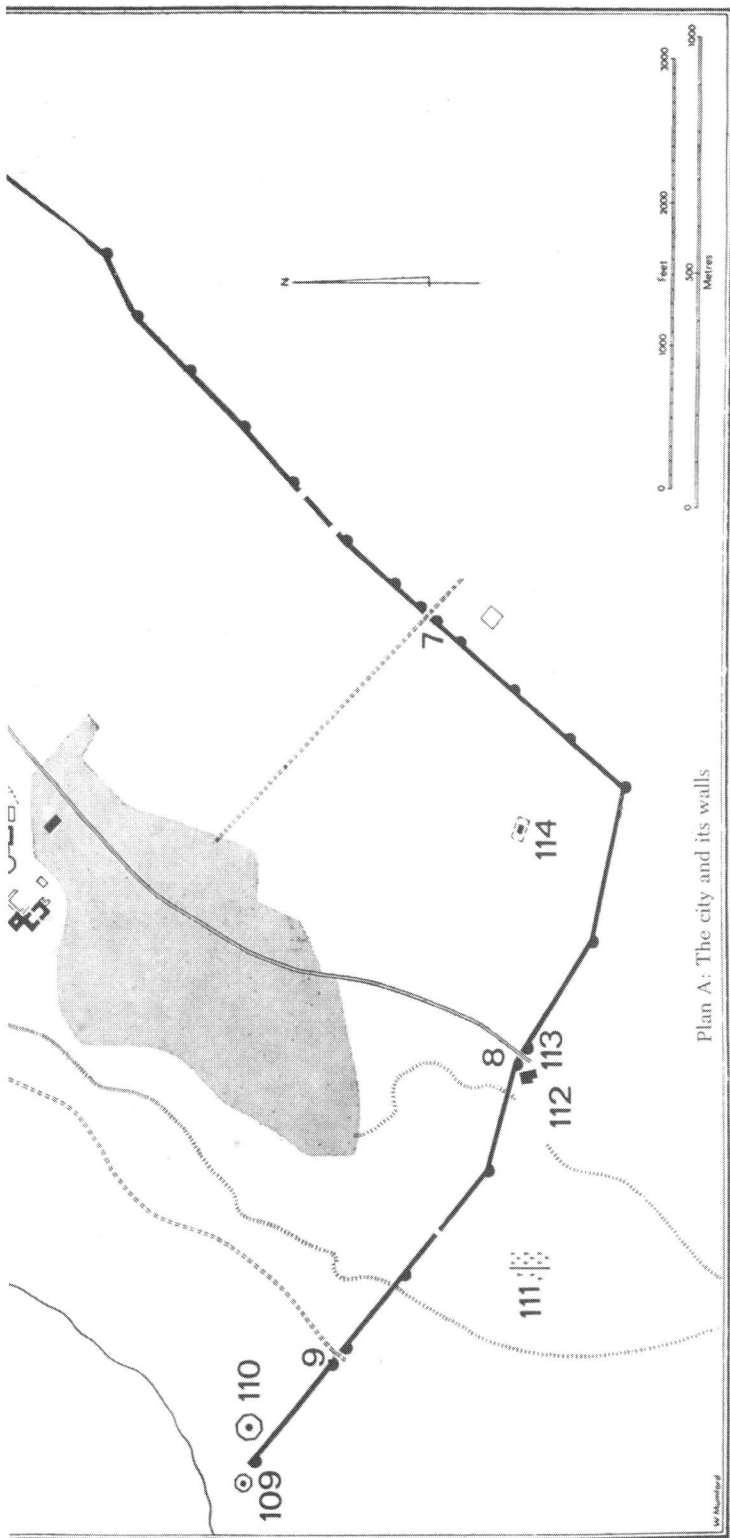

1. Fatehpur-Sikri: the city and its walls. From *Fatehpur-Sikri*, p. 5

Plan A: The city and its walls

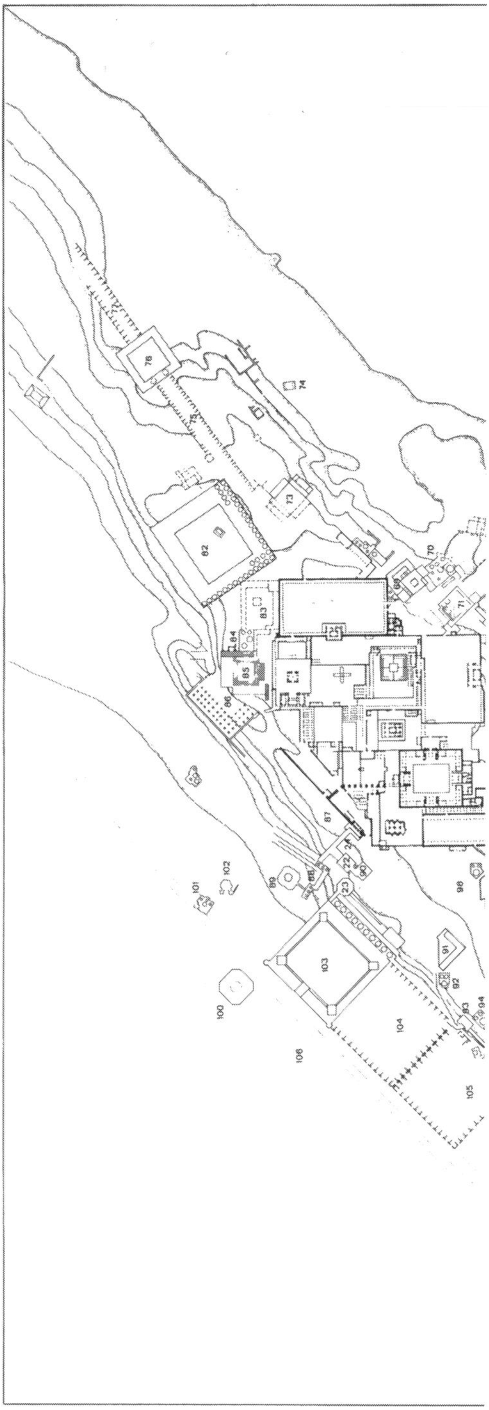

76
74
73
62
83
84
85
86
70
71
87
88
89
23
91
92
93
94
100
101
102
103
104
105
106

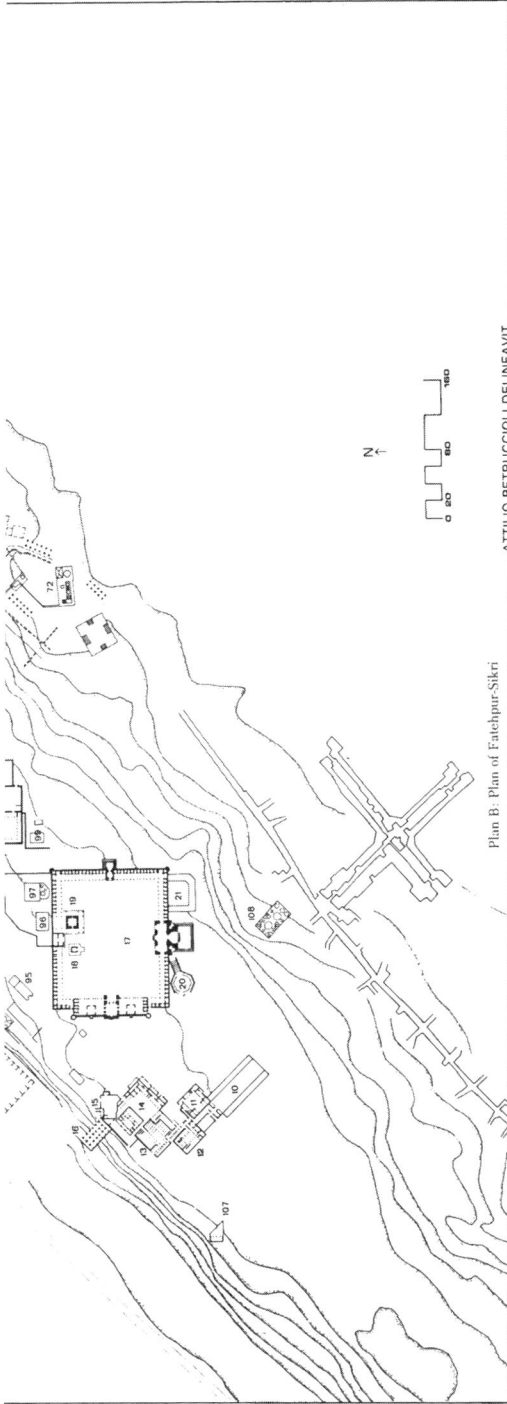

Plan B: Plan of Fatehpur-Sikri

ATTILIO PETRUCCIOLI DELINEAVIT

2. Plan of Fatehpur-Sikri. From *Fatehpur-Sikri*, p. 6

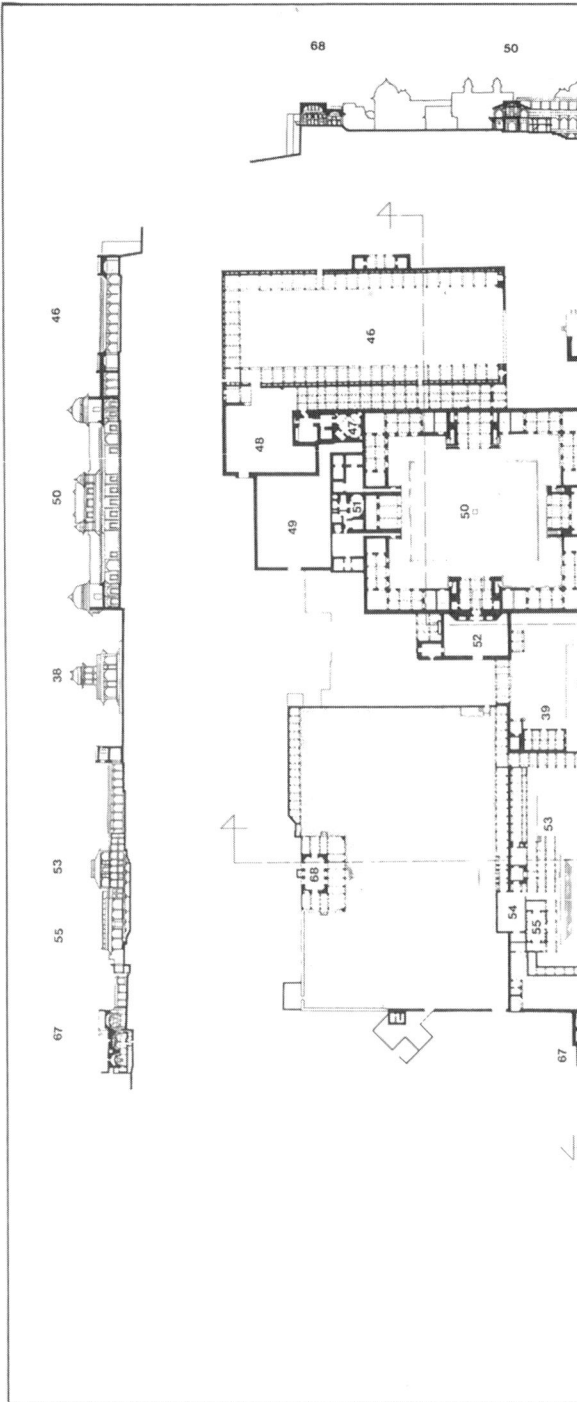

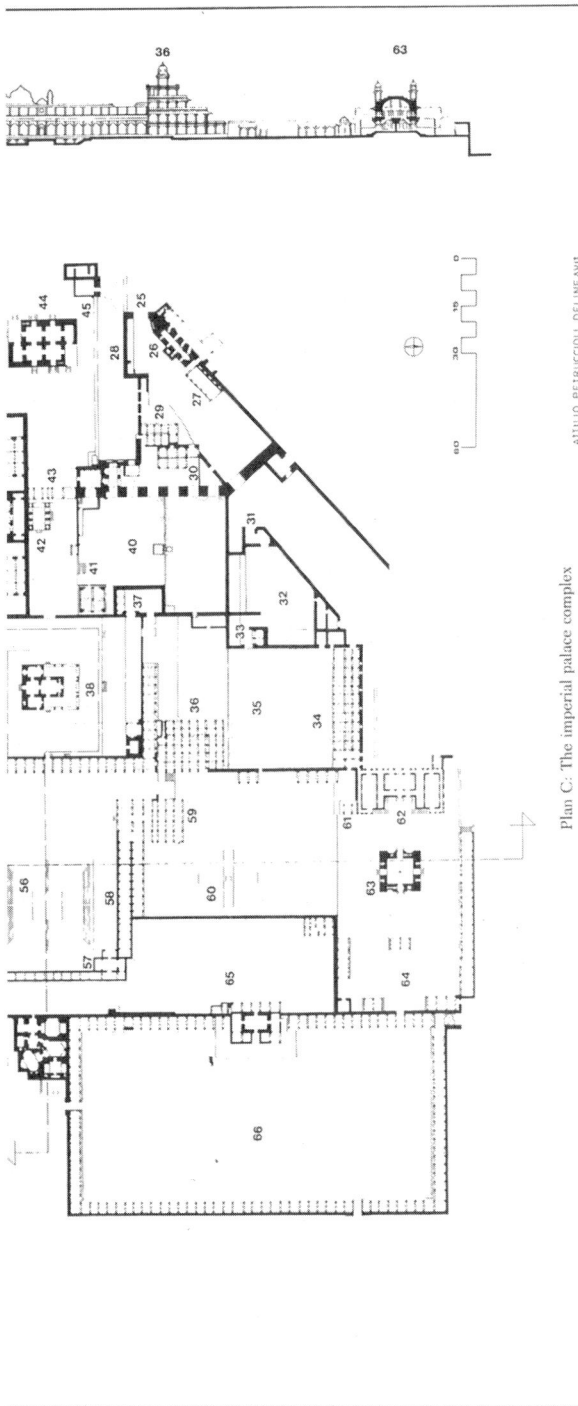

Plan C: The imperial palace complex

ATTILIO PETRUCCIOLI DELINEAVIT

3. The imperial palace complex. From *Fatehpur-Sikri*, p. 7

daulatkhana-i anuptalau. In the latter area the *khilvatkada-i khas* (imperial chambers) and the *khvabgah* (resting quarters) of Akbar are located.[84] Then the building popularly called the "Turkish Sultana's house" (57) is located in the center of the courtyard. To the south of the *talau,* connected through a cloistered passage, is a structure that has been identified as "Abdarkhana and Fruit Store" where fruits and beverages were stored for the emperor.[85]

A wall separates this part of the complex (the courtyard with the pond and the structures around it) from the *haram.* Along this wall is a covered row of pillars, a five-storeyed pavilion called the *Panch Mahal* (36, and facing the central courtyard).[86] A gallery (now locked) above this thick wall connects the *Panch Mahal* and also overlooks the courtyard from above. Behind this wall is the *haram.* Most buildings in this area are clearly marked in the scheme. These are, for instance, *Maryam's* quarters (38), *Jodh Bai's* palace (50), several baths, tanks, and some unidentified gates.[87] Rezavi suggests that *Maryam's* quarters (38), popularly known as the *Sunahra makan* (the golden house) or *Maryam ki kothi,* were originally bracketed from the rest of the *haram* with the help of walls. Thus, *Maryam's* house, although outside the *daulatkhana,* was not a part of the *haram.* Based on the depiction of hunting, battle, and siege scenes in this building, and following Monserrate, Rezavi suggests that this house might be the dining area of Akbar.[88]

In the extended plan of Fatehpur-Sikri, plan 2, we find that through the *haram,* following the unidentified baths, a passage leads to the religious-spiritual complex – almost square in shape. This area consists of the *Jami Masjid* (17), the tomb of Shaykh Salim Chishti (18), and the tomb of Navvab Islam Khan (19), son of Salim Chishti. Facing the tomb of Salim Chishti is the *Buland Darvaza,* built to construct the victory of Akbar over Gujarat (not indicated in the plan). The two possible entrances to the entire complex (official and non-official) are either from the side of the *Buland Darvaza,* a popular entry for tourists today, or the point where we began our description of the site.

The Sikri complex was intended to be a register of permanence, whatever its subsequent history. Its durability and power were manifested not merely in the grand stone palaces, but also in the monarchical construction of order in that entire space. According to Abu-l Fazl, just as everything revolved around

---

[84] S. Ali Nadeem Rezavi, "Revisiting Fatehpur Sikri: An Interpretation of Certain Buildings," in Irfan Habib (ed.), *Akbar and his India* (Delhi, 2000), p. 175.

[85] "the so-called "Turkish Sultana's chamber" and the cloistered verandah around it are the structures which Badauni calls by the name of *hujra-i Anuptalau.* The cloisters, apart from being used to seat the people called for interview by the emperor, also shielded the area of the *daulatkhana-i Anuptalau* from the *daulat-khana-i khas*"; Nadeem Rezavi, "Revisiting Fatehpur Sikri," p. 176.

[86] For the architectural details of the *panch mahal,* see Koch, "Architectural Forms," p. 131.

[87] For an early but detailed description of several other buildings in this area, see S. A. A. Rizvi, *Fatehpur Sikri* (New Delhi, 1992).

[88] Nadeem Rezavi, "Revisiting Fatehpur Sikri," p. 179.

Akbar, Fatehpur-Sikri too sparkled as a new sacred space designed by the virtuous monarch. Thus:

As the Khedive of the world is an architect of the spiritual and physical world, and is continually engaged in elevating the grades of mankind, and making strong the foundations of justice ... so also does he strive for increasing the glory of the earth, and cherishes every place in accordance with its condition. ... In a short time there was a great city, and there were charming palaces. ... H. M. gave it the name of Fathabad, and this by common use was made into Fathpur. [89]

Some of the European accounts point to the exact planning of the dwellings in Akbar's time. Monserrate comments on the "four great royal dwellings, of which the king's own palace is the largest and the finest." The second palace according to the Jesuit Father belonged to the queens; the third to the royal princes; and the fourth was used as a storehouse. He also discusses the tomb of Salim Chishti and other buildings erected by Akbar in various parts of his dominions.[90] Monserrate's narrative is concerned with the strictly planned allotment of the palaces and of different quarters. He points to the same kind of order in his discussion of other themes too, such as those relating to the imperial counselors, the embassies, the officers, sources of revenue, justice, and other matters in the empire of Akbar.[91]

In De Laet's *Description of India and Fragment of Indian History*, a similar sense of order appears. In the first line on the section on political and civil government, he notes: "The emperor of India is an absolute monarch: there are no written laws [*sic*]: the will of the emperor is held to be the law."[92] The above observation may well be an impression of a later time but the point that De Laet makes about the environment of prescription and command is important.

At any rate, this was the first time that demarcated zones of activity – including the first set of segregated women's quarters – were so carefully planned. In theory, everyone appeared to have an allotted space in the complex: the emperor, the Shaykh, the courtiers, women, servants and others. These spaces were continually to resonate kingly authority; note this in the names of the buildings: *daulatkhana-i khas, daulatkhana-i anuptalau, khilvat-kada-i khas, Sunahra makan, Maryam ki kothi*, amplifying the sanctified context of the empire in which the king was the center.

Or consider the religious-spiritual complex, mentioned above, consisting of the *Jami Masjid*, the tomb of Shaykh Salim Chishti, the tomb of Navvab Islam Khan, and the *Buland Darvaza*. Akbar's centrality in this part of the complex is manifest in many ways. By placing the saint's tomb in the *Jami masjid* complex, as Richards notes, "Akbar was able to draw upon the sanctity adhering to it, and to assimilate it in his own authority." Moreover,

---

[89] *Akbarnama*, II, pp. 530–531.   [90] Monserrate, *Commentary*, pp. 199–200.
[91] *Ibid.*, pp. 199–209.   [92] *De Laet*, p. 93.

Akbar encouraged the descendants of Shaykh Salim to enlist as high-ranking officers in imperial service and not simply remain caretakers and heirs of the shrine. In this way, the emperor was able to attach the "Chishti mystical aura entirely to Fatehpur-Sikri. Its eventual subordination to the emperor was an essential part of the religiosity Akbar claimed for his reign."[93]

The devout Muslims who would come to pray at the mosque would be under the protection of God and of the King. Juneja points out that "Unlike a Christian church, where every significant action converges at the altar, there is no liturgical center in the mosque, for the sacred centre is not within the edifice but outside it." Hence at the time of prayer, a Muslim is reminded of "belonging to a larger community transcending political frontiers ... a refuge from the outside world within which class antagonisms, dissidence, rivalries and differences dissolve through the constitution of a homogenous community held together by pity and brotherhood."[94] The sacred center for this homogenous community is Mecca, but the king becomes the most prominent intermediary providing an access to the most sacred core of the Islamic world.

One can see how Tusi's proposition of correlation and balance might have been harnessed here. The idea was that the norms established by the king's being and demeanor should run through harmoniously in other domains. In practice, a great deal happened to make the discipline tilt from its design. For a historian of gender relations the contest between the prescriptive and the possible denial of those prescriptions is best seen in how the inhabitants of the *haram* negotiated this arrangement in their everyday lives. Like the normalizing of the king's body and its comportment, the careful construction and separation of spaces for different activities and rituals serves to increase the sense of imperial power and control. The organization of an exclusive women's zone and of women's sacredness was in line with Akbar's new regime. Despite the declared physical demarcation of the public/outer (court) and private/inner (*haram*) spaces for the first time, there was much movement, spatially, and in the carrying out of different public and private activities. I shall discuss these at length in the next chapter.

The structure of empire (iii): the network of marriages

Let us now turn to the network of Mughal marriages, which I take as an instance of the third domain of Tusi, and as another sign of the emperor's inhabiting (and enveloping) the entire world. What is the significance of the 300 wives (Monserrate)[95] or 5,000 women (Abu-l Fazl)[96] – depending on one's source – that Akbar is supposed to have had? While the emperor's chroniclers differ in reporting the number of women in his *haram*, they are unanimous in writing about his large *haram*. It is notable that Babur, even in

---

[93] Richards, "The Imperial Capital," p. 66.   [94] Juneja, *Architecture*, p. 81.
[95] Monserrate, *Commentary*, p. 202.   [96] *A'in-i Akbari*, I, p. 46.

his wanderings and situation of many homes, is said to have had no more than ten wives. Humayun probably had five.[97] What purpose does the great increase in the number of marriages contracted by Akbar serve?

Several historians have stressed the political aspect of Mughal marriages.[98] Marital alliances were often key to the forging of political partnerships, and required for the production of royal heirs (as was clearly recorded in imperial regulations on matrimony). They might also have served as an important mark of the empire's strength, its virility, as a symbol of its regality and new imperial position. In this section, however, I consider Akbar's marriages (and those of his family members) to suggest that they might perhaps be read in another way: symbolically demonstrating that the world was under the emperor's protection.

Since Akbar was constructed as the center of a realm, upon whom was premised the making of other domains of his empire, it was likely that those who married him were seen as blessed simply by the fact of such union. As Abu-l Fazl tells us, imperial marriages were exalted because of the emperor. The sheer number and variety of these marriages is striking.

Several of the emperor's matrimonial alliances project the process of empire formation, especially those with the Rajputs. Many of these are recorded as having taken place in the early part of his reign when the need to cement his power was greatest. This was the time when Akbar's kingdom was not yet a dominant imperial entity, and its general circumstances were fluid. Even if this was a self-consciously Muslim polity, seeking legitimacy as a "Muslim" kingdom, the rules that should govern it were not strictly laid down, either in the *Shar'ia* or in the laws of the illustrious forefathers. A great deal of negotiation, and the making of many new traditions, was therefore necessary in the course of the making of the empire.

Abu-l Fazl discusses the marriages of Akbar at this time. The following one was contracted in 1556, when Akbar was at Delhi, in order to "soothe the minds of the Zamindars." Among the zamindars was Jamal Khan, the cousin of Hasan Khan of Mewat. Abu-l Fazl informs us that Jamal Khan was "one of the great zamindars of India." He had two beautiful daughters. Akbar married the elder sister, and gave the younger in marriage to Bayram Khan Khan-i Khanan (Akbar's guardian, and later *vakil* or vice-regent of his empire).[99]

Then in January 1562, Chaghatai Khan, an intimate courtier of Akbar, discussed with him the exceptional loyalty of Raja Bihari Mal who was the head of the Kachwaha clan.[100] According to Chaghatai Khan, Bihari Mal had "been loyal to the sublime family," and "had conducted himself as one

---

[97] See Beveridge, *Humayun*, Appendix A.
[98] See A. L. Srivastava, *Akbar the Great: Political History, 1542–1605*, vol. I (Agra, 1962), pp. 62–63; K. S. Lal, *Mughal Harem*, p. 25; Richards, *Mughal Empire*, pp. 19–25; and Nath, *Private Life*, ch. III, to take only a few examples.
[99] *Akbarnama*, II, p. 76.   [100] *Akbarnama*, II, p. 240.

of those who were firmly bound to the sublime saddle-straps," but had suffered a great deal on account of Mirza Sharaf al-Din's behavior.[101] The latter wanted to take possession of Amber, which was in Marwar, the seat of Raja Bihari Mal's ancestors.[102] Bihari Mal was brought into Akbar's presence along with several relations and leading men of his clan. Akbar's "discerning glance read devotion and sincerity in the behaviour of the Rajah and his relatives," and the Raja was elevated as one of the distinguished members of the court.[103] To cement this political alliance, the Raja offered his daughter in marriage to Akbar. The emperor accepted the proposal, and Bihari Mal conducted the wedding "in the most admirable manner and brought his fortunate daughter to this station and placed her among the ladies of the harem."[104] The dominance of the Kachwaha clan was an obvious incentive for Akbar to consolidate his connection with the local ruler. Akbar's apex position, his illustrious lineage and the growing grandeur of his court were no less consequential for Bihari Mal. But note Abu-l Fazl's presentation of this case as the "elevation" of Bihari Mal and the fortune of his daughter, both of whom are said to be uplifted by the "discerning glance" of the emperor even in this early and fluid time in his monarchical career.

Other such matrimonial alliances followed. Badauni notes that in 1562–63, when Akbar was pursuing Shah 'Abdul Ma'ali, a rebel, it was in Delhi that Akbar's "intention of connecting himself by marriage with the nobles of Dihli was first broached," and "Qawwals and eunuchs were sent into the harems for the purpose of selecting daughters of the nobles, and of investigating their condition."[105] Again in 1568, when Akbar was at Mandu (to deal with the troubles regarding 'Abdullah Khan Uzbik), several zamindars of the neighborhood of Mandu expressed their allegiance to him. Miran Mubarak Shah, the ruler of Khandesh, "sent valuable presents, with a written representation to the imperial court."[106] Later on, an imperial *farman* was sent to Miran Mubarak, "that he should send one of his daughters whom he may consider to be deserving of doing service to the emperor [*sic*] to the court."[107] Miran Shah was joyous, according to Nizam al-Din Ahmad, and considered the proposal to be a great honor.[108] In 1570–71, Akbar also married the niece of Raja Kalyan Mal of Bikaner, and the daughter of Raja Har Rai of Jaisalmer.[109]

The first half of the 1560s was uncertain for Akbar on several fronts. The only territory that he held securely was "a compact region" between Lahore, Delhi, Agra, and Jaunpur, the old "Hindustan," though this had been

---

[101] Married to Akbar's daughter Bakhshi Banu.
[102] *Akbarnama*, II, p. 240.   [103] *Ibid.*, p. 242.   [104] *Ibid.*, pp. 242–243.
[105] *Muntakhab*, II, p. 59.   [106] *Tabaqat*, II, p. 285.   [107] *Ibid.*
[108] *Ibid.* According to the *Akbarnama*, it was Miran Mubarak Shah who wanted his daughter to be included among Akbar's *haram*, *Tabaqat*, II, p. 285, n. 1.
[109] Nath, *Private Life*, p. 23.

extended to include Gwalior and Ajmer to the west.[110] Gujarat, central India, Khandesh and the states of Rajputana were independent. The descendants of the Sur dynasty and other Afghan families held Benaras, Chanar and the provinces of Bengal and Bihar. Similarly, southern India was completely outside the sphere of Akbar's suzerainty. Additionally, Akbar had to establish his own primacy among the Muslim nobility that held power in the Mughal domains, at this time when he had shed the tutelage of Bayram Khan, his tutor and vice-regent.

It is hardly surprising therefore that current historical investigations emphasize Akbar's need for a strong political base through his marriages, and that he sought numerous new marital alliances to win political allies. What is perhaps not sufficiently underscored in the received historical literature is the presence of a unique conception of kingship that was being proclaimed through the making of these marital alliances. Marriages with Akbar were not only politically valuable, but "elevating," and "blessed."

Akbar and his close associates entered into several different kinds of marital alliances. Some of the earliest ones reinforced links with major noble families of Central Asian background. Others forged connections with well-established communities in the subcontinent – most prominent among these being the Rajputs. It will help to examine a few of these marriages in a little more detail. Akbar's marriage, on the death of Bayram Khan in 1560–61, to the latter's wife, Salimeh Sultan Begum, is one striking example. The marriage signaled Akbar's loyalty and commitment to those who were close to the Mughal court. It can have done his cause no harm that the Begum was also the daughter of the well-connected Nur al-Din Muhammad Chaghaniyani and the granddaughter of Babur.[111]

Similar considerations seem to underlie other royal marriages, such as the marriage of Akbar's sister, Bakhshi Banu to Mirza Sharaf al-Din Husain. The reasons for this alliance are given as follows in the *Akbarnama*: Mirza Sharaf al-Din Husain was of "very exalted lineage," so Akbar had given him a "lofty rank" in order to enable the mirza to be "a prop of the Sultanate." "As the high connections and the reputation of the Mirza were visible to all the world," Akbar gave him in marriage "the cupola of chastity," Bakhshi Banu Begum, who was the "Shahinshah's pure sister." By this alliance, says the chronicler, "the position of the Mirza was enormously exalted."[112]

In the marriages of Akbar's daughters, Shakr-un-Nisa Begum and Khanim Sultan, the importance of illustrious connections is emphasized again. Shakr-un-Nisa Begum was married to Shahrukh Mirza in 1594.[113] The groom was a son of Ibrahim Mirza, and grandson of Mirza Sulayman of Badakhshan.[114] This was the famous Badakhshani family (of the same ancestry as that of the

---

[110] Richards, *Mughal Empire*, p. 12.
[111] Beveridge, *Humayun*, Appendix A, p. 276.   [112] *Akbarnama*, II, p. 197.
[113] *Akbarnama*, III, p. 990.   [114] *Ibid.*, Index, p. 54.

Mughals) with whom the Mughals had had close contacts, especially during Humayun's reign. Similarly, Khanim Sultan, was given in marriage to Muzaffar Husain Mirza,[115] a son of Ibrahim Husain and Gulrukh Begum, Humayun's stepsister.[116]

Many of these marriages were conducted with households that had been connected with the Mughals for a long time. The genealogical and political concerns – "of very exalted lineage," "high connections and reputation," the potential of a Mirza as a possible "prop of the state" – are clearly stated (nevertheless, the emphasis is on the rewards that the Mirza reaped from this matrimony, not the other way round).

There were many considerations behind the marital alliances the Mughals forged: political advantage or sagacity, the nobility of the family, lofty lineage, and sound abilities. Another, the desire for offspring, is clearly stated in the official statement on marriage.[117] In recording the regulations regarding marriages, Abu-l Fazl emphasizes that the institution was a "means of preserving the stability of the human race and ensuring the progress of the world."[118] He restates a version of the same regulation before providing the account of Akbar's son, Salim's marriage: "If, as in the case of those who have chosen celibacy, there be no marriages, then the great fountain-head of humanity shall become choked, and the stream of Divine benevolence shall sink into the sand."[119]

Reproduction was necessary for the purposes of an empire, even if the preservation of a famous line that might become extinct (a potential concern in the earlier Timurid–Uzbik conflict) was no longer an overriding fear. The emperor needed heirs: and there was something divine too in the fact that several of these heirs were the offspring of unions between leading Muslim and non-Muslim families. Jahangir was the son of Akbar and Harkha (later called *Maryam-uz-zamani*), the daughter of Bihari Mal, the Raja of Amber; Shah Jahan, the son of Jahangir and Jagat Gosain, a granddaughter of Raja Maldeo of Jodhpur.

Salim married into several Rajput households: to the daughter of Raja Bhagwan Das (son of Raja Bihari Mal of Amber), and with Jodhbai (the daughter of Mota Rai Udai Singh of Jodhpur), as well as to the daughter of Rai Raisingh of Bikaner.[120] Similarly, Prince Sultan Danyal was married to the daughter of Rai Mal,[121] who was the son of Rai Maldeo, a strong ally of Akbar.[122]

In relation to Salim's marriage with the daughter of Raja Bhagwan Das, Abu-l Fazl notes the importance of forging marital alliances and building connections with prestigious families. His introductory remark is significant: those who are "profoundly intelligent" ought to follow certain methods as the

---

[115] *Ibid.*, p. 990.   [116] *Ibid.*, Index, p. 43.   [117] *Ibid.*, p. 287.   [118] *Ibid.*   [119] *Ibid.*, p. 677.
[120] Nath, *Private Life*, p. 23.   [121] *Akbarnama*, III, p. 1040.
[122] *A'in-i Akbari*, I, pp. 330, 331, 474, 475.

will of God.[123] Abu-l Fazl then elucidates five points that need to be followed. The fifth required that in arranging marriages the question of background, i.e., the need for superiority of both the bride and the groom, should be attended to, "so that there may be good offspring."[124]

In line with this, the Raja's daughter is described as having a "purity [that] adorned her high extraction, and [she] was endowed with beauty and graces; and that it was the wish of her family that she should be united to the prince."[125] The bride was the daughter of a noble official, who had an eminent lineage, and was therefore likely to produce "good offspring." Besides, the family was politically important. Akbar had gained the allegiance of the Kachwaha clan as early as January 1562 when, after the introduction of Bihari Mal to Akbar, his first Rajput marriage was solemnized with this house. Several Kachwahas had thereafter been appointed to high office.[126] Although the association with the clan fitted requirements of a marriage in the Mughal family, the desire of the woman's family for a marital alliance with the Mughals is also emphasized.

Accounts of the marriages of Prince Murad and Prince Danyal bring out the same concern with lineage and reproduction as may be seen in that of Salim.[127] Murad was married on 5 May 1587 to the daughter of 'Azim Mirza Kukeh, a foster-brother of Akbar, of whom the emperor was "exceedingly fond."[128] In the *Akbarnama*, encomiums on the reproductive function of marriage precede the account of Prince Danyal's wedding: "As marriage is a means of cultivating the garden of creation ... especially in a ruling family, H.M. arranged that an union should take place between the prince and the chaste daughter of Sultan Khwaja."[129]

What is most striking about these imperial marriages is their range. It is as if the emperor was accommodating the entire world through a marital grid. Daughters of kings and nobles of all cultures and every domain were seeking his protection, and Akbar was extending shelter far and wide.[130]

Not surprisingly, doubts were expressed in various quarters about the legitimacy of the kinds of marriages being contracted and the kind of

---

[123] *Akbarnama*, III, p. 677.

[124] *Ibid.*, and n. 11.   [125] *Ibid.*, p. 678.   [126] *Akbarnama*, II, p. 244.

[127] In his description of Murad's marriage, the spirit of Abu-l Fazl's introductory remark is identical to the one he makes for Salim. See *Akbarnama*, III, p. 791.

[128] *Akbarnama*, III, p. 61. Mirza Kukeh was the son of Akbar's wet-nurse Jiji Anageh, see *Akbarnama*, III, Index, p. 18, "Aziz Kokaltash (Mirza) Khan A 'zim."

[129] *Ibid.*, p. 806. The Khvajeh came from the line of renowned saint Khvajeh Asir al-Din Ahrar. Sultan Khvajeh was appointed *Mir-i Hajj* (the leader of the Pilgrims' Caravan), and commanded a numerous party of courtiers during a pilgrimage to Mecca. On his return he was made Commander of One Thousand and was appointed the *Sadr* (Chief Judge, Chancellor), an office he held till his death (*A'in-i Akbari*, I, p. 466).

[130] These different marital links also show the range of political connections that were deemed necessary for the making and maintenance of the empire. This process of political marriages would continue well after the empire was triumphantly and securely established; see Thackston, *Jahangirnama*, Preface to the *Jahangirnama* by Muhammad-Hadi, p. 6.

marriage network that the emperor was establishing. Badauni reports in the *Muntakhab-ut-Tavarikh* that there was an extended debate on the question of how many wives the emperor was allowed to have.[131] At one of the meetings in the ʿIbadat Khana, he writes, Akbar asked how many free-born women a man was legally allowed to marry (by *nikah*).[132] The jurists answered that four was the limit fixed by the prophet.

Akbar is reported to have remarked that he had not restricted himself to that number, and "in justice to his wives ... he now wanted to know what remedy the law provided for his case." The emperor also added that Shaykh ʿAbd-un-Nabi had once told him that one of the Mujtahids had as many as nine wives. The ʿUlama present there replied that the Mujtahid alluded to was Ibn Abi Laya; indeed some had even allowed eighteen from a literal translation of the Quran verse: "Marry women of your choice, two, three, or four. But if ye fear that ye shall not be able to deal justly [with them] then only one (Quran, Sura. IV, 3)."[133] Akbar then sent a message to Shaykh ʿAbd-un-Nabi, who replied that he had simply pointed out to the emperor that a difference of opinion existed on this point among lawyers, and that he had not given a *fatwa* in order to legalize irregular marriage proceedings. According to Badauni, this annoyed Akbar very much. After considerable discussion on this subject, it was decreed, Badauni says that by *mut ʿa*[134] (not by *nikah*) a man might marry any number of wives he pleased; and, secondly, Imam Malik allowed *mut ʿa* marriages. "The Shi ʿahs, as was well known, loved children born in *mut ʿah* wedlock more than those born by *nikah* wives, contrary to the Sunnis and the Ahl-i Jamaʿat."[135]

The debate on legal marriages did not end there. On another night, Badauni notes, Akbar invited Qazi Yaqub, Shaykh Abu-l Fazl, Haji Ibrahim, and others for further discussion. Abu-l Fazl was selected as the opponent of the group and he laid before the emperor several traditions regarding the *mut ʿa* marriages. Badauni was also asked for his opinion. He replied that since conclusions had to be drawn from contradictory traditions and customs, he could only provide the following interpretation: that Imam Malik and the

---

[131] This entire episode is taken from *Muntakhab*, II, p. 212. Other references are indicated separately.

[132] ʿIbadat Khana, literally the house of worship, instituted by Akbar in the late 1570s, for spiritual, theological, and religio-legal discussions.

[133] This *Sura* is taken from John L. Esposito, *Women in Muslim Family Law* (Syracuse, 1984), p. 4. W. H. Lowe translates the *Sura* in the *Muntakhab* as follows: "Marry whatever women ye like, and two and two, and three and three, and four and four."

[134] Literally, "enjoyment; in law, temporary marriage, also called nikah al-mut ʿa, a marriage which is contracted for a fixed period," P. J. Bearman *et al.* (eds.), *The Encyclopaedia of Islam* (Leiden, 2000), p. 294. For a detailed discussion on the question of *mut ʿa* marriages, see Shahla Haeri, "Temporary Marriage and State in Iran: An Islamic Discourse on Female Sexuality," *Social Research*, 59 (Spring 1992), p. 204; and Shahla Haeri, *Law of Desire: Temporary Marriage in Shiʾi Iran* (Syracuse, 1989).

[135] Mawlawi Ali, *Muntakhab*, II, p. 207; cited in *Aʾin-i Akbari*, I, pp. 182–183. A version of the quotation above may also be found in *Muntakhab*, II, pp. 211–213.

Shi'as unanimously looked upon *mut 'a* marriages as legal, and that Imam Shafi looked upon the *mut 'a* marriages as illegal. Badauni added, "but, should at any time a Qazi of the Maliki sect decide that a Mu'tah is legal, it is legal according to the common belief, even for Shafi'is and Hanafis."[136] This, in Badauni's words, pleased Akbar, after which a Maliki *qazi* was appointed, who gave a decree on the spot and pronounced *mut 'a* marriages legal.[137] However skilful or contrived the judgment in favor of Akbar may be seen to have been, it is clear that in order to maintain his vision of a magnificent empire, the emperor was not going to be restricted by narrow legalisms.

The ambition of imperial monarchs, with aspirations to take in the world (literally or metaphorically), is not a new phenomenon. There are numerous examples from different parts of the world, and different ages, of the large *harams* maintained by royalty as a sign of imperial power and dominance. The *haram* of the Sasanian king Khusrau I (531–79 C.E.) is said to have consisted of some 12,000 women. It is written that Alexander vastly increased the size of his *haram* after he defeated King Darius of Persia in 333 B.C.E. The *haram* that he captured from Darius included the king's mother and wife, attended by their own troops of women on horseback; fifteen carriages carrying the king's children, their nurses, and a large number of eunuchs; and other carriages carrying Darius's 365 concubines. In imitation of the captured ruler, henceforth, Alexander kept his *haram* of exactly the same number of concubines as Darius.[138] Many such examples can be found in Mesopotamian, Persian, Hellenic, Christian, and Islamic cultures. Or to turn to Akbar's not so distant forerunner: Ghiyas al-Din of Malwa (1469–1500) had 1,600 women. Or take another example from the time of the Delhi Sultanate: Qazi Mughis al-Din is supposed to have advised Sultan Ala al-Din Khalji (1296–1316) to increase the expenses of his *haram* tenfold because "a large and magnificent harem would inspire awe and enhance respect for the king in the minds of the people."[139]

These large *harams* may well be seen as signs of the virility and power of kings or rulers. However, the presence of the large number of women in Akbar's *haram* is perhaps better read as a sign of the supremacy of the monarch as the center of the empire. The reach and protection of Akbar's empire comes to be stretched through his marriages in quite extraordinary terms. In part this had to do with being able to watch over the many different kinds of people who made up the empire. Kin, fellow-believers, and people of the book mattered, but the rest of the world – non-believers, *kafirs*, other races, subjects – came to be of crucial importance too. Thus Akbar's marriages with the Rajputs and other Hindu nobles become an index of a power that incorporated the universe in quite unprecedented ways.

[136] *Muntakhab*, II, p. 212.   [137] *Ibid.*, pp. 212–213.
[138] Leila Ahmed, *Women and Gender in Islam* (New Haven, 1992), pp. 14, 17, 18.
[139] Lal, *Mughal Harem*, p. 25.

To start with, Akbar's closest supporters, friends and nobles were Muslim (Mughals, Turks, Afghans, Persians, Hindustanis) but the majority of the population in the country that he now ruled was non-Muslim. The support of some of these local non-Muslim rulers was crucial in the design of the grand empire that Akbar was building. In his project of establishing a far-flung "world empire," he had married numerous Hindu women. But if the *Shari'a* allowed only four marriages, what would be the status of all these Hindu (and indeed many Muslim) wives? What, one might also ask, was to be the place of a Hindu wife in a Muslim *haram*? One way of approaching these questions is to consider how Hindu rulers, and their chroniclers and bards, responded to the marital network established by Akbar.

In his study of the local institutions and political culture of the Rajputs, Norman Ziegler asks what enabled the Rajputs to transfer their loyalties to the Mughals, "with whom they formed not only patron–client ties, but also marital alliances."[140] Ziegler's central argument is that the support and loyalty of the Rajputs rested upon a congruence between their traditional ideals, myths and symbols, and their loyalties, as well as their cultural conception of rank, authority, and sovereignty.[141] He says,

> It is important to note that the Muslim was also included within this hierarchical scheme as a Rajput. ... This category of "Muslim" within the Rajput jati did not include all Muslims, but only those who were warriors and who possessed sovereignty and power equal to or greater than the Hindu Rajput. The Muslim emperor in particular, held a position of high rank and esteem, and the traditions often equate him with Ram, the pre-eminent Ksatriya cultural hero of Hindu Rajput.[142]

During the Mughal period, there were two primary units of reference and identification for a Rajput, according to Ziegler: one of these was his brotherhood (*bhai-bamdh*) and the other his relations by marriage (*saga*).[143] The second unit seems to be of particular relevance here. The act of marriage united the woman with her husband's brotherhood, on the one hand, and created an alliance, on the other.[144] Given the political culture and notions of the Rajput community that he outlines, it seems that the marriages of the Rajput women with the Mughals would serve both purposes of the *saga*. The more interesting point is the cultural exchange that would develop in times of "fit," as Ziegler calls the balance between Rajput valorization of their local culture and the Mughal demand for service and allegiance.[145]

The Rajput bardic tradition equating Akbar with Ram is the most striking instance of Ziegler's "fit," but it is perhaps more than that. Akbar here comes to be seen as the monarch of all monarchs – even the God of Gods (since there are many Gods in the Hindu tradition). The elevation of Akbar to the status

---

[140] Norman P. Ziegler, "Some Notes on Rajput Loyalties During the Mughal Period," in Richards (ed.), *Kingship and Authority*, p. 263.
[141] *Ibid.*, p. 276.   [142] *Ibid.*, p. 269.   [143] *Ibid.*, p. 253.   [144] *Ibid.*, p. 254.   [145] *Ibid.*, p. 276.

of Ram amounts to an amazing acceptance of Abu-l Fazl's projection of the great new empire and its unique center. It was as if his "spiritual and temporal khedive" had arrived – as protector, lord, and master.

This context of monarchical magnificence and order had deep implications for the domestic life of Akbar. His *haram* became indubitably "sacred and hidden," a *sanctum sanctorum* marking a return to the very origins of the term in early Islamic history. In this radically redefined and resituated (physically demarcated) *haram*, with new institutions and regulations of the empire at work for all and sundry, new imperial women subjects would be fashioned too. We shall see in the next chapter how the inhabitants of the domestic world translated and recast this vision.

CHAPTER 7

Settled, sacred, and "incarcerated": the imperial *haram*

In *A'in 15*, Abu-l Fazl, the imperial chronicler, wrote the regulations regarding the imperial *haram*.[1] This was the first time in the career of the Mughal dynasty that an official statute on the royal household was issued. In this, the women were officially designated *pardeh-giyan*, the veiled ones. In current Mughal historiography, the sequestered character of the *haram* has come to be viewed as the mark of the Mughal women's life. This development needs to be seen in the context of the routinization of imperial spaces and practices and the creation of new subjects (especially female) in the making of Akbar's new regime. Chapter 6 explored the processes that went into the making of Akbar's monarchy and empire, by probing how Abu-l Fazl constructed the imperial monarch as sovereign and masculine, and conjured up the empire and its structures around the figure of the awesome monarch. The following discussion focuses more specifically on the ordering of domestic life that accompanied, and was constitutive of, this wider restructuring.

One of the most interesting developments of this period was the institutionalization of the *haram*, not only in its physical laying out at Fatehpur-Sikri, but in its conceptual framework as well. Courtly and domestic spaces came, for the first time, to be distinctly separated from each other. A neatly compartmentalized *haram* (*shabistan-i Iqbal*) was designed to place women in a strictly segregated space – for "good order and propriety," as Abu-l Fazl has it. As part of the process of the institutionalization of the imperial *haram*, the term itself came to be the most common description of the women's sphere, signifying important changes in the Mughals' domestic life.

One of the central tasks of this chapter is to show how the meaning and resonance of the term *haram* now change from the usage in Humayun's time. *Haram*, in Akbari chronicles, refers both to physical structures, the secluded quarters where royal women lived, and to the women themselves who lived in those dwellings. The usage of *haram* in the contemporary chronicles marks a return to the origins of the term in early Islamic history (*haram* as a *sanctum sanctorum*) and to the sanctity that extends to not only the inner quarters, but

---

[1]   *A'in-i Akbari*, I, p. 45.

also to the *haram* folk: this is not altogether surprising, given the divine connections now repeatedly drawn up for the emperor. What are the implications of all these changes?

The construction of order in different arenas and activities – what Abu-l Fazl, in the preface to the *A'in-i Akbari*, describes as the proper order of the household, army, and empire – was a major hallmark of Akbar's empire.[2] In the drive to coordinate all aspects of imperial life, domestic life had to be carefully regulated too. A neatly compartmentalized women's domain appeared in physical structures, ritual practices, and in imperial regulations. With that, courtly and domestic spaces came to be distinctly separated from each other.

A significant effect of the new arrangements was to increase the invisibility of the royal women, now more elevated and at the same time more secluded than before. However, the theory of the new empire, which was to find tangible form in the sacred, incarcerated *haram*, was never so successful as to wipe out contradictions, tensions, human volition, or unexpected departures – that is, the stuff of human history. Although in the changing environment of Akbar's reign a great deal happened to alter domestic arrangements, there is (as one would expect) considerable evidence to show how women and men continued to negotiate the prescribed, and the everyday. The initial part of this chapter indicates how Abu-l Fazl represents the domestic life of Akbar, establishing the new norms. The latter part of the chapter investigates how Mughal women responded to the new imperial constructions of the normative, and how women's negotiation of the new sovereign ideals was to be a crucial element in the making of the monarchy – at times, by the rupturing of those very ideals.

One extraordinary moment in which the power of the new regime, on the one hand, and the contrary nodes of (women's) power, on the other, converge is the pilgrimage to Mecca undertaken by the women of Akbar's *haram* in 1578. Gulbadan Banu Begum, our memoirist, led this pilgrimage, which included numerous "senior" and "respectable" women of the *haram*, under the protection of three older men and a few servants. While this *hajj* may be constructed as a sign of the "Islamic" claims of this polyglot empire, this journey simultaneously maps the desires and agency of imperial women, and shows us the nature of activities still possible in the red sandstone palaces of Fatehpur-Sikri and Agra. Like the seeking of Khanzadeh Begum's opinion on the matter of kingship (the reading of the *khutba*), this collective women's *hajj* remains an unparalleled example in the annals of the Mughals. The point that it highlights for us is that while Akbar's *haram* was secluded, sacred, and even inaccessible to most people, it was by no means closed off from the world, unconcerned with politics, or bereft of power or interest in public affairs.

---

[2] *A'in-i Akbari*, I, Preface, p. 9.

Sacred idiom, sacred domain: the organization of the *haram*

His Majesty is a great friend of good order and propriety in business. ... For this reason, the large number of women [*pardeh-giyan*] – a vexatious question even for great statesmen – furnished his Majesty with an opportunity to display his wisdom, and to rise from the low level of worldly dependence to the eminence of perfect freedom. The imperial palace and household are therefore in best order. ... His Majesty has made a large enclosure with fine buildings inside, where he reposes. Though there are more than five thousand women, he has given to each a separate apartment. He has also divided them into sections, and keeps them attentive to their duties. Several chaste women have been appointed as *daroghas*, and superintendents over each section, and one has been selected for the duties of writer. Thus, as in the imperial offices, everything is here also in proper order.[3]

In this discussion of the new sanctity that was to be created through the seclusion of women, Abu-l Fazl also refers to the arrangements for the security of the *haram* by what he calls "sober and active women." According to Abu-l Fazl, the trustworthiest women were placed at the quarters of Akbar. The eunuchs guarded the outside enclosure and, at some distance from them, the Rajputs formed another line of watchmen. Besides, on all four sides of the complex, there were "guards of Nobles, *Ahadis*."[4] He then gives the salaries of the women guards: the women of "highest rank" received 1,610 to 1,028 rupees per month, and those of the servants varied between 51 rupees and 2 rupees. If a woman wanted anything "within the limit of her salary," she had to apply to the cash-keepers (*tahwildars*) of the *haram*. It was the General Treasurer, however, who made the payments in cash.[5]

As far as visitors were concerned, Abu-l Fazl says, whenever "the wives of the nobles, or other women of chaste character" desired to visit the *haram*, they had to notify their wish to the servants of the *haram*, and wait for a reply. From there the requests were sent to the officers of the palace, and "those who ... [were] eligible" were given permission to enter the *haram*. Some women "of rank" could be given permission to remain in the *haram* for a whole month.[6]

The public pronouncement of spatial living arrangements of the imperial women is a first step in Abu-l Fazl's narrative, from where he anticipates the ascription of the veiled status, and the carefully segregated allocation of women's quarters, as a vital hallmark of the grand empire. There are various ways in which he follows this declaration.

While recording the events of the thirty-ninth year of Akbar's reign, Abu-l Fazl notes that Akbar had sent a letter addressed to the emperor of Persia.[7] The letter, incorporated in the *Akbarnama*, is prefaced with praises "of the

---

[3] *A'in-i Akbari*, I, pp. 45–46.   [4] *A'in-i Akbari*, I, pp. 46–47.   [5] *Ibid.*   [6] *Ibid.*, p. 47.
[7] *Akbarnama*, III, p. 1008. The name of the "Shahinshah of Persia" is not clarified at the beginning of the letter. Judging by the time of the letter, the addressee should be Shah 'Abbas (1588–1629), a contemporary of Akbar.

glorious company of the prophets and apostles who led mankind to better ways."[8] Akbar draws subtle connections between bounteous God and the rulers on earth (himself as well as the Persian monarch), as "shadows of Divinity" or God's representatives who were to discipline and guard mankind.[9] In one of the passages to the Safavid monarch, he says,

Let us proclaim in the pulpits of publicity; firstly, their glorious condition [of Divine humans, with the help of divine aid], and secondly ... let us tell of the bounties and noble qualities of the "members of the household" (*Ahl-i-bait*) who are confidants of the great secrets, and unveilers of the mysteries of the prophets, and let us, relying thereupon, implore new mercy![10]

The citation evokes the sacredness of the Prophet's family and, by extension, of his earthly descendants – a significant parallel in the context of what is presented as the holy empire of Akbar. This ideal of the Prophet's household, it has been argued by several scholars, became key in the assertions of Muslim monarchs who vied with each other to appropriate genealogical legitimacy as descendants of the Prophet's family.[11]

Ahl-i bayt, the Persian term used for household in Akbar's letter, incorporates two words, *ahl* and *bayt*. As noted in chapter 5, *ahl* may be understood as companion or relative, persons, people of distinction, servants, and attendants. In the plural, the word means kinsmen (*kisan*), relatives (*khvishavand*), race or tribe (*qawm*), and friends (*payruvan, yaran, ashab*).[12] *Bayt* means a house, a temple, edifice, fabric.[13] As a compound word, *ahl-i bayt* renders the sense of a household – an expression that is also found in Babur's autobiography in the context of extended familial structures.

The term *bayt* is used fifteen times in the Quran to describe God's house: aside from a simple house, it is also designated as "the first house," "the ancient house," and the "sacred house (*al-bayt al-haram*)."[14] Most of these Quranic references to God's house derive from the period after Muhammad and his followers had settled in Medina[15] – the time after the revelations when the Prophet's new religio-political community (*ummah*) was being formed. The phrase *ahl-i bayt* occurs only three times in the Quran, and in each instance, it is connected with the household of a major prophet, and involves references to female members of the household. Eduardo Juan Campo tells us that the "most important aspect of the 'people of the house' phrase is not its use in the Quran *per se*, however, but what Muslims later

---

[8] *Akbarnama*, III, p. 1008.   [9] *Ibid.*, p. 1012.   [10] *Ibid.*, p. 1008.
[11] See the following as examples: Juan Eduardo Campo, *The Other Sides of Paradise: Explorations into the Religious Meanings of Domestic Space in Islam* (Columbia, 1991), p. 19; Peirce, *Imperial Harem*, p. 162.
[12] *Loghatname*, II, p. 3149.   [13] Steingass, *Persian*, s. v. "bayt."
[14] Campo, *The Other Sides of Paradise*, p. 9. The materials for the discussion that follows on the religious meanings of domestic spaces is taken from Campo, unless indicated otherwise.
[15] *Ibid.*, p. 13.

made of it." After Muhammad's death, the term came to designate the Prophet and his family, as well as his "noble" descendants.[16]

Abu-l Fazl too seems to be invoking a Prophetic-familial association for Akbar. Interestingly, the emperor is represented as making this connection alongside a community of divine monarchs, enhancing thereby what Abu-l Fazl refers to at one point as the "spiritual relationship" between Akbar and the Safavid king, both of whom are described as the members of the *ahl-i bayt*.[17]

Once the spiritual connection with the *ahl-i bayt* was spelled out, the virtues of such a "divine household," highly praised by the monarch (the members of which are "confidants of the great secrets") would then become the model for his own, earthly one – both in expectation and portrayal. The term *ahl-i bayt* is not frequently used in the contemporary chronicles of Akbar's time. Its spirit, however, is amplified by other terms used to project Akbar's domestic world. These terms include, *dudman-i quddusi* ("holy family"),[18] *dudman-i vala* ("sublime family")[19] and *dudman-i dawlat* ("illustrious family"), to take only a few examples.[20]

The word *dudman* is of some interest. In discussing the context of Babur's domestic life, we came across the word *khandan*, which pertains to an illustrious family. For Babur, who emphatically called upon his Timurid lineage, *khandan* was an important term; it entailed the following meanings: *dudman* or genealogy, *tabar* or extraction, *dudeh* or genealogy, and, as a compound noun (*khanivar*), *khandan* indicates the people of the same house.[21] The invocation of *dudman* or genealogy was of a different order in the construction of Akbar's empire: here, the imperial chronicler called upon the Prophetic ancestors (not Timurid) in order to establish close connections with them.

None of the terms discussed above is encountered as frequently as the *haram*, officially designated as the *Shabistan-i Iqbal* (literally, "the fortunate place of sleep or dreams") in the *A'in-i Akbari*.[22] The etymology of the word *haram* is critical to understanding its various associations, some of which Akbari chroniclers might be drawing from. R. B. Serjeant informs us that closely linked with the holy family is the institution known in ancient Arabia as the *haram* (and in contemporary South Arabia as *hawtah*).[23] He explains that in ancient Arabia, at the top of the social stratification were the armed

---

[16] *Ibid.*, 19.   [17] *Akbarnama*, III, p. 1009.

[18] Maulawi, *Akbarnamah*, II, p. 217; *Akbarnama*, II, p. 335.

[19] Maulawi, *Akbarnamah*, II, p. 289; *Akbarnama*, II, p. 426.

[20] Maulawi, *Akbarnamah*, I, p. 6; *Akbarnama*, I, p. 16.

[21] *Loghatname*, I, pp. 82–98. There is another term, *Khanivadeh*, which has several meanings: *khandan*, *dudman*, *tabar*, *dudeh*, *khanivar*; see *Loghatname*, I, pp. 82–98. The term is used once in a discussion of the *'Ibadat Khana*, but the reference is not to Akbar's family, *Akbarnama*, III, p. 366; Maulawi, *Akbarnamah*, III, p. 253.

[22] *Persian A'in*, p. 39. See also *A'in-i Akbari*, I, p. xxi. The title *Shabistan-i Iqbal* is rendered "The Imperial Harem" in H. Blochmann's translation of *A'in 15*.

[23] R. B. Serjeant, "Haram and Hawtah, the Sacred Enclave in Arabia," in Abdurrahman Badawi (ed.), *Mélanges Taha Husain* (Cairo, 1962), p. 43.

tribes, ranging from camel-owning desert tribes to tribesmen living in settled villages. Customary law was central to how these tribal units governed their relationships. Since there were always times when tribesmen needed greater authority than their own, they turned to the holy family, which derived its power from the divine – perhaps through the medium of a prophet or a saint. According to Arabic hagiologies, a member of the holy family declared a certain piece of land a sacred enclave, a *hawtah*. It was incumbent upon people to show it respect (*ihtiram*), and any infringement or violation of the sanctity of this domain was likely to bring "condign punishment."[24] In and around this sacred, sanctified space, authority reposed clearly in the creator of that space. Serjeant explains that if the Medinean tribes ("self-governing but linked to the haram") disagreed at any point, the disagreement was to be referred to Muhammad, who knew the law.[25]

Among the Bedouin, *haram* was "a sacred area around a shrine; a place where the holy power manifests itself." As an adjective, the term represented "everything that is forbidden to the profane and separated from the rest of the world. The cause of this prohibition could be either impurity (temporary or intrinsic) or holiness, which is a permanent state of sublime purity."[26] The *haram* subsequently came to accumulate many more meanings. Aliakbar Dehkhoda's *Loghatname* lists the following: those behind the curtain, not to be seen (*pardeh-giyan*); that which is inside, internal, within, intrinsic (*andarun, andaruni*); house where the wives and the household live (*haramsara*); place of sleep (*shabistan*, used as a synonym for *haram*); Mecca, Medina, the area around the *Ka'ba*, and the garden of the Prophet Muhammad (*Ruzayi Rasul*).[27]

The fabric of invocations for Akbar's dwellings and of its habitants is thus woven around the Prophet, including the holy sites associated with him: his garden, Mecca, Medina, and the *Ka'ba*. In this construction, the centrality of Akbar in the *haram* is absolute; like that of Muhammad in his *haram*. The parallel between Muhammad and Akbar is significant. This is yet another component of the claim to be a hallowed and "blessed" empire – here, premised upon domestic order. The frequent use of a vocabulary resplendent with divine invocations is therefore hardly unexpected.

One other thing must be said of this vocabulary – including less commonly used expressions for Akbar's domestic life – that the sacred adjectives used as prefixes or suffixes often appear to overshadow the word indicating the familial. Thus *quddusi* ("holy"), *vala* ("sublime"), or *dawlat* ("illustrious") capture our attention first, rather than the substantive *dudman*. What is most fascinating about this language is its advertisement of the purity and sanctity attached to the notion of the familial. The pure and prophetic associations of the *haram* seem now to be deeply imbricated in the happenings

[24] *Ibid.*, pp. 43–44.   [25] *Ibid.*, p. 50.   [26] *Encyclopaedia of Islam*, p. 129.
[27] *Loghatname*, VI, pp. 7786–7789.

recounted in the chronicles of the time. Consider the following account from the *Akbarnama*. This is a description of the arrival of the "chaste" royal women from Kabul to Hindustan (1557):

When the news of the chaste ladies reached the royal ears, H.M. [His Majesty], the Shahinshah was delighted and sent that *cupola of chastity* [*'Ismat qubab*], Maham Anaga, the mother of Adham Khan, who, on account of her abundant sense and loyalty, held a high place in the esteem of the Shahinshah, and who had been in his service from the time of the cradle till his adornment of the throne, and who trod the path of good service with the acme of affection, to welcome the cortege of H.M. [Her Majesty] Miriam Makani [Hamideh Banu Begum] and other chaste ladies [*hazrat saradiq-i 'Ismat*]. That *cupola of chastity* [*'Ismat qubab*] entered on the auspicious service of the ladies in Lahore, and after informing them of H.M., the Shahinshah's eagerness to see them, proceeded with them towards the camp of fortune. . . . The auspicious conjunction took place at one stage from the fort (Mankot), and H.M. Miriam Makani's wishful eyes were gratified by the world-adorning beauty of H.M. the Shahinshah. There were mutual rejoicings, and the next morning H.H.M. Makani, Haji Begum, Gulbadan Begum, Gulcahra Begum, Salima Sultan Begum and a number more of the relations and connections of the noble family [*dudman-i 'ali*] and of the soldiery, arrived at the camp.[28]

Akbari chronicles commonly deployed reverential titles and forms of address for the women; the *Akbarnama* and the *A'in-i Akbari* are particularly resplendent with such honorifics for the women of Akbar's *haram*. The elder women were evidently the most revered ones. Note in the above citation: Hamideh Banu Begum, the mother of Akbar; Maham Anageh, his foster-mother; Haji Begum, his stepmother; Gulbadan Begum and Gulchihreh Begum, his aunts; Salimeh Sultan Begum, his older (and therefore senior) wife, all elder relatives of Akbar were referred to with illustrious titles. But while the women were revered and invoked as chaste and pure, they were at the same time (explicitly) referred to as the *pardeh-giyan*, the veiled ones.

Hamideh Banu Begum, Maryam Makani, was also referred to as the veil of chastity,[29] and pillar of purity.[30] Maham Anageh was called the cupola of chastity, and Akbar's stepsister, "the chaste" Bakht-un-Nisa Begum.[31] Similarly, Haji Begum was also called "the cupola of chastity,"[32] and Gulbadan Begum, Gulchihreh Begum, Selimeh Sultan Begum were all "connections of the noble family."

The veiled status of imperial women was now officially encoded in the imperial conventions.[33] The publicly declared, "required" veiling of women fits in with the larger rendering of them as perfect and hence secluded. The

---

[28] *Akbarnama*, II, p. 86; Maulawi, *Akbarnamah*, II, pp. 54–57. Nizam al-Din Ahmad records the same event, and uses the following expressions: "*Khalifa-i Ilahi*" for Akbar, "*pavilion of chastity*" for women and so on. See *Tabaqat*, II, p. 222.
[29] *Akbarnama*, II, p. 85.   [30] *Akbarnama*, I, p. 130.
[31] *Akbarnama*, III, p. 518. For details of the Begum, see Beveridge, *Humayun*, Appendix A, p. 214.
[32] *Akbarnama*, I, p. 343.   [33] *A'in-i Akbari*, I, *A'in 15*, p. 45; *Persian A'in*, I, p. 39.

veiled women thus serve as icons of the sacred empire, and their veiling preserves the sanctity of the empire. The emperor too represents his empire, but as a very visible emblem, the focus of all matters, spiritual and mundane, of institutions, as well as of other people's lives. As if to balance this intensely visible, omnipresent hallmark of a new (sacred) power, the *haram* emerges as a particularly secluded, sacred space.[34] In other words, Akbar appears both to sanctify the secluded space as well as to draw sustenance from the segregation of imperial feminine subjects and their dwellings.

In the sacredness of the empire and its *haram*, women were honored and cloistered at the same time. An aspect of this development was the invisibility of the Mughal women – or of most of them – in the public pronouncements and activities of the empire. This invisibility is very striking indeed in the case of Akbar's wives, including the mothers of his sons.

Births in the *haram:* the absence of mothers

Consider Abu-l Fazl's account of the "auspicious birth of the world-illuminating pearl of the mansion of the dominion and fortune, the night-gleaming jewel of the casket of greatness and glory, viz., of Prince Sultan Selim."[35] The author begins by writing about the keen desire of Akbar for the "great boon"[36] of a son and successor. Before Salim's birth, several children had been born to Akbar, "but they had been taken away for thousands of wise designs, one of which might be the increasing joy in the acquisition of the priceless pearl."[37] Salim was conceived with the blessings of Shaykh Salim Chishti, who lived near Fatehpur-Sikri. The pregnant wife was taken to repose in the shelter of the Shaykh's hospice, where she gave birth to Akbar's son.[38]

So when "the unique pearl of the Caliphate," Salim, was born in Fatehpur-Sikri, great joyousness and celebration followed.[39] The prisoners of the imperial domains were released, horoscopes were cast, and poets composed congratulatory odes: "a pearl of Shahinshah's mansion," "a pearl of Akbar Shahi's casket, *gawhar-i-durj-i Akbar Shahi*."[40]

One of the most startling features of this narrative on Salim's birth is that it does not so much as mention the name of the mother. Nowhere in the official history is this information provided. Salim's birth was the only event that was cast in the visual folios of the *Akbarnama*. Two of those illustrations are available in the Victoria and Albert Museum copy of the *Akbarnama*: "News of Selim's Birth Being Brought to Akbar" (Plate 2) and "Rejoicings on the

---

[34] On subsequent development of the notion of *purda* and the seclusion of women in the Islamic societies of the sub-continent, see Hanna Papanek and Gail Minault (eds.), *Separate Worlds: Studies of Purdah in South Asia* (Delhi, 1982).

[35] *Akbarnama*, II, p. 502.   [36] *Ibid.*   [37] *Ibid.*, p. 503.

[38] *Ibid.*, p. 503; *Jahangirnama*, p. 21.   [39] *Akbarnama*, II, p. 503.

[40] *Akbarnama*, II, p. 507; Maulawi, *Akbarnamah*, II, p. 347. Beveridge's Persian rendition is *gohar-i-daraj-i Akbarshahi*.

Plate 2: "News of Selim's Birth Being Brought to Akbar"

Birth of Prince Selim at Fatehpur" (Plate 3).[41] The first of these is set in court-like quarters and marks a general joyous mode, where the emperor Akbar is receiving the messenger in the midst of performing dancers and drummers. Great gaiety is visible here: the message in the folio is very direct. The second folio, "Rejoicings ... " depicts the inner section of the *haram*. A part of the folio contains the birth-chamber. In the center the musicians play their instruments. Just above the outer wall, a royal retainer (helped by another retainer, who is holding a bag) is distributing money to people. The detailed depiction of the birth-chamber, post-natal care of the mother, the attention being paid to the infant, are all crucial manifestations of the act of reproduction, and the centrality of the mother in child-birth.

In the congratulatory notes, however, it is the father (Akbar) alone who is glorified in the birth of his son; Salim is *"gawhar-i-durj-i Akbar Shahi."* The reproductive power of a wife should surely be recognized as a major contribution. It is all the more noteworthy that even in the performance of that single act of consequence, her name is missing from the records. There are metaphorical references to her: "shell of her womb"; and then, "it was determined that the matrix of the son of fortune [the pregnant mother of Salim] together with several of the officials attached to the Zenana should be conveyed to Fatehpur and should enjoy repose in the vicinity of the Shaikh."[42] The only contemporary document that names the mother of Jahangir is a later *hukm* (edict) issued by Maryam-uz-Zamani.[43] The seal on the *hukm* says, *"Vali Ni'mat Begum, valideh Nur al-Din Jahangir,"*[44] thus clearly identifying Maryam-uz-Zamani with Vali Ni'mat Begum, and unequivocally declaring her the mother of Jahangir.[45]

This is an extraordinary moment in imperial history. The wife remains unnamed even at the birth of the imperial heir. Most chronicles of the time tell us that Salim was the long-prayed-for son, and the first surviving child of Akbar. While encomiums were composed in praise of this event, the person glorified was only the king. Thus:

God be praised for the glory of the King
A splendid pearl came ashore from the ocean of justice ...
The just and perfect Muhammad Akbar, Lord of Conjunction

---

[41] Victoria and Albert Museum, *Akbarnama*, MS I. S. 2/1896, Acc. No. 115/117, and I. S. 2/1896, Acc. No. 78/117; Geeti Sen, *Paintings from the Akbarnama: A Visual Chronicle of Mughal India* (Varanasi, 1984), pp. 19 and 129. Salim's birth also appears in the second series of *Akbarnama*, completed nearly ten years later. See the double-page composition by Lal at the Chester Beatty Library. MS No. 3., fols. 142b and 143b. A folio at the British Library *Akbarnama*, MS Add. 26203, fol. 311a, shows "Daniyal as an infant with his mother (1572)." The folio corresponds to 1572, which is the year of Daniyal's birth (see the Persian text on the miniature). The simplicity with which this folio is cast is worth noting, especially when compared to the scene of Salim's birth. The title of "Daniyal's birth" is taken from Titley, *Miniatures*, p. 2.
[42] *Akbarnama*, II, p. 503.
[43] For detailed discussion of the term, see S. A. I. Tirmizi, *Edicts From the Mughal Harem* (Delhi, 1979), Introduction, especially p. xvii onwards.
[44] Tirmizi, *Edicts*, Persian text overlooking p. 10.   [45] *Ibid.*, p. xxii.

Plate 3: "Rejoicings on the Birth of Prince Selim at Fatehpur"

The renowned King, seeking and attaining his desires . . .
May our King be permanent and also the Prince
For countless days and unnumbered years.   (Khvajeh Husain of Marv)[46]

Abu-l Fazl recounts some other births in the *Akbarnama*. In these instances, too, noble wives remain unnamed producers of noble children. Two-and-a-half months after Prince Salim, in November 1569, a daughter was born in Akbar's *haram*. The girl was named Khanum, and Akbar "ordered rejoicings."[47] No other details of the celebration are available to us. The name of the mother is not given. Similarly in the cases of the births of Shah Murad and Prince Danyal,[48] the mothers remain unnamed. However, in discussing the birth of Murad, Abu-l Fazl emphasizes the union of "celestial fathers" and "the terrestrial mothers" that results "every spring [in] a fresh flower [that] blooms in the garden of fortune." It must be acknowledged that there is at least some indirect reference to the mother, the "terrestrial mother," the necessary instrument in this royal birth. In June 1570, once again, a noble son, on "whose forehead the lights of high fortune were visible, appeared in the fortunate quarters of Shaykh Selim in Fatehpur." He was named Shah Murad. Encomiasts composed verses and chronograms for this birth, and received rewards. Two horoscopes were cast, one according to Greek methods and another according to Indian rules.[49]

In what might ostensibly appear as similar descriptions of births, a fine difference may be noted between the narratives of the births of Salim and Murad, on the one hand, and that of Khanum, on the other. The birth of a daughter was not of the same order as that of a son. The quality of the celebration as reported is telling. The casting of horoscopes, the celebratory odes, and the general environment of overflowing joyousness is absent in the writing on Khanum's birth. The moment of birth is simply recorded, not anticipated as an important event for the dynasty and its future. In line with the make-up of Khanum's birth is the trace of the "uneventful" birth of Aram Banu Begum, in December 1584, one that simply "glorified the harem of the Shahinshah . . . , and the world's lord conferred on her that great name."[50]

---

[46] *Akbarnama*, II, pp. 507–508. See also *Muntakhab*, II, pp. 124–125; *Jahangirnama*, Preface, p. 4; and *Tabaqat*, II, pp. 357–359.

[47] *Akbarnama*, II, p. 509. Jahangir refers to her as Shahzadeh Khanum, *Jahangirnama*, p. 37.

[48] *Akbarnama*, II, pp. 542–543. According to Abu-l Fazl, an order was issued that once Danyal became one month old, he should be conveyed to the town of Amber and committed to the care of the Rani of Bihari Mal. Beveridge proposes that the transfer of Daniyal to the care of the Rani would imply that the mother of Danyal was related to her (*ibid.*, p. 543, n. 2); but this might well have to do with the foster-care of Danyal by the Rani. Nizam al-Din Ahmad also records Murad's birth, *Tabaqat*, II, pp. 360–361.

[49] *Akbarnama*, II, pp. 514–515. Badauni records the *qit'ah* of Mawlana Qasim Arsalan, composed especially for the occasion of Murad's birth. The first hemistich refers to the birth of Salim and the second to that of Murad. *Muntakhab*, II, p. 136.

[50] *Akbarnama*, III, p. 661. Jahangir also records the births of Shahzadeh Khanum, Murad, and Danyal; all three born of "serving girls." No names or details of the mothers are given; *Jahangirnama*, p. 37.

From the reign of the first two *padshah*s onwards, certain aspects of the lives of senior and junior women remained unchanged. As we shall see in a later section, royal mothers continued to be significant persons in public-political affairs, but this was markedly so only in the case of the elders, especially the mother of the emperor. Obviously, the reproductive function of a wife was also vital for the survival of the empire that was coming into being. However, the active participation of women, both senior and junior, was rendered comparatively trivial. They were present but hidden away, crucial to the maintenance of the empire but unnamed in its annals.

An examination of another aspect of Mughal domestic life under Akbar – the fostering and care of the imperial children – underlines the blessings that women were supposed to have obtained through any service or attachment to the emperor. Not least among these was the act of feeding and nursing of the infant king, which emphasized the centrality of the new axis of the empire – the great monarch himself.

The foster community of Akbar's *haram*

A folio from the British Library *Akbarnama*, "Akbar and Miryam Makani in Humayun's Camp (1542)" (Plate 4),[51] portrays the nurses and the infant Akbar. The miniature captures the environment of several nurses feeding the child. There is brisk movement, as well as caution and supervision here, in an attempt to bring out the diverse meanings of feeding the newly born. The very capturing of the moment of feeding in this visual representation attests to its great symbolic significance: the presence of several nurses simultaneously, the flurry of activity that surrounds the feeding, and the centrality of the noble child, carry their own importance.

Anthropologists have laid emphasis on breast-feeding as far more than a merely biological act: it is an aspect of "mothering," the culturally constructed bonding between mother and child, "grounded in specific historical and cultural practices."[52] They have also stressed that power relations within the family and extended kin relations determine the structure of breast-feeding.[53] Or consider briefly, what one anthropologist has to say about men in relation to breast-feeding: "in many societies, it is men (fathers,

---

[51] British Library, *Akbarnama*, MS Or. 12988, fol. 22a, and Titley, *Miniatures*, p. 4.

[52] John Carmi Parsons and Bonnie Wheeler (eds.), *Medieval Mothering* (New York and London, 1996), p. x, quoting Nancy Scheper-Hughes, *Death Without Weeping: The Violence of Everyday Life in Brazil* (Berkeley and Los Angeles, 1992); see also Vanessa Maher, "Breast-Feeding in Cross-cultural Perspective: Paradoxes and Proposals," in Maher (ed.), *The Anthropology of Breastfeeding: Natural Law or Social Construct* (Oxford and Providence, 1992). For an excellent review of current anthropological and historical writings on breast-feeding, see Avner Giladi, *Infants, Parents and Wet Nurses: Medieval Islamic Views on Breastfeeding and their Social Implications* (Boston and Cologne, 1999), especially the Introduction.

[53] See, for example, Vanessa Maher, "Breast-Feeding in Cross-cultural Perspective."

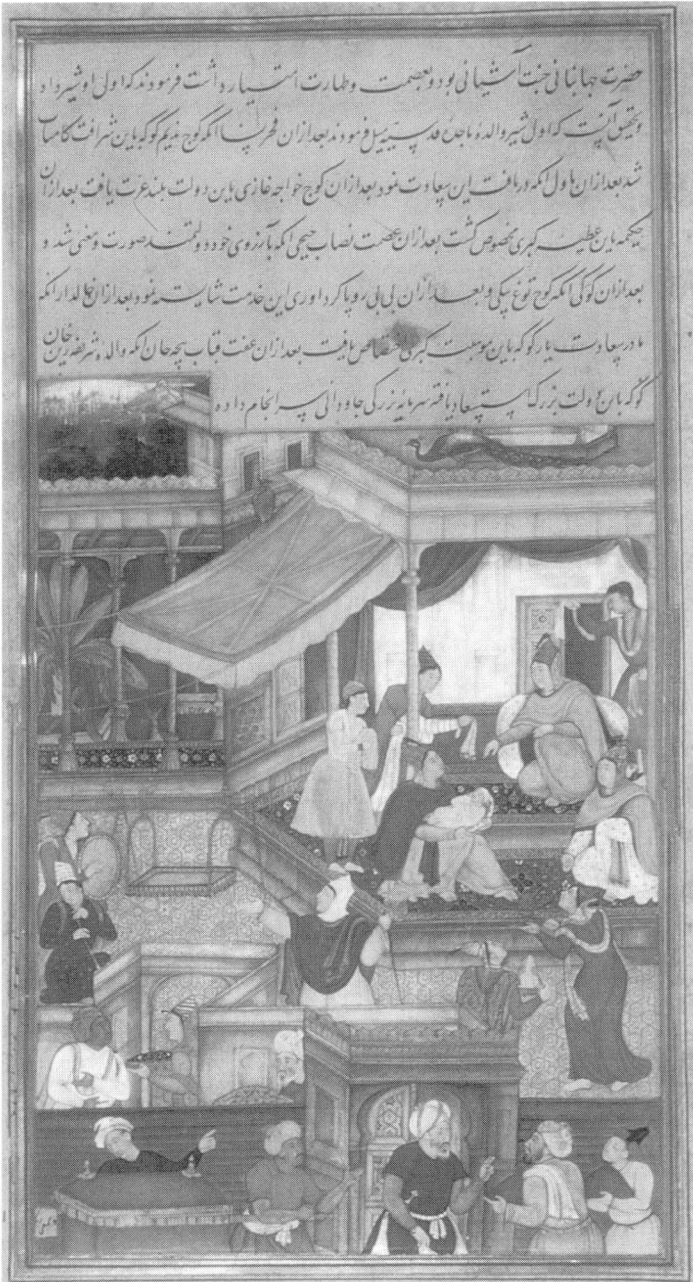

Plate 4: "Akbar and Miryam Makani in Humayun's Camp"

wet-nurses' husbands) rather than women (mothers, wet-nurses) who determine which and how much food women and children may consume. ...
Men also decide whether the mother herself will breastfeed her baby or
whether this will be done by another woman, a wet-nurse. In the latter case,
it is the father, not the mother, who is responsible for selecting the wet-
nurse ... ."[54]

Although a pre-modern historian does not generally have "access" to the
sorts of "texts" available to an anthropologist of recent societies, it is worth-
while examining the rules and practices specified in the Akbari literature.
Given the importance of feeding the divine emperor, the selection of nurses
was undertaken with extreme care. Abu-l Fazl records that they had to be
"even-tempered, spiritually-minded" nurses from whose breasts Akbar's
"mouth was sweetened by the life-giving fluid."[55] Sufistic overtones interlace
his description of the act of feeding, establishing the exceptional privileges of
the nurse. Abu-l Fazl writes that through feeding the young Akbar, "it was
as if there were Divine wisdom in thus implanting varied temperaments
[masharib] by this series of developments so that the pure entity advancing by
gradations [vujud], might become familiar with the divers methods of Divine
manifestation."[56]

Two words here call for special attention: masharib and vujud. Masharib
(plural of mashrab) means "dispositions."[57] It is also used for beverages, and for
dishes or trays, as well as for stages or degrees, "so that apparently one of the
intended meanings is "divers beverages in diverse vessels" signifying the varied
nature [and qualities] of nurses milk."[58] Vujud is discovering, procuring, finding; it also means substance, essence, existing, and "beginning to exist."[59] The
act of feeding an infant, as projected in the above expressions, thus becomes
more than providing nourishment; it has to do with fostering – and fostering in
a manner appropriate to a chosen one.[60] Of course, the act itself gets more
sanctified because of its association with the divine child. Clearly the act of
feeding was no small task. The honored names of the "blissful nurses and
spiritually moulded cherishers [qalib-i rawhani-i-qavalib]"[61] were likely to be
carefully probed.

In order to elaborate the point I am making here, let us list the nurses of
Akbar.

[54] *Ibid.*, pp. 6, 8, 18, 23.   [55] *Akbarnama*, I, p. 129.   [56] *Ibid.*, p. 131.
[57] Steingass, *Persian*, s. v. "Masharib," and *Akbarnama*, I, p. 131, n. 5.
[58] *Akbarnama*, I, p. 131, n. 5.   [59] Steingass, *Persian*, s. v. "Vujud."
[60] The idea that through milk the infant absorbs the physical as well as "spiritual" qualities of the
      nurse can be encountered widely in the Quranic literature. For a discussion of Prophet
      Muhammad and his relationship with his wet-nurse Halimeh, see Giladi, *Infants, Parents
      and Wet Nurses*, pp. 33–39, and also ch. 2, "Breastfeeding in Arabic-Islamic Medicine."
[61] *Akbarnama*, I, p. 129. Henry Beveridge writes the Persian for "the honoured names of the
      blissful nurses ... " as *qawabil-i -rawhani-qawalib*.

Jiji Anageh

"Jiji" in Turkish means a child's plaything, or handsome.[62] "Anageh" seems primarily to mean a wet-nurse, though we are told that it does not always have this meaning.[63] Jiji Anageh was the wife of "the nobly-born" Shams al-Din Muhammad of Ghazni, who was in the service of Humayun. Shams al-Din had helped Humayun up the steep banks of the Ganges when the latter was defeated by Sher Shah.[64] His wife, Jiji Anageh, was therefore "clothed with the glorious head-dress ... and mantle of distinction, by obtaining the auspicious service of nursing this new fruit of the spring tide of sovereignty and fortune, and should have the blissful charge [*hizanat*, charge of a child] of the nosegay of the house-garden of greatness and glory."[65] This was a recompense for the "noble-deed" performed several years ago. However, since the "period of pregnancy of this purely framed nurse was not yet fulfilled,"[66] Hamideh Banu Begum ordered that Daya Bhaval would feed the infant. Jiji Anageh may, however, have been the principal nurse, in the sense that Akbar drew most of his milk from her, for we are told by Abu-l Fazl how other nurses accused her of "practicing incantations" so as to prevent the infant Akbar from accepting anyone else's milk but her own.[67]

Daya Bhaval

Referred to as "a special servant" of Humayun, and distinguished for her "virtue and purity – to suckle the infant."[68]

Fakhr-un-Nisa Anageh

She seems to have been Humayun's attendant from his childhood.[69] Gulbadan Begum lists her as one of those who attended the wedding-feast of Hindal Mirza – "Fakhr-un-nisa Anaga, the mother of Nadim Kuka."[70] She is incorrectly referred to as the wife of Nadim Kukeh in the *Akbarnama*;[71] the latter was her son, and in the service of Humayun.

Bhaval Anageh

No details are available, though she is listed as a wet-nurse in the *Akbarnama*.[72]

---

[62] *Akbarnama*, I, p. 130, n. 2.   [63] *Ibid.*, p. 134, the translator's note on Maham Anageh.
[64] *Ibid.*, p. 130, n. 1.   [65] *Ibid.*, p. 130.   [66] *Ibid.*   [67] *Ibid.*, p. 384.
[68] *Ibid.* Daya is a Persian word for wet-nurse. See, "Daya," *Encyclopaedia Iranica*, VII, pp. 164–166.
[69] Beveridge, *Humayun*, p. 185; cf. Gulbadan, *Ahval*, fol. 71a.
[70] Beveridge, *Humayun*, p. 122; cf. Gulbadan, *Ahval*, fol. 26a.
[71] *Akbarnama*, I, p. 130.   [72] *Ibid.*

Wife of Khvajeh Ghazi

Mentioned in the *Akbarnama* as a nurse, and as the wife of Khvajeh Ghazi.[73] Nothing more is mentioned about her in the chronicle. Bayazid Sultan lists Khvajeh Ghazi as one of the officers who came to India with Humayun.[74] Abu-l Fazl says Khvajeh Ghazi was distinguished for his knowledge of accounts and made a *divan* by Humayun. He was thereafter "excluded" from the court of Humayun, but returned to the court of Akbar.[75]

Hakimeh

Though her name is included in the list of nurses, no other details are found about her in the records of the time.[76]

Kuki Anageh

She was the wife of Tuq Begi, who is referred to as Tuq Begi Saqi, i.e., page or cup-bearer by Bayazid.[77]

Bibi Rupa

Like some nurses above, no details of Bibi Rupa are available to the reader, except the rather obvious inference that may be drawn from her name that she was probably a Hindu.[78]

Khaldar Anageh

"Khaldar" means mole-marked,[79] and her name may have been associated with such a physical feature. Her son was Sa'adat Yar Kukeh, mentioned several times in the *Akbarnama*. He was one of the persons who accompanied a royal cortege of women for a pilgrimage to Mecca. Akbar gave his daughter in marriage to Abu-l Fazl's son. Sa'adat Yar died of excessive drinking and Abu-l Fazl records Akbar's visit at that time to condole Sa'adat Yar's sister.[80]

Pija-jan Anageh

Pija-jan Anageh was married to Khvajeh Maqsud of Herat.[81] Abu-l Fazl calls him "a man of pure disposition and of integrity."[82] He was a close servant of Hamideh Banu Begum, "ever assiduous in her service."[83] Pija-jan Anageh

---

[73] *Ibid.*   [74] *Ibid.*, pp. 130–131, n. 6.   [75] *Ibid.*   [76] *Ibid.*, p. 130.
[77] *Ibid.*, p. 130, n. 1.   [78] *Ibid*, p. 131, n. 2.   [79] *Ibid.*, p. 131.
[80] *Akbarnama*, III, pp. 192, 579, and 656; also, *Akbarnama*, I, p. 131, n. 3.
[81] *Akbarnama*, I, p. 131, n. 4.   [82] *Ibid.*, p. 448.   [83] *Ibid.*

and Khvajeh Maqsud had two sons: Siyf Khan, who died during the conquest of Gujarat, and Ziyn Khan Kukeh, "distinguished for fidelity and intelligence," became one of the great officers.[84]

Maham Anageh

Though we are told that Maham Anageh was in the service of Akbar since his childhood,[85] her name does not occur in the list of Akbar's nurses. Henry Beveridge suggests that she might have been named under some other appellation, such as Khvajeh Ghazi's wife, whose name is not given. This is possible since Maham Anageh was a title and not a proper name.[86] The stronger possibility, according to Beveridge, is that Maham Anageh was probably the head or the superintendent of the nurses rather than chief nurse. He also says that she certainly was not the chief nurse in the sense of providing nourishment to the infant prince, for we are told by Abu-l Fazl that Jiji Anageh was chief in this respect.[87]

The list of Akbar's nurses is illuminating not only for what it tells us about feeding practices – selection and background of nurses, their virtues, hierarchy among nurses by dint of feeding the royal child (who the child drew most of his milk from) – but also for the affinal (or "confused affinal" given the associations established through the act of feeding, if one considers feeding as one of the characteristics attached to practices of descent) links that it helps visualize in the time of Humayun as well as that of Akbar. Almost all the nurses were closely tied to the family of Humayun, either directly or through their relatives. Jiji Anageh was married to Shams al-Din of Ghazni, a "nobly born servant"; Daya Bhaval herself was a "special servant"; Fakhr-un-Nisa was Humayun's attendant from his childhood; Khvajeh Ghazi came to India with Humayun, whose wife also nursed Akbar; and Pija-jan was married to Khvajeh Maqsud of Herat, a man of "pure disposition and integrity."

A striking characteristic of Akbar's *haram* was that kinship networks were extended to form new extra-kin communities: here, milk becomes the *raison d'être* for the creation of other intimate relationships. The talk of blood remained, but a new idea of consanguinity was built around practices such as wet-nursing and notions of fostering. Many of Akbar's nurses and their husbands became influential in his court. Their many-sided participation in the affairs of the monarchy show how these new relationships and communities had shaped, and continued to shape, notions of family and kinship, and court politics itself. Maham Anageh, the head nurse, would soon be a major force in the politics of Akbar's court. Shams al-Din Muhammad of Ghazni, husband of Jiji Anageh, and their son, 'Aziz Kukeh (foster-brother of Akbar),

---

[84] *Ibid.*, p. 448.   [85] *Akbarnama*, II, p. 86.
[86] *Akbarnama*, I, p. 134, "Maham Anaga."   [87] *Ibid.*

both rose to be *vakils* (vice-regent) under Akbar.[88] They received the titles of *Atkeh Khan* (foster-father, Shams al-Din) and *Khan-i A'zam* ('Aziz Kukeh) from Humayun and Akbar respectively.[89] Both Prince Murad and Khusraw, sons of Akbar, married a daughter each of 'Aziz Kukeh.[90] Then Khvajeh Maqsud of Herat, "the tried servant of Hamideh Banu Begum," and his wife Pija-jan, the nurse of Akbar, had two sons. Of these two foster-brothers of Akbar, Siyf Khan died during the conquest of Gujarat, as mentioned earlier, while Ziyn Khan Kukeh was highly favored by Akbar.[91]

The significance of Akbar's relationship with his foster-community may best be judged from a comment attributed to the emperor himself: "Between me and 'Aziz ['Aziz Kukeh] is a river of milk that I cannot cross."[92] The ties formed by the bountiful milk were crucial. The divine emperor was fed first, but the bounties that were to come to the feeders and their associates were endless:

He [Akbar] drew forth milk by the bounty of his lips
Milk and sugar were commingled.
It was not milk he drank from the breast of hope,
'Twas water from the Sun's fountain that he imbibed.[93]

The representation of Akbar's *haram* in the chronicles of his time is not entirely different from projections of the domestic life of his grandfather, Babur. In the expansive community of Akbar's *haram*, matters of kith and kin, and notions of blood and genealogy, remained vital, but these were not the only essential elements. The emperor's foster-community pushed the boundaries of what would normally be recognized as blood-relations and relationships of marriage and birth. What Akbar's words, ascribed to him by his chronicler – "Between me and 'Aziz ['Aziz Kukeh] is a river of milk that I cannot cross" – point to is a relationship between two people that is made through milk, but is actually on a par with blood-relationships. Akbar's statement seems to be invoking a *hadith* attributed to Prophet Muhammad – "What is forbidden as a result of blood-relationships is forbidden as a result of milk-relationships as well" – credited also to 'Ayisheh, the Prophet's wife: "milk relationships prohibit precisely what blood relationships do."[94]

An argument of the same kind could be made about the servants of the empire, an important part of the structure of the domestic life, the center of power in many ways. Although Abu-l Fazl divided the servants of the empire into four categories: nobles of the state ("*nuyinan-i dawlat*"); friends of victory ("*awliya-i nusrat*") who include "all those who dealt with the collection and

[88] Steingass lists prime minister as one of the meanings of *vakil*; Steingass, *Persian*, s. v. "vakil."
[89] *A'in-i Akbari*, I, pp. 337–338 and 343–346.   [90] *Ibid.*, pp. 344–345.
[91] *Ibid.*, pp. 367–369.   [92] *A'in-i Akbari*, I, p. 343.   [93] *Akbarnama*, I, p. 130.
[94] Avner Giladi, *Infants, Parents and Wet Nurses*, pp. 21 and 71. According to several Quranic traditions and in subsequent commentaries to do with wet-nursing, milk and blood enforce similar relationships, similar privileges, and similar restrictions and regulations. This issue of uncompromising identification between blood and milk is discussed in detail in Giladi above. See, for example, pp. 24–26, 30, 70–71.

disbursement of state funds"; companions of the emperor ("*ashabi-i suhbat*"); and servants who "waited upon the emperor and his family in the Imperial household" ("*arbab-i khidmat*"),[95] it is important to remember that none of these categories was formalized until the imperial chronicler wrote about it. What is perhaps of greater significance is the fact that there was some movement from one category to another.

Take the example of Bayram Khan, who entered the service of Humayun at the age of sixteen, and was later appointed the *ataliq* (guardian) of Prince Akbar. Humayun referred to him as "a faithful servant."[96] His services are well known from the histories of the time.[97] On Akbar's accession he was appointed the *vakil* (vice-regent) and the *Khan-i Khanan*.[98] The chronicles tell us that Bayram Khan served Akbar in various capacities: as the *vakil* and the *Khan-i Khanan*, as well as the more personal task of acting as regent and guide of Akbar in his early years, his *Khan Baba*.[99] He was one of the most powerful political figures in the Mughal court until 1560–61, when he lost royal favor and was sent on a pilgrimage; soon after that he was stabbed to death by a Lohani Afghan called Mubarak.[100] In what category of servants might we best include Bayram Khan, given especially that most grandees of the empire were in one form or another servants of Shahinshah Akbar?

Consider also the example of *Khvajeh sara* (the title of the chief eunuch of the *haram*), I'timad Khan.[101] His real name was Phul Malik. After serving Salim Shah (1545–53), he entered Akbar's service. At the death of Shams al-Din Muhammad Atkeh Khan, Akbar's foster-father, the emperor appointed I'timad Khan "to remodel the finances, making him a commander of one thousand, and conferring upon him the title of I'timad Khan.'"[102] Abu-l Fazl reports that he performed his duties to Akbar's satisfaction. In 1565, he conveyed the daughter of Miran Mubarak, the king of Khandesh, to Akbar's *haram*, distinguished himself in the conquest of Bengal, and in 1576 he was appointed the governor of Bhakkar. When Akbar went to Punjab in 1578, I'timad Khan desired to join him. In order to equip his contingent, I'timad Khan collected the rents and outstanding payments, "with much harshness," it appears. This led to a conspiracy against him and he was murdered, in the same year, by a man named Maqsud 'Ali.[103]

[95] Blake, "Patrimonial-Bureaucratic," pp. 294–295.   [96] *A'in-i Akbari*, I, p. 330.
[97] For a summary on Bayram Khan, refer to the *A'in-i Akbari*, I, pp. 329–332. Also see the relevant sections of the *Akbarnama*, the *A'in-i Akbari*, *Muntakhab-ut-Tavarikh*, and the *Tabaqat-i Akbari*. The reader might also want to refer to any of the large number of biographies of Akbar that always have a discussion on Bayram Khan.
[98] *A'in-i Akbari*, I, p. 330.   [99] *Ibid.*
[100] *Ibid.*, pp. 329–332; also, *Akbarnama*, I, Index, p. 6. In fact, both the *Akbarnama* and the *A'in-i Akbari* suggest that part of the reason for Bayram Khan's loss of political power was Maham Anageh's growing influence at the Mughal court (*Akbarnama*, I, Index, p. 6; *A'in-i Akbari*, I, pp. 329–332).
[101] *Akbarnama*, III, p. 131, and *A'in-i Akbari*, I, p. 13, n. 1.
[102] *A'in-i Akbari*, I, p. 13, n. 1.   [103] *Ibid.*

Badauni makes a scathing comment on I'timad's various appointments. He quotes a tradition to make his point: "A time will come on men, when none will become favourites but profligates ... and then the government shall be by the counsel of women, and the rule of boys, and the management of eunuchs."[104] At the same time, he applauds I'timad's "enterprise and economy" as being quite unprecedented. Recording the events from 1562–63, Badauni says, in that year I'timad Khan "obtained the highest consideration in the haram, and even in state matters became the sovereign's confidant."[105] Two things emerge in Badauni's comments. One, a clear intersection of many kinds of services that I'timad Khan undertook that led to this high consideration of him in the *haram* as well as in state matters. At the same time, the tension produced by I'timad Khan's appointment is apparent in the citation. Though the *Khvajeh sara* was a "man of sense and discretion,"[106] what he had achieved led to some uncertainty, and even disapproval.

This brings me once again to the point about the negotiation and the unease that might underlie the non-kin (or other than blood) relationships in Akbar's *haram*. I have already mentioned the high-ranking appointments of Shams al-Din Muhammad of Ghazni and his son 'Aziz Kukeh (the *Atkeh Khan* and the *Khan-i 'Azam*), and of Khvajeh Maqsud of Herat and his sons Siyf Khan and Ziyn Khan Kukeh. These too will have produced uneasy moments like those that Badauni makes visible in the case of I'timad Khan. It might be worth reflecting a moment, therefore, on the extraordinary examples in the records that enable us to think about the new expectations and the new rigors of behavior in these intimate relationships of Akbar.

Akbar's *haram*: networks and practices

There are many moments in the Akbari chronicles that render the imperial regulations on the *haram* unstable. Although the royal women were expected to be *pardeh-giyan*, not just in donning the veil, but also in their conspicuous absence (by their elevation to an inaccessible and invisible status), it is remarkable how they repeatedly interrupt the narratives on politics or public affairs.

A thought-provoking story narrated in the chronicles is the punishment of Adham Khan, the son of Maham Anageh. We are told in the *Akbarnama* that Adham Khan had killed Shams al-Din Muhammad Atkeh Khan, the *vakil* of the empire, on the instigation of Munim Khan, who himself coveted the seat of the *vakil*. After the murder, Adham Khan went to the *haram* where Akbar was sleeping. Akbar woke up in this hullabaloo, and a servant called Rafiq explained to him the details of the matter. It appears from Bayazid Bayat that

---

[104] *Muntakhab*, II, pp. 63–64.   [105] *Ibid*.   [106] *Ibid*.

Rafiq was a house-born servant of Akbar's great-aunt Khanzadeh Begum.[107] The expression *Sahib-i chahar mansab*, used for Rafiq, literally means "owner of four offices," and indicated that he had served four generations. Rafiq's important place in the *haram* may be envisioned by references to his intimate relationship with the monarch – Jawhar mentions that the young Akbar was willing to undress and bathe in his presence[108] – as well as by his service to four royal generations, clearly a matter of no small importance.

Some other servants are depicted in the folios of the Victoria and Albert Museum *Akbarnama*, centering on the death of Adham Khan, "Akbar Orders the Punishment of his Foster Brother" (Plate 5).[109] The scene is cast at two levels: the emperor emerges from the doorway, his hand gripping the scimitar. His body is ablaze with "noble indignation." Before Akbar stand two attendants named Farhat Khan and Sangram Husnak, who obey his command to bind and throw down Adham from the terrace. The three figures on the upper level of the terrace seem to restore authority, somehow balancing and providing a "deliberate contrast to the chaotic frenzy embodied in the figures below in the hall." The cantilever staircase serves as a "brilliant symbolic device," to underline Adham Khan's fall from power.[110]

Rafiq, Farhat Khan, and Sangram Hasnak (all of whom belonged presumably to the *arbab-i khidmat*, category four of the servants according to Abu-l Fazl) seem to be involved here in an event of considerable public significance. The crisscrossing of many kinds of services by imperial servants is no novel feature of the empire under Akbar. As we are told, Darvish 'Ali, a *piyadeh* (footman, footsoldier) and *tufang-andaz* (matchlock-man) had taken the news of Hindal's birth to Babur. Mir Khurd, *bakavul*, an overseer of the kitchen was made Hindal's guardian. Jawhar, the famous ewer-bearer of Humayun, continually accompanied the *padshah* during his critical time in exile, and was the recipient of exceptional trust from him.

Let us turn to the events surrounding the death of Adham Khan. The major actors in Abu-l Fazl's commentary on the death of Adham Khan include the emperor, his foster-mother, foster-father, foster-brother, and a number of servants. In 1560–61, Adham Khan along with Pir Muhammad Khan was sent to Malwa, where he defeated Baz Bahadur, the ruler of Malwa. In doing so, he took possession of Baz Bahadur's treasure and his dancing girls.[111] The treasure (including the dancing-girls) was presented to Akbar, and the emperor generously rewarded Adham Khan.

However, Abu-l Fazl records, since everyone was engrossed in preparations for departure, Adham Khan prevailed upon his mother, "intrigued with his mother's servants who waited in the royal *haram*, and spirited away from the

---

[107] *Akbarnama*, II, p. 270, n. 1.   [108] Jouher-Stewart, *Tezkerah*, pp. 118–119.

[109] Victoria and Albert Museum, *Akbarnama* MS fol. I. S. 2/1896, Acc. No. 29/117. The description of the scene is paraphrased from Sen, *Paintings*, p. 79.

[110] Sen, *Paintings*, pp. 77–79.

[111] *A'in-i Akbari*, I, pp. 340–342; and *Akbarnama*, II, pp. 220–221.

Plate 5: "Akbar Orders the Punishment of his Foster Brother"

Shahinshah's enclosures two special beauties from among Baz Bahadur's women and who had been recently exhibited to his Majesty."[112] When Akbar heard about this, he recalled Adham Khan, and appointed Pir Muhammad to the governorship of Malwa.[113] Meanwhile, Adham Khan had turned away, and the two women he had taken were killed at Maham Anageh's orders, for "a severed head makes no sound."[114]

Matters became more complicated later on when Adham Khan killed Shams al-Din Muhammad Atkeh Khan, another foster-father of Akbar. The *A'in-i Akbari* suggests that the reason for the murder was that Shams al-Din was appointed the *vakil*, either by "supersession" or "usurpation" of what could have been Munim Khan's seat.[115] Munim Khan was a grandee from the time of Humayun and had continued in imperial service under Akbar. Munim Khan therefore intrigued with Adham Khan and instigated the latter to carry out the murder.[116]

Abu-l Fazl constructs the murder of Atkeh Khan as follows in the *Akbarnama*. Atkeh Khan was in a meeting, transacting business, when Adham Khan walked in and stabbed him to death.[117] Adham Khan then marched towards the *haram*. Akbar was sleeping there. Adham Khan tried to force his way into the *haram* but Ni'mat, the eunuch, bolted the door promptly. The emperor woke up because of the uproar and inquired after the reasons for the clamor. Rafiq told Akbar the details and pointed to the blood-stained corpse of Atkeh Khan.[118]

Abu-l Fazl's image of the moment when Akbar took Adham Khan to task after hearing of the murder is graphic:

From a divine inspiration he [Akbar] did not come out by the door where that demented wretch was standing and meditating evil, but by another way. As he was coming out, a servant of the seraglio put into his hands, without his asking for it, the special scimitar. His Majesty took the scimitar and went on ... he saw that villain [Adham Khan], and there issued from his holy lips the words, "Son of a fool [*bachcheh-i lawdeh*] [119] why have you killed our ataga?"[120]

Adham Khan tried to attack Akbar, but the latter took hold of him, and struck him a blow on his face, so that "that wicked monster turned a somersault and fell down insensible."[121]

[112] *Akbarnama*, II, p. 221.   [113] *A'in-i Akbari*, I, p. 341; and *Akbarnama*, II, p. 235.
[114] *Akbarnama*, II, p. 221.   [115] *A'in-i Akbari*, I, p. 338.   [116] *Ibid.*, pp. 333–334.
[117] *Akbarnama*, II, p. 269.   [118] *Ibid.*, pp. 270–271.
[119] The correct Persian of the "son of a fool" or the "son of a bitch" is *bachcheh-i lawdeh*, which is incorrectly read by Beveridge as *bacha-i-lada*. *Lawdeh* (*Lada*, according to Beveridge) means a bitch, apparently a nick-name for Adham's father. "Bayazid says that Akbar called Adham *gandu*, i.e., a catamite. His words are "*Hazrat ba zaban Hindustani farmudand ke ai kandu* [i.e. *gandu*] *cara Atkah mara kashti*"; see *Akbarnama*, II, p. 272, n. 3.
[120] *Akbarnama*, II, p. 271.
[121] *Ibid.* Badauni also records the episode of the death of Adham Khan, see *Muntakhab*, II, pp. 43–51.

Abu-l Fazl picks up the various strands of Akbar's relationships with his foster-kin and intricately knots them around the event of Adham Khan's death: the relationship of a son and a mother (Adham Khan and Maham Anageh), of foster-father and a foster-son (Atkeh Khan and Akbar), of foster-brothers (Adham Khan and Akbar), and of a foster-mother and her foster-son (Maham Anageh and Akbar). Although Maham Anageh's conspiratorial engagements are clearly spoken of in the *Akbarnama*, her response in the aftermath of her son's death is built up in a more complicated fashion.

After the death of Adham Khan, the first news that Maham Anageh heard was that her son had committed an act of violence and he was therefore imprisoned. Later, when Akbar went to meet her, he said, "Adham killed our Ataga, we have inflicted retaliation upon him"; to which she answered, "you did well."[122] When she was told the exact detail of the episode, according to Abu-l Fazl, "she by virtue of her wisdom preserved her respect for his Majesty and did not complain or lament, but she became inwardly wounded by a thousand fatal blows .... The colour left her face ... forty days after this occurrence ... she went to the sacred abode of non-existence."[123]

The conversation between Akbar and Maham Anageh finely generates the embedded conflict of loyalty, milk, blood, of filial respect and of parental affection, quite apart from the fear and deference Maham will likely have felt in the face of the power of the emperor. At the same time, through a delineation of her comportment and behavior, Abu-l Fazl simultaneously presses her affection for her son, as well as reverence for her foster-son.

Akbar's mixed responses likewise are in keeping with his own close relationship with Shams al-Din Atkeh Khan, and in accordance with his duties as a monarch. The emperor was familiar with the activities of Adham Khan, and according to Abu-l Fazl, overlooked a lot of his follies: in the stealing of the beauties of Baz Bahadur and other such instances, Akbar "overlooked this gross outrage ...."[124] The emperor's relationship with Maham Anageh may have been an important factor in these considerations. Nevertheless, after the murder of Atkeh Khan, punishment could not be avoided any longer. After all, Shams al-Din was Akbar's foster-father and, quite clearly, Adham Khan's behavior had crossed all permissible limits. His breaking open of the door to the *haram* and attack on the emperor himself were acts of ultimate culpability.

A folio from the Victoria and Albert Museum *Akbarnama*, "The Celebrated Dancers from Mandu Perform before Akbar" (Plate 6),[125] captures a moment in the series of episodes above. The two women depicted dancing in the court perhaps refer to the beauties that were abducted by Adham Khan. The

---

[122] *Akbarnama*, II, p. 274; and *Muntakhab*, II, pp. 49–50.
[123] *Akbarnama*, II, pp. 274–275.   [124] *Ibid.*, p. 221.
[125] Victoria and Albert Museum, *Akbarnama*, MS fol. I. S.2/1896, Acc. No. 16/17. The title of the folio is taken from Sen, *Paintings*, p. 67.

Plate 6: "The Celebrated Dancers from Mandu Perform before Akbar"

emperor is shown with his head tilted, his face marked by a concerned expression. Whilst the dancers perform, Maham Anageh stands in a corner, her face covered. The emperor, the dancers, and Maham Anageh form a triangular relationship, indexing the tension of the event in this portrayal. The bodily postures of these three protagonists also suggest their complex relationships in the context of the events enveloping them. This miniature is once again an index of a structure of relationships that are marked by intense ambiguities.

The narratives on the death of Adham Khan are particularly instructive for two reasons. First, for the chroniclers' crafting of a complex range of activities and emotions that seem to be intricately woven in Akbar's domestic life. And secondly, for the elaborate depiction of the structure of the sacred *haram* with its variety of affiliations, entitlements, and claims. The events surrounding Adham Khan's death suggest a peculiar mix of political ambition, intrigue, the aspirations of people close to the emperor seeking to achieve higher ranks, as well as the emotional bonds and relationships that made up the world of the *haram*.[126]

In addition, something else is manifest here: that the theory of sacred incarceration of the *haram* was far from perfect when put into practice. People did not always conform to the prescribed discipline. On the contrary, the *haram* of Akbar remained a contradictory and complex place, and the women in the *haram* remained living and conflicted human beings with diverse aspirations and desires. Although, according to the decrees of the empire, the divine monarch was to be at the center of everything, in the everyday life of the *haram*, Akbar was inevitably not the only point of initiative and control. All activities were not premeditated and performed around him.

The visible mothers: the matriarchs of the empire

There are other areas of tension and instability in the new dispensation. Not least among these were the activities of the older imperial women. Hamideh Banu, the revered mother of the emperor, was not inappropriately christened "Empress Dowager" in W. H. Lowe's translation of Badauni's *Muntakhab-ut-Tavarikh*. Every so often in the Akbari accounts, one finds fragments related to Hamideh Banu Begum, about how her opinion was sought on many matters and how her intervention counted for a great deal. These fragments are

---

[126] In this context, to suggest the exclusively political texture of this event, as several biographies on Akbar have continued to do, is hardly enlightening. The death of Adham Khan is regarded as a case of political intrigue and faction fighting by most historians writing on Akbar. See, as examples, Qureshi, *Akbar*, pp. 60–62; and, most recently, Richards, *Mughal Empire*, pp. 14–15.

scattered all over the imperial chronicles; on their own, these might remain marginal, but when put together, they make for an instructive statement.

Consider the example of Shaikh Ilahdad Faizi Sirhindi's comment that Prince Salim had committed great faults owing to "loss of prudence" and because of "the intoxication of youth and of success."[127] The crime referred to here is Salim's plotting and putting to death of the distinguished courtier and chronicler, Abu-l Fazl.[128] It was hard for anyone to speak in favor of Salim, but "the great lady of the age" Maryam Makani, Hamideh Banu, and "the Khatun of the chamber of chastity," Gulbadan Begum, pleaded his forgiveness from the emperor. Akbar granted their wishes and gave an order for the coming of the prince to court. He also ordered that "the cupola of chastity," Salimeh Sultan Begum, should give Salim the news of forgiveness, and bring him to court. Salimeh, "in order to soothe the prince's apprehensions," took from Akbar an elephant named Fath Lashkar, a special horse, and a robe of honor and went to fetch the prince.[129]

The above fragments in the *Akbarnama* address the influence and authority of elders – or at any rate of the most senior among them. Other chroniclers and travelers of the time also refer to Hamideh Banu Begum's high status and public role. On 20 July 1580, Father Rudolf Aquaviva, the Jesuit priest, wrote from Fatehpur-Sikri, to Rui Vicente Provincial, regarding Akbar's "inadequate attention to the word of God."[130] In this context, he referred to the opposition of Akbar's own people to Christian leanings. This included the king's immediate family and other close associates: "On the one hand he has his mother, wives and friends to importune him, and on the other are those who wish him ill."[131]

Again, on 30 July 1581, Rudolf Aquaviva wrote to Father Everard Mercurian, informing him of the benefits they had received from the emperor and his mother. He wrote, "To us the king grants many favours and so do the Queen Mother, and the princes ...."[132]

Even though the sources are fragmentary, the exalted status and frequent public appearances of Hamideh Banu Begum and Gulbadan Banu Begum are highlighted. Note the anticipation of Akbar's own responses towards Hamideh Banu at several different junctures in the records. In April 1578 when the emperor was hunting in the neighborhood of the town of Bhira, near Shahpur district of Punjab, it was announced to him that Hamideh Banu had arrived at the camp and was anxious to see him. Akbar was much delighted, says Abu-l Fazl, and "made arrangements for doing her honour." He also ordered that Salim should go and meet her, along with other officers. After that

---

127 *Akbarnama*, III, p. 1217.
128 For details of Abu-l Fazl's murder, see *Akbarnama* III, ch. CL.
129 *Akbarnama*, III, pp. 1222–1223.   130 John Correia-Afonso, *Letters*, p. 64.
131 *Ibid.*, p. 65.   132 *Ibid.*, p. 96.

Akbar went to receive the "visible God (his mother), an act of worship of the true Creator."[133]

The etiquette and the delight of the emperor in honoring this "visible God" amplify the mother's status. Again, in September–October 1581, when Akbar visited the tomb of Humayun and went on to see his stepmother Haji Begum, Hamideh Banu Begum followed him. At the end of the day, Akbar was informed that his mother had arrived. Akbar treated her with great respect. This time Prince Danyal was in attendance on her.[134]

On another occasion, Maryam-Makani arrived while Akbar was on an expedition to Punjab. It is not clear from the *Akbarnama* whether she came from Delhi or from another city. The date was December 1585, and Fatehpur-Sikri would have been abandoned by then. Abu-l Fazl records, that "on account of her great love" for Akbar, Hamideh Banu Begum could not remain (*niyarastand*) in the capital. Akbar is said to have been delighted at this news of her arrival, and he welcomed her with the utmost respect.[135]

Likewise, during Akbar's expedition to Afghanistan (1589), Hamideh Banu Begum, in her "desire to behold" Akbar, set off for Kashmir, along with Gulbadan Begum and several other ladies. When they heard that Akbar had gone to Kabul, they followed him there. On being given the news of the arrival of women, Akbar first sent Prince Danyal and some officers to meet the women, and afterwards Prince Murad, and finally Prince Salim. Then he himself went and received the Begums near Begram.[136]

Hamideh Banu Begum's persistent and unannounced journeys to see her son are not the only index of her central presence in the imperial order. The English traveler, Thomas Coryate, noted Akbar's devotion to his mother more specifically. Coryate says, Akbar never denied her anything *except once*. At some stage Hamideh Banu demanded of Akbar that the Bible should be hung around the neck of an ass, which should be paraded around Agra. This, because in a ship of the Portuguese a copy of the Quran was found, tied about the neck of a dog, which was then beaten about the town of Ormuz. Akbar apparently denied her request by saying "that if it were ill in the Portugals to doe so to the Alcoran, it became not a king to requite ill with ill, for that the contempt of any Religion was the contempt of God, and he would not be revenged upon an innocent Booke."[137]

Alongside the clear visibility of the matriarchs in the records is a corollary: a declining mention of the public presence of younger and less centrally placed women. This is not altogether surprising, given that there were now hundreds of royal women in the *haram*, and that their activities were more regimented than before. These are conditions that stand out against the peripatetic Mughal domestic life of Babur and Humayun, in which the smaller groups of women in the *padshah*'s camp – more dispersed and less

---

[133] *Ibid.*, p. 348.   [134] *Akbarnama*, III, p. 547.   [135] *Ibid.*, p. 709.   [136] *Ibid.*, p. 859.
[137] Cited in Correia-Afonso, *Letters*, p. 65, n. 5.

permanently settled – probably had greater opportunities for initiative and intervention.

It is notable that we find no trace of a loved one or a favorite wife associated with Akbar, in legend or in the contemporary literature. The presentation of the emperor on a sanctified pedestal meant that he could not be reached by a single, mortal woman – in the public narrative at any rate.[138] Instead, the woman who emerges as an outstanding figure – an elder, a matriarch, and an authority in her own right – is the mother of the emperor. Yet mothers were not the only privileged seniors in the *haram*.

Intercession and counsel of senior women

It is recorded in the *Akbarnama* as well as the *Muntakhab-ut-Tavarikh* that one Khvajigi Fathullah, "reposed for a while in the shelter of the chaste ladies, who were returning from the Hijaz (the pilgrimage to Mecca undertaken by a number of royal women). Now by their intercession he was pardoned, and laid hold of the skirt of daily increasing fortune."[139] Khvajigi Fathullah's offense was that he had gone off to Mecca without leave.[140]

On one occasion, even the *Sadr* (chief Judge) of the empire, Shaykh 'Abd-un-Nabi had sought "protection from the secluded ladies."[141] 'Abd-un-Nabi was the grandson of 'Abdul Qaddus Gangohi,[142] a great saint of his time. Akbar had appointed 'Abd-un-Nabi the *Sadr* of the empire but found cases of bribery and murder against him,[143] and therefore gave his position to Sultan Khvajeh.[144] 'Abd-un-Nabi was banished to Mecca. It was after his return that he sought refuge with the women. In due time Akbar gave orders for his arrest "in such a manner that the ladies should not know of it." 'Abd-un-Nabi was later put to death:[145] but it is interesting that Akbar had to do all this quietly, without crossing swords with the senior women of his *haram*.

In speaking about the intercession of senior women, chroniclers often emphasize the age of the women, as well as their experience. In several instances, the focus is upon the privileges conferred upon the elder women by the monarch, the male head of the household and the empire. These privileges are made manifest in several ways: for example, in the honor and

---

[138] The *Jahangirnama* records Ruqayya Sultan Begum as Akbar's "chief wife" (*Jahangirnama*, p. 437). No more details may be found in the text regarding this status ascribed to the Begum; in reporting her death, the *A'in-i Akbari* calls her "Akbar's first wife" (*zan-i kalan*, *A'in-i Akbari*, I, p. 321), though not in the sense of the most important or "favourite" wife. See also, Beveridge, *Humayun*, Appendix A, p. 274, "Ruqaiya Begam *Miran-shahi*." Findly also calls Ruqayya Sultan Begum Akbar's "principal wife" (Findly, *Nur Jahan*, p. 32).

[139] *Akbarnama*, III, p. 571.   [140] *Ibid.*, p. 571, n. 2; cf. *Muntakhab*, II, p. 323.

[141] *Akbarnama*, III, p. 572.

[142] *Ibid.*, Index, p. 2. For a discussion of the life of 'Abd-al-Qaddus Gangoh, see especially Simon Digby, "'Abd-al-Qaddus Gangohi (1456–1537 A.D.): The Personality and Attitudes of a Medieval Indian Sufi,' in *Medieval India: A Miscellany*, vol. III (Delhi, 1975).

[143] *A'n-i Akbari*, I, pp. 279–281.   [144] *Ibid.*, p. 282.

[145] *Akbarnama*, III, p. 571–572, and n. 2.

respect (and time) accorded to women (Hamideh Banu Begum), in seeking their advice, and in backing their unusual initiatives (such as the *hajj* to Mecca that Gulbadan Banu Begum performed along with several women of the *haram*).

The example of Salimeh Sultan Begum, Akbar's older and hence senior wife, is perhaps one of the most captivating in relation to the construction of seniority. On one occasion, the reader will recall, Salimeh Sultan Begum was sent to appease Jahangir, who had rebelled against Akbar and gone into hiding after being involved in Abu-l Fazl's murder.[146] While Abu-l Fazl emphasizes the intervention of Hamideh Banu Begum and Gulbadan Begum, Muhammad Hadi, in his preface to the *Jahangirnama*, places more weight on Salimeh Sultan Begum's involvement in the affair of Salim. He says,

His Majesty Arsh-Ashiyani [Akbar] sent the lady Salima-Sultan Begam to him to appease him with imperial condolences, get him out of his seclusion, and bring him to pay homage. An elephant named Fath-i-Lashkar and a royal horse were awarded the prince [*sic*] and sent with the begam. When she arrived within two stages of Allahabad, His Highness [Jahangir] went out to greet her, meeting her with the greatest of respect, humbling himself immeasurably before His Majesty Arsh-Ashyani's representative, and returning to the city with the begam in great pomp. When she had promised the prince all sorts of imperial favors and removed all traces of apprehension from his mind, His Highness accompanied the lady to court.[147]

Sakineh Banu Begum, another senior woman of Akbar's *haram*, gave counsel to Hakim Mirza.[148] Sakineh Banu Begum and Mirza Hakim were both children of Humayun and Mah-chuchak, hence stepbrother and stepsister of the emperor. Sakineh Banu was married to Naqib Khan Qazvini, "a personal friend of Akbar."[149] Akbar's relations with Mirza Hakim require a little elaboration. For most of his life, Mirza Hakim was the ruler of Kabul. This is in itself of some significance. Mirza Kamran had operated in much the same area, and "as such it remained poorly incorporated into Mughal territories."[150] On two occasions Mirza Hakim had allied with rebels in Akbar's Hindustan, and at one time, the *khutba* was read in his name. In both instances, Akbar had marched against him.

Sakineh Banu Begum was sent to Kabul in 1578, before Akbar's second march on that city. The Mirza at that point seemed to have conducted negotiations with the Abulkhairi Uzbek state of Mavra-un-nahr, and with the Safavids "who treated him as a sovereign ruler," and with another Timurid potentate, Mirza Sulayman.[151] The "veiled one of the palace of

---

[146] *Akbarnama*, III, pp. 1222–1223.   [147] *Jahangirnama*, p. 11.   [148] *Akbarnama*, III, p. 351.

[149] Beveridge, *Humayun*, Appendix A, p. 275, "Sakina-banu Begam *Miran-shahi*."

[150] Subrahmanyam, "Structure or Process," p. 298. Subrahmanyam suggests that "Mirza Hakim represented an alternative power-centre, and an alternative focus of authority and patronage to Akbar; … even if the challenge from him did not wholly mature, we cannot dismiss it out of hand" (*ibid.*).

[151] Subrahmanyam, "Structure or Process," p. 299.

chastity,"[152] Sakineh Banu Begum was sent to pacify the Mirza and was advised to offer Prince Salim's marriage to his daughter as an incentive.[153]

The jostling for position between Mirza Hakim and Akbar continued for a long period. Father Monserrate has a passage in his memoir about the intervention of another woman later on in these proceedings. At the time of the defeat of the Mirza, Bakht-un-Nisa (also called Najib-un-Nisa and Fakhr-un-Nisa[154]), also the Mirza's sister, went up to Akbar, and "asked for pardon, and begged him [Akbar] to have mercy on his conquered brother and to give him back his kingdom, for he [Mirza Hakim] was sorry for what he had done. The result of her interceding was that the king, in reliance on her virtue, faithfulness and tact, handed over the kingdom to her charge." Having thus obtained the kingdom of Kabul through her intercession, Bakht-un-Nisa quietly handed it back to her brother.[155]

The handing over of Kabul to Bakht-un-Nisa Banu Begum is a fact of no little significance. It portrays the extremely high profile of some of the senior Mughal women, and the power they could sometimes attain. Among such examples of Mughal women's initiative and influence is another prominent case: Hamideh Banu Begum's charge of Delhi when Akbar marched to Kabul in order to suppress a conspiracy, led by several rebels, to install Mirza Hakim as the ruler of Hindustan.

Monserrate comments on the arrangements made by Akbar before his departure. Hamideh Banu Begum remained at Fatehpur-Sikri with her youngest grandson Danyal. 'Aziz Kukeh was made the viceroy of Bengal and Qutub al-Din Khan of Gujarat. "The king's mother was to be superior to both of these, and was to have charge of the province of Indicum or Delinum [Delhi]." Ten thousand cavalry were left as a garrison in Gujarat and twelve thousand with the king's mother. Akbar also left his infant daughter (Ximini Begum, according to Monserrate[156]) with her grandmother at Fatehpur-Sikri. He took with him a few of his principal wives and his older daughters. "On the day of his [Akbar's] departure his mother set out with him, and spent two days in camp with her son, in his immense white pavilion."[157]

Senior imperial women stand out time and again in the chronicles. They took over positions of public authority at several junctures. In addition, they counseled and mediated between dissenting kinsmen. Their advice was constantly sought, and they frequently arbitrated and made suggestions on public matters. Although many senior women were the privileged participants of the empire, the emperor's mother, the "Queen Empress," seems to have inhabited an especially honored position during Akbar's reign. Her tenure as the governor of Delhi in 1581 is only the most striking illustration of this.

[152] *Akbarnama*, III, p. 352.   [153] *Ibid.*, p. 353.   [154] Monserrate, *Commentary*, p. 135, n. 207.   [155] *Ibid.*, p. 153, n. 231.   [156] Monserrate, *Commentary*, p. 75, n. 121.   [157] *Ibid.*, pp. 74–75.

Gulbadan Begum's *hajj*[158]

According to the *Akbarnama*, Akbar was the apex and the center of every-thing that happened in his empire. I argued in the previous chapter that the figure of the monarch was the force behind the order and discipline of the empire, not excluding the sphere of domestic life. In this chapter, I have discussed how the image of the monarch at the helm of affairs was contested and shaken particularly in relation to Akbar's *haram*.

It is appropriate thus to conclude this chapter with one other destabilizing moment in the Akbari chronicles – perhaps the most arresting of all. There are only brief allusions to it in the histories of the time. The event is a pilgrimage to Mecca undertaken by the women of Akbar's *haram* in 1578, a journey that raises many questions about the newly emerging monarchy of Akbar, the power of his new regime, the centrality of the emperor, the obstacles still encountered in these processes, the making of the *haram*, and paradoxically in a confined *haram* the unusual initiatives of women.

Abu-l Fazl discusses the pilgrimage undertaken by Gulbadan Banu Begum in 1578 along with several other women of Akbar's *haram* as the "visit to the Hijaz[159] of the veiled ladies of the Caliphate."[160] Gulbadan Begum, Akbar's paternal aunt, had "long ago made a vow to visit the holy places."[161] The *Akbarnama* records that she had not been able to fulfill this vow owing to the insecurity of the route to be traveled (this refers especially to Gujarat). However, when there was relative calm in Gujarat, and after the "masters of the European islands ["*amiran-i-jazair-i-farang*"], who were a stumbling block in the way of the travellers to Hijaz" became submissive, Gulbadan Begum discussed her desire for a pilgrimage with Akbar.[162] Akbar sent Gulbadan Begum a large sum of money and goods, and gave her permission to proceed.[163] Abu-l Fazl says that the caravan left on 8 or 9 October 1575,[164] and stayed for three-and-a-half years in Mecca.[165]

---

[158] *Hajj* has the following meanings: "setting out," "tending towards," "going on a pilgrimage to Mecca," and "performing the ceremonies there"; see Steingass, *Persian*, p. 411.

[159] Mecca, Medina and the adjacent territory, Steingass, *Persian*, p. 411.

[160] *Akbarnama*, III, p. 205; see also, *Muntakhab*, II, pp. 216, 320.

[161] *Akbarnama*, III, p. 205.   [162] *Ibid*.   [163] *Ibid*.

[164] *Ibid*., p. 206. Beveridge actually translates two different dates of the women's departure: 8 or 9 October 1575 (*Akbarnama*, III, p. 206) and October 1576 (*Akbarnama*, III, p. 570, n. 1).

[165] *Akbarnama*, III, p. 569. There is some confusion about the dates of departure and return of Gulbadan Begum and her companions. However, the date of their return is given as 13 April 1582 in the *Akbarnama* (*Akbarnama* III, p. 206, n. 3), which is clearly not compatible with the suggestion that the pilgrimage lasted three-and-a-half years. Henry Beveridge, the translator of the *Akbarnama*, works out this discrepancy by pointing to the confusion of the dates in the chronicles and concludes that it must have been about 1580 or beginning of 1581 when she might have started her homeward journey. Then the voyage to Surat, the detention in Gujarat, and the journey to Ajmer, where they performed a supplementary pilgrimage, and then on to Fatehpur-Sikri, would take another year (*Akbarnama*, III, p. 570, n. 1).

The cortege of royal women accompanying Gulbadan Begum on the *hajj* included the following women from the imperial *haram*:

- Salimeh Sultan Begum, widow of Bayram Khan, and now the senior wife of Akbar;
- Haji Begum and Gul'azar Begum, the daughters of Mirza Kamran (Akbar's stepcousins);
- Sultanam Begum, the wife of Mirza 'Askari (Akbar's step-aunt, who looked after him when Humayun was in exile);
- Umm-Kulsum Khanum, the granddaughter of Gulbadan Begum (perhaps the daughter of Gulbadan Begum's son Sa'adat Yar, though this is not entirely clear);
- Gulnar Agha, a wife of Babur *padshah*, one of the two Circassians sent as a present to him by Shah Tahmasb in 1526.[166] (Akbar's step-grandmother);
- Bibi Safiyeh, Shaham Agha, and Sarv-i Sahi, the servants of Humayun. Bibi Saru-qad, also called Sarv-i Sahi (Straight Cypress) had later married Munim Khan-i Khanan. A widow by the time of this journey, she had been, according to Annette Beveridge, a singer, a "reciter," and a "reliable woman."[167] Bibi Safiyeh and Bibi Saru-qad, "sang in the moonlight on the road to Laghman in 1549."[168]
- The last named member of the group was Salimeh Khanum, daughter of Khizr Khvajeh Khan,[169] Gulbadan Begum's husband. Whether Gulbadan was the mother is not known.[170]

Prince Sultan Murad, aged six, was directed to lead the pilgrims up to the shore of the southern ocean[171] – the clearest possible statement on appropriate hierarchies of age and gender! In a hierarchical and patriarchal world, a little boy was, by virtue of his gender alone, "senior enough" to escort the senior-most women of the dynasty to lands across the seas. It is noteworthy that, on hearing of this, Gulbadan Begum requested that he might be kept back, precisely on account of his tender age.[172] Akbar agreed. Three older men accompanied the convoy along with some servants: Baqi Khan, the elder brother of Adham Khan; Rumi Khan of Aleppo, possibly an artillery officer under Babur who accompanied the group perhaps as an interpreter;[173] and 'Abdur Rahman Beg, a nephew of Haydar Mirza (Babur's cousin), who had married one of Mirza Kamran's daughters.[174]

The composition of the party of pilgrims is very interesting. The voyage was led by one of the most senior and respectable women of the *haram*: "the shining chaste one," the aunt of the emperor. Other members of the group were mainly elder members of the Mughal family: close connections and relatives of Babur, Humayun, 'Askari, and Akbar, as well as reliable servants. On such a special, and privileged, occasion – a pilgrimage to Mecca organized for, and by, the royal women – it is noticeable that Hamideh Banu Begum and a long-time confidential servant, Bibi Fatimeh, did not take part.

---

[166] Beveridge, *Humayun*, p. 70.   [167] *Ibid.*   [168] *Ibid.*   [169] *Akbarnama*, III, p. 206.
[170] Beveridge, *Humayun*, Appendix A, p. 280, "Salima Khanam *Chagatai Mughal.*"
[171] *Ibid.*, p. 71.   [172] *Akbarnama*, III, p. 206.
[173] Beveridge, *Humayun*, p. 71; *Akbarnama*, III, p. 206, n. 2.   [174] *Ibid.*, p. 206, n. 3.

The evidence of the intercessory activities of women in the records makes it possible for us to conjecture the reasons for Hamideh Banu Begum's absence from the *hajj*. Senior women of Akbar's *haram* were called upon for several intercessory roles: to advise, to intervene, to conciliate, and indeed to conduct the administration on certain occasions. The presence and support of senior women was clearly vital at many critical moments; and since many senior *haraman* were going away on the pilgrimage, it may have been decided that one or two of the most important should stay behind to support Akbar if the need arose. The event of Hamideh Banu Begum taking charge of Delhi indicates that such possibilities always had to be taken into account. Such a consideration may have led Hamideh Banu Begum (and the trusted Bibi Fatimeh) to stay on in Fatehpur-Sikri, whilst the others performed the *hajj*.[175]

The composition of the women pilgrims once again points to the significance and privileges of senior women: of mothers, aunts and other senior generations in the Mughal family. Gulbadan Begum conducted the *hajj*. The others who joined her were mainly elder women: Salimeh Sultan Begum, granddaughter of Babur, now married to Akbar; the daughters of Mirza Kamran; the stepsisters of Akbar; a wife of Mirza 'Askari; and old servants. Perhaps the only relatively young people in this gathering were Gulbadan's granddaughter and Salimeh Khanum. As for the former, we know practically nothing about her and it is difficult to guess her age. Salimeh Khanum was the daughter of Khizr Khvajeh Khan, but as no other details are available (even about her maternal parentage), it is hard to make anything of her inclusion. Salimeh Sultan Begum was the only wife of Akbar who accompanied the pilgrims. She was a few years the emperor's senior.[176]

No young wife of Akbar accompanied the *hajj* pilgrims who consisted mainly of elder women. This appears to be another illustration of the special status of senior women. But it might be as well that the elders felt a more urgent need to go on the pilgrimage, and may also reflect the view that younger women needed to be kept at home for their protection.

When the women returned, there was much rejoicing. In Abu-l Fazl's words, when the litter of "that chaste lady" Gulbadan Banu Begum reached Ajmer, Prince Salim, "the pearl of the crown," was sent off to meet her. Every day one of the court grandees was also sent to convey salutations. And once Akbar joined the cortege of women, "there were hospitalities, and that night they remained awake and in pleasing discourses." Next day was the glorious return to Fatehpur-Sikri. The ladies had been away for three years and six months.[177]

---

[175] One might suggest that Hamideh Banu did not accompany the pilgrims perhaps because of her old age. It should be noted, however, that she was fifty-one years or so in 1578, at the time of the *hajj* (born in 1527), and lived on for another thirty years or so (d. 1604). For a brief biographical sketch of Hamideh Banu, see Beveridge, *Humayun*, pp. 237–241.

[176] Beveridge, *Humayun*, Appendix A, pp. 276–279, "Salima-sultan Begam *Chaqaniani*."

[177] *Akbarnama*, III, p. 569; see also a description of the return of the women from Hijaz in *Tabaqat*, II, p. 557.

Father Monserrate also noted the return of the chaste ones: "When his [Akbar's] aunt returned from Mekka, the king had the street-pavements covered with silken shawls, and conducted her himself to her palace in a gorgeous litter, scattering largesse meanwhile to the crowds."[178]

The *hajj* of the senior women indicates very clearly the multitude of concerns and interests that animated the activities and initiatives of the *haraman*. The historians who notice it tell us only of Akbar's generous support to women for this journey.[179] The details of the journey in the chronicles show that women themselves took a large part in planning the trip. Gulbadan, while "preparing for a journey to Mecca,"[180] was staying at Surat. To ensure friendly treatment from the Portuguese, she went as far as to give them the town of Butsar (or Bulsar), Butzaris as Monserrate calls it.[181] Then Gulbadan's decision not to include Prince Murad as their escort, Hamideh Banu Begum's (and Bibi Fatimeh's) resolve to stay back – one that may be read as a consensus decision among the *haraman* – as well as the shipwreck and the consequent stay of women in Aden for one year on their return journey (no details of which are found in the contemporary texts), are all signs of a most unusual enterprise.

Badauni comments that the two possible routes through which the *hajj* could be undertaken were rather inaccessible at the time.[182] One of these lay through Shiʿa Iraq, and the other through Gujarat, across the Arabian Sea, that required a pass which "bore the idolatrous stamp of the heads of the Virgin Mary and of Jesus Christ ('on whom be peace')."[183] Other chroniclers also discuss the difficulties of this journey. Abu-l Fazl notes that Akbar was familiar with these problems: he had, in fact, instructed "the great amirs, the officers of every territory, the guardians of the passes, the watchmen of the borders, the river-police, and the harbour-masters" to perform "good services" for the travelers.[184] In such circumstances, the permission to perform the *hajj* came perhaps because it served a crucial political purpose, but also, surely, because the elder women expressed their keenness in no uncertain terms.

In order to fully appreciate the unique character of Gulbadan's *hajj*, its narratives have to be placed by the side of the portrayal of the 1570s, the time when the debates on spirituality and religion were at their peak in the ʿIbadat

---

[178] Monserrate, *Commentary*, p. 205.

[179] Richards, in *Mughal Empire*, observes that the *hajj* gave evidence of Akbar's "Islamic piety by actively organising and sponsoring an official pilgrimage to Mecca each year" (Richards, *Mughal Empire*, pp. 30–31). The point about the emperor's sponsorship that several contemporary chroniclers (Badauni and Nizam al-Din Ahmad, for example), as well as recent scholars (N. R. Farooqi, "Mughal-Ottoman Relations: A Study of Political and Diplomatic Relations Between Mughal India and the Ottoman Empire, 1556–1748," unpublished Ph.D. diss., University of Wisconsin, Madison, 1986) emphasize, is also made evident in the *Akbarnama*. But what emerges in the official chronicle is the exceptional detail on royal women's endeavor, the complete omission of which, by Richards and others, is troubling.

[180] Monserrate, *Commentary*, p. 167.   [181] *Ibid.*, p. 166, n. 255.

[182] *Muntakhab*, I, p. 480.   [183] Beveridge, *Humayun*, p. 72.   [184] *Akbarnama*, III, p. 207.

Khana – literally the house of worship, instituted by Akbar to hold discussions among representatives of various religions. Badauni's *Muntakhab-ut-Tavarikh* marks out his own resentment regarding Akbar's growing interest in different religions, and the nature of religious-social-legal debates in the 'Ibadat Khana. Given the panegyric nature of the imperial history, Badauni's text is crucial to understanding the resentment that might have been generated by Akbar's eclectic interests more generally. At such a time, Gulbadan's pilgrimage is likely to have helped reinforce the Islamic face of the empire. It is interesting to note that Haji Begum, a wife of Humayun, had also undertaken a pilgrimage to Mecca and Medina in 1564. Her return from the *hajj* (1567) is recorded by Abu-l Fazl,[185] but the visibility and the importance attached to the organization and finer details of Gulbadan's *hajj* are missing in relation to Haji Begum's pilgrimage.

Gulbadan's *hajj* was organized as a spiritual journey for the participants, the records tell us: but it was perhaps more than that. What the *hajj* seems to mark is a moment of critical change in the structures of Mughal rulership: from relatively fluid political structures to a more settled, consolidated government. The *hajj* was one among the many pietistic activities supported by the emperor – part of a series of moves that he and others in his court may have found necessary for the consolidation of Muslim support in this uniquely polyglot empire. The undertaking (and the imperial sanction for it) may thus be seen as another sign of the ideological tension that marked this stage of the formation of the Mughal Empire. This tension is evident again in Badauni's comments on the debates in the 'Ibadat Khana.[186] The empire was seeking different forms of legitimacy. The *hajj* presumably helped to signal its "Muslim" character.

In addition, the *hajj* is a crucial indicator of the volition of women. At the time of the making of Akbar's empire, when its mechanisms and procedures were still being drawn, a group of the senior-most royal women was able to travel across the seas as pilgrims. Although women continued, individually, to make trips to Mecca,[187] such a *hajj* by a large group of imperial women was never heard of again – later in Akbar's reign, or under any of his grand successors.

A royal women's *hajj* was no mean venture, its organization no meager task. The women's initiative and decision-making lay not only in bringing forward their wish to the emperor to undertake the pilgrimage, but was seen all along in its organization and in the way that the women faced the ensuing hazards. The *hajj* in the late 1570s is an extraordinary statement in the Mughal chronicles. First, it is a comment on the exceptional enterprise of royal women in rather restrictive circumstances. Secondly, and as a corollary to the first point, it dismantles the premises and understanding of historians writing on the Mughal *haram*.

---

[185] *Ibid.*, p. 107.
[186] See, for example, *Muntakhab*, II, pp. 200, 203, 204, 215, 219, 262, 294.
[187] In 1617, Jahangir sent his sister, probably Shahzadeh Khanum to Mecca; W. Foster (ed.), *Thomas Roe*, p. 418. Then Tavernier reports, sometime later in the century that the Queen of Bijapur had visited Isfahan on her way back from Mecca. See Findly, *Nur Jahan*, p. 121.

There is yet another inference to be drawn from this evidence. The collective royal women's pilgrimage to Mecca, like Khanzadeh Begum's mediation in the matter of reading the *khutba*, is an exceptional moment in the annals of the Mughals – a dream moment for an historian of pre-modern women, and gender relations. It is only such moments that rupture the male-centeredness of the texts of the time. While Akbar and Abu-l Fazl were perhaps successfully fabricating a carefully circumscribed *haram* world, the *haram* folk were responding to those constructions in rather unexpected ways; the *hajj* of Gulbadan Begum, alongside other undertakings of royal women, may be considered one of those unpredictable rejoinders. In the many messages conveyed by Gulbadan's journey, perhaps this one is the most pertinent: that the domestic world of the Mughals could not be so easily domesticated after all.

CHAPTER 8

Conclusion

The projections of the Mughal family and how these alter from time to time and from text to text have been the primary focus of my investigation in this book. I have emphasized the fluidity of the domestic life of the early Mughals. The domestic world and the *haram* that the historians have written about came to be constructed over a long period, in the context of the establishment of a new imperial formation in a new land. One of the main propositions of the book is that the institutionalization of the *haram* and a more general regulation of the Mughal domestic world mirrored the making of a new imperial order under Akbar. The inhabitants of the *Shabistan-i Iqbal* were pivotal in this move towards glorification of the empire and its written prescriptions.

The conditions under which the *haram* became the officially designated "domestic" space of the Mughal empire have been discussed in detail in chapter 7. Recall the other terms that were used in earlier Mughal chronicles for parallel arrangements, and for the king's intimate circle, before the term *haram* came to be commonly deployed. Terms like *ahl-va ʿayal, khanivadeh, kuch va oruk, khvishan va ʿazizan, nasab, khvishan va mardum*, and *ahl-i haram* or *haraman-i padshah* of Babur and Humayun's time invoke an array of changing physical-political-cultural conditions and with these a diversity of "royal" communities and forms of associations. For me, these terms have been key to thinking through the diverse units of reference and the varied kinds of power relations through which domestic life may be imagined.

The point about changes over time relates to another important argument advanced in the preceding pages: that the Mughal empire was not a ready-made regime, fully formed from its birth. Its establishment was of course processual. It was also troubled and multi-tonal. A great deal of trial-and-error, negotiation and conflict went into its emergence. Abu-l Fazl's construction of a genealogy that sought to make Akbar the fulcrum of Mughal life, the commissioned histories, the extended rules and regulations that were brought in to set the normative in Akbar's court and the *haram*, the physical grandeur of the court – the court laureates, the presence of distinguished clerics, Jesuit priests, ambassadors and other dignitaries – the hunts, feasts and other paraphernalia, are all instances of new institutions that were developed as part of the building up of a new imperial polity. The changes that occurred under Akbar's rulership did not mark a complete break from the lives and practices of his immediate predecessors; yet they signaled the establishment of a much more confident and secure regime, the results of a long-term consolidation of political power and social solidarity, symbols of sovereignty and rituals of governance.

Akbar's domestic life was obviously conditioned by the mediations and processes – and unease and arbitration – that went into the making of the empire more generally. The imperial regulations now marked a move towards the confinement of the royal women, and a constriction of the space available for their activities and agency. It was a step towards making them invisible. The honoring and seclusion, or should one say, honoring *by* seclusion, of the *haraman* became a major aspect of the new imperial order; the remains of the grand complex of women's quarters in Fatehpur-Sikri stand testimony to that. A development that is surely no less striking is that the *Shabistan-i Iqbal* (Akbar's *haram*) came to have hundreds of women. I have said that this development may be seen in many ways, not just the fact numerous historians have noted, that these multiple alliances were contracted on account of the political needs of the empire. There is no doubt that the need for political alliance was at the heart of several of Akbar's marriages. In addition, the large number of his marriages may also be read as a sign of the strength and virility of his empire. More crucially, I have argued, the several marriages of the emperor speak to a vision of empire in which the emperor was the center of the universe: by a marital union with this near-divine ruler, women were marvelously blessed – as were all others who came under the protection of his umbrella.

I have pointed out that the use, one might even say, the invocation of the term *haram* in Akbar's reign marks a return to the original Quranic meaning of the concept: the *sanctum sanctorum*, the "most inaccessible of the inaccessible."[1] At the same time, paradoxically, in what might be described as a major departure from the "Islamic" conception of the marriages, Akbar's marriages might be said to have transformed the character of the *haram*. Consider the fact that the *Shariʿa* prescribes a maximum of four wives, an issue that had to be debated extensively in Akbar's inner circle in relation to the number of women in his *haram*. Akbar, a Sunni Muslim king, resorted to *mutʿa* marriages for some of these women. Etymologically *mutʿa* means enjoyment or pleasure. "The custom of mutʿa of women, as it has been called, was outlawed in the seventh century by the second caliph, ʿUmar, who equated it with fornication," writes one scholar, pointing out that in theory temporary marriage is forbidden among Sunnis.[2]

---

[1] In addition, it referred both to the living quarters of the royal women, and to the women of the *haram*, the *haraman* themselves.

[2] Haeri, "Temporary Marriage," p. 210.

In addition, the presence of large numbers of "Hindu" wives in a Muslim *haram*, the introduction of "Hindu" customs and ceremonials into Mughal practices, the relationships among the "Hindu" and Muslim wives of the monarch, the children born out of these marriages between Mughal and Rajput noble households, and the relationships between the families of the bride and the groom, all contributed towards making this an unusually eclectic site. I suggest that what is most remarkable in the history of these marital alliances is the mixing of rituals, symbols, and activities – between those that did, and those that did not belong to a recognizable Islamic heritage. What still remains to be investigated are the details of how the emperor and other inhabitants of the Mughal *haram* came to negotiate and inhabit these mixed ritual and religious worlds – this must be the subject of another book or books.

Comparing Mughal India, Ottoman Turkey, and Safavid Iran

Through the findings outlined above, I seek to carry forward a point that has been made in a number of recent scholarly interventions: that one cannot turn away from the specifics that went into the making of different Islamic societies and polities. There is no eternally established model of Islamic social, political, and cultural forms. All such forms are historically constituted, and the argument stands for the Islamic world as much as for Christendom, the Buddhist lands of East and South East Asia, and other "traditions." As several scholars of Islamic history have demonstrated, even what is known as Classical Islam (elaborated by Prophet Muhammad and his immediate successors) is conditioned by local practices, traditions – and histories. The history of Islam and of Islamic polities and societies obviously does not stop with the making of that classical form.

Scholars have made the point that the Mughal, Ottoman, and Safavid idioms were distinct articulations of their shared inheritance of Central Asian political traditions either in Mongol or Turkish form.[3] Recent writings emphasize the different routes taken by different monarchs in their drawing up of political syntheses, their construction of illustrious genealogies and the invocation of religious and political ideologies. Note the recasting of Imami Shi'ism in Safavid Iran with a public rejection of Sufism and other syncretic forms of cultural practice as heretical and a move towards *Shari'a* as the legitimate form of social order; Akbar's experimentation with religion as a "way of life" by means of the *Din-i Ilahi*, his so-called new religion, based upon his regular meetings and conversations with representatives of different religions on every Thursday in the 'Ibadat Khana; and the Ottoman disassociation in the fifteenth century from Mongol tradition, denigrating even the

[3] Peirce, *Imperial Harem*, pp. 160–161; Babayan, "The 'Aqa'id al-Nisa," p. 352.

Muslim ruler Timur, followed by a claim of descent from the Prophet as a ground for legitimacy.[4]

Paradoxically this context of distinctness, continual enunciation and revaluation of traditions seems to have left untouched formulations on imperial women and their places and spaces. Take the instance of the "powerful" Timurid and Mongol matriarchs that have been referred to in scholarly literature as the exemplars for later Ottoman, Safavid, and Mughal women.[5] Although scholars have suggested the point about the particularity of later matriarchal traditions, pointing out that these were not a simple carryover of the Timurid Mongol antecedents,[6] the matter has not been pursued in any detail.

The problem to a certain extent has to do with the generalized ways in which we approach questions related to pre-modern societies. For example: as long as there are "powerful" women contributing to the making of the monarchy by advising the monarchs, by counseling young kings on their marriages, and directing their wives to produce children to carry forward the name of the dynasty, there is no further question about projections of power and exercise of sovereignty. The women are simply there. Both the more visible matriarchs and younger women too are, quite similar in what they do across the board: the Mughal queen Nur Jahan is *like* the domineering Ottoman queen Hurrem, and Hurrem is *like* the influential Safavid princess Pari Khan Khanum. And the activities of these imperial women are reminiscent of the influential Mongol and Timurid predecessors – Ho'elun (Chingiz Khan's mother), Borte (Chingiz Khan's wife), Saray Mulk Khanum (Timur's principal wife), Gawharshad Begum (Timur's daughter-in-law) – as if it runs in the blood. Only the kings are historical, individual subjects.

Here is a good example of this kind of generalizing:

The general roles assigned to women in Timur's family appear similar to those ascribed to females in other nomadic Mongol and Turkic groups of eastern Iran and Central Asia. Women were expected not only to care for children, but also to be able to manage other aspects of family life in the absence of their husbands, fathers or brothers. Their duties included overseeing the production or procurement of food and clothing needed by the household. Given their broad responsibilities, it is logical that such women also exercised considerable personal freedom.[7]

---

[4] Babayan, "The 'Aqa'id al-Nisa," pp. 357–358; Peirce, *Imperial Harem*, pp. 156–162. For an extensive bibliography on Akbar's *Din-i Ilahi*, see Iqtidar Alam Khan (ed.), *Akbar and His Age* (New Delhi, 1999). For an example of comparative writing on the Mughal-Ottoman-Safavid empires, especially in relation to political-administrative-institutional structures, see M. Athar Ali, "Political Structures of the Islamic Orient in the Sixteenth and Seventeenth Centuries," in Irfan Habib (ed.), *Medieval India I: Researches in the History of India 1200–1750* (New Delhi, 1999).

[5] Cf. ch. 1, n. 25.

[6] See, for example, Babayan, "The 'Aqa'id al-Nisa," pp. 352–353; Peirce, *Imperial Harem*, pp. 160–161.

[7] Soucek, "Timurid Women," p. 200.

Let me reiterate that in much of the received literature, the domestic is equated with the women's quarters and women's activities. In the writings on Mughal India, and until recently in Ottoman and Safavid historiography, this domain has been generally summed up as the *haram* – a sequestered world, behind the wall, its women veiled. In its most common form it is also described as a highly sexualized, mysterious (hidden) realm of perverted, even orgiastic, pleasure. It is the argument of this book, however, that there is a crucial element of experimentation and creativity that goes into the making of the monarchies and societies of which these *harams* are a part – their new political arrangements, their domestic lives, their social hierarchies, and their sacred symbols.

Note the very major differences in ritual place and political practice ascribed to the women of Mughal, Ottoman, and Safavid kingdoms. Concubines dominate the history of the Ottoman *haram* and its dynastic politics. In the Safavid case, by comparison, sovereignty rested "in the ruling family as a whole."[8] The projection of the social importance of women at the court also marks the Safavid *haram* as distinct from its Mughal and Ottoman counterparts. The prominent women include not just the royal mothers and wives, but unmarried (and thus childless) daughters. Such women, as Rizvi notes, rarely appear in the histories of other Islamic societies.[9] For the Mughals, at least by the time of Akbar, it is the invisibility of women that is most striking.[10] It may help to spell out these differences in a little more detail.

The available literature on practices related to Timurid and Mongol women already indicates something of the specific inflections of the domestic ethos of the Mughal, Ottoman, and Safavid women. As Leslie Peirce has pointed out, it is difficult both to denote a distinct Timurid-Mongol strand, and mark a clear-cut departure in the domestic culture of the Mughal, Ottoman, and Safavid worlds in some visibly recognizable way.[11] However, neither she nor I am suggesting the coming together of different traditions in any easy synthesis. This book demonstrates how the early Mughal domestic life was articulated differently at different times – in the wandering ethos of the peripatetic kings, in an accommodation of Quranic and Prophetic traditions, in reference to ethical, juridical, and courtly norms together with invocations of illustrious Timurid-Chingizid forefathers – sometimes candidly, at other times hesitantly. What I emphasize in this book, and in this conclusion, is those hesitant, variable traditions sitting beside each other presenting different

---

[8] Babayan, "The 'Aqa'id al-Nisa," p. 352.
[9] Kishwar Rizvi, "Gendered Patronage: Women and Benevolence during the Early Safavid Empire," in D. Fairchild Ruggles (ed.), *Women, Patronage, and Self-Representation in Islamic Societies* (Albany, 2000), p. 128.
[10] As we have seen in the previous chapter, the invisibility of Mughal women under Akbar is in the sense of seclusion of their persons (incarceration) as well as in the suppression of their names in the records. This invisibility is broken time and again, most notably by senior women like the mother of the emperor.
[11] Peirce, *Imperial Harem*, p. 157.

possibilities of understanding the Mughal domestic ethos in which it becomes hard to represent any patterns as "inevitable." Very much the same thing can be said for the domestic lives of the Ottoman and Safavid monarchs.

The Ottoman *haram*

Let us begin by considering the very location and inhabitants of the Ottoman *haram*. The Ottoman *haram* (*haram-i humayun*), the living quarters of the sultan, was initially the inner precinct of the royal palace, dwelt in only by males. Towards the end of the sixteenth century, the sultan built a second set of private quarters in this palace to house women and children, and this area also began to be called "the imperial harem *because of the presence there not of women but of the sultan*" (emphasis mine).[12]

The imperial *haram* rose to importance not only because of the presence of the royal family in the capital but also because of the integration of the domestic (mainly female) into the imperial residence. Until the reign of Sulayman I (1521–66), entitled the Magnificent, the royal residence, *saray-i atik* or the Old Palace, were the principal quarters of the women. By 1468 Mehmed II (1444–46, 1451–81) had taken residence in the splendid New Palace (called today Topkapi Palace), constructed on the dramatic confluence of the Sea of Marmara, the Golden Horn and the Bosphorous. The *haraman* remained in the Old Palace for another century, which was incorporated into the New Palace (*saray-i jedid*) only when Hurrem (Sulayman I's "favorite") took residence there (she appears to have been living there by 1534[13]). "The enormous growth in the population of the harem [now] created the need for greater hierarchical organization and differentiation of function that had previously been necessary." "It is this expanded harem," Peirce notes, that we can appropriately call "the harem institution."[14]

And it was this expanded *haram*, a manifestation and part of Ottoman Empire's shift from a conquest state to a sedentary, bureaucratic state, that became the source of the power of women, especially the sultan's concubines and his *valide sultan*, the queen mother. The Old Palace now came to house the "retired harems": after the sultan's death, the women associated with him, his servants, concubines, and their servants and others would be sent to the Old Palace. This palace also became the center for "royal urban ritual" from where daughters of the sultans were married, where statesmen and other dignitaries were often received, and where sultans often went for a "change of air."[15]

Even more striking is the Ottoman dynasty's "devotion to concubinage"[16] in its politics of reproduction – an unparalleled feature of pre-modern Islamic history. Until the last quarter of the fifteenth century the Ottoman sultans married daughters of the Balkan and Anatolian dynasties (they also married their own daughters to Anatolian dynasts) for political linkages and to

---

[12] *Ibid.*, p. 5.   [13] *Ibid.*, p. 121.   [14] *Ibid.*, p. 119.   [15] *Ibid.*, pp. 122–123.   [16] *Ibid.*, p. 31.

strengthen the military and diplomatic alliances.[17] After 1451, no foreign marriages were conducted. From 1451 until the reign of Sulayman I, the sultans pursued a reproductive policy of "one mother, one son."[18] After producing a son, a concubine would leave the *haram* and accompany her son to the provincial governorate. Sulayman put an end to this policy by making his Ukrainian concubine Hurrem his favored partner, and eventually marrying her. "Hurrem's title – *haseki*, the sultan's favorite – broadcast her unique status."[19] This gradually became the common practice among sultans after Suleyman and paved the way for the acceptance of primogeniture in the seventeenth century. It was only after the death of Sulayman's son, Salim II (1566–74), that the *valide sultan* emerged as the most powerful figure among royal women and more generally in the political life of the empire.[20]

Leslie Peirce's central engagement in fact is to delineate the political power and public prominence of Ottoman imperial women that was most striking particularly after the accession in 1520 of Sulayman I. Nurbanu, the *haseki* of Salim II (son of Suleyman I), was the first of the "great *valide sultans*."[21] When Salim died in 1574, Murad III, his son from Nurbanu, continued his relationship with his *haseki* Safiye, although unlike Hurrem and Nurbanu, Safiye did not become the sultan's legally married wife. This did not affect her prominence because by Safiye's time there was "Hurrem's career in establishing the model that influenced the expectations of the generations following her." At any rate, "within two generations, the once-disturbing *haseki* and even the marriage of the sultan had become expected [influential?] features of dynastic life."[22] There are several examples from the Ottoman empire: the making of the tradition of *hasekis* and *valide-sultans* – *hasekis* as powerful wives of the sultans and later as influential mothers, *valide sultans* – is persuasively illustrated by Peirce.[23]

Note also, Ottoman women's "public culture of sovereignty," as illuminated in the moment with which Peirce opens her book (set in 1599), when Sunullah Efendi, the foremost guardian of Islam, "publicly lamented" a number of harmful and disruptive developments in Ottoman society. Among his several criticisms, one was "that women should have nothing to do with 'matters of government and sovereignty'."[24] Sunullah, in his disapproval, recalled a *hadith* (tradition) attributed to Prophet Muhammad, which spoke to the harmful consequences of women's sovereignty: "[A] people who entrusts its affairs to a woman will never know prosperity."[25] It was this depraved "sultanate of women" that became the favorite version of the popular and scholarly literature where the *haram* was seen as a site of "illegitimate usurpation of power that resulted from a weakening of moral fibre and institutional integrity of the Ottoman society," especially since the

---

[17] *Ibid.*, p. 29.   [18] *Ibid.*, p. 58. The phrase is used at several other places in the book.
[19] *Ibid.*, p. 63.   [20] For details of concubinage, see *ibid.*, chs. 2 and 3.
[21] *Ibid.*, p. 92.   [22] *Ibid.*, pp. 94–95.   [23] *Ibid.*, chs. 3–4.   [24] *Ibid.*, p. vii.   [25] *Ibid.*, p. 267.

time of Sulayman when his *haseki* and then the *valide sultan* became considerably more prominent than their predecessors had ever been.[26]

The political presence of women stimulates debates not only in the writings of the 'ulama but also in other ethical digests and treatises to do with etiquette often written by statesmen.[27] Out of this appears the "near-universal view of Ottoman society that regards the influence of harem women as illegitimate." And out of this emerges Hurrem as a "powerful schemer selfishly manipulating the sultan to secure the succession of one of her sons, and thereby jeopardizing the welfare of the empire."[28]

The Safavid *haram*

Compare the Ottoman instance with the example of the Safavids. As they became sedentary, the Safavids had to work at creating a universe that balanced the relationship of the imperial house with the Iranian landed elite, the clergy, and the slaves. This resulted in an unusual blend of local practices and mores in the making of the monarchy, and of the royal household and its traditions.[29] The Safavid monarchs strengthened ties with the Qizilbash tribesmen of Anatolia through matrimonial alliances. In these partnerships, it was not just the king who was held in high regard, "but his entire family, including the women."[30] The esteemed position of royal women is seen not only in cases of matrimony: it is premised more broadly upon an "air of sanctity" that attached to the household and that emerged in their association with Prophet Muhammad. Safavid men and women were highly respected, being "elevated," in Rizvi's words, "almost to sainthood." Strikingly, although Shah Isma'il (1500–24) never explicitly assumed the role of a religious leader, his family came to be identified as the *ahl-i Muhammad* (the family of Muhammad).[31]

Fatimeh, the daughter of Muhammad, wife of 'Ali and mother of Hasan and Husain became the reference point for Safavid princesses. Thus, Pari Khan Khanum, daughter of Shah Tahmasb (1524–76), was not only the "queen of the age" (*maleka-i zamani*), but also the "Fatima of the age" (*Fatima-i zamani*). Mahd-i 'Ala, the mother of Shah 'Abbas (1587–1629), was called the "queen of the times," "the chaste" (*'afifa*), "the radiant" (*zahra*), "the lawful progeny of the leader of the women" (*dhariya tayiba sayyida al-nissa*) and "the great Maryam" (mother of Jesus).[32] Simultaneous emphasis on prophetic associations and political authority – what Babayan

---

[26] *Ibid.*, pp. vii–viii.   [27] *Ibid.*, p. 273.   [28] *Ibid.*, p. 89.

[29] Babayan, "The 'Aqa'id al-Nisa," pp. 349–351.   [30] Rizvi, "Gendered Patronage," p. 123.

[31] *Ibid.*, p. 125.

[32] *Ibid.*, pp. 125–126. I have retained the spellings and transliteration as used by Kishwar Rizvi. For an extended discussion of the titles of imperial Safavid women, and the larger context in which those titles were ascribed to them, see Maria Szuppe, "La participation des femmes de la famille royale à l'exercice du pouvoir en Iran," *Studia Iranica*, 23, 2 (1994), pp. 240–242.

sums up as "an eponymous dynastic clan and a sacrosanct *dudman* (family)"[33] – remained crucial to the Safavid dynasty from the beginning of its career.

Maria Szuppe argues that in this royal *haram*, the mother of the Shah was theoretically the most important person. Usually the mothers resided at the imperial *haram*. However, there are two striking examples of mothers who left the *haram*. The first is that of Shah Isma'il's wife Tajlu Khanum who was "sent" to Shiraz. The second that of Sultanum Begum who "left" the *haram* to reside in Qum.[34] It should be noted that the association of Safavid women with the city of Qum is a recurrent theme in the writings of the contemporary chroniclers.[35] The palace in this city was a "surrogate, winter residence" for the Safavids and "the site of retreat and exile from the court, especially for the women." Shah Tahmasb had sent his mother to Qum in 1528 when she had aided his brother Bahram Mirza against him. According to Rizvi, Sultanum Begum, the mother of Shah 'Abbas, was "banished" to Qum when she sided against her son in a political intrigue. Rizvi also provides other examples of women who were sent away to Qum.[36]

What these examples help to do is to highlight the point that the Safavid *haram* was a complex institution, with its own distinctive qualities. Among these, historians of sixteenth-century Iran have underlined the Safavid women's exercise of authority, their patrimonial rights, and their freedom of movement.[37]

Pari-Khan Khanum, the daughter of Shah Tahmasp (contemporary of Humayun), and Shahzadeh Sultanum, his sister, whom we encounter during Humayun's wanderings in Persia, are frequently cited examples of Safavid imperial women who wielded considerable authority.[38] We are also told that Zainab Begum (d. 1642), daughter of Shah Tahmasb, held great sway over courtly politics.[39] The examples of Safavid women exercising enormous imperial power are, as several scholars have shown us, in fact several. Both Safavid men and women were "believed to be laced with divinely-bestowed charisma." Along with their brothers, princesses in the seventeenth century were blinded for fear that they might lay claim to the throne. "This is a phenomenon peculiar to the Safavids," Babayan argues. "In theory then, all females, whether they were descended through male or female lines, could rule."[40] Pari Khan-Khanum (d. 1578) aspired to rule in this context. Her involvement in the succession politics following her father's death "reveals the

---

[33] Babayan, "The 'Aqa'id al-Nisa," p. 357.
[34] Szuppe, "La participation des femmes," p. 219 and n. 40.
[35] Rizvi, "Gendered Patronage," p. 134.   [36] *Ibid.*, pp. 133–134.
[37] Witness the repeated visits made by royal women to the winter palaces and their active participation in hunting and archery. For details see, among others, Babayan, Szuppe, and Rizvi cited here.
[38] For details of Pari Khan Khanum's political engagements, see Shohreh Gholsorkhi, "Pari Khan Khanum: A Masterful Safavid Princess," *Iranian Studies*, 28, 3–4 (Summer/Fall 1995), pp. 143–156.
[39] Rizvi, "Gendered Patronage."   [40] Babayan, "The 'Aqa'id al-Nisa," p. 352.

extent to which the Safavids regarded sovereignty as being vested in the ruling family as a whole."[41]

Shah Tahmasp, Pari Khan Khanum's father, gave her considerable responsibility and extensive powers as his confidante, entrusting her with difficult affairs.[42] After his death, Pari Khan Khanum's status was enhanced even more. She plotted her brother Shah Isma'il's (at the time incarcerated in Qahqahah for the previous twenty years) accession to the throne. Isma'il waited for the auspicious moment to enter the capital. Meanwhile, the nobility continued to pay obeisance to Pari Khan Khanum at her residence first ("indicating that she had a separate residence from the harem in Qazvin") and then turned to the new king.[43] The king was apparently displeased with this conduct of the nobles and with his sister's "meddling" in the affairs of the state. He asked the nobles: "Have you not understood, my friends, that interference in matters of state by women is demeaning to the king's honor ... ?"[44] Or as Babyan's reading of the comment of the Shah has it, the "exercise of political power tarnished male honor."[45] These were aspersions quite similar to the Ottoman Sunullah Efendi's in 1599.

In the Safavid case, however, by the side of the predictable male critique sits the unusual argument for women's authority, namely that Safavids considered that both male and female descendants were "cloaked with authority." Thus Safavid women engaged to preserve the imperial realm "as their patrimony."[46] Maria Szuppe puts it a little differently: that the domain that was "natural" for women's activities was politics – "Le domaine d'activité naturel était celui de la politique"[47] – an exceptional formulation for the place of premodern imperial women.

The Mughal *haram*, by way of comparison

The rule of the Ottoman concubines finds no parallel in the Mughal or the Safavid worlds. In neither case are concubines described as "favorites" or as eminent mothers; and mothers are scarcely mentioned in the discussion of royal births in the contemporary chronicles of Mughal India. The absence of the name of the mother of the emperor Jahangir, the much-longed-for and (according to the chronicles) miraculously conceived son of Akbar, is perhaps the most striking example of this breathtaking silence.

The "naturalness" of royal women's political authority that historians have suggested for the Safavids also finds no parallel among the Mughals. On the

---

[41] *Ibid.*
[42] Gholsorkhi, "Pari Khan Khanum," pp. 149–150; Babayan, "The 'Aqa'id al-Nisa," p. 353.
[43] Babayan, "The 'Aqa'id al-Nisa," p. 353.
[44] Gholsorkhi, "Pari Khan Khanum," pp. 149–150.
[45] Babayan, "The 'Aqa'id al-Nisa," p. 354.   [46] *Ibid.*, p. 352.
[47] Szuppe, "La participation des femmes," p. 253.

contrary, it was only the uncommonly determined, talented and lucky women – even among royalty – who gained political prominence and visibility here.

The presence and exercise of power by such women should not be underplayed, especially among the seniors. Recall some of the matriarchs from the Mughal world discussed in the preceding chapters. Isan Dawlat Begum: Babur's grandmother, known for her "strategy and tactics"[48] in Babur's words; Maham Begum: Babur's "wife of affection" (and later the influential mother of Humayun) as Annette Beveridge casts her; Khanzadeh Begum: known in the chronicles of her time for the great "sacrifice" she performed by marrying Shiybani Khan Uzbik in order to help establish peace between the Mughals and the Uzbiks. Gulbadan Banu Begum records the special position Khanzadeh Begum, the *akeh-janam*, the "oldest paternal aunt and my royal father's eldest sister."[49] Khanzadeh's part, in the matters of reading the *khutba* in the conflict for power between the sons of Babur, is memorable.

Then there is Hamideh Banu Begum: she is elevated already in her refusal to marry Humayun, particularly the clarity with which she retorted to the proposal of marriage: "Oh yes, I shall marry someone; but he shall be a man whose collar my hand can touch, and not one whose skirt it does not reach."[50] She was to be the domineering mother of emperor Akbar: her repeated arrival in the distant camps set up by the busy monarch, as well as her charge of the empire when the emperor was away, are illustrations of her assertive motherhood. And finally, the unforgettable Gulbadan Banu Begum, Akbar's aunt, who organized and led the *hajj* of imperial women, and also left behind the critical memoir that inspired this book.

It is out of such a tradition of matriarchal authority that the emergence of a figure like Nur Jahan, the renowned "Empress of Mughal India," might be best understood. It is worth remembering that the gaining of this new place has been portrayed as smooth, uncomplicated, and sudden.[51] The speed with which Nur Jahan gains prominence has often been ascribed to her close relationship with Jahangir. This is portrayed in the received historical writings as *the* singular romance of the emperor.[52] In the light of our findings on the domestic life of the early Mughals, it seems appropriate to suggest that Nur Jahan's "centrality" – whether premised upon a special romance or not – becomes possible only in the track of the powerful women who had gone before her.

---

[48] Thackston, *Baburnama*, p. 49; cf. Thackston, *Memoirs*, p. 59, and Beveridge, *Baburnama*, p. 43.

[49] Beveridge, *Humayun*, p. 103; cf. Gulbadan, *Ahval*, fol. 15b.

[50] Beveridge, *Humayun*, p. 151; cf. Gulbadan, *Ahval*, fol. 43a.

[51] Findly, *Nur Jahan*, p. 3. As noted earlier, Findly sums up chronologically the details of Nur Jahan's life in the prologue to her book, and argues for the quick (and unusual?) centrality that she acquired in the court. See a detailed discussion of Findly's work in the Introduction.

[52] For references, see the Introduction. Even the details of exchanges between Jagat Gosain (another wife of Jahangir) and Nur Jahan cited by Findly suggest the undecided, contested basis of romantic primacy and authority between them (Findly, *Nur Jahan*, pp. 116–125).

In relation to imperial women like Nur Jahan, it is to be noted that there was a continuous process of experimentation and negotiation as the new regimes and new cultures came into being. What stands out is the tension and the changeability, one might even say fragility, before the glorious *harams* at Istanbul, Fatehpur-Sikri, Agra, and Herat and Isfahan came to don their colorful new garbs – and the women's splendid dwellings, and all the legends surrounding unusual women, emerged. It is in these changing and contested arenas that a more satisfactory portrayal of the lives of imperial women like Maham Begum, Hamideh Banu Begum, Khanzadeh Begum, Gulbadan Banu Begum, Nur Jahan, Pari Khan-Khanum, Shahzadeh Sultanum, Hurrem and Safiye, may be located.

Yet, in spite of the ascription of unusual influence and power of particular Mughal women, one's overwhelming sense remains that of the women's profound invisibility – especially once Akbar's power and his statutes came to be in place. In the introduction to his new translation of the *Jahangirnama*, W. M. Thackston asks the interesting question why Jahangir himself in his memoirs wrote so little about Nur Jahan,[53] despite her oft-cited centrality in imperial affairs. As a matter of fact, the emperor does not even make a mention of his marriage with Nur Jahan.[54] One may propose at least a speculative answer to Thackston's question. Would it be entirely wrong to say that, like the historians of later years, the men of the Mughal family thought in very hide-bound and conventional ways, and composed their memoirs along inherited patterns? In these inherited, patriarchal terms, the presence of a woman has often been erased – even when the woman was of enormous importance. This is precisely what happens when it comes to the births of Salim and other leading princes. The names of the mothers of these much-coveted royal heirs are not so much as mentioned in the most import-ant official histories of the time. The absence of Nur Jahan in the *Jahangirnama* is like the absence of Jahangir's mother in the *Akbarnama* and other chronicles of Akbar's reign. It is a powerful comment on the patriarchalism of Mughal sources, not unlike the patriarchalism of our own history-writing regarding the Mughals.

Final thoughts

What I have suggested in this conclusion is that very particular kinds of lived experience, and particular political, cultural, and historical struggles, pro-duced different practices of domestic life, and different kinds of *harams* in Mughal India, Ottoman Turkey, and Safavid Iran – *harams* that are all accepted as Islamic. It is scarcely a revelation to say that different configura-tions were produced by different contexts and conditions. Yet, these

---

[53] Thackston, *Jahangirnama*, p. xxv.   [54] *Ibid.*, pp. 37–38.

variations do not seem to have prevented commentators from ascribing the assumed qualities of one *haram* to all *harams*, without exception.

The diverse modes of adaptation to local circumstances and the ongoing struggles that the three imperial "Islamic" domestic worlds of the sixteenth century were engaged in necessitates some rethinking about the ways in which Islamic societies and peoples have responded to diverse conditions and challenges – a point that may have a certain contemporary political as well as historiographical relevance. By opening up the question of how one set of Islamic traditions and institutions was forged in one pre-modern kingdom, this book invites researchers to re-examine not only the assumed normality and universality of our own domestic and political arrangements, but also the essentialized representations of other lives and other cultures.

Bibliography

Primary sources

Manuscripts and translations

Ahval-i Humayun Badshah, by Gulbadan Banu Begum, British Library MS Or. 166.
  Beveridge, Annette Susannah (trans.), *The History of Humayun: Humayun Nama* (1902; rpt. Delhi, 1994).
A'in-i Akbari, by Abu-l Fazl 'Allami, ed. Henry Blochmann *The A'in-I Akbari by Abul Fazl-I-'Allami*, vols. I–III, Persian text (Calcutta, 1872–77).
  Blochmann, Henry (ed.) and H. S. Jarrett (trans.), *The A-in-I Akbari*, vols. I–III (1873, 1894; rpt. Calcutta, 1993).
Akbarnama, by Abu-l Fazl 'Allami, ed. Maulawi 'Abd-ur-Rahim, *Akbarnamah by Abul-Fazl I Mubarak I 'Allami*, vols. I–III, Persian text (Calcutta, 1873–86).
  Beveridge, H. (trans.), *The Akbar Nama of Abu-l-Fazl*, vols. I–III (1902–39; rpt. Delhi, 1993).
  British Library *Akbarnama*, MS Or. 12988.
  Victoria and Albert Museum MS I. S. 2/1896: Acc. Nos. 16/17, 115/117, 29/117, and 78/117.
Akhlaq i-Nasiri, by Nasir al-Din Tusi, trans. and ed. G. M. Wickens, *The Nasirean Ethics* (London, 1964).
Baburnama, by Zahir al-Din Muhammad Babur, British Library, MS Or. 3714.
  Thackston, W. M. (trans. and ed.), *Zahiruddin Muhammad Babur Mirza: Baburnama*, Parts I–III, Turkish transcription, Persian edition, and English translation (Cambridge, Mass., 1993).
  Beveridge, Annette Susannah (trans.), *Babur-nama (Memoirs of Babur) of Zahiru'd-din Muhammad Babur Padshah Ghazi* (1921; rpt. Delhi, 1997).
  Thackston, W. M. *The Baburnama: Memoirs of Babur, Prince and Emperor* (New York, 1996).
Qanun-i Humayuni, by Khvandamir, ed. M. Hidayat Hosain, *The Qanun-i Humayuni of Khwandamir*, Bibliotheca Indica Series 260, no. 1488 (Calcutta, 1940). Persian edition.
Tazkireh-i Humayun va Akbar, by Bayazid Bayat, ed. M. Hidayat Hosain, *Tadhkira-i Humayun wa Akbar of Bayazid Biyat*, Bibliotheca Indica Series 264, no. 1546 (Calcutta, 1941). Persian edition.

Stewart, Major Charles (trans.), *The Tezkereh al Vakiat or Private Memoirs of the Moghul Emperor Humayun* (1832; rpt. Lucknow, 1971).

Jahangirnama, by Nur al-Din Muhammad Jahangir, trans. W. M. Thackston, *The Jahangirnama: Memoirs of Jahangir, Emperor of India* (New York, 1999).

Meer Hasan Ali, *Observations on the Mussulmauns of India*, ed. W. Crooke (1917; rpt. Karachi, 1974).

Muktabat-i 'Allami, by Abu-l Fazl 'Allami, Mansura, Haidar, *Muktabat-i-Allami (Insha'i Abu'l Fazl) Daftar I* (New Delhi, 1998).

Muntakhab-ut-Tavarikh, by 'Abd al-Qadir Badauni, trans. and ed. George S. A. Ranking, W. H. Lowe, and Sir Wolseley Haig, *Muntakhabu-t-tawarikh* vols. I–III (1884–1925; rpt. Delhi, 1986).

Tabaqat-i Akbari, by Khvajeh Nizam al-Din Ahmad, trans. B. De, and Baini Prasad, *The Tabaqat-i Akbari of Khwajah Nizammudin Ahmad*, vols. I–III (1936; rpt. Delhi, 1992).

Tarikh-i-Khandan-i Timuriyyan, MS of the Khuda Bakhsh Oriental Public Library, Patna, India.

Tarikh-i Rashidi by Mirza Muhammad Haydar Dughlat, trans. Sir E. Denison Ross and ed. N. Elias, *The Tarikh-i Rashidi of Muhammad Haidar Dughlat: A History of the Moguls of Central Asia* (London, 1895).

Tirmizi, S. A. I. *Edicts from the Mughal Harem* (Delhi, 1979).

Mughal Documents 1526–1627 (Delhi, 1989).

European travel accounts

Camps, Arnulf, *An Unpublished Letter of Father Christoval Ce Vega, S. J. Its Importance for the History of the Second Mission to the Mughal Court and for the Knowledge of the Religion of Emperor Akbar* (Cairo, 1956).

Constable, Archibald (ed.), *Travels in the Mogol Empire AD 1656–1668 by François Bernier* (1891; rpt. Delhi, 1968).

Correia-Afonso, John (ed.), *Letters from the Mughal Court* (Bombay, 1980).

Foster, William (ed.), *The Embassy of Sir Thomas Roe to the Court of the Great Mogul 1615–1619*, vols. I–II (London, 1899).

Early Travels in India 1583–1619 (New Delhi, 1985).

Grey, Edward (ed.), *The Travels of Pietro Della Valle in India: From the English Translation of 1664, by G. Havers: In Two Volumes* (London, 1892).

Hoyland, J. S. (trans.), *The Empire of the Great Mogol: A Translation of De Laet's "Description of India and Fragment of Indian History"* (Bombay, 1928).

Hoyland, J. S. (trans.) and S. N. Banerjee (ed.), *The Commentary of Father Monserrate, S. J. On his Journey to the Court of Akbar* (London, 1922).

Irvine, William (trans.), *Storia Do Mogor or Mogul India 1653–1708 by Niccolao Manucci Venetian* (London, 1907).

Markham, Clements R. (ed.), *The Hawkins' Voyages during the reigns of Henry VIII, Queen Elizabeth, and James I* (London, 1878).

Moreland, W. H. and P. Geyl (trans.), *Jahangir's India: The Remonstrantie of Francisco Pelsaert* (Cambridge, 1925).

Oaten, E. F. *European Travellers in India during the 15th, 16th and 17th Centuries* (Lucknow, 1973).

Purchas, Samuel, *Hakluytus Posthumus or Purchas His Pilgrims: Contayning a History of the World in Sea Voyages and Lande Travells by Englishmen and others*, vol. X (Glasgow, 1905).

Secondary sources (select readings)

Abu-Lughod, Lila, *Veiled Sentiments: Honor and Poetry in a Bedouin Society* (Berkeley, 1986).

Ahmed, Leila, *Women and Gender in Islam* (New Haven, 1992).

Alam, Muzaffar, "Akhlaqi Norms and Mughal Governance," in Muzaffar Alam *et al.* (eds.), *The Making of Indo-Persian Culture: Indian and French Studies* (New Delhi, 2000).

"The Pursuit of Persian: Language in Mughal Politics," *Modern Asian Studies*, 32, 2 (1998).

Alam, Muzaffar and Sanjay Subrahmanyam, *The Mughal State, 1526–1750* (2nd edn, Delhi, 2000).

Asad, Talal, "Conscripts of Western Civilization," in Christine Gailey (ed.), *Dialectical Anthropology: Essays in Honor of Stanley Diamond* (Ithaca, 1992).

Babayan, Kathryn, "The 'Aqa'id al-Nisa: A Glimpse at Safavid Women in Local Isfahani Culture," in Gavin R. G. Hambly (ed.), *Women in the Medieval Islamic World: Power, Patronage, and Piety* (New York, 1998).

Beach, Milo Cleveland, *Early Mughal Painting* (Cambridge, Mass., 1987).

Bearman, P. J. *et al.* (eds.), *The Encyclopaedia of Islam* (Leiden, 2000).

Bennett, Jane, *The Enchantment of Modern Life: Attachments, Crossings, and Ethics* (Princeton, 2001).

Beveridge, Annette Susannah, "Life and Writings of Gulbadan Begam (Lady Rosebody)," *Calcutta Review*, 106 (1892).

Beveridge, H. "The Memoirs of Bayazid (Bajazet) Biyat," *Journal of the Asiatic Society of Bengal*, 62, 1–4 (1898).

Blake, Stephen P. *Shahjahanabad: The Sovereign City in Mughal India 1639–1739* (Cambridge, 1993).

Brand, Michael and Glenn Lowry, *Akbar's India: Art from the Mughal City of Victory* (London, 1985–86).

Burke, Peter, "The Philosopher as Traveller: Bernier's Orient," in Jaś Elsner and Joan-Pau Rubies (eds.), *Voyages and Visions: Towards a Cultural History of Travel* (London, 1999).

Butler, Judith, "Against Proper Objects" and "More Gender Trouble," *Differences*, 6, 2–3 (1994).

Campo, Juan Eduardo, *The Other Sides of Paradise: Explorations into the Religious Meanings of Domestic Space in Islam* (Columbia, 1991).

Chatterjee, Partha, *The Nation and Its Fragments: Colonial and Postcolonial Histories* (Princeton, 1993).

Cohn, Bernard S. "The Command of Language and the Language of Command," in *Subaltern Studies IV* (Delhi, 1985).

Contamine, Philippe, *War in the Middle Ages*, trans. Michael Jones (New York, 1984).

Das, Veena, "Wittgenstein and Anthropology," *Annual Review of Anthropology*, 27 (1998).

Dale, Stephen F. "Steppe Humanism: The Autobiographical Writings of Zahir al-din Muhammad Babur, 1483–1530," *International Journal of Middle East Studies*, 22 (1990).

"The Poetry and Autobiography of the *Babur-Nama*," *The Journal of Asian Studies*, 55, 3 (August 1996).

The Garden of the Eight Paradises: Babur and the Culture of Empire in Central Asia, Afghanistan and India, 1483–1530 (Leiden and Boston, 2004).

Davis, Natalie Zemon, *Society and Culture in Early Modern France* (Stanford, 1975).

Dehkhoda, Aliakbar, *Loghatname, 1879–1955*, in Mohammad Mo'in and Ja'far Shahidi (eds.), *Encyclopedic Dictionary*, vols. I–XIV (Tehran, 1993–94).

Elias, Norbert, *The Court Society*, trans. Edmund Jephcott (Oxford, 1983).

"The Concept of Figurations," in Johan Goudsblom and Stephen Mennell (eds.), *The Norbert Elias Reader* (Oxford, 1998).

Elliot, H. M. and John Dowson, *The History of India as told by its own Historians*, vols. I–VIII (1867–77; rpt. New Delhi, 1996).

Elphinstone, Mountstuart, *The History of India* (2nd edn, London, 1843).

Esposito, John L. *Women in Muslim Family Law* (Syracuse, 1984).

Ethé, Hermann, *Catalogue of Persian Manuscripts in the Library of the India Office*, vol. 1 (Oxford, 1903).

Falk, Toby and Mildred Archer, *Indian Miniatures in the India Office Library* (London, 1981).

Faubion, James D. (ed.), *Michel Foucault: Aesthetics, Method, and Epistemology*, vols. I–II (London, 1998).

Findly, Ellison Banks, *Nur Jahan: Empress of Mughal India* (New York, 1993).

Foucault, Michel, *The Use of Pleasure: The History of Sexuality*, vol. II (New York, 1990).

Fuss, Diana, "Reading Like a Feminist," in Naomi Schor and Elizabeth Weed (eds.), *The Essential Difference* (Bloomington, 1994).

Geertz, Clifford, *Negara: The Theatre State in Nineteenth-Century Bali* (Princeton, 1980).

Gholsorkhi, Shohreh, "Pari Khan Khanum: A Masterful Safavid Princess," *Iranian Studies*, 28, 3–4 (Summer/Fall 1995).

Giladi, Avner, *Infants, Parents and Wet Nurses: Medieval Islamic Views on Breastfeeding and their Social Implications* (Boston and Cologne, 1999).

Gomes, Rita Costa, *The Making of a Court Society: Kings and Nobles in Late Medieval Portugal*, Trans. Alison Aiken (Cambridge, 2003).

Goodman, Dena, "Public Sphere and Private Life: Toward a Synthesis of Current Historiographical Approaches to the Old Regime," *History and Theory: Studies in the Philosophy of History*, 31 (1992).

Gordon, Daniel, *Citizens without Sovereignty: Equality and Sociability in French Thought, 1670–1789* (Princeton, 1994).

Guha, Ranajit, "The Small Voice of History," in *Subaltern Studies IX* (Delhi, 1996).

Habermas, Jürgen, *The Structural Transformation of the Public Sphere* (Cambridge, Mass., 1989).

Haeri, Shahla, "Temporary Marriage and State in Iran: An Islamic Discourse on Female Sexuality," *Social Research*, 59 (Spring 1992).

Haider, Mansura, "The Mongol Traditions and their Survival in Central Asia (XIV–XV Centuries)," *Central Asiatic Journal*, 28, 1–2 (1984).

Haim, S. (ed.), *The Shorter Persian–English Dictionary* (3rd edn, Delhi, 1998)
    Dictionary English–Persian Persian–English (rev. edn, New Delhi, 2000)
Helly, Dorothy O. and Susan M. Reverby (eds.), *Gendered Domains: Rethinking Public and Private in Women's History. Essays from the Seventh Berkshire Conference on the History of Women* (Ithaca, 1992).
Hodivala, Shahpurshah Hormasji, *Studies in Indo-Muslim History: A Critical Commentary on Elliot and Dowson's History of India as Told by its Own Historians*, vols. I–II (Lahore, 1979).
Juneja, Monica (ed.), *Architecture in Medieval India* (Delhi, 2001).
Khan, Iqtidar Alam (ed.), *Akbar and his Age* (New Delhi, 1999).
Khoury, Dina Rizk, "Slippers at the Entrance or Behind Closed Doors: Domestic and Public Spaces for Mosuli Women," in Madeline C. Zilfi (ed.), *Women in the Ottoman Empire: Middle Eastern Women in the Early Modern Era* (Leiden, 1997).
Koch, Ebba, "The Architectural Forms," in Michael Brand and Glenn D. Lowry (eds.), *Fatehpur Sikri* (Bombay, 1987).
Lal, K. S. *The Mughal Harem* (Delhi, 1988).
Lal, Ruby, "Historicizing the *harem*: The Challenge of a Princess's Memoir," *Feminist Studies*, 30, 3 (Fall/Winter 2004).
    "Mughal India: 15th to Mid-18th Century," in Suad Joseph (ed.), *Encyclopedia of Women and Islamic Cultures: Methodologies, Paradigms and Sources*, vol. 1 (Leiden and Boston, 2003).
    "The 'Domestic World' of Peripatetic Kings: Babur and Humayun, c. 1494–1556," *Medieval History Journal*, 4, 1 (January–June 2001).
Lane-Poole, Stanley, *Aurangzeb* (Oxford, 1893).
    Medieval India under Mohammedan Rule A.D. 712–1764 (London, 1903).
Lentz, Thomas W. and Glenn D. Lowry, *Timur and the Princely Vision: Persian Art and Culture in the Fifteenth Century* (Los Angeles, 1989).
Maher, Vanessa, "Breast-Feeding in Cross-cultural Perspective: Paradoxes and Proposals," in Vanessa Maher (ed.), *The Anthropology of Breastfeeding: Natural Law or Social Construct* (Oxford and Providence, 1992).
Manz, Beatrice Forbes, *The Rise and Rule of Tamerlane* (Cambridge, 1989).
Marshall, D. N. *Mughals in India: A Bibliographical Survey*, vol. 1 (London, 1967).
Meredith-Owens, G. M. *A Handlist of Persian Manuscripts (acquired by the British Museum): 1805–1966* (London, 1968).
Mernissi, Fatima, *Dreams of Trespass: Tales of a Harem Girlhood* (Reading, Mass., 1994).
Metcalf, Barbara D. (ed.), *Moral Conduct and Authority: The Place of Adab in South Asian Islam* (Berkeley, 1984).
Milano, Lucio (ed.), *Drinking in Ancient Societies: History and Culture of Drinks in the Ancient Near East* (Padua, 1994).
Mill, James, *The History of British India*, ed. Horace Hayman Wilson, vols. I–II (London, 1858).
Misra, Rekha, *Women in Mughal India 1526–1748 A.D.* (New Delhi, 1967).
Mukhia, Harbans, *Historians and Historiography During the Reign of Akbar* (New Delhi, 1976).
Nath, R. *Private Life of the Mughals 1526–1803 A.D.* (Jaipur, 1994).
Nath, Renuka, *Notable Mughal and Hindu Women in the 16th and 17th Centuries A.D.* (New Delhi, 1990).

Nelson, Cynthia, "Public and Private Politics: Women in the Middle Eastern World," *American Ethnologist*, 1, 3 (August 1974).

Najmabadi, Afsaneh, "Gender and the Sexual Politics of Public Visibility in Iranian Modernity", in Scott, Joan W., and Keats, Debra (eds.), *Going Public: Feminism and the Shifting Boundaries of the Private Sphere* (Illinois, 2004).

O'Hanlon, Rosalind, "Kingdom, Household and Body: Gender and the Construction of Imperial Service under Akbar" (unpublished paper).

Parsons, John Carmi, and Bonnie Wheeler (eds.), *Medieval Mothering* (New York and London, 1996).

Peirce, Leslie P. *The Imperial Harem: Women and Sovereignty in the Ottoman Empire* (New York, 1993).

Petruccioli, Attilio, "The Geometry of Power: The City's Planning," in Brand and Lowry (eds.), *Fatehpur Sikri* (above).

Philips, C. H. (ed.), *Historians of India, Pakistan and Ceylon* (London, 1961).

Ray, Sukumar, *Humayun in Persia* (Kolkata, 2002).

Raychaudhuri, Tapan, *Bengal under Akbar and Jahangir: An Introductory Study in Social History* (Delhi, 1969).

Reiter, Rayna (ed.), *Toward an Anthropology of Women* (New York, 1975).

Rezavi, S. Ali Nadeem, "Revisiting Fatehpur Sikri: An Interpretation of Certain Buildings," in Irfan Habib (ed.), *Akbar and his India* (Delhi, 2000).

Richards, John F. "The Formulation of Imperial Authority under Akbar and Jahangir," in John F. Richards (ed.), *Kingship and Authority in South Asia* (Madison, 1978).
   The Mughal Empire (Cambridge, 1993).

Rieu, Charles, *Catalogue of the Persian Manuscripts in the British Museum*, vols. I–III (London, 1879, 1881, and 1883).

Rizvi, Kishwar, "Gendered Patronage: Women and Benevolence during the Early Safavid Empire," in D. Fairchild Ruggles (ed.), *Women, Patronage, and Self-Representation in Islamic Societies* (Albany, 2000).

Rizvi, S. A. A. *Religious and Intellectual History of the Muslims in Akbar's Reign* (New Delhi, 1975).

Rosaldo, Michelle, "The Use and Abuse of Anthropology: Reflections on Feminism and Cross-Cultural Understanding," *Signs*, 5 (Spring 1980).

Rosaldo, Michelle and Louise Lamphere (eds.), *Woman, Culture, and Society* (Stanford, 1974).

Rossabi, Morris, "Kublai Khan and the Women in his Family," in W. Bauer (ed.), *Studia Sino-Mongolia* (Wiesbaden, 1979).

Rubies, Joan-Pau, *Travel and Ethnology in the Renaissance: South India through European Eyes, 1250–1625* (Cambridge, 2000).

Saksena, B. P. "Memoirs of Baizid," *Allahabad University Studies*, 6, 1 (1930).

Saxena, B. P. "Baizid Biyat and His Work – 'Mukhtasar," *Journal of Indian History*, 4, 1–3 (1925–26).

Scherer, M. A. "Annette Akroyd Beveridge: Victorian Reformer, Oriental Scholar" (Unpublished Ph.D. diss., The Ohio State University, 1995).
   "Woman to Woman: Annette, the Princess, and the Bibi," *Journal of the Royal Asiatic Society*, Ser. 3, 6, 2 (1996).

Sedgwick, Eve Kosofsky, *Epistemology of the Closet* (Berkeley, 1990).

Serjeant, R. B. "Haram and Hawtah, the Sacred Enclave in Arabia," in Abdurrahman Badawi (ed.), *Mélanges Taha Husain* (Cairo, 1962).

Shakeb, M. Z. A. *A Descriptive Catalogue of Miscellaneous Persian Mughal Documents from Akbar to Bahadur Shah II* (India Office Records and Library, 1982).

Sinha, Mrinalini, *Colonial Masculinity: The "Manly Englishman" and the "Effeminate Bengali" in the Late Nineteenth Century* (Manchester, 1995).

Smith, Bonnie G. *The Gender of History: Men, Women, and Historical Practice* (Cambridge, Mass., 1998).

Soucek, Priscilla P. "Timurid Women: A Cultural Perspective," in Hambly (ed.), *Women in the Medieval Islamic World* (above).

Spiegel, Gabrielle M. *The Past as Text: The Theory and Practice of Medieval Historiography* (Baltimore, 1997).

Stagl, Justin, "The Methodising of Travel in the 16th Century: A Tale of Three Cities," *History and Anthropology*, 4 (1990).

Steingass, F. *A Comprehensive Persian–English Dictionary* (2nd edn, New Delhi, 1981).

Storey, C. A. *Persian Literature: A Bio-Bibliographical Survey*, vol. I, Parts 1–2 (London, 1927–39 and 1953).

Subrahmanyam, Sanjay, "The Mughal State – Structure or Process? Reflections on Recent Western Historiography," *Indian Economic and Social History Review*, 29, 3 (1992).

Subtelny, Maria Eva, "Art and Politics in Early 16th-Century Central Asia," *Central Asiatic Journal*, 27, 1–2 (1983).

Szuppe, Maria, "The Jewels of Wonder: Learned Ladies and Princess Politicians in the Provinces of Early Safavid Iran," in Hambly (ed.), *Women in the Medieval Islamic World* (above).

"La participation des femmes de la famille royale à l'exercice du pouvoir en Iran," *Studia Iranica*, 23, 2 (1994).

Tambiah, Stanley J. "What did Bernier Actually Say? Profiling the Mogul Empire," in Veena Das *et al.* (eds.), *Tradition, Pluralism, and Identity: Essays in Honour of T. N. Madan* (New Delhi, 1999).

Teltcher, Kate, *India Inscribed: European and British Writing on India 1600–1800* (Delhi, 1995).

Titley, Norah M. *Miniatures from Persian Manuscripts: A Catalogue and Subject Index of Paintings from Persia, India, and Turkey in the British Library and the British Museum* (London, 1977).

Warner, Michael, *Publics and Counterpublics* (New York, 2002).

Woods, John E. "Timur's Genealogy," in Michael Mazzouni and Vera Moreen (eds.), *Intellectual Studies on Islam* (Salt Lake City, 1990).

Ziegler, Norman P. "Some Notes on Rajput Loyalties During the Mughal Period," in John F. Richards (ed.), *Kingship and Authority in South Asia* (Madison, 1978).

Index

Cambridge Studies in Islamic Civilisation

Other titles in the series